GORAU YMGAIS GWYBODAETH

ONE HUNDRED YEARS OF EDUCATION AT ABERAERON

Argraffiad cyntaf—Mai 1996

ISBN 1 85902 363 0

Argraffwyd gan Wasg Gomer, Llandysul

CYNNWYS - CONTENTS

Ysgol Gyfun Aberaeron

GOLYGYDDOL / EDITORIAL

Mr. Eifion Davies, Cadeirydd / Chairman

Penderfynodd Pwyllgor Dathlu Canmlwyddiant Ysgol Gyfun Aberaeron mai da o beth fyddai cael llyfr i gofio'r achlysur.

Braint fawr oedd cael paratoi'r llyfr hyn sy'n bwrw golwg ar addysg yn Aberaeron dros y can mlynedd diwethaf.

Diolch i aelodau'r Is-Bwyllgor am eu hawgrymiadau buddiol ac i'r lliaws o bersonau sydd wedi cyfrannu i'r llyfr.

Hefyd, fy nyletswydd yw diolch yn ddiffuant iawn i genedlaethau o ffotograffwyr a wnaeth yr orchwyl yn un mor bleserus. Bu llawer o gyfeillion a chyn-ddisgyblion yn hael iawn yn rhoi benthyg hen ffotograffau.

Y mae arnaf ddyled arbennig i'r canlynol:

Miss Marina James, y Pennaeth, am ei chymorth, ei chyfarwyddyd a'i chyngor.

Mrs. Christine Venville am deipio'r gyfrol ac am ei holl gwaith diflino.

Mr. Robert Brierley am y gwaith cysodi.

Mrs. Lona Brierley a Mrs. Ellen Llwyd-Evans am ddarllen a chywiro'r proflenni.

Mr. Lyndon Thomas am gynllunio'r clawr.

Gwasg Gomer am ymgymryd â chyhoeddi'r llyfr ac am eu cyd-weithrediad parod.

Gwerthfawrogaf eu cymorth yn fawr iawn. Gobeithio y cewch fwynhad o ddarllen yr hanes.

Ysgol Gyfun Aberaeron Centenary Committee decided it would be appropriate to publish a book celebrating the occasion.

It has been a privilege preparing this volume which records one hundred years of secondary education in Aberaeron.

I would like to express my thanks to the members of the Sub-Committee for their support and advice and to the numerous people who have contributed to this volume.

Thanks to the generations of photographers who have made the task such a pleasant one. Sincere thanks also to the many friends and past pupils who parted with precious photographs.

I am particularly indebted to the following:

Miss Marina James, Headteacher for her advice, guidance and assistance.

Mrs. Christine Venville for typing the volume and for her commitment and hard work.

Mr. Robert Brierley for typesetting the book.

Mrs. Lona Brierley and Mrs. Ellen Llwyd-Evans for reading and correcting the proofs.

Mr. Lyndon Thomas for designing the cover.

Gomer Press for their ready cooperation at all times.

Their assistance is greatly appreciated. I hope you enjoy the book.

AELODAU IS-BWYLLGOR LLYFR Y CANMLWYDDIANT
MEMBERS OF THE CENTENARY BOOK SUB-COMMITTEE

Mr. Eifion Davies (Cadeirydd/Chairman)
Mrs. Christine Venville (Ysgrifennydd/Secretary)
Miss Marina James
Miss Rhiannon Davies
Miss Maria Evans
Mr. Geraint Davies
Mr. Prosser Evans
Mr. Eifion Gruffudd
Mr. Graham Hope
Mr. Denys Gwynne Hughes
Mr. David Jones
Mr. Gareth Owen
Mr. Hywel Thomas

PRIFATHRAWON / HEADTEACHERS

Mr. G. G. Jones B.A. 1896-1899
Mr. C. J. Hughes B.A. 1899-1917
Mr. H. T. Evans M.A. 1917-1944
Mr. J. T. Owen O.B.E., M.A. 1944-1965
Mr. G. G. Davies B.A. 1965-1973
Mr. D. J. Thomas O.B.E., B.Sc. 1973-1993
Mr. J. E. Lewis B.Sc. 1993-1995
Miss J. M. James B.Ed. 1995-

RHAGARWEINIAD

Cynog Dafis A.S.

Rwy'n ei chyfri hi'n fraint fawr i gael cyfle i lunio ychydig o ragarweiniad i gyfrol mor bwysig â hon.

Yn y 1940au, blynyddoedd fy machgendod cynnar i, 'roedd y "Cownti Sgŵl", ei hathrawon a'i disgyblion, ac yn wir yr adeilad ei hun, yn destun parchedig ofn i blant bach tref Aberaeron. Peth rhyfedd ac ofnadwy oedd y broses o baratoi ar gyfer y "scholarship", dan gyfarwyddyd medrus Mr. Ellis yn yr Ysgol Gynradd, a diwrnod mawr iawn oedd hwnnw pan fydden yn cerdded y rhiw i sefyll yr arholiad yn neuadd yr hen ysgol (y llyfrgell nawr).

Erbyn diwrnod y canlyniadau, 'roedd y dref (a'r holl ddalgylch am wn i) yn ysu am gael gwybod pwy oedd wedi pasio, ac yn enwedig, efallai, pwy oedd wedi methu. 'Roedd cymaint yn dibynnu ar yr un digwyddiad tyngedfennol hwnnw.

Wedi'r rhyfel, daeth to o athrawon ifainc newydd i wasanaethu'r ysgol ac i gyfoethogi bywyd tref Aberaeron a'i sefydliadau. (Bryd hynny, 'roedd rhaid i bobl fyw gerllaw eu man gwaith!). Annheg fyddai enwi rhai heb roi'r rhestr yn llawn, ond go brin bod modd gorfesur fy nyled i a'm cyfoedion i'r bobl ragorol ac ymroddedig yna. Rhaid wrth gwrs cyfeirio'n arbennig at y brenin ei hun, J. T. Owen; yr oedd naws ei bresenoldeb yn hydreiddio'r holl le.

Ef a gafodd y cyfrifoldeb mawr o lywio'r ysgol drwy gyfnod y trawsnewid o fod yn ysgol ramadeg, â dwy "fform" go academaidd y flwyddyn, i fod yn ysgol "ddwyochrog" ac yna'n ysgol gyfun go iawn. Mae diwrnod gosod carreg sylfaen yr adeilad newydd yn eglur yn fy nghof. Mynych y gwersi rhydd a fwynhawyd yn ystod fy ail flwyddyn oherwydd rhu'r peiriannau wrth eu gwaith. Erbyn fy nhrydedd, 'roedd yr adeilad newydd ar gael, a ninnau'r disgyblion yn gorfod gwisgo daps (ar orchymyn yr hybarch W. A. Jones) rhag crafu'r llawr. Ystyr y cyfan hyn wrth gwrs oedd estyn i holl blant yr ardal y cyfle i gael addysg uwchradd a fu gynt yn gyfyngedig i élit cymharol fach. Daeth y "moderns" i'w teyrnas.

Yn 1980, mi es nôl i sefydliad go wahanol ar lawer cyfrif. Hyfrydwch mawr i mi oedd cael bod yn aelod o'r un staff â rhai o fy nghyn-athrawon ac yn enwedig mentor blynyddoedd fy nglaslencyndod, yr hynaws-ddiffuant Mr. Jack Rees.

Pan adewais yn 1984, yn ddigon anfoddog, 'roedd addysg ar drothwy cyfnod o ddiwygiadau di-dor a osododd straen go ddifrifol ar yr athrawon. Fyddai neb yn gwadu gwerth llawer o'r syniadau a'r gofynion newydd, ond nid bendith ddi-gymysg fuon nhw. Rhaid i unrhyw newidiadau pellach fod yn fwy graddol o lawer, yn seiliedig ar ddefnyddioldeb pragmataidd yn hytrach nag ideoleg, ac yn sensitif i farn athrawon yn ogystal â lles plant. Heb broffesiwn diddig, ni chawn ddarpariaeth o'r safon orau.

A gaf i ddymuno'n dda i Ysgol Gyfun Aberaeron wrth iddi wynebu canrif newydd a her oes o gyfnewidiadau mawr. Os ceir yr un ymroddiad eto ag y gafwyd yn y ganrif gyntaf, aiff hi ddim ymhell o'i lle.

❖

PREFACE

Cynog Dafis M.P.

It is a very great privilege for me to have been asked to pen a brief preface to such an important publication.

During the 1940s, the years of my early boyhood, the County School, its teachers and pupils, and indeed the building itself, were the objects of awe to the younger children of the town of Aberaeron. Preparation for the scholarship examination, under the expert supervision of Mr. Ellis at the Primary School, was a serious business, and the day when we walked up the hill to take the examination in the old school hall (the present library) was a momentous occasion. On the day when the results were made public, the whole town (and the catchment area as a whole, I am sure) was bursting to know who had passed, and perhaps even more so, who had failed. So much depended on that one fateful event.

After the war, a new generation of young teachers came to serve the school and to enrich the life of Aberaeron town and its institutions. (In those far off days people had to live near their work place!) It would be unfair to name some of those excellent and dedicated people without listing them all, but I and my contempoaries are more in their debt than we could ever measure. Mention must of course be made of the king himself, J. T. Owen, the aura of whose presence penetrated the entire establishment.

It is he who had to face the great responsibility of steering the school through the period of transformation from being a grammar school with an academic two-form entry to being first a bilateral and then a fully fledged comprehensive school. The day when the foundation stone of the new building was laid is still clear in my memory. Many were the free periods that we enjoyed during my second year because the noise of machinery made work impossible. By my third year, the new building was in place and we pupils entered it, wearing daps in order to protect the floor from scratch and scuff (the awesome W. A. Jones saw to this). The meaning of these events of course was that secondary education formerly available only to a relatively small elite, was now to be provided for all the children of the area. The "moderns" had inherited their estate!

In 1980, I returned to a pretty different institution. However, it was a particular delight to find myself a member of the same staff as some of my former teachers, in particular the mentor of my adolescent years, the excellent Mr. Jack Rees.

When I left in 1984, not all that willingly, education was on the threshold of a period of unbroken reforms that imposed considerable strain on the teachers. No one would deny the value of many of the new ideas and requirements, but they were certainly not an unmixed blessing. Any further changes must be far more gradual, based on pragmatic usefulness rather than ideology, and sensitive to the opinions of teachers as well as the welfare of children. There can be no educational provision of the highest standard without a contented profession.

May I wish Aberaeron Comprehensive School all the very best as it faces a new century and the challenge of a constantly changing age. If there is the same degree of dedication as the first century saw, the school will not go far wrong.

❖

NEGES ODDIWRTH / A MESSAGE FROM

John Ellis, Dyfed Director of Education

Pen blwydd nodedig iawn mewn hanes unrhyw un neu unrhyw achos yw canmlwyddiant. Pan ystyriwn effaith a dylanwad ysgol am gyhyd, ar gymdeithas a chenedlaethau lawer o blant, mae lle i longyfarch ac i lawenhau. Dyna, felly, a wnawn ar ran Ysgol Gyfun Aberaeron.

During the hundred years of the existence of Aberaeron Comprehensive School, education has gone through revolutionary changes. The school has been in being for the whole duration of free public secondary education in Wales. Established as a result of the Welsh Intermediate Education Act of 1889, students in the early years were being prepared for the twentieth century. Today, its current students are being prepared for the new millenium. For those responsible for the school, today's challenges are in many ways similar to those faced by their predecessors; to strive for achievement, provide stimulation, maintain high standards and establish an environment for constant development. The fact that the school has been able to accept and adapt to such challenges is manifest not only in its survival but also in the many generations of successful citizens it has produced. They have contributed and still continue to contribute locally, regionally and nationally. It has a proud and successful record, but it also has qualities of leadership and purpose that will motivate the current generation of students. That is a firm foundation for a long, successful history and for another hundred years of contribution to the Welsh educational scene.

Wrth gyrraedd y garreg filltir arbennig hon, dymunwn bob llwyddiant a bendith am y dyfodol. Ein gobeithion yn sicr yw can mlynedd arall o effaith da a dylanwad cryf ar blant yr ardal, fel y bydd iddynt hwythau ymfalchïo, fel y rhai a fu yn yr ysgol o'r blaen, o gael bod am gyfnod yn aelodau o Ysgol Gyfun Aberaeron.

Y Ddolen / The Link 1926

Gorau Ymgais Gwybodaeth

CANRIF AERON

Donald Evans

Mae eleni'n gan mlynedd
A rheini eleni'n wledd:
Gwledd y Cof o atgofion:
Daeth i'w lys er dathlu hon.

Ac o'r Cof daw'r atgofion
Yn bêr drwy freuder y fron:
Afon rhawd a fu i'n rhan;
Afon dŵr funud arian:
Hen win yr afon a aeth;
Afon Aeron o hiraeth.

A Chof sy'n eich cofio chwi
Na wêl loniant eleni:
Hon a hwn a gofiwn gynt -
Heno 'does gip ohonynt,
Ond heno oll maent yn ôl
Yn dyner o adunol.

A Chof am rai na chofiwn
Ar dir y byw ydyw hwn:
Y brwd a fu'n ysbrydiaeth
Fan hyn ar gychwyn y gwaith:
Hen lewion, mor oleuwedd
O anwel ŷnt yn y wledd.

Ysgol Gyfun Aberaeron 1896 - 1996

A Cho'r iau, y dechreuad
Y bore hwn o barhad:
Mae'n dathlu canrif ifanc;
Mae'n lasoed yr oed di-dranc:
Fel pob doe ac echdoe gwiw
Dydd pob dydd ydyw heddiw.

A Chof o ddiolch hefyd
I Dduw'r Grog am go' gyhyd:
Canrif sy'n para i lifo,
Y llif sy'n ganrif o Go'!
(1995)

❖

TEACHING STAFF 1896 -1996

Geraint Gwyn Jones	**Headmaster**	**1896-1899**
Miss Hooke		1896-1899
G. Senior	Science	1896-1897
Frank Standish Fenton	Science	1898-
Elizabeth Evans		1898-1899
Mabel Kitching		1898-1899
Mr . Nathan	Science	1898-1899
Charles J. Hughes	**Headmaster**	**1899-1917**
Miss K. A. Scott		1899-1902
James Dewhurst	Science	1899-
H. Bertha Jones	Cookery (part-time)	1900-1912
David Williams	General Subjects	1900-1907
R. A. Scott	Science	1902-
Miss G. S. Pole-Evans		1902-
R. Robson	Science	1902-1904
Miss L. C. Bennison		1902-1905
E. O. James	Latin/Welsh	1903-1921
C. K. Barnes	Science	1905-1908
Miss Maddock	English/History	1904-1907
Miss Richards	French	1904-1906
Miss M. Owen	French	1906-1915
Miss Ethel Thomas	English/History	1908-1914
W. J. Jones	Science	1908-1944
Miss M.F. Watson	English/Geography	1911-1916
Miss Hilda Jones	Cookery (part-time)	1911-1920
Miss E. M. Davies	English/History	1914-1916
Miss V. F. Ferguson	French	1915-1916

Miss M. E. Thomas	French	1916-1927
Miss Doris M. Davies	English/History	1916-1923
Miss G. E. P. Furby	French	1916
Miss K. W. Wild	English/Geography	1917-1919
Howell T. Evans	**Headmaster**	**1917-1944**
Mr. S. B. Porter	Science	1917-1918
Mr. S. H. Ross	Science	1918
Miss A. Richards/Gordon	English/Geography	1919-1921
Miss E. A. Roberts	English	1919-1922
Miss Megan Williams	Goegraphy/Mathematics	1921-1923
Stephen J. Williams	Welsh	1922
W. E. Roberts	English	1922-1929
J. T. Owen	Welsh	1923-1944
	Headmaster	**1944-1965**
Miss Hannah Williams	Geography/Mathematics	1923-1926
Miss N. M. Turnell	Mathematics	1923-1924
Miss E. Greenhalgh	Mathematics	1924-1927
Miss I. M. Harry	Domestic Science	1925-1929
Miss Aeronwen Jones	Geography/Botany	1927-1932
Miss Catherine E. Thomas	Mathematics	1927-1929
Miss Nansi Timothy	French	1927-1935
W. A. Jones	English	1929-1970
Miss B. I. Treharne	Mathematics	1929-1933
Miss Elaine Lewis	Domestic Science	1929-1969
T. H. Fox	Latin	1930-1959
John Evans	Agriculture/Botany	1933-1966
Miss L. Wood	Geography	1933-1939
Miss Kathleen M. Evans	Mathematics	1933-1937
Miss Ethel M. Davies	French/Welsh	1935-1942

Miss Olwen Richards/Thomas	Mathematics	1937-1942
W. J. Griffiths	Physics/P.E.	1939-1947
W. M. Meredith	English	1939-1941
Miss M. K. Clayton	Geography/P.E.	1939-1945
Miss E. M. Morgan		1945
Miss Olive John/Rees	Physics/Mathematics	1940-1952 1962-1976
Miss Joan Evans	English	1941-1943
Miss Maria Evans	Biology	1942-1976
Miss Nesta Lewis	Mathematics	1942-1945
Miss Mabel Hughes	French	1942-1944
Miss G. Parry/Matthews	Welsh	1944-1952
		1971-1979
Miss Nansi Jones	Latin	1944-1947
Miss M. M. Jones/Griffiths	French/P.E./Welsh	1944-1979
Emlyn W. Jones	English	1944-1946
W. Alcwyn Evans	Geography	1944-1975
Miss Mary Thomas	History	1944-1947
John A. M. Davies	Chemistry	1945-1947
Morgan Price	Mathematics/Physics	1945-1954
Miss Gweneirys Iorwerth	General Subjects	1945
E. Morgan	Music (part-time)	1945-1951
Miss Mary Thomas	History/English	1945-1947
Mrs. N.M. Evans	Crafts	1946-1974
T. V. Michael	Chemistry	1947-1955
R. D. Matthews	History	1947-1983
I. Gwynfil Rees	Welsh	1947-1973
W. Sydney Evans	Physics	1947-1956
W. J. Lewis	English	1948-1964
		1965-1983

Miss Rhiannon Davies	Domestic Science	1948-1984
D. Hughes Jones	P.E./Art	1950-1961
Miss M. Williams	English	1950-1957
Miss Dulcie Jones	Social Studies	1950-1953
Jack A. Rees	R.E.	1950-1982
John Roberts	Woodwork	1950-1982
Miss V. Benjamin/Hubbard	Music	1951-1954
		1974
Mrs. M. L. Simpson	Commercial Subjects	1951-1959
Tudor Jones	R.E.	1951-1978
Mrs. A. M. Lewis	P.E.	1951-1954
Robert Armstrong	Woodwork/Metalwork	1951-1954
Mervyn Griffiths	Mathematics	1951-1967
H. D. Johnstone Jones	French	1952-1955
Miss S. Ann Jones/James	Welsh	1953-1982
Mrs B. A. Jones	Social Studies	1954-1955
D. M. Henry	Music	1954-1973
Miss O. R. Jones/Owen	P.E.	1954-1960
Mrs D. F. Davies		1954
D. W. Matthews	Mathematics	1955-1968
D. Myrddin Evans	Metalwork	1955-1986
D.J. Thomas	Chemistry	1955-1973
	Headmaster	**1973-1993**
Hugh Hayward	French	1955-1958
Miss A. Harries/Lewis	Social Studies	1955-1960
		1975-
Mrs. M. E. Jones	Music	1955-1959
Miss B. Davies/Griffiths	English	1958-1961
		1962-1984

Alan Pascoe	French	1958-1987
Arwyn Lewis	P.E./Careers	1959-1987
Mrs. Nance James	General Science	1959-1962
D. R. Evans	Physics	1959-1988
G. Alun Davies	Commercial Subjects	1959-1983
Paul Kline	Latin	1959-1961
Mrs Valmai Jones	P.E.	1960-1965
John Jones	Art	1961-1985
Miss Ceril Jones	English	1961-1967
Meurig Evans	Latin	1962-1972
Miss L. McCann	Geography	1962-1968
Mrs. K. Pascoe	English	1963-1995
Miss Ann Davies	Welsh	1964-1969
G. G. Davies	**Headmaster**	**1965-1973**
Miss Pat Rees/James	P.E.	1966-1970
Mrs. G. K. Lewis	Remedial	1966-1976
Mrs. M. Kitchener Davies	English	1967-1971
E. D. Williams	Agriculture	1967-1974
Mrs. Megan Lewes-Daley	Biology	1968-1987
Iorwerth Evans	Mathematics	1968-1990
David Lloyd *	P.E./Special Needs	1968-
Mrs. Margaret Evans	Domestic Science	1969-1975
Miss G. M. Jones	Welsh	1969-1970
Miss Janice Ledger	P.E.	1970-1972
Mrs. Margaret Jones	Crafts/Games	1970-1972
		1985-1986
Mrs. Mair Lewis	English	1971-1978
Miss Jean Parry	P.E.	1972-1987

Miss Gwenda Evans/Davies *	Special Needs	1973-1978
		1990-
Wynne Harries *	Chemistry	1973-
John Evans *	Mathematics	1973-
Brynach Parri	German	1973-1977
Wynford Edwards *	Woodwork/D.T.	1974-
Mrs. Daisy Williams	Crafts	1974-1985
Richard Champion	Pottery	1974-1977
Bryn Jones *	Science	1974-
Mrs. Jean S. Evans	Food Technology	1975-1993
Mrs. Rayanne Lewis	Science	1975-1990
Mrs. Heywood	History/R.E.	1975-1977
Ken Griffiths	P.E.	1975-1980
G. Hughes Jones	Music	1975-1981
Tudor Thomas *	Geography	1975-
Clive Harpwood	Drama	1975-1978
Stuart Lloyd	Mathematics	1976-1977
Helen Eirian Jones	Domestic Science	1976-1981
Lowri Morgan/Jones *	French	1976-1983
		1988-
Geraint Davies *	History/Geography	1976-
Mostyn Leyshon	Science	1976-1980
Lyndon Thomas *	Art	1977-
Barbara Mathias/Crawford	Welsh/Geography	1977-1981
Christopher Jones *	P.E.	1977-
Elin Owen	German/French	1978-1978
Denise Beard	German	1978-1980
Annabel Owen/Aynsley	English	1977-1978
Bethan Phillips	English/History	1977-1986

Wynne Rogers *	Mathematics	1977-
Diane Jones	English	1978-1980
Susan Roberts *	R.E.	1978-
Malcolm Williams	Drama	1978-1979
Diane Thomas	English/P.E.	1979-1986
Gwenan Owen	History	1979-1984
Sue Hindson	Music/Mathematics	1979-1982
Eifion Gruffudd *	Welsh	1979-
Meurig James	Welsh/Geography	1979-1993
Neville Evans	Drama	1979-1984
Richard Griffiths *	Physics	1980-
Ellen Llwyd-Evans *	Welsh	1980
Cynog Dafis	English	1980-1984
Alun Rees	P.E.	1981-1989
Lona Davies/Brierley *	Music	1981-
Delyth Davies	Welsh	1981-1984
Carol Harris	Music	1982-1987
Ian ap Dewi	Special Needs	1982-1984
Robert Fry *	German	1982-
Emyr Llewelyn	Welsh	1982-1995
Gerwyn James	C.D.T.	1982-1986
Linda Badham	Mathematics	1983-1987
Jennifer Horgan	Mathematics	1983-1987
Keith Barrett	French	1983-1989
Eifion Davies *	History	1983-
Lena Daniel	Mathematics	1983-1990
Glyn Howells	Computer Studies	1983-1994
Stella Jones	English	1983-1987
Barbara Swain	Commercial Studies	1983-1987

Wendy Williams *	English	1983-1984
		1989-
Marina James *	Food Technology	1984-1995
	Headteacher	**1995-**
Cherry Davidson	English	1984-1991
Jean Jones *	Welsh	1984-
Noreen Kay *	Computer Studies	1984-
Mary Parry	History	1984-1985
Catryn Rees *	English	1984-
Nest Thomas *	Special Needs/Art	1984-
Ann Williams	Textiles	1984-1987
Nerys Ll. Davies *	Welsh	1985-
Stewart Gibbs *	Art	1985-
Robert Brierley *	C.D.T./Careers/Drama	1985-
Suzanne Herbert Evans	Geography	1985-1992
Elizabeth Nicholas *	Media Studies/English	1986-
Gerald Duford	C.D.T.	1986-1987
Anne Hubbard *	P.E.	1986-
Graham Hope *	Physics/Mathematics	1987-
Janice Parry/Rees *	Music/Games	1987-
Tracey Smith/Edwards *	Mathematics	1987-
Alison Round	English	1987-1988
Anne Lewis *	Biology	1987-
Chris Raybould	C.D.T.	1987-1989
Siôn Walker *	C.D.T.	1987-
Buddug Thomas *	Geography/Business	1987-
Elizabeth Pollock *	Chemistry	1988-
Françoise Davies	French	1988-1995
Anne Ebenezer *	Science	1988-

Anne Knowles *	English	1988-
Haydn Harries	C.D.T.	1988
Meirion Jones *	Country Skills	1989-
Beth Thomas *	Mathematics	1989-
Dawn Thomas *	C.D.T.	1989-
Mair Rees	Canolfan Iaith	1989
Mari Dalis	Canolfan Iaith	1990
Elan Bolton/Dafis *	Welsh	1990-
Margaret Howells *	Science	1990-
Rhys Roberts *	Science	1990-
Beryl Morgans *	Textiles	1990-
Frances Sumner *	English/G.N.V.Q	1990-
Jennifer Oliver	Canolfan Iaith	1991
Dorothy Jones	Typing	1991-1994
Chris Prosser	Art	1991-1993
Alwena Williams	Welsh	1991-1993
Nicola Davies *	French	1992-
Pat Jones *	Geography	1992-
John Lewis	**Headteacher**	**1993-1995**
Helen Jones	Art	1993-1994
Anwen Jones *	Welsh	1993-
Non Bowen	Food Technology	1994-1995
Lynne Rees *	Geography	1994-
Noriko Yoshida	Japanese	1994-1995
Michael Vobe *	Health Education	1994-
Catrin Jones *	English	1995-
Eleri Lloyd *	Food Technology	1995-
Mieko Kobayashi *	Japanese	1995-

* denotes current member of teaching staff.

Major Price Lewes, D.L., J.P.
Tyglyn Aeron
Chairman 1894-1911

Dr. John Davies
Tanyfron
Chairman 1911-1915

Alderman J. M. Howell, J.P.
Chairman 1915-1927

Mr. G. Gwyn Jones, B.A.
Headmaster 1896-1899

Neuadd y Dref lle agorwyd yr ysgol ym mis Mai 1896
The Town Hall where the temporary School opened on May 12th 1896

Mrs. Price Lewes yn agor yr Ysgol newydd
Mrs. Price Lewes (with bouquet) opening the new School on September 19th 1898

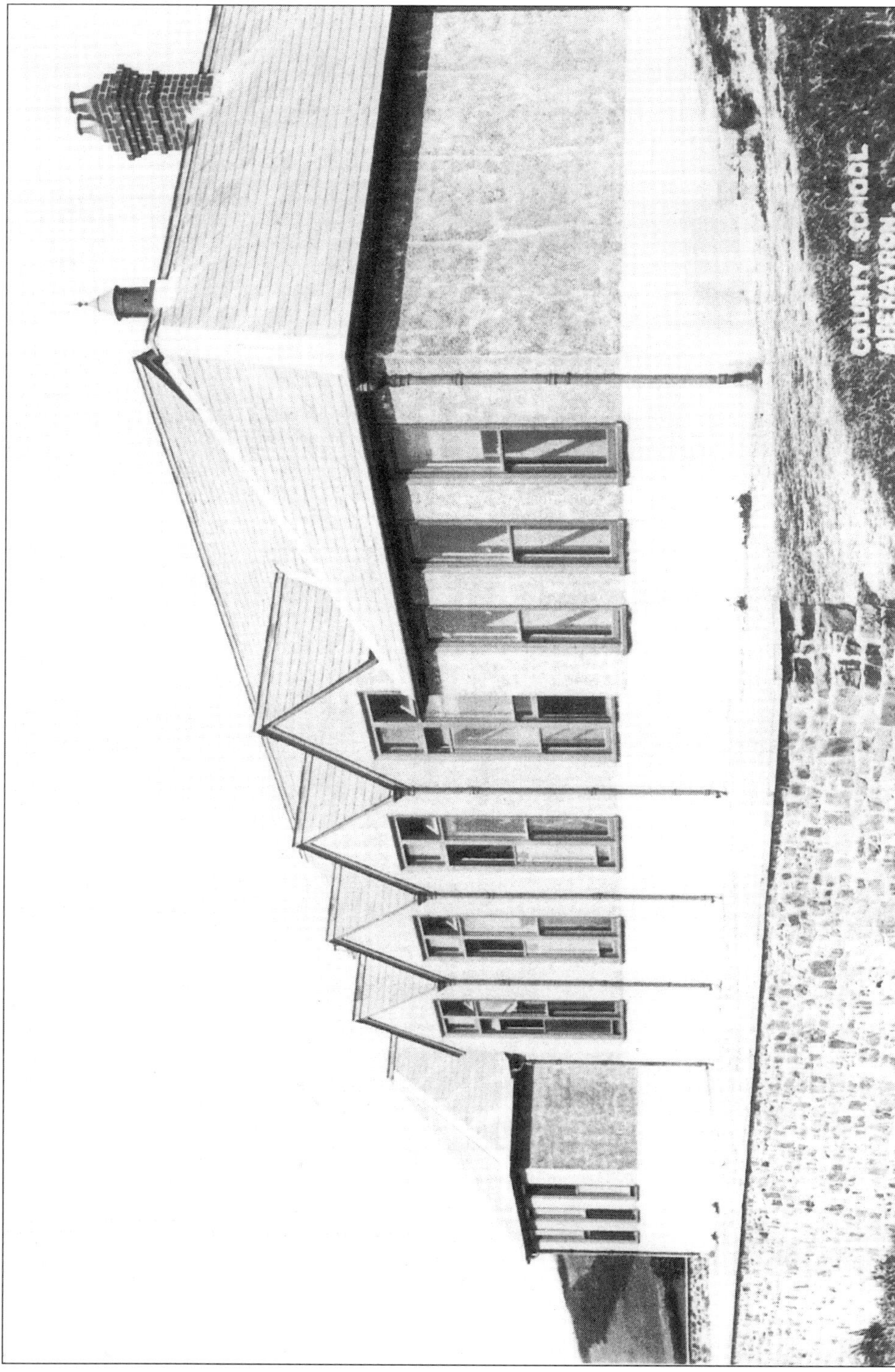

Yr Ysgol Newydd
The New School

NEW

Intermediate School Buildings

- - ABERAYRON. - -

THE

- Opening Ceremony -

Monday, Sept. 19th, 1898, at 2.30 p.m.

Chairman - - - Major PRICE LEWES, Tyglynaeron.

For Progr mme, See Page 3. *For Programme See Page 3.*

"The Cottage by the Bridge."

Picturesque Aberayron. - An - Illustrated Guide to Aberayron and District - - - 6d.

By Miss EVELYN LEWES, Tyglynaeron.

Rhaglen yr Agoriad
Opening Ceremony Programme

IN THE BEGINNING: 1889 - 1898

R. Gareth Owen

J. M. Howell, one of the founding fathers of our school, grasped with admirable clarity the significance and impact which the Welsh Intermediate Education Act of 1889 was to offer educationalists in Wales. In The Link, in 1908, he explained:

> *"The earliest years of institutions, as of men, are interesting.*
>
> *The establishment of the University College of Wales at Aberystwyth in 1872, its incorporation in 1890, and the establishment of the Bangor and Cardiff Colleges, made the creation of Intermediate Schools a necessity.*
>
> *There were no means of transit from the Board Schools to College.*
>
> *The Welsh equivalent for school is 'ladder'. It is a suggestive name. A school to a Welshman is a ladder. And I am referring to a period when the ladder had rungs at the upper and lower ends, with a long gap in the middle.*
>
> *By the passing of the Local Government Act in 1889, the necessary machinery and tools were supplied by the Legislature for fixing rungs in the gap."*

Overnight, elementary education could proceed with intermediate education and hopefully onwards to university graduation -

> *"Yn agor priffordd o ddrws y bwthyn i deml yr athrofa."*

The Welsh Intermediate Education Act placed upon the recently created County Councils the obligation to prepare educational schemes particularly tailored to their locality and, for that purpose, to create a Joint Education Committee consisting of Councillors and other nominees who would undertake the responsibility of determining the number of schools to be established and their location and regulation.

In Cardiganshire, the first Joint Education Committee consisted of Arch Deacon Edmunds, Principal of St. David's College, Lampeter, and Colonel Davies Evans, Lord Lieutenant for the County, who were appointed by the Charity Commissioners. They were assisted by the nominees of the County Council, being Alderman M. Evans J.P. of Oakford, the Reverend LL. Edwards M.A., and Alderman Peter Jones J.P., both of Aberystwyth.

There was little doubt that a school would be sanctioned in Aberystwyth and in Cardigan. Similarly, a school would be founded in Llandysul and, at a later date, Tregaron also. The coast and centre of the county was very much open to debate. Which location would more appropriately serve this area of Cardiganshire? It was clear from the outset that there would be considerable rivalry between the claims of New Quay, Llanarth and

Aberaeron as the appropriate location for a school.

The leading light in the organisation of Aberaeron's appeal was L. J. Roberts, then an under-graduate at St. David's College, Lampeter, later one of Her Majesty's Inspectors of Schools, and a renowned musical composer. He was well qualified to prepare, with meticulous detail, the necessary proposals to place before the Joint Committee. He orchestrated these activities and in the year 1890 a series of public meetings took place in and around Aberaeron with a view to testing the temperature and enthusiasm for the founding of an Intermediate School. They set about obtaining subscriptions or promises and pledges of financial help so as to satisfy the Joint Committee in due course that the necessary guarantee of a contribution of £1,500 could be raised locally, if consent was forthcoming.

There already existed at Aberaeron a private Grammar School formed in 1887 under its Headmaster Mr. G. Gwynne Jones B.A. of London University. Also, catering for the seafaring fraternity, was a Commercial and Navigation School under the care of T. Beynon Rees. The girls' needs were met by a private Grammar School under the supervision of Mrs. T. Z. Jones.

On the 25th July, 1890, the Cambrian News reported that a meeting had taken place in the Assembly Room, in what was then the Town Hall and is now the County Hall, to further promote Aberaeron's claims. By then the Building Subscription Fund, albeit mainly in promises, amounted to £900 and enquiries were in hand for a suitable site where the school could be located.

However, the rumblings from New Quay and Llanarth as possible rivals were noted and the meeting concluded:

> *"Too great to allow this important project to dwindle into a squabble for local prominence. The school is not for a town, but for a radius of country with 15,000 inhabitants."*

The Fund Raising Committee, or to give it its full title, the Aberaeron Intermediate School Committee, consisted of the Rev. W. O. Edwards B.D. (Chairman); Mr. Munro Hughes (Treasurer); the Rev. William Evans, Peniel; the Rev. Morgan Evans, Rector of Llanddewi Aberarth; the Rev. E. Morris; Dr. J. Davies; Dr. J. A. Jones; Mr. J. M. Howell; Mr. Thomas Davies, Compton House; Mr. J. H. Jones; Mr. Evan Jones, Feathers Hotel; Mr. J. Davies, London House; Mr. E. Lima Jones; Mr. T. H. Maddy; Mr. B. C. Jones, Financial Hon. Sec; and Mr. L. J. Robert, Hon.Sec.

They met virtually weekly and their Minutes illustrate the efforts which were made. The town was sub-divided into collection districts and members of the Committee were accorded responsibility for canvassing their own particular area. They appealed to exiled Aberaeronians and every businessman in their midst wrote off to each commercial company with whom they traded to beg financial assistance. They organised an Eisteddfod, ran bazaars and concerts. They canvassed the Regatta Committee for a subscription, canvassed would-be parliamentary candidates, and even approached the Bishop of Bangor who resided at Llanarth - *"His Lordship"*, however, *"could not see his way clear to grant a subscription"*, no doubt because the Church was reluctant to support or endorse the new Intermediate School movement. Similarly, they conscripted help from the outlying areas and ensured that Llanon and Llanrhystud particularly, were wholly committed to Aberaeron's cause.

By December of 1890, the Joint Committee were in a position to entertain the rival arguments as to the location of the new school. Two meetings took place, at Aberaeron and Lampeter, to which delegates were invited to put their case. On the 7th December of 1890, the Cambrian News recorded that some speakers at these meetings:

> *"made unwise and ludicrous assertions which were not calculated to advance the claims of the places which they were sent to represent. Facts only should be stated and laid before the Committee from which, and from their personal knowledge of the various places, the members of that Committee should decide the locale of each school.*
>
> *No predilection in favour of any particular place, no extraneous pressure brought to bear upon them, no party, political or church feeling should influence them in their decision."*

It is clear from the report written by one describing himself Guillaume, (I suspect no other than J. M. Howell) that he was most concerned at the misrepresentations made by the New Quay advocates. Guillaume pressed the Aberaeron cause maintaining that their:

> *"delegates at the various meetings which are held to further our cause represented a total population of 10,000 without including either Llanarth or New Quay, which we have a greater right to include in our scheme than the Reverend Mr. Griffiths of New Quay had to many places which he included in the huge scheme he presented at Lampeter."*

The arguments seemed to have rested principally upon the fact that New Quay was equidistant between Aberystwyth and Cardigan and if a school were to be located in Tregaron, New Quay enjoyed arguably a more central position. This correspondent, however, dismissed such a contention with the words:

> *"Is this paltry difference of four miles to exclude Aberaeron from having one of the schools? Is this distance to be of such import as to shift the locality of a school to a place that is most inaccessible on all sides from one whose convenience and means of access cannot be surpassed? Are all the solid claims and arguments in favour of Aberaeron to give way to such a small consideration? We are sure that a school established here will be an undoubted success and a greater success than if established in an un-get-at-able place a few miles lower down in the County."*

Guillaume concluded his plea to the Joint Education Committee:

"Taking all these considerations into account, we fail to see how the Joint Committee can ignore our claims. A school is sadly needed, the advantages which the place offers are all that can be desired, a guarantee has been given as to school buildings, the centrality of its position is indisputable. These are the facts which we wish the Reverend Llewellyn Edwards and his associates on the Committee to reflect upon. Are they going to ignore them? Are they going to shut out a large and important section of the County from the enjoyment of a privilege which should be theirs by right and by reason?"

Given the antagonism that had existed, it was hardly surprising that J. M. Howell, reflecting at the eventual opening of the school, stated that the age old rivalry between Aberaeron and New Quay had to it much of the bitterness which characterised the biblical squabbling which existed over centuries between Samaria and Jerusalem in their struggle for supremacy in the Holy Land.

In the Spring of 1891, the recommendation of the Joint Education Committee was that Aberaeron be the location at which the new school should be built, and on the 23rd March 1892, the Cardiganshire Draft Scheme was published and eventually, and not without difficulty and amendment, it received the Royal Assent on the 1st August 1896.

The declaration of March did not mark the entire end of the rivalry between the two protagonists. Indeed, as late as the 2nd December 1892, an anonymous correspondent to the Cambrian News, signing his name as 'Anti Twaddle' continued to open old wounds when he wrote:

"That an intermediate school should be established in Aberaeron for the purposes of teaching navigation and the three 'R's is, on the face of it, preposterous and is due to some desire by the district, fostered by the leading men, to share the money devoted by government towards the support of intermediate schools in each County. Aberaeron has, I believe, collected some £500. What is £500 when an intermediate school is to be established? The buildings of an intermediate school worthy of the name would cost £5,000. What then is £500? It will be said that a school of this sort is not wanted. The answer then is that an intermediate school is not wanted. An ordinary grammar school would more than meet the case. What is true of Aberaeron is true of other places. It might in truth be said that Aberaeron should avail itself of the Elementary Education Act before aspiring to an intermediate school. But that is not the question. There is a sum of money to be devoted towards the establishment of intermediate schools in Cardiganshire and Aberaeron is going to have a share of that money. That is what the question resolves itself into. Aberaeron, an insignificant place in an out of the way part of the County, where people drink sewage out of wells, where there is no system of drainage, where there is no local government, where the Elementary Education Act has not been adopted. Is this a fit and proper place to establish an intermediate school in? The whole thing is preposterous on the face of it and the result will be that Aberaeron will establish, granting that completest success crowns its efforts, only a very inferior grammar school."

The battle though was won and 'Anti Twaddle' remained unanswered. The architect of this early effort, Lewis Jones Roberts, Secretary of the School Committee, resigned from his office having overcome the first hurdle and on the 14th January 1893, wrote a letter of resignation to the Chairman, Dr. Davies. In it, he interestingly gave an outline of how matters had developed and of the efforts made. He wrote:

> *"As I am now leaving Aberaeron, it becomes necessary for me to resign the Secretaryship of the Intermediate School Committee which I have held since the inception of the movement in May of 1890. It is with extreme reluctance that I send in my resignation, as I had hoped before severing my connection with the movement, to see it brought to a triumphant issue in the erection of the school buildings to which all have been, and are, so eagerly looking forward. On a review of the work since May 1890, I cannot see that the Committee have been lax in their efforts in any way, but rather they appear to have done everything in their power to forward the movement. Nor have the people generally been wanting in support, although it must be acknowledged that the subscriptions have not flowed in with that readiness with which they were promised. But this tardiness is in most cases due not to the want of will, but to the want of means. The comparative poverty of the district, the absence of any great centres of industry where wealth rapidly accumulates, and the paucity of rich gentry in the neighbourhood - these are sufficient to account for the slowness with which our building fund mounts up. A cheque of £100 from one or two rich gentlemen would materially alter the position of affairs, but these are not to be had and the Aberaeron Committee must rely on subscriptions (however small they be) from the hard earned savings of working men. That over £500 (the exact amount is £529.15s.19d) has already been paid into the Bank is a matter for congratulation. If all will only 'possess their souls in patience', the remainder will surely, though slowly perhaps, come in in the course of the year. The townspeople generally ought to feel that the matter is one that affects each of them personally and the burden of responsibility ought not to be allowed to remain on the shoulders of a few individuals, however willing those may be to bear it. In laying down my insignia of office, I feel I ought to thank the members of the Committee one and all for the uniform courtesy which they showed towards one. I can only trust that they will pull as well together in the future as we have done in the past, for in this respect we were quite unique among Aberaeron Committees. A strong, strong pull and a long, long pull together will be the best means of bringing the vessel safely into port. If the various mariners on the Committee will allow a landsman to use a nautical metaphor! My regret in abandoning the vessel whilst still battling with the waves in mid ocean, is partly mitigated by the confidence which possesses me that I leave it in trusty and experienced hands. With yourself as Captain, Mr. John Howell as Chief Mate, Mr. Munro Hughes as Boatswain, Mr. B. C. Jones as Steward, and so many Captains, Councillors, Surveyors and able hands among the crew, I really feel no compunction at my compulsory desertion of the vessel. Wishing the gallant crew a*

pleasant voyage, and the vessel whose course will be watched with greater interest by no-one than by myself, a speedy arrival in port, I am, dear Dr. Davies,

Yours sincerely,"

In his place, the fund raisers appointed Mr. G. Gwynne Jones Headmaster of the private Grammar School, and Mr. B. C. Jones, to continue as Joint Secretaries.

The first meeting of the Aberaeron Intermediate School Managers under the County Scheme was held at the County Hall on Thursday, 12th April of 1894. The Committee convened with Major Price Lewes as Chairman; Mrs. Captain Jones, Rosalind, Llanon; Mrs. Munro Hughes; Mrs .T. Z. Jones; and Messrs. John Jones, Cwmere; Morgan Evans J.P., Oakford; Reverend W. Griffiths, Maenygroes; Mr. E. Lima Jones, Chemist; William Williams, Draper; John M. Howell; and Dr. John Davies, Aberaeron, as its members.

The two Committees now worked in harmony together, but from time to time indications came to the surface that the original fund raisers were somewhat impatient with the local Management Committee. Strangely, there were members who served on both, but nevertheless hints of friction appeared between the two as if to suggest that 'he who paid the piper called the tune'.

On the 9th April, 1894, the Managers received from the fund raisers a report on the financial situation and their recommendations to them, the fund raisers intent on moving things on. They reported:

"No.1

The present financial position:

Total amount promised - £1,142.19s.0d.

Total amount collected - £624.4s.11d.

In addition to the above amount, the sum of £100 has been deposited in trust for the Intermediate School Building Fund."

"No.2

That the Committee are prepared to continue the work of collecting subscriptions towards the Building Fund <u>if they can rely upon the co-operation of the Governors. It is hoped too, that the Governors will solicit fresh subscriptions in their several districts</u>." (My Underlining)

"No.3

A strong feeling animated the Committee, that it would be exceedingly desirable that the work of the school should be commenced in temporary premises, if possible in

January 1895. The Committee feel that a further long delay in commencing the work would be greatly prejudicial and injurious to the interests of the school."

This advice met with some caustic reaction from the Governors. The inference that the Governors would not themselves launch into their own fund raising was hard to tolerate. Mr. Morgan Evans and The Reverend W. Griffiths strongly resented the conditional tenor of Paragraph No.2 and eventually the latter part, from the words...... 'if they can rely upon the co-operation of the Governors etc...........' was erased from the record. It had the desired effect though of pushing the Managers towards creating a temporary school.

There could be only one location suitable for such use and that was the Town Hall Assembly Room where, in the main, the Fund Raisers, and indeed the Managers, met from time to time. This room constituted accommodation behind the open market which took place within what was then the open arches of the Town Hall. Improvements would have to be carried out in order to bring the accommodation up to the requirements of the Charity Commissioners, but it was certainly pressed upon the Managers that such a course should be adopted.

The premises were described by E. Lima Jones, Secretary of the Managers in a report to the Commissioners as follows:

"These premises form part of the Aberaeron Town Hall buildings, namely the room on the ground floor situated at the back of the market hall and known as the Assembly Room. This room, which has been used for the purpose of a secondary school during the last six years, is thirty-seven feet long, twenty feet wide and thirteen feet high. It is lighted by three large windows on the north side looking out upon a large garden, which can be utilised as a play ground and in which the School Managers will have the necessary offices erected.

On the first floor of the building and above the Assembly Room, is a large room known as the Magistrates' Room. Now seldom used, the use of which as a classroom has, it is confidently hoped, been granted by the County Council.

On this floor also is a lavatory which, subject to the consent of the County Council, will be set apart for the use of the girls attending the school.

These premises will afford ample accommodation for over fifty pupils, which number, in the opinion of the Managers, is not at present likely to be exceeded."

As he mentioned, it had already been used by Mr. Gwynne Jones for his private School and it seemed therefore logical that it should be the appropriate accommodation for the first, temporary Intermediate School. Reports were obtained from the Sanitary Inspector, negotiations concluded for the use of the garden at the rear as a school play ground, and all was conducted to the satisfaction of the Charity Commission so that on the 1st February, 1896, they granted their approval to open the school there.

What was now required was staff, and in due course advertisements were circulated for the appointment of a Headmaster and Headmistress.

On this issue, again some friction arose between the fund raisers and the Managers, but by the 13th April of that year the Managers were in a position to select from the applications to hand the respective Headmaster and Headmistress. Before the meeting took place, however, Major Price Lewes had received a letter or petition, circulated by six of the local Committee of Fund Raisers, endorsing the excellence of two of the candidates and containing a veiled threat that, if their views and recommendations for the Headship were not observed, there might well be difficulty in collecting the remaining financial contribution by way of bond in the final balance required of £350. The Minutes of the meeting of the 13th April record the anger of Major Price Lewes:-

> *"The Chairman called the attention of the Local Governors to a circular letter he had received from the local Committee ....he strongly protested against the tone of the concluding paragraph, referring to the bond of £350 which the local Committee had to provide before opening the school.*
>
> *He regarded it as a pistol levelled at their heads.*
>
> *If their request would not be complied with under these circumstances, he suggested that the appointments be delayed until the £1,000 and the building site were in their actual possession."*

Others, such as Lima Jones, sought to excuse this injudicious intervention in the appointments as he thought the circular :

> *"Was one which they should consider in a friendly and conciliatory spirit, for it was couched in respectful terms and was signed by people whose opinion as workers in the cause of the school should receive every consideration."*

Dr. J. Davies, however, was not so easily pacified and it was decided there and then to adjourn the meeting to enable Major Price Lewes and Dr. Davies to visit the National Provincial Bank, over lunch, to propose other names to the Bank Manager who would be acceptable to the Bank as bond guarantors.

This was done, and the afternoon proceeded with the appointment of Miss Hook of Ipswich as Headmistress and the existing private Grammar School Headmaster, Mr. G. Gwynne Jones B.A. of Aberaeron, as Headmaster of the new school. If the Fundraisers had achieved nothing more than to accelerate the founding of the school, by perhaps disruptive means, they had certainly sparked the Managers into immediate action.

G. Gwynne Jones, in a letter of 30th April, 1946, to the Jubilee Number of The Link, recalled the first day of its opening on 12th May, 1896, with the words:

> *"There was no formal gathering on that first day. The staff consisted of two, myself and Miss Hook whom, to the deep regret of all who knew her, the school lost under sad circumstances after only a short period of service.*

> *Between thirty and forty pupils presented themselves. The number of pupils steadily increased, and so also did the number of the staff; one disadvantage of the temporary premises was the lack of means for practical work in science; also more than one class had to be taught in the same room."*

The late Miss Olive M. Jones, recalled her experiences too in the new school. She was, in fact, the first registered pupil in the Aberaeron Intermediate School Register and, like all children, recalled the Magistrates' Room upstairs and the mischief of her fellow pupils with affection:

> *"What was of far greater importance to those early pupils was the thrill of sliding down the slippery bannister of those steep stairs, in reckless pursuit of one another, into the flagged 'pashet' below, heedless of the exasperated threats of the then 'Mrs Mop', with her broom and unique vocabulary."*

Matters moved apace to the acquisition by the Managers of the present site of the old school, purchased on the 22nd May 1896. This land had been within the ownership of the Llanayron Estate. Mrs. Lewes, then the tenant for life of that Estate, regrettably could not make a gift of any land under the terms of the legal arrangements affecting the property and so, after negotiation, one and a quarter acre was to be acquired at a price of £160 and the formalities were left in the care of the Estate solicitors, Messrs. Busk & Mellor of 45 Lincoln's Inn Fields, London.

The specification for the new school had to be circulated to architects. On the 14th October, 1896, the general invitation was issued on behalf of the Managers as to their requirements.

> *"Plans, sections and elevations must be drawn to a scale of 8 foot to 1 inch and not mounted. The buildings are to be erected on a plot of 1 and 1/4 acre in extent, situated at an elevation of about 80 feet above the level of main road, with a gradual descent to the road. The buildings must embrace accommodation for sixty boys and forty girls, with separate entrances, to include Assembly Room, two Class-rooms, Laboratory, Laundry, Cooking Kitchen, Workshop, Music and Sewing Room, Cloakroom, Master and Mistress Rooms and usual offices, to be so planned so as to afford facilities for easy extension. Estimated cost not to exceed £1,600."*

The winning design was submitted by a local architect, Mr. LL. Banks Price B.A., of Lampeter and his projected drawings were accepted on 5th December 1896, agreed by the County Governing Body, and finally approved, after some discussion with the Charity Commissioner's Architect, by that body on the 26th April, 1897. On the 18th May 1897, eight tenders for the erection of the buildings were opened and the tender of Mr. E. Evans of Llanybydder was accepted in the sum of £1,525. In the course of construction there were to be extras approved in the sum of £75, and the boundary walls, gates, and water supply involved a further unanticipated expenditure of £200.

Matters did not go, however, without difficulty, for most of the stone used in the construction was quarried from the Cwmmins Quarry, the property of the Monachty Estates.

The Clerk to the Managers received a letter on the 19th November 1898 from Messrs. Roberts & Evans, solicitors for the Monachty Estates, complaining:

"The number of loads you return to us seems quite inadequate to the extent of walling. We are informed that there are 800 perches of walling at least in the boundary walls, culvert and dry wall and if this is so, the number of loads should be at least 1,200 - not to speak of what Elias Jones carted. We understand that the Managers consider that Mr. Gwynne should make a present of the stone, or a part of them, but we can assure you that he is not in a position to do so, much as he would like to further any forward movement in Aberaeron. We have much hesitation in not accepting your return. At the same time we are informed from several sources that a far larger number of loads have been taken and cannot help thinking that you have made a mis-calculation."

These were minor and insignificant problems and by the 1st August, 1898, the buildings were completed.

The official opening ceremony was set for 19th September 1898. Major Price Lewes, Chairman of the Local Governing Body presided. In commenting on the physical appearance of the school, he remarked that there might be some who would be:

"somewhat disappointed by the outward appearance of the building, but the local Governors had .... rightly decided not to spend money on ornate decoration to the outside of the buildings, but rather to provide spacious accommodation in the classrooms. They would admit that they had succeeded in their object."

The Architect, Mr. Lloyd Banks Price of Doldrement, Lampeter and the Contractor, Mr. E. Evans of Llanybydder, were present, as were a number of local dignitaries and educationalists. Mrs. Price Lewes was to perform the opening ceremony and in due time, at 2.45 p.m. that afternoon, the Architect handed her a silver key in a velvet case, with which she immediately opened the chief entrance door and, in a clear voice, gave expression to a schoolmaster's dream:

"I now declare this building to be open. I wish the school great success. I trust the pupils who come here from time to time will be obedient boys and girls and that they will obey their masters and mistresses and that they will make good men and women. I again wish the school and its Managers, its staff and its pupils, very great success."

The list of all who attended would be too numerous to relate, but the stalwarts of the cause, Major Price Lewes, John M. Howell, and Dr. Davies, were present and spoke to the assembled crowd of around 200 people. They, in due time, would be immortalised for their contribution by the adoption of their respective homes, Tyglyn, Portland and Tanyfron, as the constituent houses of the school.

Having commenced by referring to J. M. Howell's contribution, published in The Link in 1908, what better way to conclude than by again referring to his aspirations:

> *"We only began to make history when we built our County School. Here is a starting point - and a propelling force. It remains with the pupils to add by their records to the momentum. They will do so by their careers. By-and-bye many of them will become rich people. They will give of their treasures. They will build a tower and workroom and extend the laboratories and endow scholarships, and thus add the name of Aberayron to the list of names of Cardiganshire townlets which have given the world men and women."*

❖

YSGOL ABERAERON YN GANMLWYDD OED

Geraint Bowen

Ei hanes sy'n dal ynof
Fel cynt yng ngafael y cof.
Yn gêl yn ffrwd y galon
Mae enwau y llanciau llon
A'r merched dirifedi
Fu rhwng ei hen furiau hi,
Morynion, meibion y môr
A geirwon draethau'r goror,
Bugeiliaid defaid a da
O Lan-non i Lanina,
Anhuniog a Henfynyw,
Llannarth, Aber-arth a'u rhyw.
Mae hiraeth yng nghwm Aeron
A saeth yn y fynwes hon.
Mae'n ganrif, eto'n ifanc,
Fel pe bai'n ddi-drai, ddidranc.
Yn lân ymhen y lonydd,
Yn deg yn heulwen y dydd.
Er yn hen mae'i rhin i hyd
A'i hasbri yn ei hysbryd
(1995)

Staff tua 1898 / Staff about 1898
G. Gwyn Jones, Miss Bessie Evans, Mr. Findon, Miss Kitchen

Charles J. Hughes, B.A., Prifathro, 1899-1917

Tîm Hoci / Hockey team
1909

Tîm Pêl-droed / Soccer team
1910

War Memorial Number.

1922.

THE LINK.

A Magazine supported by the Past and Present Pupils of the Aberayron County School.

" Rhai ar wasgar o'r ysgol—gu unir
A'r genedl bresennol :
Goreu gadwyn gre' gydiol,
Ddaw i ni a ddoe yn ol."

WEST EALING, W.13:
Francis A. Perry, Printer, 4, Kirchen Road.
1922.

The Link 1922

ABERAERON COUNTY SCHOOL 1898 - 1973

David L. Jones

The early years 1898-1917

Thc day chosen by the Managers for the official opening of the new School building was Monday, 19 September 1898, with the ceremonies commencing at 2.30 p.m., provided that this day suited the Principals of Saint David's College, Lampeter, and of the University College of Wales at Aberystwyth. The day proved suitable for both Principals. The new school building, i.e. the central part of the "old school", contained a hall, classrooms, a laboratory and a kitchen, with a small plot of grass, enclosed by a medium sized wall, in front of which trees were planted. Through the fields below, a path ran up to the School and, to the wrath of the Headmaster and the owner, the more mischievous of the boys would run through these fields on their way to and from the School. On the opening day, Llewellyn Price, the architect, presented a silver key to Mrs. Price Lewes and she opened the main entrance door. "I now declare this building to be open", said Mrs. Lewes, "I wish the School great success. I trust the pupils who will come here from time to time will be obedient boys and girls, that they will obey their masters and mistresses, and that they will make good men and women." Principal Bebb from Lampeter and Principal Roberts from Aberystwyth, together with a number of the Managers spoke, the chief theme of their addresses being the value of education. Tea was then served in the School by Mrs. Lewes, her daughters, her son and others to around 200 guests.

A new school year began in a new school building. The Assembly Room had fulfilled an useful purpose but it had not been satisfactory, especially from the point of view of discipline. In the circumstances, the results of the teaching carried out in the Town Hall were good; there had been a number of successes in the London and Welsh matriculation as well as in other examinations. The excitement of moving into the new School had scarcely died down when three of the four teaching staff resigned. Gwyn Jones and Mabel Kitching resigned on 13 February 1899; Jones had been appointed Headmaster of Llandeilo County School and Miss Kitching took up a post at the same school. Charles Nathan, the Science Master, resigned on 14 March. Why Jones moved to Llandeilo is unclear, but his departure was amicable; a large party of pupils and friends gathered in the new School Hall where, after several speeches of appreciation, a presentation was made to Jones.

By a coincidence, the day on which Gwyn Jones handed his resignation to the Managers was also the day on which the Central Welsh Board inspector first visited the School. In 1896, the Joint Education Committees in Wales had united to found the Central Welsh Board as an examining and an inspecting body. The Board's inspector reported that there were 46 boys and 30 girls at the School; 41 pupils could not travel home in the evening and they stayed in lodgings at Aberaeron. The teachers were Gwyn Jones, Charles Nathan, Mabel Kitching and Elizabeth Evans. The inspector noted that the School had entered new premises "on a very eligible and suitable site". At the time of the inspection, the School was fitting up a chemical laboratory, a manual instruction room and a kitchen. The general comment was that the "School continues to do very good work". The inspector noted that Welsh was taught and, while translations were well done, the work in grammar was weak and in composition weaker.

Commendable despatch was shown by the Managers in selecting a successor; Jones resigned on 13 February 1899 and a new headmaster was elected on 21 March. The advertisement for the vacancy had been approved at the meeting which received Jones' resignation; the Board accepted a motion that the Headmaster "must speak Welsh and this to be in the advertisement". The salary was £150 a year with a captitation fee of £1; in March, the School had 71 pupils which brought the salary up to £221. Seventeen applicants sent in their names and four were placed on the short-list: Charles J. Hughes of New Quay; David Rees of Llanelli; W. H. Jenkins of Rhyl; and, J. W. Jones of Gelligaer. Ten members of the Board of Managers were present on 21 March and the Clerk recorded the voting figures. John Lee Davies, a pupil at that time, recalled that "It was fervently hoped on all side that sectarian motives should not play such an important part in this second appointment. However, the battle on this occasion again was as keenly contested between the various denominations as had been the previous one, ...". We know how many votes were cast for each candidate, but we do not know how each member of the board voted. The Clerk's arithmetic is also uncertain. From the voting figures, it is probable that only nine members cast their vote and that the Chairman did not take part. On the first round of voting, each member was allowed three votes and the result was as follows: Charles J. Hughes (6); David Rees (9); W. H. Jenkins (8); J. W. Jones (5). The result produces a total of twenty-eight votes which leaves one a little suspicious of the Clerk's arithmetic; it also appears that some members split their votes between two candidates. The candidate with the least number of votes was now eliminated and each manager was allowed two votes: Charles J. Hughes (6); David Rees (8); W. H. Jenkins (4). The last round was between Hughes and Rees and each manager was allowed one vote. Charles J. Hughes was elected headmaster by 5 votes to 4. The two main denominations on the Board of Managers were Congregationalists and Methodists; Hughes was a Congregationalist and his chief contender was probably supported by the Methodists. At the same meeting, Miss K. A. Scott was appointed the Second Mistress.

Hughes was only narrowly elected Headmaster which indicates that the strength of denominational loyalty led four of the managers to discount an overwhelming argument in Hughes' favour: he was, like Gwyn Jones, the headmaster of a private grammar school for boys, but in New Quay. As a result of his appointment, six pupils from New Quay came to Aberaeron and this served to dissipate the animosity lingering from the battle over the site of the new intermediate school. A native of Brecon, Hughes was forty-eight years old when he became Headmaster at Aberaeron. Following two years at sea during his youth, Hughes studied for a Teacher's Certificate at the Normal Training College in Bangor. He then held a number of temporary posts while he studied for a degree in the University of London. These temporary posts included the headship of the British School at New Quay and the headship of Llanarth British School. On completing his studies for a B.A. of the University of London, Hughes established, in February 1875, a grammar school in New Quay. Little has been written on the history of the private grammar schools in nineteenth-century Wales; the glimpses of these schools which appear in the memoirs and autobiographies of the period show that they provided a valuable service to their communities. Hughes' school in New Quay was a typical example; "Ysgol Huws" provided a basic education to pupils from the New Quay area and boarders from other parts of Wales. Hughes' pupils became doctors, lawyers, colliery managers, master mariners, clergymen, and ministers; the Rev. Josiah Towyn Jones, the Member of Parliament for Llanelli 1912-1922, describes his education in *Dod's Parliamentary Companion* as "New Quay Grammar School and Presbyterian College, Carmarthen". The main problem for Hughes' school, like many other private schools, was financial support; Hughes charged fifteen shillings a quarter which, in a successful year, would produce an income of £50. However, this income would not allow the employment of an extra master and the curriculum was necessarily limited. Hughes did not regard his school as a business; a boy who showed promise was given an education on the basis of "You will pay when you can?"; J. M. Howell saw the school's account books and noted that the number who "could not pay" was considerable.

The vacant science post had been advertised at a salary of £120, an increase of £20 over Nathan's salary; the successful candidate was James Dewhurst. Changes in the staff of the School continued to be a problem: Miss Elizabeth Evans resigned at the beginning of the autumn term. The Managers deferred the question of replacing Miss Evans until their next meeting, at the beginning of 1900, when they postponed the appointment of a replacement fourth teacher because it would result in a deficit of £34. However, Miss Scott's salary was increased by £10 a year, presumably in view of the extra teaching burden she was carrying. The Managers did not have a problem in recruiting teachers, but it was difficult to keep these teachers for more than a brief period. The establishment of several intermediate schools in the late 1890s meant that there was plenty of opportunity for an ambitious young teacher, especially one with some experience of teaching in a secondary school. Aberaeron was a remote place, difficult of access before the coming of the railway. Moreover, teachers without a knowledge of Welsh must have found it difficult to live in a Welsh-speaking district; the Managers had already discovered that a teacher without a knowledge of Welsh had difficulties, especially a difficulty over discipline. Equally, the children with a poor knowledge of English would not have found it easy to be taught by a teacher who only spoke English. But the School was making good progress. The results of the important Science and Arts examination in the summer of 1899 had been praiseworthy:

Theoretical and Inorganic Chemistry

3 First Class Pass

5 Second Class Pass

2 Failure

Mathematics Stages 1, 2, & 3

7 First Class Pass

8 Second Class Pass

5 Failure

Because the School had a small staff with a high turnover, the curriculum had to be limited: Chemistry, Mathematics, History, English, French, Latin and Welsh. The Headmaster took a full share in the teaching work. The Managers, as we have already noted, tried to extend the curriculum by adding to the list of qualifications required from new teachers; the favoured additional subjects were instrumental music, vocal music, and drawing. This approach demanded too much from individual teachers and it was not successful. Individual teachers were encouraged to obtain extra qualifications; Gwyn Jones was allowed to shorten the Easter holidays and to extend the summer holidays in 1897 so that he could attend a six week manual training course in Sweden. Elizabeth Evans was recommended to receive the grant offered by the County Council for manual training.

The encouragement given by the Managers shows that they were aware that the curriculum was biased towards those pupils intending to enter higher education and that it failed to provide for the needs of those pupils whose experience of secondary education would be brief. One solution to this problem was the employment of part-time teachers. Towards the end of 1898, the Managers were looking for a "travelling teacher" to teach cookery and laundry work; the successful candidate was Miss H. Bertha Jones, the daughter of B. C. Jones, Clerk to the Managers, who was appointed a part-time cookery mistress. This appointment proved to have a wider benefit when, a year later, evening classes were held on Friday after 6 p.m. - the fees for the classes included the cost of Miss Jones' time and the cost of the use of the kitchen, utensils and coal. The Managers also looked towards the University College at Aberystwyth and, for a short period, Mr. Pickard, the Lecturer in Horticulture, visited Aberaeron to deliver lectures and demonstrations in horticulture.

The Joint Education Committee had a legitimate interest in the provision of technical education; the Welsh Intermediate Schools Act of 1889 was "to make further provision for the intermediate and technical education of the inhabitants of Wales and the county of Monmouth." The Act included a wide definition of technical education:

(i) any of the branches of science and art with respect to which grants are for the time being made by the Department of Science and Art;

(ii) the use of tools, modelling in clay, wood, or other material;

(iii) commercial arithmetic, commercial geography, book-keeping, and shorthand;

(iv) any other subject applicable to the purposes of agriculture, industries, trade, or commercial life and practice, ... suited to the needs of the district; but it should not include the teaching the practice of any trade, or industry, or employment.

The County Council also had an interest in that the Technical Instruction Act of 1889 allowed the council to levy a rate for technical education which could be applied under the Welsh Intermediate Education Act or under the Technical Instruction Act. Fryer, the clerk to the Joint Education Committee in Cardiganshire, was also the Clerk to the Technical Instruction Committee and he gave permission, as clerk to the Technical Instruction Committee, for Miss Bertha Jones' evening cookery classes. The Managers showed little enthusiasm for the more practical aspects of technical education and this reflected the views of many parents who saw secondary education as the pathway by which their children could enter a white-collar occupation. Pressure from Fryer's committees was probably responsible for Bertha Jones' appointment and for Pickard's lectures. Later in 1900, Fryer asked if the managers were exercising supervision over Miss Jones' work and what were they doing about laundry work, carpentry and similar subjects. The Managers declared that the boiler had been fixed and they were at that moment prepared to start laundry work. Miss Bertha Jones, they added, was giving satisfaction. A room had been built and reserved for the "manual labour class", but the Managers lacked the means to provide the necessary apparatus. They were anxious to proceed and they were glad that the county body was disposed and able to help. The ball was neatly thrown back to Fryer and his Committees.

Sport had not been neglected. From the first year of the School, the Managers had rented a playing field in Aberaeron and they provided the necessary games equipment for both boys and girls. When the materials for games were purchased in 1897, the Managers pointed out the advantage of "games of recreation" for girls as well as boys. The fields rented in the early years included part of the Square Field, Cae Prince and the field near Llyswen Mill. The last two fields are now the School's permanent games fields. Physical exercises were added to the School's curriculum in 1899 when dumb-bells, a horizontal bar and quoits were purchased.

In the four years to the end of the nineteenth century, the Managers had laboured well. The School building had been completed and the School itself established on a sound basis. An attempt had been made to extend the curriculum. Scholarships were awarded regularly and they were monitored; pupils with a scholarship had to stay in school for a year. Books and other prizes were given to pupils who achieved a mark of 60%+ in an external examination. From the end of the autumn term 1900, the pupils were given an annual party of tea and cake out of the school funds.

A new century brought new arrangements in the organisation of education at a national level. The Charity Commissioners had been drawn into the administration of the intermediate schools because of their existing interest in educational charities. On the whole, the Commissioners did not intervene greatly after the county schemes had been approved. Fryer drew, in May 1897, the attention of the Managers to the Commissioners' insistence on "an uniform system of nomenclature being adopted for Grades or Classes in the intermediate schools and the name 'Form' should be adopted and that the relation should be from the lowest Form as number one to the highest." The Clerk was tartly instructed to point out to Fryer that this was already being done at Aberaeron. The Science and Art Department in South Kensington intervened in the provision of scientific and technical education through inspection and the provision of grants which brought £35.12s.2d. to Aberaeron in 1899. There was a confusing organisation of education authorities both at the national and at the local level.

By 1899, the government had realised that a single authority for education was necessary at the centre before local organisations could be re-constituted. In the same year, the Education Department that looked after elementary education and the Science and Art Department were consolidated into a Board with its own President, for the "superintendence of matters relating to education in England and Wales." The new Board of Education also took over the powers and duties of the Charity Commissioners in education. The Education Act of 1902 allowed County Councils to create local education authorities, and education thus became a normal and usual function of local government. These reforms were common to both England and Wales and simplified the administration of education, especially elementary education, in that central government could now pay grants to 318 local education authorities instead of 2,658 school board and 14,238 committees of voluntary school managers. Considerable lobbying by Welsh Members of Parliament and others led in 1907 to the creation of the Welsh Department of the Board of Education with its own Permanent Secretary and its own inspectorate. Unfortunately, the Act that created the Board of Education had also confirmed the powers of the Central Welsh Board to inspect schools which had been established under the Welsh Intermediate Education Act. There was room for friction and, under Alfred T. Davies, the first Permanent Secretary of the Welsh Department, there was considerable friction between the Department and the Central Welsh Board. This division had more effect on the general development of Welsh education than on the daily administration of individual schools. However, after the intermediate schools accepted the grants available under the 1902 Education Act, these schools had to accept an annual inspection by Her Majesty's Inspectors of Schools from the Welsh Department as well as an annual inspection by the Central Welsh Board.

The Central Welsh Board inspectors visited Aberaeron on 10 May 1900 and they recorded that 71 pupils attended the School, with 31 of these pupils living in lodgings. The four teachers were C. J. Hughes, James Dewhurst, John A. Enoch and Katharine Scott; Enoch was a temporary appointment. The inspectors complained that the room set apart for manual instruction was still not furnished. A considerable number of new pupils entered the School in January and the School's authorities were urged to secure a larger entry in September. Boys were needed at home in the autumn for the harvest. The lessons showed evidence of careful and painstaking work; oral French was taught by Miss Scott in a particularly bright and animated manner. However, the work in languages could gain much if the School laid stress on the teaching of Welsh. A year later, the inspector noted that a bookcase had been added for the library and very good progress had been made with the library since the last inspection. A field was provided for school games, but a tennis court for the girls was very desirable. Discipline and order were good. The School suffered from the premature removal of pupils; ten of the twenty pupils in Form II would probably leave at the end of the first year. The inspector noted, without comment, that the examiner's report recorded three pupils as being entered for the Stage 3 Welsh examination.

The inspector's reports reveal a School marking time and they mask some turmoil in the School's affairs during the first two years of Hughes' headmastership. Hughes was not working well with the other two teachers. In October 1900, he was compelled to report that Miss Scott was not prepared to continue instructing the girls in drill and he asked for the Managers' instructions in the matter. E. Lima Jones intervened to inform his fellow Managers that Mr. Dewhurst was willing to undertake these duties on a temporary basis. The Managers accepted this offer. This dispute should have been settled within the School; Lima Jones' intervention was humiliating for the Headmaster.

Some progress was made. Miss Scott and Mr. D. Williams arranged an entertainment which raised £9.11s.4d. towards books for the School library. The creation of the library had been prompted by the Central Welsh Board inspectors. However, Miss Scott, whose salary had been reduced to its previous level after the appointment of D. Williams in September 1900, left at the end of the summer term 1902. The Headmaster reported to the Managers that he was not satisfied with Dewhurst's work and it was decided that Dewhurst should be given a term's notice to leave; but if he wanted to leave at once, then this was acceptable. Mrs. T. Z. Jones, one of the Managers, complained that history and literature for the matriculation examination of the University of Wales was not adequately taught. The Managers recommended that, if the pupils had gone through the full course of the School and desired to sit any examinations other than the Central Welsh Board, they should be assisted as far as possible by the School staff. The Managers also recommended that the Headmaster was empowered to deal with his subordinates as having the complete authority of the Managers. Hughes was a weak man and he found it difficult to work with his staff. Mrs. T. Z. Jones complained because her daughter, Alice Grace, intended to enter an university; the solution to her complaint was unfair in that the Managers required the teachers to cope with an extra burden.

The School opened the autumn term of 1902 with two new teachers: Mr. R. A. Scott for science and Miss G. S. Pole Evans as mistress. In less than two months, Mr. Scott had resigned and Miss Pole Evans was found to be unsatisfactory. The Headmaster was authorised to test Miss Evans' work while Dr. John Davies and Lima Jones interviewed Mr. Scott in order to prevail upon him to change his mind. Scott refused to alter his decision and Miss Pole Evans agreed to resign after the Headmaster found that she could not control her classes. The position of science master was offered to W. H. Griffiths who declined, as did the next candidate, and the post was given to R. Robson; Miss L. C. Bennison was appointed mistress.

The Central Welsh Board inspector visited the School early in 1902. The only aspect of School work he found praiseworthy was the teaching of Latin and Greek. He noted that the examiner's reports were on the whole fair, which was faint praise. Miss Bertha Jones, who had recently received a salary increase, was described as weak in her method of teaching and the knowledge of cookery possessed by the pupils was very limited. When the inspector visited again, on 19 March 1903, after the several changes in staff, his report was far more critical. The teaching of chemistry was described as thoroughly bad with some pupils knowing nothing. The examiners had asked in their report "why is there only one pupil offering Welsh in a School situated in such a thoroughly Welsh-speaking district as Aberayron?" This question had prompted the inspector to investigate language teaching and he complained that nearly all the pupils in the School received instruction in French, but only one pupil was receiving instruction in Welsh. Several pupils who were not likely to stay in the School for more than a year were wasting their time on a foreign language when this time could be diverted with more profit to the study of the home language. The inspector recommended that serious consideration be given to the position of Welsh in the School curriculum. An additional teacher was required because the Headmaster was wholly involved in teaching and had no time for general supervision. The report was not entirely gloomy; the inspector recorded that "he received the impression that a fair amount of good work was being done." The teaching of physical exercise needed attention but, on the other hand, hockey had been added to the School's games. The grants for science teaching, formerly awarded by the Department of Arts and Science, were now disbursed by the Board of Education and, in the early years, the inspectors from the Board concentrated on the teaching of science. Their reports press for an additional laboratory for physics and the purchase of extra equipment for the teaching of the physics part of the syllabus. Ominously, the inspectors pronounced the standard of work as yet only moderately good in science.

The Managers took action after the reports from both inspectors. E. O. James, a native of Glynarthen, was appointed the fifth teacher and David Williams' salary was increased to £105. A sub-committee considered "the teaching of the principles of agriculture", and the Board agreed that these principles should be taught at Aberaeron. This resolution was not acted upon for many years. B. C. Jones sent the plan of the proposed new physical laboratory to the Board of Education on 30 July 1903 and he received the required approval on 5 October. Despite these efforts, 1903 ended on a gloomy note; the Central Welsh Board inspectors wrote that the School had been exceptionally recognised for the present session, but continued recognition would depend upon the development of a three years' course and the implementation of the requirements of the Board of Education.

In the following year, the Central Welsh Board inspectors complained that the School needed painting and decorating and that the facilities for drawing were limited. The attention of the governing body was drawn to the omission of Geography - an obligatory subject - from the School timetable. The Central Welsh Board made a more thorough inspection a year later on 25 May 1905 when a triennial inspection took place. The School was sharply criticised both as regards buildings and curriculum. The inspectors noticed sign of neglect everywhere and judged the condition of certain parts of the School to be a grave menace to health. The gravel walks at the entrance were overgrown. There was an unpleasant smell in most of the rooms and the ventilation was judged to be defective. The curriculum was not organised satisfactorily in that the School followed a three years' course and not four as required by the Regulations. Almost half the School was in Form 1 which appeared to the inspectors to be the class for pupils staying only for one year in the School. This form was divided into 1A and 1B, with 1B containing the pupils who were not staying after one year. Form 1A was taught all subjects but, as both sections were taught together, satisfactory teaching was "well nigh impossible". There were some good aspects; except for mathematics, each teacher was responsible for one subject throughout the School. English was well taught; Latin, taught by E. O. James, was sound and energetic; French was not so good; History was well arranged. However, the Welsh language was again a problem: "taking into consideration the requirements of the district, the course in languages was not well arranged. Welsh only one hour a week in one form while Latin and French taken throughout. This is a School in which a large proportion of time given to languages in the lowest Form should be English and French." The teaching of science was satisfactory with the Chemistry practical done in good style. Turning to the reports on science teaching prepared by the inspectors from the Board of Education, we find that the 1903/04 report noted with satisfaction that the physics laboratory had been completed with a fair supply of equipment and that a suitable demonstration table had been purchased for the science lecture room. The timetable was not satisfactory in that the usual School hours had to be extended for some of the practical classes and the pupils taking these classes were deprived of the usual morning interval. In the following year, the Board of Education was in agreement with the Central Welsh Board - good work in science teaching was being done at the School. The Board of Education's reports also reveal the range of subjects included in the School's curriculum during 1903/04: Composition, English language, English literature, History, Arithmetic, Additional

Mathematics, Elementary Mathematics, Latin, Welsh, French, Chemistry, Geography, Drawing. If we compare this list with the list for 1901/02, we find that Welsh and Geography had been added to the curriculum while Elementary Science and Mechanics had been omitted. Geography had been added after the inspectors reminded the Managers that this was a compulsory subject; a copy of the amended timetable was supplied to the Board as proof in September 1904.

Robson, the Science Master left at the end of 1903; he was replaced by D. J. Parry who did not take up the appointment and the post was not filled until 30 March 1905, when Mr. C. K. Barnes M.Sc. was appointed at a salary of £130 p.a. Miss Bennison left in July 1905 and David Williams in August; Miss Richards was appointed to teach French and Miss Maddock to teach History and English.

At the end of 1905, the Managers granted permission for a Reunion of Old Pupils to be held in the School on 26 December 1905. A Past and Present Pupils Association had been formed in 1904, but little is known of its activities until this reunion. At this Reunion, a Magazine Committee was elected to establish a school magazine; the staff were later invited to join the committee. A concert, organised in August, produced about £10 to defray the expenses of producing the magazine. *The Link: a magazine supported by the past and present pupils of the Aberayron County School* was first published in the late autumn of 1907. The editor was D. W. Fenwick Jones, a medical student in London, and the school editor was J. Seymour Rees, later a Congregationalist minister. E. O. Jones composed an *englyn*:

"Rhai ar wasgar o'r Ysgol - go unir

Â'r genedl bresennol;

Gorau gadwyn gre' gydiol,

Ddaw i ni a ddoe yn ôl."

This verse was published in every edition of *The Link* until 1971. The contents of the new magazine included a profile of Major Price Lewes DL, JP, the first Chairman of the Board of Managers; an address written by the first Headmaster, G. Gwyn Jones; "A brief sketch of the school's early days" by J. Lee Davies; together with School notes and letters from the various universities. T. H. E. wrote from Aberystwyth to record that in his first year, 1905/06, there were three *Aeronians* at the University College. These included Miss Alice Jones, the daughter of Mrs. T. Z. Jones and later better known as Miss A. Gower Jones, who completed her History degree in 1906 with Honours; she was the first Aberaeron pupil to graduate from the University of Wales. In the current year, there were six pupils from the School at Aberystwyth: four women and two men. T. H. E. pleaded that the pupils at Aberaeron should not be so disloyal to their native county as to enter Cardiff and Bangor Colleges, "in preference to what ought to be their own College in their own County." There were seven old pupils taking the arts course at Cardiff, according to J. M.

D., and two following a medical course. The two medical students were Garfield Evans, the son of Captain John Evans of Milford House who built the Aeron Express, and Milton Davies, the son of Dr. John Davies of Tanyfron, and both were in the Soccer Eleven, the former being the vice-captain. Miss Eleanor Beckett was "a dashing forward" in the Ladies Hockey team; born in Denver, Colorado, Eleanor Beckett, later Mrs. John Hugh Jones of Llanon, had returned to Aberaeron with her parents to live in the house called Denver in Portland Place. The early copies of *The Link* now held by the School were donated by Mr. and Mrs. J. H. Jones. A late contribution to the magazine was a letter from London, signed by *Bwrw* and dated 15 November 1907; *Bwrw* was an old pupil who had lived in Panteg Villas but whose identity is now lost. In the 1908 issue of *The Link, Weros* wrote the London letter; he was probably the Garfield Evans mentioned above. He reported that D. W. Fenwick Jones had succeeded in securing his Inter M. B. and had joined the London Welsh choir in the summer and "with his pal "Bwrw" make a strong pair." Willie Lewis was now a fully qualified solicitor; he returned to practice in Market Street, Aberaeron. On Sunday, most of the old pupils made "a special effort to attend the evening service at his favourite chapel." After the service, they met at a restaurant for "News from home" and supper. Naturally, the conversation is always in Welsh, and the foreigners on the nearest tables have heated arguments on the nationality of our little group."

The 1909 issue of *The Link* included a survey of the careers achieved by past pupils during the first ten years of the School's existence:

60 in teaching (12 being graduates)

20 ministers in various denominations

8 in medicine

4 in the legal profession

30 bank clerks

12 sailors

6 music teachers

5 engineers

1 newspaper reporter

1 policeman

100 in trade or commerce.

The rest were following the father's occupation, chiefly farming, at home or, in the case of women, keeping house and waiting for marriage. There was still a lack of obvious careers, outside teaching, for women; an article in the 1911 *Link* outlined the choice of the careers as teaching, medical work and secretarial work. By 1909, the old pupils included fifteen university graduates: nine at the University of Wales (five of these, including the first, were women); three at London University; three at Oxford University; and three at Saint David's College, Lampeter. The vision of those who had campaigned for intermediate education had been fulfilled at Aberaeron: young Welsh women and young Welshmen were being given an opportunity to obtain an university education.

The *School Notes* in the early issues of the school magazine reveal that the School had developed an active social and sporting life. A Debating Society was established in the winter of 1906: "with our worthy Headmaster President, success was only what might be expected. A high tribute of obedience and of reverence was paid by the pupils in all meetings." E. O. James, the Latin and Welsh Master, was elected President for the 1907/08 session; his presidential address was given on 9 October 1907 when he spoke on the "Vitality of the Welsh Language." J. Seymour Rees, the school editor, reported that "when listening to Mr. James, we felt proud of the fact that we were Welshmen, and as long as the *Welsh language* will be taught by gentlemen who are enthusiastic in their work and as patriotic as he is, we further add that it will be practically an impossibility for the Welsh language to die out." Later in the same issue, the editor noted "we feel grateful to the School Managers for the change which they have brought about by the introduction of Welsh in the school timetable." In late July, the School Debating Society, thirty-two in all, journeyed down over the cliffs to Gilfach-yr-Halen. After a picnic, prepared by Miss Maddock and Miss Owen, various games were played, the Headmaster both superintending and participating. Barnes, the Science Master, took a photograph and James wrote an englyn:

"Swil, dewisol lodesi - a bechgyn

Bochgoch yn ymloni

'Arholiad' yn yr heli

A foddwyd, anghofwyd hi."

This event was a welcome break in the summer examinations.

E. O. James was the "propelling force" behind the School's first Eisteddfod held on 8 April 1908. The subject for the Chair Competition was *Cymru*: James gave a careful analysis of the four competitors and awarded the prize to J. Seymour Rees. The ritual of chairing the bard at the National Eisteddfod was followed: James presided as the Archdruid Arthen and he was supported by Ap Gwryn, Llew o'r Fron, Cei-Fab, Gwallter, Ap Galed, Ap Cenin, Ap Trichrug, Glanymor, Onen Arth, Ap Micah, Aeronia (Rees James) and the Manager J. M. Howell who could never resist the lure of a platform appearance. Evan Jones won the competition for tenor solo and for music reading; M. D. Morgan the competition for baritone solo; J. Llew Lewis the competitions for ear test, Welsh essay, impromptu speech and the lyric; W. Owen Davies the competition for the englyn; E. T. Griffiths the competition for the Welsh recitation; D. Albert Lewis the competition for the limerick; T. Irenaeus Jones the competition for English translation; J. Seymour Rees and W. B. Williams shared the prize for the Welsh-English translations while Miss Nesta Howell and W. B. Williams shared the prize for the English-French translation. All the members of staff participated as adjudicators and the Managers attended as part of the audience. Thus, concluded the school editor in the 1908 *Link*, "have they identified the School with Wales's cherished institution."

The Managers faced a number of difficulties from 1906. Barnes applied for a salary increase and he was given an extra £10 a year, bringing his annual salary to £140. James was also awarded an extra £10, bringing his annual salary to £110. However, Miss Richards left after a year and she was replaced as French teacher by Miss Owen. At a special meeting in September, Hughes reported that, with 107 pupils attending the School, it was impossible for the five teachers to carry on the work of the School. The Managers resolved to appoint a certified teacher to take English subjects at £100 a year. An immediate order was placed for three desks, each to seat four pupils, and six dual desks. The new post was later altered to a temporary position and, in early 1907, William Owen Ellis was appointed to teach English subjects, drawing and drill. This decision was prompted by a financial crisis. When the Central Welsh Board enquired as to the progress on a workshop, the Clerk was instructed to answer that the unsatisfactory position of the school funds made it impossible to comply with the Board's request. The School's bank account was overdrawn by £274.8s.9d. and D. G. Munro Hughes, the Treasurer, persuaded the Managers to enter into a guarantee bond with the Bank for £350. Letters were sent to the other intermediate schools in Cardiganshire asking for their support in obtaining more revenue from the County Council. Three months later, Major Lewes, Dr. Davies and the Headmaster were appointed to place the School's financial situation before the County Education Authority in the hope that the authority would grant additional aid to the Managers. The existing income being much less than the School's expenditure, it was decided that the staff would be reduced by one teacher at the end of the term - the Headmaster would select the person to be dismissed. The school fees were increased from 4 guineas to £4.10s.0d. from September 1907; this was still a moderate fee compared to other intermediate schools, but the poverty of the area made it a significant increase. The provision of tea and cakes to the pupils after the annual distribution of prizes was no longer to be paid from school funds. On 10 August 1907, the Managers discussed the new code of regulations issued by the Board of Education and they concluded that the new grants would bring in an increased annual income. The school fees were restored to four guineas and the provision of a workroom was placed on the agenda of the next meeting. A reduction in the teaching staff had been avoided by managing without the temporary sixth teacher. The next meeting reverted to a pessimistic mood; the subject of a workroom was not raised and it was decided not to appoint a sixth teacher. An additional teacher was only required for teaching the two or three candidates for the honours certificate. The Clerk was directed to ask the Chief Inspector not to insist on the requirement in the Central Welsh

Board regulations which laid down that the timetable should show the time allocated to the teaching of honours subjects. At the end of 1907, Miss Ethel Thomas was appointed to replace Miss Maddocks and E. O. James' salary was raised by £10 to £120 following the Managers' agreement that two hours a week be devoted to the teaching of Welsh to pupils for the Senior Certificate. The teaching of Welsh appears to have been intermittent and the few pupils who took the subject in the Central Welsh Board examinations may well have received instruction outside the School. The Managers' decision on this occasion was warmly congratulated, as we have seen, in *The Link.* This does appear to be the first serious attempt to provide for the teaching of the Welsh language. A month later, at the end of January 1908, the Headmaster placed before the Managers a letter from the Central Welsh Board on the teaching of Welsh and on the need for a workroom for manual work. On the first subject, the Managers had forestalled the Central Welsh Board; on the second subject, the Clerk was told to reply that the present building lacked accommodation for the teaching of manual work and that an adverse balance of £305.2s.3d. in the School's fund prevented the building of a new room.

The letter from the Central Welsh Board arose from the triennial inspection due in 1908 and held on 29 October 1907. The inspectors complained that the accommodation provided by the School was inadequate for 103 pupils in six forms. The central hall was in constant use as a class room and, on occasion, two classes were held in the hall at the same time. The other class rooms and laboratories were too small. Cookery, the only technical subject on the curriculum, was only taught once a week for 3 or 4 hours to 28 girls in form II or IIA. The teaching staff was inadequate for the size of the School. Honours pupils were taught out of school hours and this was only exceptionally sanctioned by the Central Welsh Board for the school year 1907-08. The teaching staff were all engaged with a class during the whole of a school day and this left no time for marking or for the preparation of experiments. The appointment of an extra teacher would solve the problem and enable the creation of an extra form with the happy result that all forms would be homogenous in composition and of a convenient size for the classroom. James was praised for good teaching in Latin and Welsh although the time allotted to Welsh should be increased. The teaching of science by Barnes was described as capable with an admirable scheme of instruction. Barnes left Aberaeron in the following year and he was replaced on 31 July 1908 by W. J. Jones, a Welsh-speaker from Swansea. Other aspects of the teaching were not so well received by the inspectors: the teaching of geography was divided between four teachers while drill lessons were held with a large class of 30-40 pupils once a fortnight which was not enough time and too many pupils. The results in drill were politely described as "not good." Compared with the last triennial inspection, the corporate life of the School was much more vigorous; football and hockey were played while a School Debating Society had been founded.

The Managers did not consider the triennial report until 28 July 1908. We have already seen that they had forestalled, a fortnight before the inspection, the adverse comments on the teaching of Welsh; the Local Sub-Committee, which dealt with immediate problems between Board meetings, had recommended an increase in the number of hours on 14 October 1907 and this had been approved by the Board on 13 December. The main topic under consideration was the Central Welsh Board's requirement for extra accommodation. The Managers were astute enough to take advantage of the new administrative arrangements for education: "in view of the fact that both elementary and secondary schools are now controlled by the County Education Committee, the Clerk was directed to ask the County Clerk whether the services of the County Architect may be requisitioned to advise managers in regard to an extension of premises now somewhat severely pressed by the Central Welsh Board Inspector." On the advice of the County Architect, the question of a partition in the Hall was quietly dropped and the Managers decided, at the end of the year, to proceed with a new laboratory for 24 pupils and a new workroom while the existing laboratory would be converted into a classroom. The Board of Education also took an interest in the School's accommodation; the Board's officials noted that the existing building together with the new extensions would provide an assembly hall; a chemical laboratory for 22 pupils; a physical laboratory for 10 pupils; a manual workshop for 16 pupils; a kitchen and a laundry room for 15 pupils; two classrooms each holding 20 pupils; a classroom for eighteen pupils; a classroom for 16 pupils; and a restroom for the mistresses. The Managers added a turret above the central hall to the County Architect's plans. Because the cost of the new building could not be met from the school funds, the managers applied to the Local Education Authority for the necessary sanction to raise a loan of £800 "for the benefit of new buildings to comply with the urgent requirement of the Board of Education." The Authority agreed and a tender of £748.10s.0d. was accepted by the Managers; the Director of Education then applied to the Board of Education for permission to raise a loan of £750 on the security of the County Fund. The Board reduced the amount of the loan to £697 to be repaid within 30 years; permission was granted in March 1910 for an extra £60 to be added to the loan.

Following the 1902 Education Act, three outside bodies had an influential interest in the School: the Central Welsh Board, the Local Education Authority and the Board of Education. The School was subject to frequent and separate inspections by the Central Welsh Board and by the Board of Education; moreover, the results of the Central Welsh Board were passed on to the Board of Education. It is unfortunate that the minutes of the Board of Management do not record the discussion on 5 December 1908 when the Clerk laid before them a copy of the resolution passed by the Portmadoc County School Managers objecting to the dual inspection by the two boards. The constant pressure for improvements must have been irksome to a Board consisting of busy men and women. The Local Education Authority also began to intervene in the running of the intermediate school; the Clerk tabled a letter from the Director of Education seeking the observations of the Managers on amendments to the County Scheme for Intermediate Schools and a letter from the managers of the schools at Tregaron and Cardigan asking for co-operation in opposing the amendments. An answer to the Director was postponed for a few weeks, presumably while all the managers were consulted, and then the Board of Managers indicated a general lack of enthusiasm for the suggested amendments and a decided opposition to both the alteration of the method for appointing Headmasters and to the proposed abolition of capitation which provided a significant part of the Headmaster's salary. The attention of the Local Education Authority was drawn to the advisability of amending clause 39 and Schedule IV of the county scheme on the "Percentage of grants from general funds on basis of population;" the Managers advocated that a more equitable basis would be the number of pupils - this would provide more money for Aberaeron. Three years later, at the beginning of 1911, the draft scheme for amending the county scheme was laid again before the Managers, as was a copy of the amendments suggested by the Aberystwyth governors. The new draft did not interfere with the Managers' power to appoint a new headmaster nor did it alter the capitation scheme for paying the Headmaster and the Managers approved the draft, with the Aberystwyth amendments. The Local Education Authority had limited influence over the intermediate schools and the Managers at Aberaeron were determined to maintain this situation. A number of pupils intending to become teachers after obtaining the Senior Certificate had their fees paid by the Local Education Authority. At the beginning of 1910, the Director of Education sent a memorandum to the intermediate schools on the need to adapt the curriculum to meet the specific requirements of intending teachers. The Aberaeron Managers responded tartly: "it was the opinion of the Managers, that it behoved the County Education Committee to amend or modify the curriculum of intermediate schools with the primary object of meeting the requirements of the ordinary pupils" rather than the specific requirements of pupil teacher candidates. The increased number of pupils was a testimony to the School's success, only ten years after its foundation, in providing a means of advancement for the able child; this success stretched the resources available to the Managers uncomfortably.

Although the chief concern of the inspectors, especially the Central Welsh Board inspectors, was the quality of the teaching provided, it is a little surprising that the Board of Education inspectors did not consider the question of pupils in lodgings until 1910. At a small number of intermediate schools, particularly those on the west coast of Wales, a large number of pupils had to stay, for lack of transport home, in lodgings during the week. The Central Welsh Board recorded the number of pupils at Aberaeron and the number of pupils in lodgings:

1898	76	(46 boys, 30 girls; 41 in lodgings)
1899	71	(39B, 32G; 40L)
1900	71	(39B, 32G; 31L)
1900	56	(29B, 27G; 30L)
1900	54	(30B, 24G; 26L)

1901	53	(36B, 17G; 20L)
1902	70	(44B, 26G; 34L)
1903	72	(44B, 28G; 41L)
1904	79	(47B, 32G; 38L)
1905	71	(37B, 34G; 35L)
1906	110	(59B, 51G; 65L)
1907	106	(57B, 49G; 67L)
1908	90	(50B, 40G; 60L)
1909	73	(41B, 32G; 47L)
1910	81	(45B, 36B; 47L)

School attendance was erratic over a school year, as can be seen in the figures for the three terms in 1900. This was not unusual in the rural intermediate schools where an extra pair of hands was required on the farm at certain times of the year. The total number of pupils show a marked trend upwards which made the Board of Education sound an alarm about the School's accommodation. Ironically, before the additional accommodation was complete, the number of pupils dropped significantly. At least half of the pupils at Aberaeron were in lodgings throughout the years 1898-1910. The Board of Education inspector visited the School on 22 March 1910 and decided to investigate the condition of children in lodgings. He found that 40 pupils were staying in lodgings in Aberaeron on that day - the Central Welsh Board figures for 1910-11 are 47 in lodgings. These children paid 1/6d or 1/9d a week, but they either brought or bought their own food, while fires in winter were an extra charge. Two or three pupils lodging together had a separate sitting-room. In a few cases, a single child boarded with a family as a "kitchen-boarder", but the Headmaster assured the inspector that the kitchen in such cases was comfortable and the household did not contain any other children. Dinners, i.e. lunches, were not provided in town or in School. A few pupils living two miles away from town brought their own lunch and the inspector gathered that they obtained a cup of tea in town. The lodgings were not registered and they were not inspected by the Headmaster or his assistants. The women teachers informed the inspector that they were of the opinion that the lodging houses should be registered and supervised. B. C. Jones explained to the inspector that the first Headmaster had introduced a system of registering and supervising lodgings but this system had lapsed about four years previously. Jones produced a form of agreement which the lodging house keepers then had to sign. The Managers had already listened to Dr. John Davies' complaint about the laxity prevailing in the supervision of children out of school hours and they acted promptly when they were informed of the inspector's strictures. The Headmaster was instructed to arrange for the teaching staff to visit the lodging houses where pupils resided and approved lodging houses had to be registered. Pupils were expected to be in their lodgings not later than 7 p.m. during the Michaelmas and Lent terms and not later than 8.30 p.m. during the Midsummer term. The instruction does not appear to have been successful because fuller instructions were laid down in October 1910:

a. all lodging houses to be registered;

b. no pupils to lodge in appartments [sic] not registered;

c. not more than two pupils were to occupy a bedroom;

d. boys and girls were not to lodge in the same house, except in the case of a brother and a sister;

e. not more than four pupils to lodge in the same house;

f. all houses to be inspected by the Headmaster regularly;

g. all registered lodging houses to be visited once a fortnight by a member of staff and any irregularities to be forthwith reported to the Headmaster.

In the following year, on 20 May 1911, the Managers adopted the recommendations of the local sub-committee that pupils in lodgings not later than the stipulated time would be fined 6d. for the first offence; 1/- for the second, and would appear before the governors for the third offence.

In *The Link* of 1933, *Unohonynt* recalled his generation at Aberaeron, a generation which spanned the years of the First World War. He recalled himself as a country boy entering a class of thirty strangers and a boy who found staying in lodgings a fresh experience, dull at first, but later fruitful of opportunity for mischief-making. He remembered, but unfortunately did not detail, many escapades in "Miss Evans' lodgings" in Victoria Street where Dai Lloyd struggled for the small bed with E. D., a green horn from Cribyn, and which led to that jump on the bed which sent the leg through the decayed ceiling. This would seem to indicate that Miss Evans was packing three boys into one room despite the 1910 Regulations. *Telothen*, in *The Link* of 1922, confirms the concerns expressed by Dr. Davies: "Outside school there were practically no restrictions on our liberty, and were left to find for ourselves in matters of right or wrong. ... There was no supervision over us out of school. We needed not to be labelled with school caps, so that our comings and our goings might be noticed. We would not have brooked daintily-striped caps, but we displayed our freedom and independence in wearing caps of all sizes, hues and shapes." He also notes children from the same village "sojourned under the same roof, and there was not one of the others but had a compatriot abiding by him." In *The Link* of 1910, *Penbryngoleu* recalled the journey home at the end of the week, "On Friday nights could be seen the "week-enders" slinging their bags on their backs, and making forth in all directions. Some went towards Henfynyw, bound for Llanarth, Talgarreg, and the distant port of New Quay, while others wended their way to Llanon, and were accompanied by the contingent from the plateau of Bethania, Pennant, and Cross Inn. On the Lampeter road could be seen the rest of the pilgrims returning to their mysterious fastnesses at Cilcennin, Pen Trichrug, Abermeurig, and to their homes scattered over the wide countryside around Cribyn, Dihewyd, and Mydroilyn. A motley throng we were. (I am speaking of the Lampeter road scholars, the others were, I believe and hope, a respectable lot). We talked a lot, sang a lot, and swore a little. A little mischief was indulged in, such as the occasional tapping of a window and asking the aged occupant of a house if she was in need of a lover, but no serious outrage that would set the countryside by the ears was committed. Rather were these peregrinations made memorable by the good fellowship of the company. ... To make the girls feel fully dependent on us for their safety, we always resorted to a most successful device - the product of the brain of one wicked spirit who knew far too much of the doings of this world than was good for one of his tender years. We would take the girls past Llanerchaeron Churchyard, and begin telling the most hair-raising ghosts stories. Then did the damsels shudder, and emit exclamations of horror, and then indeed, would their craven companions chuckle with delight." The opening of the Lampeter to Aberaeron Railway reduced the number of children needing to stay in lodgings. Nellie Jones of Tirbach in Cilcennin stayed in lodgings at Belle Vue Terrace before 1910; but, in the late 1910s, her youngest brother, Gwilym Jones, ran from their new home at Penwern, Cilcennin, down to the halt at Ciliau Aeron where he caught the train to School. The long return journey was uphill all the way from Ciliau Aeron. The figures in the Central Welsh Board reports show the decline in the number of pupils in lodgings from a half to a quarter of the pupils at School.

1911	93	(46B, 47G; 36L)
1912	97	(39B, 58G; 43L)
1913	103	(42B, 61G; 25L)
1914	105	(48B, 57G; 25L)

The introduction of motorised transport, especially motor buses, eventually brought the custom of lodging in Aberaeron to an end. After 1920, children who were not near a bus route would cycle to School and a bicycle became the usual reward for scholarship success.

There were fewer changes in the teaching staff after 1907: the two men teachers, E. O. James and W. J. Jones, were both Welshmen who wished to make their career in Wales and they would remain at the School for many years. Women teachers usually had a shorter career because it came to an end when they married. However, Miss Ethel Thomas, who replaced Miss Maddock at the beginning of 1908, stayed for four years. Teachers' salaries were negotiated by each school and, with a more stable staff, the Managers had to consider a more regular method of awarding increases. During the early years, increases were awarded in answer to a request from a teacher. At the beginning of the school year 1910-11, all the assistant teachers requested an increase: Miss Owen's salary was increased to £125, Miss Thomas' to £115; E. O. James' to £140; and W. J. Jones' to £140. This prompted the Managers to consider the introduction of a proper scale for salaries and this was implemented a month later: £90 for an assistant mistress; £100 for an assistant master; £110 for an assistant science master. After the first two years' service, an annual increase of £10 would be allowed for three years which would bring the relevant salaries to a maximum of £120, £140, £150. The Senior Assistant Mistress would get an additional £5 a year after the maximum. All the assistant teachers at Aberaeron were on or near the maximum of their particular salary scales. The Headmaster requested a higher capitation fee but this was deferred until information was received from the other schools in the county. Hughes' total salary had increased significantly up to 1907, but it had then declined as the number of pupils fell by around one-fifth from a peak in 1906-07. There was no further action on Hughes' request.

On 17 May 1911, Owen M. Edwards, the Chief Inspector of the Welsh Department of the Board of Education, visited the School. He noted four points for action:

1. The duration of school life for many pupils was short and the provision of free places should be extended;
2. The Board's syllabus on the teaching of English was known to the School but the teaching of English was antiquated;
3. There were no special courses only a rigid subordination to the needs of the Central Welsh Board examinations;
4. Scripture was taught only in Form 1 and the morning assembly consisted of a few verses and the Lord's Prayer read out in English; there was no hymn.

Edwards thought the Headmaster was old and past his working day. "He looks upon himself as being in the way of his senior assistant [E. O. James], and pities himself that there is no pension for him to retire on. He has two clever sons, one the Superintendent of the Denbigh Asylum and another a Fellow of the University of Wales. When he had a private school at New Quay he did well, he prepared every boy for his course in life; but now he never thinks of the boys' needs, he lives in terror of the Central Welsh Board." Edwards noted that E. O. James was "very energetic, a man of some resource, a good Welsh scholar, but his teaching is very grammatical and he has no concept of adaptation." James had recently obtained an M.A. degree from the University of Wales on the unpublished poetry of Lewis Glyn Cothi. The judgement made by Edwards on his teaching was sound; Haydn Lewis, once the Crown Poet at the National Eisteddfod, recalled that, although James was talented in writing *englynion,* he never showed his pupils how to compose in the traditional Welsh metres. He kept to the curriculum of the Central Welsh Board. Edwards was equally shrewd, as we will discover later, in judging the young master, W. J. Jones: "Mr. Jones appears to be amiable and is popular." Edwards judged the School to be well staffed, but, there were a number of serious defects:

1. There was no idea of adaptation. The children were all prepared for the Central Welsh Board examinations and no further thought seemed to be given to them, e.g., intending teachers at the top of the School had not done any geography or manual work;
2. The lower part of the School was sacrificed to the small top;
3. The library was kept in a high cupboard; a very long ladder was necessary for access and it did not contain any Welsh books of use.

Edwards concluded that the School was "a bad example of what can become when entirely at the mercy of an external exam."

The intermediate schools had been established to provide a bridge between elementary education and the universities. These schools provided, as we have seen in the case of Aberaeron, a means of advancement for the bright child. The chief criticism that Edwards made of Aberaeron was that the teaching staff concentrated on those aspects of education which benefited the bright child aiming for university and did not adapt the curriculum for the needs of the less bright child by providing those subjects, e.g. manual work or handicrafts, which would fit them for employment in their own community. Edwards believed that the intermediate schools had an important function in providing for the needs of the community; the complaints made by the Central Welsh Board inspectors over the teaching of Welsh at Aberaeron is another reflection of this view. The Managers at Aberaeron were well aware of this question because, three years earlier, John Jones of Cilcennin moved the following resolution at the Board meeting on 15 October 1910: "That as the majority of the pupils who attended Intermediate Schools do not intend to have university training, we are of opinion that the Intermediate Education Scheme for this County shall be amended so that all subjects for instruction mentioned in the scheme should be optional in order to meet the wishes of those who desire to be taught in subjects which will be useful to them in the trade, profession or industry which they intend to follow." There was a long discussion, unfortunately not detailed, on this resolution and further discussion was deferred until the next meeting on 17 December, when it was further adjourned until the recent inspection report was received. No more was heard of this resolution.

One must surmise that the lack of resources prevented the Managers from broadening the curriculum and one suspects that the Headmaster and the teaching staff were not inclined to take on an extra burden. The five teachers in the School covered the subjects required by the Central Welsh Board examination syllabus and the lengthy series of examinations held every summer dominated the School's activities. The Board of

Education pointed out, on 16 December 1911, that singing, cookery, woodwork and sewing were only taught in the lowest forms and the Managers were asked if they could see their way in the near future to extend the teaching of any or all of these subjects so that they could be taught in the higher forms. The Managers replied that cookery would be taught in the three lowest forms during the present term but it would be most difficult to introduce singing and cookery in the higher forms in the existing timetable. The teaching of sewing and woodwork only commenced at the beginning of the school year 1910-11 and the four year course would be completed in 1913-14. From the school year 1912-13, the timetable would include provision for the teaching of singing and cookery throughout the School. When the Managers considered the Board of Education's report for 1912, the Headmaster was asked to ascertain from the parents of children entering the School in September 1913 whether they wished their children to take a commercial course or the ordinary school course. The results of this survey are not known, but the Local Sub-Committee resolved that Latin and elementary science should be discontinued for first year pupils in order to devote more time to the teaching of Arithmetic and English which suggests that the parents had indicated some sympathy for vocational education. Another matter of concern to the Board of Education was the size of classes; the Managers were instructed on 2 February 1913 to ensure that all classes were limited to 30 pupils. This was solved, at little cost, by allowing Miss E. V. Beckett, the talented hockey player and an ex-pupil, to join the staff in order to gain teaching experience. Further pressure in 1914, when the number of pupils in Form II was 33, received the tart response that Managers had decided, if the Board of Education insisted that the maximum number should not exceed thirty, to dismiss three pupils from Form II because the school's funds were insufficient to employ an extra teacher. It was also pointed out to the Board that permission to enter the School had been refused to two applicants. The School clearly needed another teacher but the Managers realised that the funds at their disposal were sadly insufficient. The financial situation had worsened because the rules for payment changed under the new county scheme for intermediate schools introduced in 1913. The tuition fee was 4 guineas for each pupil but 25% of the total number admitted in one school year were to be given free places; if there were three children from the same family, then the third child was exempt from fees. The new regulations tried to solve the problem of children being withdrawn suddenly from School by requiring a term's notice of any withdrawal and a penalty of one term's fee for withdrawal without notice. The total number of pupils in the midsummer term of 1913 was 93 which, allowing for 25% free places, would bring in an annual income of c.£200, enough to meet the salaries of only two teachers. The Managers could do little to increase this income and they were dependent on the Local Education Authority if they were to increase the number of teachers. The teaching staff had remained remarkably stable since 1908; Miss Ethel Thomas who taught English and Geography had been replaced by Miss M. J. Watson in 1911 and Miss Bertha Jones had been replaced by Miss Owen as a part-time cookery teacher appointed by the Local Education Authority at a cost to the School of £20 p.a. for two days service each week. She worked for the other three days at Aberystwyth at £30 p.a. and the Aberaeron governors complained, unavailingly, that £30 for three days service was a lesser contribution than the £20 paid by Aberaeron.

In retrospect, the work of the two sets of inspectors proved beneficial to the School's progress. A signal example of their influence was the introduction and expansion of the teaching of Welsh in the School: in the 1908-09 report, the Board of Education noted, with approval, that all pupils took Welsh, except for six in Form V and one in Form IV. Therefore, it is surprising to discover that the Clerk wrote on 1 August 1913 to ask the Board whether the grant paid by the Treasury would be continued if the teaching of Welsh was to be discontinued. As was the custom, a junior official, T. G. Roberts, considered the letter and his minute notes that Aberaeron was a Welsh speaking district which came under the regulations for Welsh Secondary Schools which required that Welsh should be taught in the schools in such districts. His draft reply pointed out that one of the conditions to be fulfilled by a secondary school before a grant was awarded under the regulations was that the curriculum must be approved by the Board. In the absence of the provision for teaching Welsh, the Board would not be in a position to report to the Treasury that the conditions for payment of the Treasury grant under the Welsh Act were satisfied in the case of the School. Alfred T. Davies, the Permanent Secretary to the Welsh Department of the Board, minuted against Roberts's draft: "Might it not be well to shew them - even more clearly - the folly of this proposal." Before the final draft of the letter was approved, it was submitted to Owen M. Edwards who commented that "This is one of the most examination riddled schools in Wales. The aim of the old Head Master is to get the easy marks-getting subjects. The Governors will probably agree heartily with Mr Roberts' proposed letter." Edwards drafted an additional paragraph which was added to the letter sent out on 11 August 1913: "The Board are of opinion that the school would be more efficient if it were not so largely dominated by the desire for examination results, and if more attention were paid to the individual needs of the pupils, and to subjects which are of educational value during their school course and which will help them in their life's work. Among such subjects, Welsh is one of the most important." Only three weeks earlier, Edwards had visited the School and his brief report reflects a continued disenchantment with the administration of the School. He noted that his query regarding the provision of a midday meal received the response: "nobody has ever asked." It was, he minuted, an "examination-riddled helpless school." The Headmaster was interesting only when he talked of his experience as "a free man in his own school."

Responsibility for the request to abandon the teaching of Welsh must reside with the Headmaster and it probably arose from the difficulties he faced in covering all the subjects for the Central Welsh Board. This is revealed by the comment made to Edwards by one of the teachers, "we as teachers are at them all day to cover the work." Edwards was also right about the attitude of the Governors; it is unlikely that men like J. M. Howell and John

Jones of Cilcennin who prized the language and literature of Wales would have welcomed the Headmaster's initiative. It is also unlikely that Edwards would have visited Aberaeron without meeting J. M. Howell. There was a link between the two men through L. J. Roberts, an old friend of Edwards, who was musical editor of Edwards' journals, *Cymru* and *Cymru'r Plant* and a contributor with Howell of an annual Christmas carol to *Cymru.* Edwards' disillusionment with the old Headmaster probably reflected the views of Howell and other governors.

The Managers were not finding it easy to administer the School, especially with a defensive Headmaster. Major Price Lewes died in 1911 and he was succeeded as Chairman by Dr. John Davies. There was a considerable and obvious advantage in the Chairman living in Aberaeron. Elected Chairman at the end of 1911, Davies found the position burdensome, probably through age and indifferent health, and he resigned in October 1914. The Governors declined to accept his resignation and asked him to continue, with J. M. Howell as Vice-Chairman to assist him. Within six months, Dr. Davies was dead; he had made a significant contribution to his community and to the development of the School. The post of Chairman was left unfilled and Howell took charge as Vice-Chairman. A leading figure in the public life of Aberaeron for many years; a considerable figure in Cardiganshire politics; and a man who was well acquainted with David Lloyd George and other leading Liberals, Howell had the determination and vision to carry the School forward.

The meeting on 19 September 1914 saw the Governors, as they now called themselves, considering a circular letter regarding the proposed University of Wales Battalion in France and despatching a sharp reminder to E. O. James that, because the state of the library was unsatisfactory, they wanted him to prepare, with other members of staff, a list of suitable books for purchase and to get dilapidated books rebound. Seven old pupils had signed up with the Territorials at various places and six old pupils were with 'Kitchener's Army' in France; *The Link* proudly records that Dr. Garfield Evans, who had settled in Port Talbot in 1913, was selected, out of many applicants, for a post on the staff of the Welsh Field Hospital in France. In the following year, the school magazine devoted considerable attention to the War. Geraint Howell, the son of J. M. Howell, wrote an amusing account of life in the Royal Flying Corps: "When we two [the identity of the other old pupil is not known] joined there was general consternation, the prevalent idea being that a flight in the upper regions would be the first thing demanded of us. Horrified exclamations greeted our ears on all sides, "O, beth oe'ch chi'n joino'r hen bethe hedfan 'na", being typical." T. H. Davies wrote of his Army training at Winnal Down, near Winchester. While Howell adopted a jocular tone, Davies wrote in the style of a boy's adventure story: "Sometimes we hold little 'sing-songs' around the stoves in the huts. The programme might not be appeal to those with literary tastes, and though the songs may be poor in quality and trashy in sentiment, yet they appeal to us in a fashion which nobody can realise but those who are situated as we are. 'Futurist' music has no place on our programmes. We sing of home, "The Little Grey Home in the West", and of home fires, "Keep the Home Fires Burning", simple songs, perhaps, but sung around the camp fires, they have a charm indefinable." Davies also had school friends in the same unit: "...an order was promulgated in our battalion some time ago that the upper lip was not to be shaved, that all men were to grow a moustache, but owing to the tender upbringing of a few of us, the hairs would not grow, and among those few was "Panteryrod" which moved Dai Lloyd to poesy and apostrophise him as:-

"Un â'i flew yn rhy fain,
I flino un firain."

Davies ended on a more serious note: "What do we think about the war? Well, we seldom think about it, and we go for days without seeing a newspaper, and be none the worse for it. It is the slackers at home, the armchair critics who worry most about the affairs on the Continent. Whether it is "full pack" on the morrow, or whether it is sausage or bacon for breakfast, is a matter of far greater moment to us than the doings of Van Hindenburg or Ferdinand of Bulgaria. I have an apology to make, Miss Editor, and that is, that I am penning this screed from England and not from France, but, maybe, you have found a contributor who is already in the firing line. Before the publication of the "Link" we shall, in all probability, be out somewhere on the Continent, doing our little bit, for our School and for our country. .... In conclusion, we make an earnest appeal to any "old" pupil who has not yet joined the colours, and who has no valid excuse for remaining behind, to come forward at once, and cast in his lot with the others who have obeyed the call, so that it may be said, in years to come, that in this, the greatest crisis which our nation has ever had to face, the old School played its part, and played it well." The old pupil from Panteryrod was Evan Lewis Jones, who received a commission in the North Staffordshire Regiment in the same year and who was killed at Serre, in the Battle of Ancre, on 13 November 1916; he had graduated from Aberystwyth with First Class in Botany in 1914. *The Link* did publish a contribution from the front lines, the family of Private J. D. Jones allowed the Editor to publish a long extract from a private letter home. Jones, with E Company, Brecknock Battalion of the South Wales Borderers, wrote from Steamer Point, Aden, on 7 July 1915. He had been involved in the unsuccessful defence of the town of Lahejd when 500 British troops _ Brecknocks, Regulars and Indians _ were defeated by an army of 5000 Turks. The real enemy was the great heat. Jones describes the retreat on 5 July from Lahedj: "There were hours of suffering after another day of desert heat to fight against, no rations, and shortage of water. What grub I had was two biscuits, but about four o'clock a case of rations was dished out, and all that fell to my lot was a tin of raspberry jam, and I made a tea of that. Just by me were four men unconscious, the whites of their eyes showing and their lips blue, dying. When the heat became less and the sun was sinking we marched on again - some ten of us, with full water-bottles, and a weary walk before us. Past whitened bones, past dead horses and mules which bore testimony to the heat and the cruel desert, we ploughed our way through. Men, white and black, lay just as they had fallen, no effort was made at burial. The boy (21 years old) who breakfasted with me that morning, died on the homeward journey. ..... I stuck it well, suffered no pain, but in the heat I was half wandering in my mind, seeing rivers of water flowing by and thinking of you all on a beautiful Sunday at home. I am sure your prayers on my behalf are being answered."

The *Roll of Service* published in the same issue includes the name of 54 old boys of the School; the name of one pupil, Private T. Compton Herbert of the Welsh Guards, who enlisted under age and who survived to become the Vicar of Old Windsor; and, the name of one woman, Miss Gretta Pugh of Paris House, who was serving on board a transport ship. A tiny and determined lady, Margretta Pugh returned home, after the War, to nurse an invalid mother and her uniform as a nurse in the Queen Alexandra's Nursing Corps was still neatly folded in her trunk in the box room of 7 Alban Square when she died in the 1960s. After 1915, *The Link* was not published again until 1922; the War took up the energies of many old pupils and there was a lack of interest from the School during the last year of Hughes' headmastership.

The most direct effect of the War on the School was on staffing. Miss Owen's departure was probably not caused by the War; she received an offer to become the Senior Mistress at Holyhead County School and asked the Governors if they were prepared to increase her salary. The Local Sub-Committee explained that they did not have the power to offer an immediate increase but the Governors would probably make an advance of £5. Miss Owen resigned one week later, on 22 July 1915, and she was replaced by Miss V. Ferguson. When conscription was introduced, the Governors made an application, on 4 February 1916, to the Local Tribunal for the Aberaeron Urban District Council for the temporary exemption of Mr. W. J. Jones, science master and teacher in woodwork on the grounds that the teaching of chemistry was essential for the welfare of the School and that a person to teach the two aforesaid subjects could not be obtained. At the same meeting, the teaching staff were asked to organise a celebration of St. David's Day in 1916 and a dozen copies of the booklet on "Patriotism" by Alfred T. Davies, of the Board of Education, were ordered for distribution to the pupils. It was now realised that the War would be long and hard. Less than six months later, another application had to be made to the Local Tribunal for a further postponement in the case of W. J. Jones and an application on Form 301 to the Board of Education for the postponement on the grounds of public interest in the case of E. O. James. The Local Tribunal did not take a sympathetic view and declined a further postponement in the case of Jones; this decision was reversed by the County Tribunal after J. M. Howell appeared in person before the tribunal at Lampeter. In the same summer, Miss Ferguson resigned to be replaced by Miss G. E. P. Furley and Miss E. M. Davies also resigned to be replaced by Miss D. M. Davies. The Governors were informed that Latin and Physics, which had not been taught in 1915-16, were now to be restored to the curriculum. No reason is given for the omission of these subjects from the timetable and the omission was not noted by the Central Welsh Board inspectors. On their annual visit in 1915, the inspectors recorded that there were 105 pupils at the School (47 boys and 57 girls), with only 25 in lodgings. Forty pupils received exemption from fees. While most of the teaching was given a rating of fair, the teaching of Welsh was praised as "excellent throughout." E. O. James must have prevailed upon the Headmaster to let him drop the teaching of Latin for a time and to allow him to concentrate on Welsh. Physics had only been taught intermittently and W. J. Jones' first love was Chemistry. The inspectors noted that a tennis court had been installed at the School and the library now contained 450 books. In the previous three years, more frequent periods had been allowed for Physical Education and the Central Welsh Board inspectors were pleased with progress, although Miss Davies from the Board of Education noted that the P.E. lesson was from 12.05 to 12.20p.m. and that it encroached on five minutes of the dinner hour. Organised games were held during the last school period on a Thursday afternoon; Miss Davies remarked that the lack of swimming instruction was very odd considering the contribution of the County to the Merchant Marine Service.

Miss Furley's appointment was not a success and she resigned after less than two months at the School. All the candidates selected by the Governors accepted appointments elsewhere and, in March 1917, the Headmaster and Howell appointed Miss K. Winifred Wild to replace Miss Furley and Miss Mary E. Thomas to replace Miss Watson who had also departed. There was still a problem over W. J. Jones' deferment from military service and the Governors agreed to pay the legal expenses amounting to £5 for the cost of defending Jones under a case brought against him by the Military Authorities under the Military Service Acts and tried before the Justices at the Petty Sessions in Aberaeron. The Governors were fighting a losing battle and W. J. Jones' exemption was only extended until July 1917. On the instructions of the Board of Education, the pupils were now drawn more directly into the war; a portion of the school grounds was turned into a garden cultivated by the pupils, under the direction of the Headmaster, for food production. At the beginning of the war, the Royal Navy clung to an offensive strategy and declined to provide warships to defend merchant shipping; by 1917, the country was desperately short of food and Aberaeron County School had to do "its bit."

Hughes was now in his sixty-seventh year and he decided to resign at the end of the summer term of 1917. The Local Sub-Committee received the Headmaster's resignation on 10 May 1917 and Howell went off to consult the Director of Education and the Registrar of the University College at Aberystwyth about the terms of the advertisement. The resignation was accepted on 30 May 1917. Between the meeting of the Local Sub-Committee and the Board of Governors, the Central Welsh Board inspectors visited the School for a subsidiary inspection held every second and third year. The inspectors noted that there were six members of staff which made the School numerically one of the best, i.e. in terms of teacher-pupil ratio, in Wales. The school hours had changed because of the train times to 10-12.30 in the morning and 2-4.30 in the afternoon. The inspectors noted that Hughes was resigning at the end of the school term; he had served the cause of education in the district for the past forty-five years and during his tenure new buildings had been constructed at the School and the staff increased from four to six. The School was worthily established as a secondary school. The Board of Education did not comment on this report and it probably received lukewarm approval in London; O. M. Edwards had commented briefly on the 1916 subsidiary report: "This school is not satisfactory otherwise the upset on Welsh should not be necessary." There is no doubt that Hughes had given many years of worthy service to education but he had found, as Edwards noted, it difficult to move from being the only teacher in his own school to being the head of a larger school. The comments in the reports of the two sets of inspectors tend to suggest a lack of leadership and a lack of firmness with his staff, especially E. O. James. While the School had expanded its accommodation and its staff during Hughes's rule, this expansion owed more to pressure from the Central Welsh Board and the Board of Education rather than from Hughes' own initiatives. He had tried to establish a social life at the School with the foundation of a Debating Society but there is no evidence that this society continued for more than a few years and the admirable school eisteddfod held in 1907 was never repeated. However, it should be remembered that the Headmaster carried a full burden of teaching and for many years, Hughes had charge of mathematics teaching. Few of his pupils have recorded their impressions of Hughes; Haydn Lewis and a few others recalled that he was fond of "llinellau-cosb", the punishment of writing lines, but they also remembered him as a gentle man. The Governors paid a perfunctory tribute to Hughes which took place, rather oddly, at the start of the meeting to appoint his successor when minds were very much on another matter.

The advertisement for a new Headmaster was placed with the Joint Scholastic Agency: "B. C. Jones, Esq., Clerk to the Governors of the ABERAYRON COUNTY INTERMEDIATE SCHOOL, Aberayron informs us that a Headmaster will be wanted for this school next term - duties to begin on September 10th. The Head Master must be a graduate of a University in the United Kingdom and Welsh speaking. Salary £350 per annum. Canvassing the Governors either directly or indirectly is strictly prohibited and will disqualify the Candidate. Applications stating age and qualifications accompanied by 15 copies of three recent testimonials also references with names and addresses should be sent to B. C. Jones, Esq., Clerk to the Governors as above on or before July 7th. ....N.B. Candidates are requested to remember when making the application that letters weighed over one ounce require additional postage." Thirty-nine applications were received at Aberaeron.

Howell T. Evans, Senor History Master and House Tutor at the High School for Boys, Cardiff, posted his application on 5 June. A Cardiff friend, William Williams, reported a week later that the Aberaeron governors were making enquiries about Evans among the Methodists in Cardiff _ this lowered Evans' hopes because he was a Baptist. An old college friend of Mrs Evans came from Aberaeron; Lilian 'Lena' Howell, the headmistress of Elerch Primary School, was the niece of J. M. Howell. Lena Howell wrote on 22 June with details of the competition and she suggested that Evans should ask his friend Lord Pontypridd to write to J. M. Howell. This was done. Lena reported to Gwen Evans on 28 June that "Mr. Evans is still the favourite, but there are several in for the post with very good qualifications and canvassing (tho' prohibited) is proceeding apace." Evans was disheartened to learn that denominationalism was playing a large part in the discussion over the appointment of a new Headmaster; the Baptist cause was weak at Aberaeron.

The Governors met on 28 July 1917 to select a short list for the post of Headmaster. W. J. Jones had been given leave to join the Army and his post would be kept open for him; the Governors began by postponing the appointment of Jones' replacement as science master until the new Headmaster was in post. There followed brief thanks to C. J. Hughes before three scrutineers were appointed. Mrs T. Z. Jones and Mrs Munro Hughes moved that those who had canvassed should be excluded. An amendment was tabled by the Rev. William Griffiths and seconded by John Jones (Cwmere) that the list be taken as it stood. The amendment was carried by 5 votes to 3; 3 governors abstained. When the scrutineers reported that two of the candidates - Howell Evans and A. E. Jenkins - had an equal number of votes, Mrs T. Z. Jones and E. Lima Jones proposed that these two candidates, both with excellent qualifications, should be the short list. John Jones (Cilcennin), seconded by Mrs Munro Hughes, moved an amendment that the short list should be as agreed at the last meeting. "Thereupon the scrutineers reported that the following six names were placed on the short list:

Howell Evans, Cardiff

E. I. Griffiths, Newport (Mon.)

John Hooson, London

Owen Hughes, Wallasey

E. O. James, Belle Vue Terrace

A. E. Jenkins, Huddersfield."

The appointment was to be made on 1 August 1917. A young history teacher, R. T. Jenkins, had seen the advertisement but he did not apply because he preferred town life. However, Jenkins changed his mind when a brief note came from Owen M. Edwards: "Ewch i mewn am Aberaeron - cewch groeso." [Apply for Aberaeron - you will receive a welcome]. Jenkins still did not wish to apply but he did not wish to offend Edwards; to his great amusement, his own application did not achieve the short list. Edwards may have thought that Jenkins, an able man, would appeal to the Governors as a Methodist.

On 26 July, Evans heard that he was on the short list. A Cardiff friend, Mr. J. Rowland undertook to write to E. Lima Jones in support of his application while Evans wrote for assistance to Joseph Jones of Brecon and to the Vicar of Aberpergwm, both men with Aberaeron connections. A letter came from Lena Howells warning that someone was working against Evans at Aberaeron. On 31 July 1917, Evans cycled to Bridgend where he caught the 7.50 train to Llandysul and motored thence to New Quay where he saw the Rev. W. Griffiths and Alderman E. J. Griffiths, two of the governors. It was a glorious day and, his business complete, Evans walked, carrying his hat and coat, the seven miles to Aberaeron. He had booked a room at the Monachty Hotel opposite the Town Hall. Late in the evening, between 9 and 10 o'clock, he walked on the beach in a reflective mood. "I have doubts whether I have done a wise thing in applying for this place. However having applied, I shall like to win - my defeats are many."

All eleven governors were present at the Town Hall on 1 August. The scrutineers were re-appointed and the advertisement was read. The voting was conducted by ballot; the governors would write on the slip of paper the numbers opposite the names of the candidates on the list. On the first ballot, each governor voted for four of the five candidates; on the second ballot, for three of the remaining four; on the third ballot for two of the remaining three; and, on the fourth ballot, the candidate receiving the largest number of votes would be elected Headmaster. The details of the meeting are scanty. The six candidates appeared and were interviewed; Evans recalled that his interview lasted from eleven in the morning to three in the afternoon which suggests that some of the other candidates were given a rather cursory hearing. The one difficult point which Evans had to face in his interview related to a disagreeable incident at Cardiff High School. Under Yates, an acting head appointed in 1914, discipline had become slack and there were rumours of a financial crisis. Evans gave evidence to a sub-committee appointed by the Cardiff Education Committee; a faction on this sub-committee tried to throw the blame for the School's troubles on to the previous Headmaster and on to the staff. The *Western Mail* published an account of the incident which exonerated Yates. This incident was used, as Lena Howell warned Gwen Evans, to damage Evans' prospects at Aberaeron. Cuttings from the Cardiff papers had been supplied to the Governors and the matter was raised during Evans' interview but his explanation was successful and it earned him votes. The final result of the balloting was ten votes for Evans and one vote for Griffiths of Newport. Evans saw C. J. Hughes, B. C. Jones and J. M. Howell late on the same day and he returned to Cardiff at 11.05 on the following morning. The young R. T. Jenkins succeeded Evans as history master in Cardiff before he became an university lecturer and, in time, Professor of Welsh History at Bangor.

The Headmastership of Howell T. Evans 1917-1944

Howell Thomas Evans, the new Headmaster, was born on 6 November 1877 in Cwmbwrla, outside Swansea. He was the second son of a steelworker, John Evans, and his wife, Mary. A pupil at Swansea Grammar School, Evans went on to study at the University College of Wales at Aberystwyth, the University of London, and finally at St. John's College Cambridge where he took double honours in History and in Mental and Moral Sciences Triposes. Following his studies at Cambridge, Evans embarked on a

Howell T. Evans, M.A., Prifathro, 1917-1944

A Midsummer Night's Dream, Christmas 1917

Asgri Lân, Dydd Gŵyl Dewi 1918

Tîm Pêl-droed / Soccer team - 1917-18

Mr. Ross, Leslie ?, Jonathan Davis, Frank Evans, John Lloyd, Jonathan Jones, Mr. E.O. James
John Morgan, John Henry, Jacob Jones, Wm. Joseph Evans, Haydn Lewis, D. Ivor Jones

Tîm Hoci / Hockey team - 1918-1919

Dosbarth Chwech / Sixth Form
1918-1919

Dosbarth Chwech / Sixth Form
1922

"Ar y Groesffordd", Dydd Gŵyl Dewi, 1919

Princess Ju Ju, 1921-22

"Maesymeillion" 1924

"Cnoi Awel", 1930

Athrawon Yr Ysgol / Teaching Staff 1931-32
Mr. T. H. Fox, Miss B. Treharne, Miss E. Lewis, Mr. W. A. Jones
Miss N. Timothy, Mr. W. J. Jones, Mr. H. T. Evans, Miss A. Jones, Mr. J. T. Owen.

"H.M.S. Pinafore"
1934

"H.M.S. Pinafore"
1934

teaching career. Evans taught at Swansea Municipal Secondary School, Wellington College and Carmarthen Grammar School, before becoming Senior History Master and House Tutor at Cardiff High School for Boys. Besides his remarkable academic career, Evans had also made a significant contribution through his public and written works. While at Cardiff, he had delivered a series of University Extension lectures at Swansea and he was a regular contributor to the summer schools which were popular at that period. Evans was prominent in the work of the Welsh Language Society of the time which worked to establish the Welsh language in the schools of Wales. Through his membership of the Cardiff Welsh Sunday School Union, Evans began classes in the chapel vestries of Cardiff for Welsh learners. Evans was also an active supporter of the Liberal Party and he was on friendly terms with Sir Alfred Thomas, later Lord Pontypridd, Chairman of the Welsh Liberal Parliamentary Party and Member of Parliament for East Glamorganshire from 1885 to 1910.

Besides his busy public and professional life, Evans was also a prolific writer both at a scholarly and a popular level. In those days, the National Eisteddfod held competitions in Welsh and English; Evans won prizes in 1909 for an essay on "Welshmen in the Wars of the Roses" and in 1911 for an essay entitled "A critical examination of the works of Lewis Glyn Cothi". Evans' essay on the War of the Roses, developed from his Cambridge M.A. thesis, formed the basis of *Wales and the Wars of the Roses*, his most important scholarly work, which was published by Cambridge University Press in 1915. This was the first serious study of these civil wars in Wales and Evans was the first historian to use contemporary Welsh poetry as an historical source and one of the earliest historians to draw attention to the important chronicle, still unpublished, by Elis Gruffudd. By a happy coincidence, *Wales and the Wars of the Roses* was reprinted in 1995, with an introduction by the distinguished Welsh mediaevalist, R. A. Griffiths, who comments justly, "rarely does a monograph written by a grammar-school teacher retain substantial value for historians eighty years after its publication."

Neither the articles nor the textbooks which comprised Evans' more popular writings have stood the test of time. However, his textbooks are very important because Evans was the first man to recognise the need for school books on Welsh history as a subject in its own right and he was the first writer to compile such books. At the beginning of this century, the few teachers who taught Welsh history faced an uphill struggle because they had no assistance in the form of textbooks nor were there many histories of Wales easily available. In 1907, Evans published *An analysis of Welsh history* which he wrote to "give in outline the chief historical facts, and to trace the main lines on which development has taken place." An outline rather a narrative, this was an ideal book for teachers wishing to prepare lessons on Welsh history. The work began with the arrival of the Romans and ended with the granting of city status to Cardiff in 1905. *An analysis of Welsh history* is stronger on the earlier period, but this reflects the general weakness of Welsh historical writing at the time. A more important work was *The making of modern Wales* (1912) which covered the period from 1500. In this narrative history, Evans was the first to exploit the rich source material to be found in nineteenth century Welsh periodicals. The preparation of textbooks on Welsh history which assisted in the establishment of the history of Wales as a subject in its own right was Evans' greatest achievement. This work was noticed by his contemporaries, including Owen M. Edwards, and it is recalled with considerable respect by many historians of our day. In electing Howell Evans to be Headmaster of Aberaeron County School, the Governors had chosen a man of considerable achievement.

The main tone of the congratulatory letters received by Evans was that he had long deserved promotion. When he returned to Cardiff, he had a few weeks holiday before he took up his new post. The only urgent matter was the appointment of a science master to fill in for W. J. Jones and Evans recommended placing an advertisement in the Welsh papers with a view towards interviewing at the beginning of September. A letter came from the Baptist Chapel begging Evans to join the cause at Aberaeron but, as he confided to his diary, "it would be well for me to keep apart." He left Cardiff on the 10.20 train on the morning of 3 September and arrived in Aberaeron at 4.50 p.m. Temporary lodgings had been arranged with Mrs. Rees of 3 Belle Vue Terrace. The first week was busy with meetings. The Local Sub-Committee met on 6 September and agreed to postpone the opening of the School until 18 September, while every effort was made to obtain the release of W. J. Jones from military service or to obtain another qualified teacher. There was a shortage of science teachers because men with the suitable qualifications were required for war work. Evans was authorised to go to Aberystwyth to look for a science teacher and J. M. Howell was sent to London to lobby the Welsh Department of the Board of Education for Jones' release. At Aberystwyth, Evans met Principal Roberts, had lunch with Samuel, the headmaster of the intermediate school there, and saw the Professor of Chemistry. He was not successful. On the bus back to Aberaeron, he met Mrs. T. Z. Jones and "I had a long talk with her about men and things." There was a great deal of work at the school because "school records &c are in the utmost confusion ... There has been neither order nor system in anything it appears to me." Besides tidying the School's administration, Evans was also occupied in interviewing parents and children. He noted in his diary on 10 September that he had "finished timetable a.m." This was a difficult task in that the School did not begin until ten in the morning because the train from Lampeter which brought some twenty pupils did not arrive until ten. There was a secondary school linked with the Church of Wales in Lampeter, and some nonconformists preferred to send their children to Aberaeron County School. The majority of the twenty children would, however, have come from Felinfach and other halts down to Aberaeron.

The lack of a science master meant that Evans had to take on all the science classes as well as most of the mathematics teaching. He possessed first class South Kensington certificates in chemistry, hygiene and drawing. On Sunday, 9 September, he had tea with C. J. Hughes at Park View when the family had gone to Peniel and then went up the road to Sunnyside where he saw Mrs. T. Z. Jones who provided him with her view of the School and its affairs. The second week was less hectic and he was able to find time for fishing, "caught 4 eels", and shooting, "shot 3 partridges." Evans performed one important task on 11 September when he persuaded the Local Sub-Committee to increase the salaries of the assistant teachers; E. O. James now received £185 p.a.; W. J. Jones £185; Doris M. Davies £140; K. M. Wild £140; Mary E. Thomas £140. The Managers also agreed that the Clerk would collect the school fees in future and not the Headmaster as had been the practice.

On Sunday, 16 September, Miss Wild, the Geography Mistress, came to tea at 3 Belle Vue Terrace. Evans found her very prim, but he thought that she was a good teacher. Haydn Lewis recalled her as speaking beautiful English, but without any knowledge of Welsh or of Wales. Miss Wild pressed Evans to allow more time for Geography in the upper form. After supper, he went to see Mrs. T. Z. Jones who asked him if had "funked the chapel question!", as he had again not attended a chapel. Mrs. T. Z. Jones was keen to impress her views on the new Headmaster, but Evans was always to show an independence of judgement and action in his work. He was skilful in avoiding any involvement with the two main and rival nonconformist chapels.

The teaching staff met at Evans' lodgings on the evening of 17 September. He explained his scheme of reorganisation which was well received. He found them ready to co-operate and they appeared to welcome the changes he proposed. The School opened for the 1917-18 school year on 18 September; the total number on the School's register was about 120, which was an increase of some 50 pupils over the last term. At prayers on the first morning, Evans had decided to do exactly as had been done before. Then, after placing the old pupils in their new forms, he examined the 50 new pupils. With the help of an undergraduate from Aberystwyth, he tested them in Dictation and Arithmetic, marked their papers and allotted them to their classes by the end of the morning. On the advice of the staff, he had placed one boy in the same form as he had been in during the last year. The boy walked out of school. Evans noted, "from what I was told about him, I imagined him to be something of a bully, and sent for him on the third day. There came to my room a nervous lad who struck me as being a rather gentle specimen of boyhood. To my surprise, I discovered that he was too sensitive to bear the indignity of being kept in the same form for a second year." The boy's older sister had already been to see Evans to ask, in tears, if her brother could move up. "And so I dealt with him in the tenderness of my heart and moved him to the next form. I had some difficulty in keeping my own feelings under control." The new pupils struck Evans as only fair, with some of them poorly educated and old to be entering an intermediate school. It was still possible to remain at an elementary school until the age of 12-13. In the afternoon, Evans summoned all the pupils to the Hall where he told them to stand in their places, by forms, for prayers. He explained to the children what he wanted done at the school and then, after giving them his blessing, dismissed them for the day.

On the evening of 19 September, Evans invited E. O. James to call after tea. James had been a contender for the post of Headmaster and Evans needed to establish a good working relationship with James, especially in the absence of W. J. Jones; they had an amiable discussion about the timetable. Evans confided to his diary that James appeared very ready to work. On the following day, he offered Miss. S. B. Porter the temporary post of science teacher at £150 p.a. if she proved satisfactory. Howell had written from London to report that he had failed to prevail upon Owen Edwards and A. T. Davies to allow Jones to return.

Evans continued to make changes at the School. One simple innovation was that the girls would sing at prayers. He introduced the prefect system and, on 25 September, the prefects began to read the scripture lessons at prayers. The school was divided into three houses named after the homes of the first three chairmen of the Governors: Tyglyn (Major Price Lewes); Tanyfron (Dr. John Davies); Portland (Alderman J. M. Howell). These innovations have stood the test of time well and, as the years went by, a pleasant arrangement arose whereby children were placed in the same House as other family members from their and preceding generations. Evans also introduced a system of school diaries in which a weekly report was made on a child's progress and sent to each home for the parent's inspection and signature. Although the evidence is not clear, it is likely that Evans introduced the school colours as used in the school uniform and also devised the school's distinctive shield with the motto "Gorau ymgais gwybodaeth."

On 27 September, Evans started the term's games in the afternoon. He wrote to Mrs Evans in the evening: "School is taking shape. They had games in the afternoon. I went to see them; the girls at hockey & the boys at football and it was refreshing to hear nothing but Welsh - even at games. One boy had a statement to make to me yesterday. He stopped short in the middle of it - couldn't get it out in English, so dived into a stream of Welsh which carried him along beautifully. You had better make it a point to speak nothing but Welsh from the day you arrive. In 3 months you will be proficient par excellence. The same applies to the boys." Evans sought to interest the pupils in their Welsh heritage; on 30 October, he gave a speech to the pupils on William Williams Pantycelyn to mark the centenary of the hymnist's birth.

The one problem was still the question of science teaching. Miss Porter proved to be unsatisfactory and the Local Sub-Committee confirmed the notice given to her by the Headmaster. A Mr. Fleet of Nottingham was appointed to the post from the beginning of the Lent term but he did not appear at the School. A Miss Baldwin was approached but she also did not appear. Finally, on 23 December, Sidney Ross of Exeter was appointed at £175 p.a. to begin in the summer term "on assurance that you give in being able to do the work educationally, & that your nervous disability will not be an insurmountable difficulty." In fact, Ross did a small amount of teaching in the Lent term for which he was paid £15. At the year's end, Evans persuaded the Governors to pay a bonus of £10 for the period 1 April to 30 September to the assistant teachers. One small but important change made by Evans during the autumn of 1917, and made with the blessing of Local Sub-Committee, was the conversion of the Fourth Form room into a headmaster's room which allowed him the privacy to interview colleagues and pupils and gave him a status within the School apart from the other teachers.

Less than three months after Evans arrived at the School, the Chief Inspector from the Central Welsh Board, together with the Assistant Inspector and Miss S. Price, a temporary inspector, arrived at the School for a full inspection on 22-23 November 1917. Their detailed report supplies an excellent picture of the School towards the end of 1917. They begin with a statistical analysis of the pupils in the three years from 1915 to 1917. The total number of pupils in 1915-16 was 98, being 37 boys and 61 girls, with 5 pupils from outside the school district (i.e. Lampeter and area) and 23 pupils in lodgings; the total for 1916-17 was 100, being 40 boys and 60 girls, with 5 pupils from outside the school district and 30 pupils in lodgings; and finally, the total for 1917-18 (Evans' first year) was 120, being 48 boys and 72 girls, with all the pupils from within the school district and 47 pupils in lodgings. Evans had complained about the age of the pupils when they entered the School and this report confirms his dissatisfaction. In 1917-18, there were only 5 boys in the 11-12 age group; 7 boys and 12 girls in the 12-13 age-group; 16 boys and 11 girls in the 13-14 age-group; 13 boys and 17 girls in the 14-15 age-group; 3 boys and 12 girls in the 15-16 age-group; 4 boys and 12 girls in the 16-17 age-group; 5 girls in the 17-18 age-group; and, 3 girls in the 18-19 age-group. The pupils were concentrated in the three age-groups from 13-16, with over half the boys in the two age-groups from 13-15. Girls made up 60% of the School's pupils, as they did in the two preceding school years, and there were no boys aged 17 and over in the School. In a rural area, boys were often needed at home to help with farming activities and this need would be greater during wartime when the country was desperately in need of food. Nineteen of the pupils received scholarships which allowed them exemption from the fees and 17 pupils received maintenance allowances; the total amount expended by the School on scholarships was £65.2s.0d and on bursaries was £64.1s.0d. The inspectors listed the staff of the School and their salaries; Evans received a fixed salary of £350 - the old capitation fees had been abolished.

Once again, the inspectors remarked on the beautiful situation of the School, but they were less kind on the interior. The classrooms presented a dreary appearance and the report suggested that a few pictures would brighten the rooms and stimulate the pupils' taste and interests. The Hall was being used again for teaching but a former classroom had been converted into a "much needed private room for the Headmaster", although it could do with more furniture. There were insufficient desks and the type being used was incorrect in that they were long desks or dual desks and not the better type, i.e. a single desk with a locker. There were shortages of cupboard accommodation, of umbrella stands and of hockey stick stands. The staff room for the mistresses was small and it lacked a sofa and a rug in case of sudden illness. The inspectors were striving to bring in modern practices and the proper riposte to these criticisms was to point towards the inadequate funding of the School. The Library held 50 volumes of reference books and 300 volumes of general literature, but the inspectors noted that no new books had been purchased since 1914, except in the Welsh section which held 80 volumes. E. O. James had evidently acted after the second and sharp reminder from the Governors in 1915. The adverse remarks made in previous reports about the inaccessible housing of the Library still held good and the School was urged to place a few books, to be changed from time to time, in the classrooms so that pupils might handle these books. The Headmaster had a copy of *A Nation and its books* which the inspectors trusted would help in the choice of books relating to Wales. One must commend the advanced ideas of the inspectors both in their concern that the library books should be readily handled by the pupils, rather than being locked away in a distant cupboard, and in their wish that books on the history and literature of Wales should be available to the pupils.

The report notes that only two members of the staff were in the School before the beginning of 1917 and they hoped that there would be fewer changes in the future after the increases in salaries. The reasons for Evans' prompt actions in improving the salaries and obtaining a bonus for the staff now become clear. E. O. James' disappointment over the headmastership still rankled and he made it clear to the inspectors that he would be leaving the school soon. The pupils certainly noticed the frequent changes in their teachers; over fifty years later, Haydn Lewis recalled the confusing time caused by these changes.

The main criticism with regard to the subjects taught referred to language teaching. After earlier criticisms, the teaching of Latin had been postponed to Form II. From Form II until Form IV, all pupils took Latin, French and Welsh. Because the average age of admission was over 13, Form II consisted entirely of new admissions while two-thirds of Form III were also new admissions. Many of these pupils left before they could obtain a good grasp of Latin and French and, as the inspectors delicately pointed out, "English itself requires much care and practice in this thoroughly Welsh district." The report suggested that only one language besides Welsh and English should be taught in the first year at least. Evans had introduced the elements of navigation as an alternative to Latin in the fourth form which pleased the inspectors because it reflected the maritime nature of the locality.

The inspectors were satisfied with the standard of teaching in English, History, Latin and Geography, although they did express some concern that there was too much reliance on the dictation of notes rather than on the preparation of individual work by the pupils. The teaching of Welsh by E. O. James was praised, "the impressions obtained at the visit as to the thoroughness of the teaching, especially in composition, were distinctly favourable." However, the inspectors felt that insufficient advantage was being taken of the position of Welsh as a home language of practically all the pupils. They thought that it could be more used as a medium in the Welsh lessons and occasionally even in other subjects, such as Welsh history. One innovation that pleased the inspectors was the use of

Welsh in the morning assembly which now consisted of a hymn, a prayer and a Bible reading. These remarks betray how little the Welsh language had been used at the School before the autumn of 1917. The teaching of French had suffered because of staff changes and it was evident that the young mistress had been prevented by the War from visiting France. Form III contained 25 new pupils and it was doubtful if they would gain any proficiency in the language before they left the School, and it was difficult to teach a class composed of two sections very unequal in attainments. Evans himself took Mathematics in the upper forms while two of the mistresses coped with the lower forms. At the last annual examination, the Mathematics results had been poor and the inspectors considered the prospects of success more hopeful because the new Headmaster had made himself responsible for the subject. The School lacked a science teacher and science work had suffered. The inspector noted that Jones had taught for many years with success and that one of his pupils was now "doing useful work in the laboratories of Messrs. Nobels Works in Scotland." Woodwork had not been taught since Jones left and the inspectors were assured that the services of a local carpenter were being sought at an early date. One of the mistresses taught drawing to Forms II - IV; Form II was very crowded and on a dull November afternoon the light was bad in the Hall, where they received instruction. Only one girl in the class had received instruction in drawing before coming to the School. One can only sympathise with the mistress in charge of this class. Cookery was taught by a visiting mistress, Miss Hilda Jones, who attended for one whole day each week. The subject was taken up to and including Form IV and pupils were presented for the Junior examination of the Central Welsh Board. Needlework was taught by one of the mistresses up to and including Form III, but none of the pupils were presented for examination. The inspectors were displeased with the incomplete nature of the course in Domestic Subjects: Hygiene, Laundrywork and Housewifery were absent from the curriculum; the convenient kitchen lacked a larder and a hot water supply; the cookery mistress, a "very competent teacher", had been obliged to drop more advanced work in the upper school; Needlework should be taught throughout the School. A comprehensive course in Housecraft for girls should be provided. The School's own housekeeping came in for criticism because a school dinner was only provided on the day when the cookery class was held when "a well-cooked and well-served meal" was available for 5d. On the other hand, one of the mistresses arranged an evening class in dancing once a week for girls from Forms IV and V.

In their conclusion, the inspectors noted that the new Headmaster was previously at a large boys' school. They felt that his move to a rural and seaside mixed school was an interesting change of experience but it made many calls on his resourcefulness in contriving ways by which the differing needs of the pupils could be maintained. His intellectual abilities and his personal qualities gave the inspectors reason to hope "that he will ultimately achieve great success here." Excellent order was maintained in the School and all the teachers showed "creditable willingness to promote the interests of the School."

The inspectors noted that the prefect system had lately been established and that the pupils were divided into 'Houses', each under one of the teachers. The arrangements for supervising the fifty pupils in lodgings were very satisfactory. Evans had taken a positive attitude towards the three inspectors and there are touches in the report which plainly come from his conversations with the inspectors, e.g. the reference to the old pupil now working at the Nobel Works in Scotland. The report was submitted to the Board of Education and T. G. Roberts noted for his senior colleagues: "You have considered this school not to be satisfactory: perhaps the new head will make a difference, it is to be hoped that he will read the report carefully." O. M. Edwards commented, "Yes, the school, like other Cardiganshire schools, has been too much of a cramming place, blind to everything but examination results. This report is a good one, and the new Headmaster will understand it." A. T. Davies added, "The report is decidedly refreshing - but that is not its fault but that of the bad traditions in which the School has been raised."

After appointing Evans, the Board did not meet again until 27 March 1918 when they approved the reports of six meetings of the Local Sub-Committee. One of the most significant decisions taken by the Local Sub-Committee was that the Clerk should collect the school fees in future and not the Headmaster as previously. This removed a disagreeable task from the Headmaster and placed him in a more satisfactory relationship to the parents. Following representations from the Board of Education, the library was now made a charge on the School's funds. The Local Education Authority stopped its contributions towards the cookery teacher and the Governors agreed to employ here for two days if the Director could employ her for three days. This arrangement worked well. W. J. Jones was concerned that his salary in the Royal Naval Air Force was only 14 shillings a week and he asked the Governors to make up his salary to that which he received as a teacher. This matter troubled the Governors for some time and, because they wanted Jones back at the School, they gave him an interim payment of £25 in 1918 and, when he returned later in 1918, they paid him £50 to make up his salary and a bonus of £10 as a mark of their appreciation for returning at the earliest possible opportunity. The School's finances had improved now that there were more children on the registers.

On 30 October 1918, B. C. Jones resigned as Clerk to the Board of Governors. His resignation was received with surprise and regret, but he refused to alter his decision. J. M. Howell was formally only the Vice-Chairman and, at the end of 1918, he was elected Chairman; Daniel Jenkins, the Headmaster of Aberaeron Primary School, was appointed the Clerk; and, the Governors decided to place a portrait of B. C. Jones in the School as a mark of their appreciation for over 23 years' service. The position of Clerk was onerous in that he was responsible for much of the School's administration especially in its relationship with the regulating bodies and in handling the finances which now came to over £1000 a year.

A Central Welsh Board inspector visited the School for a subsidiary inspection on 1 July 1919. He noted that the Senior Master had returned "after doing valuable war work in connection with the use of poison gases." An additional mistress had been appointed. Evans had made an application in May 1919 for a person to teach Geography and English; it was left to the Headmaster to select two candidates from the list supplied by the agencies. He engaged Miss Richards and, the Governors agreed, after an explanation from the Headmaster, to appoint her from the beginning of the Summer Term 1919. The inspector noted that, while the accommodation was insufficient, improvements had been made in that cupboard shelves had been provided for the Headmaster while £100 was to be spent on renovation and equipment as well on science books for the Library. The teaching of science had returned to normal with the return of W. J. Jones; Sidney Ross left after only one term and the Headmaster took science in the Christmas term. All forms, except Forms V and VI, were receiving instruction in Physical Education and all forms, except Form VI, had one period for games during the first two terms of the school year. Games were not possible in the summer term because the field was required for pasture, although one form had been able to play tennis during the last period of each afternoon. W. J. Jones was in charge of games for the boys and Miss Hilda Jones, the Cookery Mistress, for the girls. The inspector was pleased to note that "espirit de corps is being encouraged by means of games competitions." During the school breaks, the girls frequently danced and there were still occasional dances in the evening. The inspector concluded that " A new spirit is being breathed into the School by the Headmaster."

Evans had certainly made a considerable impact on the life of the School. The suggestion that pictures should be hung in the School for the benefit of the pupils had been met by the purchase of four wall portraits of Welsh celebrities purchased from the profits of a dramatic production, *Ar y Groesffordd.* The complaints about the place of music in the curriculum had been met by Evans himself who took music lessons and, on occasion, took the whole School in preparation for the opening morning services. He loved music and he was delighted when he could get the whole school singing together.

The criticisms made by the inspectors regarding the curriculum at Aberaeron are mirrored in the reports made of other intermediate schools, and were raised by the Welsh Department of the Board of Education in its annual report to Parliament. Physical Education, Music and Art were neglected in many intermediate schools and the Central Welsh Board arranged for experts in music and in art to tour the schools of Wales in order to interest the pupils and to provide practical help to the teachers. Evans was fortunate in that the heavy burden of external examinations, which had harassed his predecessor, was being reduced with the reform of the system into two examinations: the Senior, taken at the age of 16, and the Higher, taken at the age of 18. Educational reform was on the political agenda. The Fisher Act of 1918 sought to establish a national system of education for the benefit of those who wished or were able to profit from education. However, the Act was not mandatory and many of the developments envisaged by the Act were curtailed for reason of economy. The Act did lead to the introduction in 1921 of an uniform school leaving age of 14 which assisted in solving the problem of children entering the intermediate schools late and leaving early.

Evans had done much to improve the salaries of his staff; the inspector noted in 1919 that additions had been made and further increases would be made in September. The two men teachers now received £230 a year and the women received £165 a year. The average salary for an intermediate school teacher was £212 for an assistant master and £162 for an assistant mistress. In 1918, the assistant staff at Aberaeron were receiving more than the average. However, the Headmaster with a salary of £350 was considerably below the Welsh average of £461.

Teachers' salaries were to prove a considerable problem for the School over the next five years. The Board of Education proposed, in 1917, a minimum salary scale, and a supplementary grant was allowed to the authorities who adopted this scale. This proposal did not affect Aberaeron. The Fisher Act contained proposals for the improvement of the status of teachers and it led to the establishment of a committee, chaired by Lord Burnham and charged with the task of developing salary scales for teachers. On 12 June 1918, all the assistant teachers at Aberaeron had presented a scale of salaries for the consideration of the Governors. This request was not accepted, but the Governors had agreed to review the salaries of assistant teachers every year and to award £10 extra to the women teachers and £5 to E. O. James for the school year 1918-19. Within five months, the teachers applied for a further increase and they were told that the matter was not to be reopened until the end of the school year.

On 15 March 1919, the first meeting of the Cardiganshire Association of Secondary School Teachers was held at Aberaeron. The Association appealed for the support of the governing bodies in pressing the County Council to follow the lead of neighbouring councils by adopting a scale of salaries for secondary schools. The Association invited the governors to send three representatives from each school to a meeting at Lampeter on 25 April in order to arrange united action in approaching the County Council for further financial help by raising the Education Rate. At a special meeting, the Aberaeron Governors selected J. M. Howell, E. Lima Jones and Mrs. T. Z. Jones to attend at Lampeter. The deputation chosen by the Lampeter meeting waited upon the County Council and they were informed that the matter would be referred to the Finance Committee. The Aberaeron Governors joined the teachers in a strong appeal to the County Council. Teachers in neighbouring counties were now receiving a provisional scale of up to £450 for men and £400 for women which was almost double the salaries of the Cardiganshire teachers. A conference of education authorities and teachers met at Llandrindod on 28 June 1919 to arrive at an uniform scale for West and Mid-Wales counties, but Cardiganshire Education Committee refused to send a representative. Another deputation went to see the Finance Committee of the Local Education Authority on 14 April 1920; D. Andrew Davies and the Headmaster represented the Aberaeron Governors. This led to the creation of a Joint Committee consisting of members of the Local Education Authority, governors and teachers with the remit of devising a county scale for secondary teachers. However, at the first meeting of this committee, the members agreed to postpone the consideration of a scale until the publication of the national scales being considered by the Burnham Committee. The teachers, certainly, and some of the governors believed that the Burnham scales would be applied in Cardiganshire. An increased higher education rate had been introduced, meanwhile, by the County Finance Committee. When E. Lima Jones and the Headmaster reported this increase to the Governors, the Clerk noted that this extra money was granted "pending the adoption of the Burnham scales." The extra £320 given to Aberaeron for 1920-21 was promptly allocated by the Governors: £45 to Headmaster; £60 to E. O. James; £50 to W. J. Jones; £45 to Miss D. M. Davies; £30 to Miss M. E. Thomas; £50 to Miss A. Richards; £25 to Miss E. A. Roberts.

Lord Burnham's committee reported in October 1920 and issued the first series of nationally negotiated salary scales for teachers. These scales were immediately adopted by 117 authorities out of 126 and eight other authorities adopted similar scales; leaving Cardiganshire, in J. M. Howell's words, as "the only defaulting authority in the kingdom." The Aberaeron teachers were prompt in appealing to their Governors for support in obtaining the Burnham scales; the cost of the new scales to Aberaeron was estimated to be an additional expenditure of £515. Cardiganshire governors had met together and agreed on steps to bring the matter to a satisfactory conclusion. This was optimistic. There followed a whole year of deadlock between the governing bodies and the County Council. On the whole, the Aberaeron Governors were sympathetic to the teachers; the adoption of a national scale would remove the burden of dealing with requests for pay increases.

A Joint Committee of governors and members of the Local Education Authority produced a draft scale towards the end of 1921. This scale was adopted by the Local Education Authority on 22 January 1922; it was the worst scale in the country and Cardiganshire teachers were to be paid £100 less than their counterparts in Carmarthenshire. However, following the elections in March, a new council scrapped the January scales and referred the matter back to the Finance Committee. Another new scale, considerably inferior to the January scale, was adopted on 26 October and it was to be put into place as from 1 October. The teachers rejected this scale and, for the first time, called in the assistance of their union.

The Aberaeron Governors considered the new scales on 13 December. Evans was ill. John Jones, Cilcennin, seconded by J. Elias Jones, both members of the Local Education Authority, proposed that these scales be adopted. Howell produced an amendment asked for more time to bring the scale into operation. This amendment was carried by four votes to three. Howell was correct in his attempt to postpone the crisis which would arise if the teachers refused to accept the scale. Precipitate action at the intermediate school in Cardigan resulted in the governors serving one month's notice to the staff to terminate their engagements on 31 December 1922.

During the past three years, Evans had worked hard to raise standards at the School. On

11 May 1921, he presented the Governors with a table which showed the results of all the intermediate schools in the county at the Central Welsh Board examinations in July 1920. The number and quality of the successes obtained by the School were strikingly in advance of those gained by any other school - on the proposition of John Jones, Cilcennin, and E. Lima Jones, the Governors decided to congratulate the Headmaster. Teaching vacancies in other counties were now more attractive to members of the staff. When Miss Richards resigned as Geography teacher in 1921, only one application was received. The Governors indicated to Miss Megan Williams, the sole and successful applicant, that they expected her to remain at the School for two years and to give three months notice if she wished to leave. Miss Williams agreed to spend the summer before she came to Aberaeron on a physical drill course in Barry. The Governors asked E. O. James to attend the Barry course. However, James resigned in November; he had been Latin and Welsh master at the School for eighteen years and he was a native of the county, but his disappointment over the post of headmaster meant that he had been searching for another position since 1917. He had accepted the post of Senior Assistant Master at the new secondary school in Quaker's Yard, Merthyr Tydfil. This school was one of the first secondary schools in Wales to offer free secondary education and the first headmaster was T. J. Thomas, the poet 'Sarnicol', and a native, like James, of the Llandysul area. Stephen J. Williams was appointed to replace James. He had a First Class Honours degree in Welsh and he also agreed to take the course in Barry. Miss E. A. James, the English Mistress, left for Whitland Intermediate School and W. E. Roberts was the successful candidate out of the thirty-six who applied for her post. S. J. Williams resigned at the end of the Christmas Term 1922 when the crisis over salaries was coming to a head; he left for Llandeilo County School and went on to become Professor of Welsh at Swansea.

Seven applications were received for the post of Welsh teacher and two men, both with first class honours, were summoned for interview. J. T. Owen from Ysbytty Ystwyth and J. Morgan Williams from Pontygwaith appeared before the Governors on 3 January 1923. It transpired that, acting on advice received from the National Union of Teachers, neither candidate was prepared to accept an appointment at the advertised salary. Both candidates withdrew their applications. When the Governors enquired why, in the face of this situation, both candidates had attended for interview, they replied that, after withdrawing their applications, they had received the Clerk's invitation to interview and interpreted this to mean that there might have been a change in the situation. Howell pointed out that if an appointment was made for a period of two months only, up to the time of the expiration of the notices already served on the assistant staff, viz. up to 28 February, it would ensure the smooth and efficient running of the School and it would only involve a payment of £3.6s. 8d. more than the new county scale. After February, the successful applicant would find himself in the same position as the other assistant teachers. The other Governors agreed with Howell and the post was offered to J. T. Owen who accepted for a probationary period of two months at a salary rate of £220.

Another meeting of all the Cardiganshire governors, held at Lampeter on 16 December, had resolved to seek another meeting with the Local Education Authority and to ask the teachers to remain in post until the end of July 1923 at the salary they would be entitled to under the October scale. After the annual Prize Day on 21 December, Howell had endeavoured to persuade the Headmaster and his staff to accept the resolutions of the Lampeter meeting. Evans and his staff rejected this proposal unanimously. On 29 December, the Chairman, seconded by John Jones (Cilcennin), moved that the Board should issue notices to each member of staff terminating his or her present engagement with a view to re-appointment from the date of the expiration of the notice at a salary in accordance with the October scale in each case; six months' notice was given to the Headmaster and two months each to the assistant teachers, all notices to date from January 1923. The Clerk then presented a revised financial estimate for 1922-23, based on the October scales, and this showed a reduction in staff salaries of £220. At a later meeting, Howell pointed out that the notices issued on 1 January were not in strict accordance with the regulations, and fresh notices were issued to the assistant staff terminating their appointments on 31 March 1923. The appointment of J. T. Owen was continued to the end of term at the same rate.

Efforts to solve the dispute continued. The Central Welsh Board inspectors appeared before the Governors on 21 March and presented a verbal report on the recent full inspection - "they emphasised the great advance made in the efficiency of the School since the advent of the present Headmaster. They also congratulated the Governors on obtaining the services of a highly-qualified staff of teachers, of whose ability they spoke in terms of high praise." Edwards referred to the lack of accommodation and he noted that the number of pupils was now 163. There was room for an extra teacher; some of the teachers worked from start to finish on each day of the week, and that was too great a strain on the voice and the energy. Robinson, the assistant inspector, remarked that he had difficulty in addressing the Governors of a school described by a leading public figure at Aberystwyth as the best school in the county. The purpose of this unusual appearance by the inspectors in front of the Governors was to underline the achievements made at the School, which could be damaged by the dispute, and to underline the concern felt by the Central Welsh Board and the Board of Education.

The teachers had been offered a revised salary scale, "the revised October scale", but it was rejected at a meeting in Cardigan on 17 March. The Governors "reluctantly decided to advertise for teachers to take up duties at the beginning of the next summer term, at salaries in accordance with the latest county scale." Only four applications were received as a result of advertisements in the *Western Mail* and the *South Wales News*. Howell explained that an objection had been raised because the advertisement specified one month's notice and he suggested that they should re-advertise without that reservation. The opening of the School would therefore be postponed until 1 May. During further discussion, Howell indignantly rebutted the suggestion that he was a teacher's man. A wily politician, Howell was gaining time in order to avoid appointing replacement teachers. Forty-three applications were received in answer to the second round of advertisements. When the Governors came to consider the candidates, they found that a number had withdrawn and that there were no applications for Geography or Welsh. The School was now closed and the assistant staff on strike. The Governors agreed that if no candidates were received for Welsh and Geography, then the Clerk could write to the Board of Education, the Central Welsh Board and the Director of Education that the Governors had failed to staff the School and that it would be closed for the summer term. The Clerk wrote in these terms on 29 April. Three governors, who were also members of the Local Education Authority, asked for an emergency meeting on 7 May to make a further effort to staff the School. Llandysul School had reopened on 2 May with new staff, appointed without consultation with the Headmaster. The pupils, in sympathy with the old staff, declined to enter the School until appealed to by the Headmaster. Cardigan was in a similar position. The dispute was now much more difficult to resolve. When E. J. Davies pointed out that those schools had obtained staff, Howell answered that the Governors were quite prepared to appoint new teachers and he invited the three governors to find applicants for the posts of Welsh and Geography. Mrs. T. Z. Jones deplored the fact that they were going to remove seven Welsh-speaking, experienced and successful teachers, all with honours degrees, to make room for inexperienced English, Irish and Scottish teachers who could not for years, if ever, adapt themselves. The Governors agreed that they would wait for the answer of the Board, while the Chairman explored fresh avenues for teachers of Welsh and Geography. The Headmaster had met the senior pupils and explained that the School might be opened in time for the Central Welsh Board examinations. He had urged them to pursue their studies. The intermediate schools at Tregaron and Aberystwyth had also managed to avoid appointing replacement teachers and the three northern schools tried to find their own solution to the dispute.

The President of the Board of Education now intervened and invited all the parties to a confidential conference at the Board on 24 May. Howell represented Aberaeron. The terms of a suggested basis of settlement were agreed: the Local Education Authority would pay the schools a sum which was not less than the aggregate amount which it would have contributed to enable the revised October scale to be paid; the school fees would be raised to, or near, £8 a year, the maximum amount authorised by the County Scheme, and which would enable the governors to pay an uniform minimum scale to be agreed between them and the teachers; the schools to be re-opened as soon as possible. This was a clever solution in that extra money was found for the teachers; the Local Education Authority was not forced to a humiliating retreat; and the governors of each school were confirmed in their relative freedom of action. The terms agreed in London were approved by the Aberaeron Governors on 5 June.

Representatives of the northern schools met at Aberystwyth, with Vice-Principal Edward Edwards, the brother of the late O. M. Edwards, in the chair. In a letter to the

Chairman, J. M. Howell, who was staying at the Hotel Majestic in Folkestone, warned against losing the Board of Education grants for the current school year. The proceedings were marred by considerable bickering, especially over the question of the old staff of the two southern schools. Mrs. T. Z. Jones, representing the Aberaeron Governors, proposed that the three northern schools should open and that the question of the two southern schools be left to the Board of Education. She appealed to the teachers to go back on any scale to the end of the school year so that the schools could be opened on 1 July. Howell Evans spoke for the teachers and he pointed out that there was nothing in the Board of Education settlement to make it impossible for the three schools to restart immediately apart from the other two schools. The Local Education Authority had already agreed to the revised October scale. Evans then referred to the proposal for raising the school fees, which was of great concern to many present, and he pointed out that fees were a matter for the governors who could reduce or increase them as they pleased. Mrs T. Z. Jones' proposal was formally put to the Conference and it was carried unanimously. The teachers from all the five schools met in Aberystwyth on 23 June and agreed, almost unanimously, to return to work on the basis of the Board of Education settlement.

Howell reported these developments to the Governors. He remarked that Aberaeron was in a privileged situation. Their staff was intact and on the spot. They were a tried and efficient staff and they had raised the school to an enviable position. He urged the Governors to re-appoint the staff on salaries in accordance with the terms of the Board of Education settlement. Howell emphasised that the School would not receive any contribution from the Local Education Authority or the Board of Education for 1922-23 unless they reopened the school for the term, which was fast dwindling out. John Jones, Cilcennin, moved that the old staff be re-appointed and he was seconded by Miss Evelyn Lewes, the daughter of the first Chairman. Concern was expressed by some of the Governors about the question of raising the school fees, but Howell assured them that this was not required for the present term. They would have time and leisure "in a less foggy atmosphere" to examine that condition. The School reopened on 27 June and the staff were paid a term's salary under the revised October scale, less the amount they had received from the National Union of Teachers.

J. M. Howell and Howell Evans had worked well during this crisis and, thanks to their efforts, the School emerged from a difficult situation without any serious damage. To conclude the sorry tale of this dispute, the Local Education Authority agreed, on 28 January 1926, to pay salaries to the secondary school teachers on the national scale from the following 1 April. The old staff at Cardigan and Llandysul had not been restored to their positions and they had been receiving payments from the union; these payments were about to lapse. The Cardiganshire branch of the National Union of Teachers tabled a motion at the Portsmouth Conference held during the Easter holidays which appealed to the Conference to ensure that payments to the old staff at the two schools were continued. Howell Evans moved the Branch's proposition with an admirable speech which outlined the crisis of 1923 and he was supported by James Davies of Rhydypennau Council School. Their eloquence led to such excitement on the floor of the conference that the Executive agreed to continue the support allowed to the displaced teachers.

Evans' position was enhanced by the reforms he had instituted at the School and by his success in bringing the School through the crisis of 1923. For the rest of his career as Headmaster, the Governors would play a lesser role in the development of the School and they were content, on the whole, to accept Evans' suggestions. Howell Evans had a vision of the School as an instrument for developing all aspects of a child's character: "to emphasise the value of examinations necessarily implies the belittlement of the school as a centre of culture - intellectual, moral, social and physical. As a matter of fact these functions are complementary." He was concerned to develop "the spirit of freedom and consequently of enterprise and self-reliance." These ideas were behind his support of the foundation of the School Club which allowed the senior pupils to organise their own meetings, to arrange concerts and social functions, and to organise the School Eisteddfod. The three school houses established in 1917 competed against each other in the Eisteddfod as well as in football, hockey and tennis. The pupils also took part in operettas and dramas organised by the Headmaster. His young colleague, J. T. Owen, proved to have a talent for acting. "We are", remarked Evans, "having a jolly time." Evans ensured that the profits from these entertainments were kept under his control and used for the benefit of the School, e.g., to purchase another piano in 1923.

The rapid turnover of staff which was a feature of School life since the middle of the War ceased to become a problem after the settlement of the teachers' dispute. The Governors, however, drew up proper agreements defining conditions of service which were signed by all the assistant staff on 13 December 1923. Evans turned his attention to the School's buildings and obtained permission to construct a concrete exercise court and to lay down a new grass tennis court. Eric Richards who brought electricity to Aberaeron established an electric supply at the School in the autumn of 1924. A wireless set and a gramophone were purchased and a typewriter was obtained for instructional purposes.

References to the reports produced by the school inspectors appear far less frequently on the agenda for the Governors' meetings. The main complaint was still over handicrafts. W. J. Jones took charge of woodwork and he was provided with 12 new steel-jack planes in 1925. The Local Education Authority declined to provide the services of the cookery teacher, for an extra half day, and the Governors decided to advertise in 1925 for a full time Domestic Science Mistress with three years' training, i.e. one with special diplomas in needlework and dressmaking. When a new post was advertised, Evans sifted the applications and presented his recommendations for the short list to the Governors. Mrs. T. Z. Jones objected to this practice and it was agreed that the Clerk should summarise the qualifications of all candidates and supply each governor with a copy. Mrs. Jones died in 1925; she had served the school well for 29 years and she played an important role in solving the 1923 dispute. Evans did not alter his practice. Towards the end of 1926, he presented the Governors with a summary of the applicants for a post and recommended three candidates for interview. He then left to take a rehearsal of *The Old Bohemian Girl* to be performed by the pupils on the following day. Left to their own devices, the Governors then proceeded to consider another application which had been brought to their notice, "and so favourably impressed were they by the high attainments and testimonials of the candidate in question, no. 10 on the list, that it was decided to add her name to the short list."

There were a number of staff changes during the years 1926-27 mainly caused by women teachers resigning after a few years service. It was still not usual for a teacher to continue her career after marriage. Miss Harry served as Domestic Science teacher for three years up to 1929, when she left to become Mrs. D. L. Jones and a valued member of the community at Aberaeron for the next fifty years. W. E. Roberts, the English master, also left in 1929 for a post in Aberdare. He eventually returned to a post at Lampeter and made his home again in Aberaeron. After his retirement from teaching, "W. E." became a popular figure in the town as Aberaeron correspondent for the *Cambrian News*. He died, at a considerable age, in 1995. Miss Harry was replaced by Miss Elaine Lewis, the first old pupil appointed to a teaching post, and W. E. Roberts by W. A. Jones.

Evans was still making improvements to the School; a sports pavilion was built out of funds raised by the School and by the Old Pupils. There was still a problem over the teaching of physical education. The Board of Education protested in 1925 when the inspector discovered that boys and girls in Forms III and IV were exercising together in the charge of a mistress. An attempt by the School, in conjunction with Aberystwyth and Machynlleth Schools, to obtain the services of the physical instructor at the University College of Wales was vetoed by the Local Education Authority which suggested that a member of staff should take on this work as an extra duty. Another urgent problem was the number of pupils in the School which had risen to 180 by the Christmas Term 1930; the Local Sub-Committee decided to recommend the appointment of an additional member of staff to teach Latin and Welsh. The Governors met on 24 September to consider this recommendation; J. M. Howell, who did so much for the welfare of the School, had died in 1927, and he was succeeded as Chairman by John Jones of Cilcennin, one of the original Governors in 1896 and the grandfather of the present writer, who retired after a year because of ill-health, but remained on the Board. The new Chairman was Dr. D. M. Davies, the son of the second Chairman. Twenty years before, John Jones had argued for the extension of vocational education at the School; he argued now for the appointment of a man qualified to teach agriculture. The Governors temporised and recommended a temporary appointment of a man to teach Latin and Physical Education. T. H. Fox was appointed. John Jones raised the question of agriculture and commercial subjects again on 21 October and he pointed out that the Central Welsh Board inspectors were in favour of such a development. At another meeting, eight days later, John Jones moved formally "that the school curriculum be reorganised so as to include the teaching of agriculture and commercial subjects." After a good discussion, approval was given to the principle of teaching agriculture, but action was deferred for a year when the Governors would reconsider it in connection with a possible re-distribution of staff. Fox was given a permanent post as Latin Master on 10 June 1931 and, on the recommendation of the Headmaster, it was decided to introduce agriculture by extending the syllabus in Chemistry and Botany so as to include the prescribed syllabus in agriculture up to School Certificate. By the end of 1932, John Jones' long-held ambition was achieved when the Local Education Authority agreed to the appointment of an additional assistant master competent in agriculture. John Evans was appointed to this post on 16 December 1932.

The Headmaster had not forgotten the school magazine. *The Link* had been revived for a brief period in the late 1920s and it was revived again in 1932 with W. A. Jones and Ben George Jones as Editors. W. A. Jones was to have charge of editing *The Link* for the next forty years; the first pupil editor became a distinguished solicitor in London, a leading member of the Honourable Society of Cymmrodorion, and an influential figure in the campaign to preserve the Welsh language. The first issue of the revived magazine introduced the practice of publishing winning entries at the School Eisteddfod. Among the items of School news was a report on the completion of the Sports Pavilion, the addition of a new classroom, and the installation of a proper water supply and drainage system. This issue also includes an account of the production of *Cnoi Awel,* a drama in Welsh by the Headmaster which portrayed life in fifteenth-century Wales and which was produced in the Memorial Hall, with J. T. Owen in the leading role as Gruffydd ap Niclas, a Welsh nobleman of the period. Evans was also engaged on a series of new textbooks on Welsh history. The 1932 issue of *The Link* was a success and it has appeared annually since this date. Most of the staff was drawn into the preparation of the magazine: J. T. Owen took charge of the Welsh entries; T. H. Fox helped with the advertisements; John Evans took the copy to Lampeter; and W. J. Jones compiled the news about the old pupils.

W. J. Jones had served the School for twenty-four years; he had no interests save the life of the School. He was an able and much-loved teacher of Chemistry and a number of his pupils went on to pursue careers in various aspects of Chemistry. Jones lodged at Maglona in Albert Street when he first came to Aberaeron and he purchased the house when his landlady died; the owners of Compton Ironmongery next door claimed that they could set their watches by the punctual time at which Jones passed their shop each morning on his way to School. On his arrival, Jones leaned on a window-sill in the Hall and his pale face could be seen by the children as they came up the school-path - girls to one side and boys to the other side of the path, and considerable wrath was visited upon the child who strayed to the wrong side. He devoted much time to the activities of the School Club and also to the organisation of the annual Reunion of Old Pupils. At weekends, he would often take some of the children to visit a place of historical interest. Evans was fortunate in his staff and they has confidence in him. School life was not without its friction as was illustrated by a fictional exchange recorded in *The Link* of 1936.

A boy from Tanyfron asserted that Mr. Evans had said that their girls' choir was by far the best in the Eisteddfod and that their big choir was better than the others provided they kept time; a boy from Portland answered that Miss Lewis had said quite the opposite, and she understood far more about the matter than the Headmaster. Miss Elaine Lewis had been made the House Mistress of Portland and she was a fierce champion of that House throughout her time at the School. There was a tremendous rivalry between Evans and Miss Lewis over the performance of their choirs at the School Eisteddfod. On one occasion, Evans flattered the adjudicator who gave the prize for the choir to Tyglyn, the Headmaster's house, when Portland's choir had given a better performance. Relations between the Headmaster and Miss Lewis were very frosty for some time.

During the 1930s, the increasing number of pupils placed great pressure on the School's accommodation. The School needed extra classrooms and a dining room now that Miss Lewis, with the assistance of the School's caretakers, Mrs. Breeze and later Mrs. Lloyd of Water Street, was preparing school dinners. The pupils, boys and girls, were expected to assist in laying the tables and clearing up afterwards. The economic climate in the early 1930s was not favourable towards extra expenditure on school buildings. By 1937, pupil numbers had reached 200 and the position was so bad that the Local Education Authority authorised the Governors to select a suitable room at the County Hall as a classroom. The required extensions were put out to tender on 3 March 1938 and they included a science room and the boys' cloakroom to the south and a domestic science room, new classrooms and a girls' cloakroom to the north. At the insistence of the Board of Education, a gymnasium was added to the plans. *The Link* recorded in 1939 that "there comes from every side the sound of lorries, creaking of pulleys, the unloading of numerous blocks." The work was completed during the Second World War which prevented the School from obtaining the necessary equipment for the gymnasium. Rhys James, the County Architect, married the new extensions to the original building very successfully and his gymnasium, in its original form, was a fine design.

The Second World War affected the School in two significant ways: difficulties over staffing and the presence of children evacuated from the large English cities. For the first year of the war, there was no problem over staffing, but when W. J. Griffiths, the Physics Master, resigned in September 1940, the Headmaster could not obtain a replacement and he had to make the best arrangements he could. W. M. Meredith, appointed as a temporary English master during W. A. Jones' illness and later appointed an extra master, was called up on 12 March 1941. The Headmaster managed to obtain a replacement for him and he asked the Governors to consent to one of the teachers being kept on after she married. John Evans was seconded to the Ministry of Agriculture and Food as a Land Commissioner in Breconshire and the teaching of agriculture was discontinued for a month until Miss Maria Evans was appointed to replace him. By 1942, three old pupils were on the staff: Miss Maria Evans, Miss Joan Evans and Miss Morfudd Thomas. T. H. Fox formed an Air Training Corps Unit , "No. 1511 Flight ATC", and the boys went on training courses at St. Athan; after Fox was called up, the corps was placed in the charge of E. J. Thomas, a local chemist. Sergeant Robinson was lent to the School as a physical training instructor by the military camp outside Aberaeron.

Mr. Griffiths wrote from his naval training establishment and Mr. Meredith, a wireless operator in the Navy, came to visit his old colleagues. William Maskell Meredith was killed on active service in the East Mediterranean in 1943, and the Headmaster called the children to the Hall to announce the sad news. Meredith was a young man of considerable academic achievement and he had been very popular both with his colleagues and the pupils; he is still remembered with fondness by pupils from that time.

Dr. D. M. Davies died in 1941; a Governor since 1919, he had been the Chairman for eleven years. He had been one of the pupils who registered on the first day the School opened. The last service "Dr. Dai" performed for the School was to assist with the purchase of the playing fields near the sea-shore. In the following year, Alderman E. J. Davies, who had been a Governor since 1896, died. Dr. Davies was replaced as chairman by J. M. Lloyd-Thomas of Llanarth; a pupil at Hughes' private grammar school in New Quay, Lloyd-Thomas had practised as a lawyer before entering the Unitarian ministry. He was a very distinctive figure because he wore a flowing black cloak. Mrs. Nesta Poulgrain was appointed a Governor in 1940; the daughter of J. M. Howell, she had been a pupil at the School and she would give good service as a Governor for many years.

The Government's plans for reconstruction after the War included plans for the wholesale reform of education: secondary education would be available to all children. This was not an imposed plan but a plan devised after a considerable period of consultation with all the interested parties. In 1943, Evans was the President of the Cardiganshire branch of the National Union of Teachers and, in his presidential address in November 1943, he discussed the Government's proposals. He was, on the whole, sceptical about several aspects of the proposed reforms and he objected strongly to the proposal for compulsory religious training in schools: "Compulsion has always been the greatest enemy of Christianity." As for Cardiganshire, Evans foresaw that the solution for the County would be the multilateral school which would provide practical, technical and academic education for secondary schools. He regarded this as "the democratic solution because it would discourage intellectual and social snobbery." For a man whose life had been devoted to raising the academic standards of the intermediate schools, this was a statement made with some reluctance. In the debate that followed, J. T. Owen noted that Evans had been against the multilateral school but that he was now wavering on the best policy for Cardiganshire. Owen believed that "the child should be trained as to become a citizen of his own locality." There was still a division of opinion over the function of education in Wales: should it be organised solely to benefit the child or should it be organised to benefit both the child and the community? The rural intermediate schools had provided a good academic education which enabled many pupils to pursue successful careers, but careers in other places and not in their native community. The effect of the intermediate schools on a small rural community was demonstrated by the late Jac L. Williams, an ex-pupil and later Professor of Education at Aberystwyth, in a study of Llanddewi Aberarth which showed that all the successful intermediate school pupils from the village had left the village which had been deprived of its natural leaders. Williams' sister, Joan Williams, obtained, like her brother, a degree in Welsh and, under her married name of Joan Davies, she has celebrated the old Cardiganshire society, which her brother was concerned to protect, in a series of fine essays published as *Trwy Gil Y Drws*, *Cawl Cennin*, *Pen Y Mwdwl*, and *Casglu'r Briwsion*.

At the end of 1942, Howell Evans told the Governors that he would be sixty-five soon and he indicated that he was considering retirement. However, he agreed to stay on for another year and he resigned at the end of August 1944. Evans was still writing and, both before and after his retirement, he was preparing scripts for BBC Radio on Welsh history. He had been a Headmaster with exceptional qualities and the School had prospered well under his stewardship. He is remembered with much affection by his pupils.

Secondary education for all: The School, 1944-1973

The Government's reforms in education were enacted in the Butler Act of 1944. The task of implementing these reforms at Aberaeron would be the first task facing the new Headmaster, John Thomas Owen. Born at Ysbytty Ystwyth in 1901, Owen had been Senior Welsh teacher at Aberaeron from 1923 to 1944. He was a keen Welshman, an adjudicator of eisteddfod recitation competitions, a good actor and a lover of field sports. He had been awarded a M.A. degree by the University of Wales for a thesis on the work of Gwallter Mechain.

Following the Butler Act of 1944, each county in Wales was expected to prepare its own plan of reorganisation for secondary education. A small rural county like Cardiganshire was circumscribed in its freedom to plan major changes by the problem of distance and by the lack of resources. The County's plans were submitted in April 1947 to the Welsh Department of the Ministry of Education which did not object to the solution proposed for Aberaeron. The radical solution of a multilateral system had been abandoned in favour of a bilateral school where the grammar side would co-exist with the new secondary modern side.

The reforms of education placed the Governors at Aberaeron in a new relationship to the Local Education Authority. The Governors of the intermediate schools had guarded jealously their independence from the county authorities. This position was eroded at Aberaeron during the Second World War. The Director of Education had been allowed to participate in the selection of a Headmaster by making enquires about the candidates and by preparing a typed list of questions which were approved by the Governors and given to each candidate ten minutes before his interview. A more significant intervention occurred over the work of the Clerk to the Governors. Daniel Jenkins was ill in the autumn of 1942

Mr. J. T. Owen, O.B.E., M.A.
Prifathro 1944-1965

Staff yr Ysgol / Teaching Staff

Nansi Jones, M. Price, M. Thomas, John A. M. Davies, Maria Evans, Alcwyn Evans, Nancy Evans, T. Morgan, Mair M. Jones, G. Parry, John Evans, Elaine Lewis, J. T. Owen, W. A. Jones, Olive John, T. H. Fox.

Agoriad y Bloc Newydd / Opening of the New Block

Rhagfyr / December 1951

Agoriad y Bloc Newydd / Opening of the New Block

Rhagfyr / December 1951

Junior Choir 1957

Cerddorfa'r Ysgol

1957

Dosbarth Chwech / Sixth Form

c. 1960

Gymnastics Team

c. 1960

Cerddorfa'r Ysgol / School Orchestra

1962

and he was replaced for two months by G. E. Ellis, his successor as Headmaster of the Primary School. Jenkins returned at the end of 1942 but his health and age forced him to retire at the end of 1944. A man from the Tregaron area, Jenkins had worked long and hard for the School. The new Chairman, Lloyd-Thomas, appealed to the Governors to accept the decision of the Higher Education Committee to centralise all intermediate school clerkships in the County Education Office. This was not acceptable to the other Governors and the Local Education Authority agreed to give the Governors a free hand in the appointment of a Clerk. The post was offered to Ellis who asked if he could consider the list of duties and consult the Education Office before he came to a decision. Ellis withdrew because the work would interfere with his duties at the Primary School. In view of Ellis' withdrawal, the Director of Education was appointed Clerk, for the time being, from 1 October 1944 at a salary of £50. This arrangement became permanent and, two years later, the School's account at the National Provincial Bank was closed and the balance was transferred to the County Fund. The Director kept the old logbook, hand-written up to the time of Jenkins' retirement, until 1949. From that year, the minutes of the Governors' meetings are published in the quarterly reports of the County Council and they became more formal, lacking the references to the views of individual governors which enliven the old logbooks. The Governors of the intermediate school had relied on the school inspectors to maintain the necessary standards; the considerable extension of secondary education required a more professional administration of the School.

W. J. Jones announced that he intended to resign from the end of the Christmas Term 1944. Because his successor was unable to join the staff at the required time, Jones stayed on until 1945. He had been at the School since 1908 and the School had been his whole life. During his retirement, Jones continued to organise the annual reunion of old pupils until his death on 11 August 1952.

By the end of the Second World War, the senior staff in the School consisted of J. T. Owen, W. A. Jones and Elaine Lewis and they would all work together for the next twenty years. Towards the end of 1945, the old name of Aberaeron Intermediate School had been abandoned in favour of Aberaeron County School. The provision of secondary education for all pupils required extra staff and extra accommodation and this would be the main concern of the Headmaster and the Governors during the next six years.

Owen was replaced as a teacher of Welsh by Miss Gwyneth Parry, later Mrs. R. D. Matthews, and Miss Olive John, later Mrs. Jack Rees, was appointed to teach mathematics. Miss Mair Meganwy Jones was appointed to teach French and Welsh in September 1944 and Mr Alcwyn Evans was appointed a general form master later in the same term. Miss Mair Jones would eventually be responsible for the teaching of Welsh; known as 'Mair fach', she was a popular and familiar figure, in her black gown, until she retired in 1979. Mr. Alcwyn Evans also spent his life in the service of the School; a devoted supporter of soccer, he became the Geography Master. Miss Maria Evans, who had replaced John Evans during his war service, stayed on as Biology Mistress. She was known for her dedication to academic standards and for her well-ordered laboratory and greenhouse where she cultivated cacti. Many of her pupils will remember the special occasions when they were shown a cactus plant that had flowered for the first time. The School acquired a part-time music teacher in 1945; Mr. Edward Morgan only stayed at the School for a few years but he re-appeared as the music adjudicator at the School's Eisteddfod in the 1950s and 1960s. The first married woman appointed to a teaching post was Mrs. Nansi Evans who became a part-time arts and crafts teacher in 1946. Before 1946, women were expected to resign from their teaching posts when they married, except in very exceptional circumstances. Mrs. Evans served as a very skilled and much loved crafts teacher for many years. The increasing size of the School and the greater role of the Local Education Authority meant more paperwork and Miss Nell Jones became the first Headmaster's Clerk in October 1946.

The most pressing problems facing the School during the years 1945-46 were school dinners and school transport. The Butler Act allowed the Local Education Authority to provide both school dinners and school transport. The old system of school dinners, whereby Miss Lewis was in charge of organising dinners, was wound up in November 1944 and the balance of £144.2s.7d. in the dinner fund was transferred to the School Library Fund. The new system had to confirm to the county scales of salaries and staffing. Mrs. Lloyd, Water Street, was the joint-caretaker and she was appointed cook with Mrs. A. Davies as assistant cook and Miss E. M. Morgan as the second assistant. These reforms occurred because a record number of 192 pupils were taking school dinners in 1944 and the School clearly needed new arrangements and new accommodation. Within a year, there were discussions on extending the new kitchen dining room which had yet to be erected and, in November 1945, the County Architect was asked to estimate for extending the kitchen for the use of 500 pupils. This was not an optimistic over-estimate for the future; 230 pupils were receiving dinner at the School in September 1946 and a new plot was sought to provide more vegetables. If children had to attend secondary schools, as laid down in the Butler Act, it was necessary to get them to school and school transport had to be provided in rural areas. Before 1945, children had to rely on public transport or they cycled to school and several children had a long cycle ride at the beginning and at the end of each school day. The first school bus was engaged in September 1945 for the Dihewid-Aberaeron route, taking in Mydroilyn, at £9 per week; in the next twelve months, buses were hired to cover Pennant, Felinfach and New Quay.

The fiftieth anniversary of the School's foundation was celebrated in 1947. The plans for the celebration were placed in the charge of a sub-committee of the Governors with E. Glyn Davies, Mrs. Poulgrain and Dr. Ernest Davies as members. They all had a special devotion to the School in that they were all old pupils and Mrs. Poulgrain was the daughter of J. M. Howell, the second Chairman, while Dr. Ernest Evans was the son of the second Chairman and the brother of the fifth Chairman. The celebrations of the Jubilee were held on 18-20 December, presumably to enable many old pupils to attend, and they began with the Annual Prize Distribution at the Memorial Hall on the Wednesday afternoon at 2.30. p.m., with Professor R. I. Aaron from the University College of Wales as guest-speaker. There followed an evening concert by the school children, with W. J. Jones in his familiar role as Chairman of a School event. On Thursday morning, a public meeting was held at which addresses were delivered by old pupils and this was followed by a service of thanksgiving and praise in the afternoon. Friday saw football and hockey matches played by the Old Pupils against the present pupils and an Old Pupils' Dance in the Memorial hall with Lu Owen and his Sextet from Llanelli in attendance. In the programme printed for the Jubilee, several old pupils recorded their memories of school days and two former Headmasters, Gwyn Jones and Howell Evans, wrote messages of support.

The Jubilee Programme included a Roll of Honour for those pupils and one Master who had fallen in the two World Wars. At their Easter reunion in 1946, the Old Pupils had chosen representatives from the various parts of the School's districts to form the School War Memorial Committee. The sum of £280.2s.7d. was collected and it was agreed that part of the money would be spent on a plaque inscribed with the names of the Fallen in the Second World War, while the surplus would be used to buy equipment for the School's Library which would, with the Governors' ready assent, be renamed the Memorial Library. The Library was originally planned to be in the new extension, but it was decided later to turn the old School Hall into the Library. The bronze plaque was unveiled in the Hall on Friday, 1 October 1948 in the presence of parents, relations and friends of the Fallen.

The School began its second half-century with 272 pupils on the register and a staff of twelve full-time teachers and one part-time music teacher. J. T. Owen noted that there would be great changes in the next few years; "Changes will also present difficulties and one of these will be to design curricula appropriate to the pupils' needs and free from the domineering role of the Universities. We shall have to provide an educational menu far more appetising and nourishing than anything yet provided in our secondary schools if we want to make all the 11+ children feel that it is better to be in School than to start work." T. H. Fox and John Evans had returned from their war service, while T. V. Michael and W. Sidney Evans had been appointed from September 1947 to teach Chemistry and Physics. R. D. Matthews came to the School as History Master at the same time, as did Gwynfil Rees as Master for Religious Education and Physical Training. Both men stayed at the School until their retirement. R. D. Matthews was in charge of history teaching throughout his time at the School, while Gwynfil Rees became a Welsh Master and a dedicated follower of country pursuits which he celebrated in his volume, *Brenin Teify*. A year later, W. J. Lewis was appointed English and Woodwork Master and, apart from a brief period of 'exile' in Lampeter, he was also to pursue his teaching career at Aberaeron and he has taken a leading part in the town life of Aberaeron. Gwynfil Rees and Bill Lewis introduced the regular playing of rugby to the School.

The School was now very short of accommodation: the Woodwork Room housed other classes as well as Woodwork; three classes were housed in the Hall; and there was only one laboratory for Botany, Zoology and Agricultural Science. Economic conditions in the immediate post-war years were not favourable towards the rapid construction of the extensions necessary before the reorganisation of the School could be completed. The Ministry of Education granted its consent for a starting date for the extensions in late 1949. The question of reorganisation was now urgent and it was decided to obtain the old Church in Wales primary school as an annexe for one year. This was only a partial solution in that only pupils of 13 years and over, some 97 in all, could be admitted. The annexe in the old primary school was ready for occupation in September 1950 and it was used by the pupils on the Modern side. Extra teachers were required and four appointments were made in May 1950 when J. C. Roberts, D. Hughes Jones, Miss Mary Williams and Miss Dulcie Jones were given positions on the staff of the School. John Roberts would teach Woodwork at the School until his retirement; D. Hughes Jones taught Physical Training and Art, and the Art alone, until his early death. Hughes Jones was an old pupil of the School and, while still in the Army as Captain D. Hughes Jones, he had brought a team of physical training experts to give a demonstration at the belated opening of the gymnasium on 26 November 1945. Mr. Jack Rees was appointed a teacher of Religious Instruction in June 1950. Jack Rees was also an old pupil and he devoted his career to the School. He enjoyed a good argument with his pupils and his colleagues; in later years, he assumed the role of a school counsellor. Jack Rees spent many years in public service as an elected representative for his home town. He also enjoyed success as a radio dramatist. Around the same time, Miss Rhiannon Davies returned to her old school as a Domestic Science teacher, specialising in needlework. She retired as Deputy Headmistress of the School.

A good picture of the School during the last year before reorganisation was painted by W. A. Jones in a characteristically thoughtful contribution to a symposium on the teaching of English: "I write from rural Wales, from a secondary day school of 350 boys and girls. The pupils are bilingual, and for many of them, English is a second language, of which little or no use is made once the four o'clock school buses have taken them home to their farms, isolated cottages and quiet villages. .... Most of my sixth-form pupils have probably never heard an orchestra, never seen a good play well produced, never been inside a really good library or art gallery. But they have the advantage of knowing something of two literatures, of living in a part of the world where knowledge is respected and widely diffused and where almost every village has its poet." Up to the Second World War, Aberaeron had been a quiet place, isolated from the rest of the country by poor transport and by a lack of affluence. When Howell Evans offered to conduct a party of pupils to the Wembley Exhibition in 1924, none of his pupils expressed a desire to go. Few could afford to go. The Second World War brought a military camp to the outskirts of Aberaeron and this dispelled the quiet isolation of the community. Increasing affluence in the 1950s and the development of better road links meant that pupils could travel more easily. Miss Mair Meganwy Jones and Miss Gwyneth Parry took nine pupils on the School's first trip abroad when they visited Paris in 1950.

The foundation stone of the new extensions was laid on 25 May 1950: the Chairman of the Education Committee presided; the Chairman of the Governors, Alderman Simon Davies of Felinfach, gave an account of the events leading up to the building work; the Headmaster offered a prayer of dedication. Extra land had been purchased and the school path was closed, while the children went up and down the back lane. The new extensions were completed by the start of the school year 1951-52. The total cost of the building work was £102,000 and some £19,000 was spent on furniture and equipment. The official opening, held on 20 December 1951, was performed by the eminent Welsh poet and academic, Sir Thomas Parry-Williams. The reorganisation of secondary education in Aberaeron was complete when the new extensions opened for use in September 1951. Additional teachers had been appointed to cope with the extra number of pupils; Mr Tudor Jones (Religious Instruction); Miss Valmai Benjamin (Music); Mr. Robert Armstrong (Metalwork); Miss A. M. Goldsworthy (Physical Training); and Mrs. Simpson (Commercial Subjects). The School was, at last, able to provide the instruction in both academic and practical subjects which had been desired by the school inspectors some forty years earlier. The large increase in the number of pupils meant that more school buses were required and nine bus routes were devised in July 1951, with two buses on the Aberaeron - New Quay route. Condiserable time was spent by the Governors on the vexatious question of a park for the buses and another piece of land above the School was purchased for this purpose and also as a playground.

The new extensions gave the School sufficient room for all its activities after a long period in very cramped conditions. The School had required new accommodation almost every ten years after the opening of the first school building. The new extension consisted of three blocks, built in a modern style with flat roofs and built up the hill on the northern side of the old School which was given a coat of paint after the completion of the extensions. The lowest block contained the Metalwork and Woodwork Workshops and laboratories for Agricultural Science, Chemistry, Physics and for Biology and Zoology with a greenhouse attached to the latter. The middle block contained cloakrooms and classrooms for French and Latin, Mathematics, History, English, Geography and Welsh. The upper block contained a large domestic science room for Miss Elaine Lewis, used on occasions as Portland's "war room"; a dental surgery where Mr. E. Byron Lloyd, the County's School Dentist, came to see the pupils; separate staffrooms for men and women; and, the School Hall with a handsome foyer containing a glass cupboard for the sporting trophies. J. T. Owen was very proud of the School Hall. Every morning, dressed in his gown, he held the School's Assembly in the Hall, with Miss Elaine Lewis and other women teachers to his right, while Mr W. A. Jones and other men teacher stood to his left. The School assembled in forms, with the most junior to the front, and with the girls to the right and the boys to the left. A row of teachers stood at the back of the Hall. During Owen's period as Headmaster, he required that the Hall be treated with great respect by his pupils who were expected not to trespass in the Hall or in its foyer after Assembly, without very good reasons. It was in the Hall that the great excitement of the School Eisteddfod took place, when the children would stay late in the evening, bellowing out their house chants as their House mascots climbed the poles at the side of the stage. It was in the Hall that the afternoon ceremony of prize-giving took place every December. These were two occasions when the School Hall was packed with pupils and with people from Aberaeron and other places in the School's districts. The Hall in the old School had not been used for many years as an assembly hall; the School was too big by the end of the War and the Memorial Hall had been used in the intervening years. The old Hall now became the Memorial Library and it was used as a sixth form classroom.

J. T. Owen delighted in country sports and he took a particular interest in developing agricultural education at the School. Discussions on expanding agricultural education began in 1951 when the Headmaster presented the Governors with a report on the successful course of agricultural education that had been provided at the School for many years. The Governors later appointed representatives at a conference on agricultural education in the County. Further developments at Aberaeron were postponed until after the opening of the new extensions and it was agreed that the 1952/53 estimates should include a ridger, a tiller, and a plough at a cost of £211. The field above the School was ploughed and sown with rape in the spring of 1952. Around seventy local farmers from the Aberaeron National Farmers Union branch visited the School at this time and the Headmaster considered that they were satisfied with the provision for agricultural education and for practical craft instruction. Later in 1952, the Governors agreed, subject to the approval of the Higher Education Committee, that £100 should be spent on the purchase of twenty sheep as an experiment in agricultural education. In the event, the Headmaster arranged for the purchase of 21 lambs at a cost of £4.4s.0d. each and he obtained permission to purchase another 20 lambs, up to the value of £100, in order to graze the land adequately. In the autumn of 1952, Owen reported to the Governors that the sheep appeared to be progressing satisfactorily, and that a temporary pen had been erected so that the weight of the sheep could be checked periodically. The Governors thanked T. Glyn Herbert for injecting 21 of the sheep free of charge and for lecturing to the pupils on the object of the injections. Thomas Glyn Herbert, an ex-pupil and the local veterinary surgeon, was a great raconteur and played a prominent part in the town life of Aberaeron. By the end of 1952, Owen had successfully established the basis for a school farm which was to provide practical experience for those pupils intending to pursue a career in agriculture. A further plot of land, approximately two acres, was purchased in 1954 and a further eight acres in 1963. On occasions, after shearing, the wool was sent to Mrs. Nansi Evans' class for spinning and colouring before it was used in practical work. Throughout the 1950s, Mrs. Evans enjoyed a number of remarkable successes when her pupils won national competitions in embroidery.

During the school year 1953-54, the Modern side of the School achieved its full complement of forms. The School had around 550 pupils on the registers throughout the

1950s. From 1952, the Headmaster was troubled by the fact that several pupils admitted to the Grammar side left at the age of 15, thus depriving others of places on the Grammar side. He suggested to the Governors that a form of undertaking should be signed by the parents that the pupils admitted to the Grammar side would not leave before the age of 16. The Education Office explained that no legal compulsion could be brought to bear on those Grammar pupils who left at the age of 15. The Governors agreed that the Headmaster should obtain an assurance that those pupils should not leave School before completing their required grammar-side course. The percentage of early leavers was a serious problem in that 22% left in 1954, 21% in 1955 and 27% in 1956 and it continued to be a problem until the early 1960s. The present writer can recall Owen emphasising this point when he placed the new entrants in their forms. Pupils could be moved from the Modern to the Grammar side, and vice-versa, if their school work showed that they merited a move.

With a larger staff and with most of the teachers taking only one subject, changes in teaching staff were infrequent and most departures were usually younger staff seeking promotion elsewhere. T. H. Fox, who had taught Latin since 1930, left in August 1959. He had been a leading figure on the staff of the School, both as a very able teacher and a firm disciplinarian. He was an old fashioned Schoolmaster. For many years, he supplied material on Aberaeron affairs to the *Western Mail.* Sidney Evans taught Physics with much charm for ten years until he left in 1959 to become the Headmaster of Beaumaris County School.

The problem of accommodation reappeared on the agenda of the Governors' meetings only seven years after the opening of the new extensions. The Nissen hut which had been used for teaching in the immediate post-war years was converted into a pottery classroom in 1958. The initial request for new buildings was for a new rural science laboratory. However, the County Architect noted that, according to the regulations, the School was entitled to a new rural science laboratory, a further science laboratory, a drawing office, a new pottery room, 4 classrooms (one for Music), and a Dining Room and a Kitchen which would replace the wartime dining room and kitchen. This was a Major Works Programme costing over £20,000. Mindful of the delays involved with a Major Project, the Governors recommended that a rural science laboratory and two classrooms should be erected as a minor project in 1961/62, provided that the cost did not exceed £20,000. After further discussions, the Architect submitted a plan for a new Crafts block containing two new manual rooms and a pottery room; the old manual rooms would be converted into laboratories. The Ministry of Education wanted more detail on the eventual size of the School and a remodelling team from the Ministry visited the School on 30 May 1961.

While the School awaited the deliberations of the men from the Ministry, attention turned to the playing fields. The seaside playing field allowed room for only one rugby pitch. The Headmaster noted that the two adjoining fields of 2.9 acres, often used by circuses visiting Aberaeron, were for sale and he persuaded the Governors to recommend the purchase of these fields. After a length period of negotiation with the County Council and the Aberaeron Urban District Council, these fields were purchased for £1,750 in 1963 and £900 was spent on preparing them as playing fields. Meanwhile, the Ministry of Education declined to allow the Local Education Authority a further allocation for the Minor Capital Works programme and suggested that the Woodwork and Metalwork Classes could be housed in the Primary School when that was vacated in 1962. Owen presented strong objections to this plan and offered instead the temporary solution of creating an additional laboratory by removing the wall of the existing storerooms and vestibule in the lower block. This was approved by the Ministry and the Governors urged the County Architect to complete the work by September 1962. The Ministry continued to consider the request for additional accommodation until 1963 when they granted permission for the work to proceed.

J. T. Owen would not supervise the completion of the new crafts block. After forty-two years service, he retired from his post as Headmaster in 1965. When he took over as Headmaster in 1944, the School had 272 pupils and 12 full time teachers with one part-time music teacher. In the year before the reorganisation of secondary education and the building of the new extension, the School had 451 pupils and 14 members of staff. After reorganisation, the number of pupils increased to 550 pupils and 28 members of staff. Ten years later, in 1960, the School had 650 pupils and 31 members of staff. The curriculum had been expanded, both in academic and vocational subjects. A good school library had been formed in the old School Hall. Extra curricular activities had also grown throughout the 1950s. The School Club was in the charge of W. A. Jones and it was remarkably successful in that over 100 pupils attended meetings. An active Chess Club had been established with the strong support of Mr. Alcwyn Evans. D. M. Henry, the Music Master, had formed a School Orchestra of some 20 pupils. There was a vigorous programme of sports activities: rugby, soccer, hockey, netball and athletics. The quiet isolation which marked Aberaeron in the pre-war period was slowly disappearing. Pupils went on regular trips abroad and to other parts of the country. Television came to the area in 1957 and this provided an ever-present window on the wider world. Rock and roll was introduced to the School Club in the same year.

Owen had presided over a great transformation of the School from a small grammar school into a secondary school providing education for all children. Unlike his predecessors, he had to work closely and maintain cordial relations with the Director of Education. After the Second World War, the role of the School's Governors was more circumscribed in that their recommendations, even on minor matters, were usually subject to the approval of the Local Education Authority and the Ministry of Education. The Headmaster and the Governors created a large and successful school during the fifteen years from 1950 to 1965. Owen was appointed O.B.E. in 1961 for his services to education. He was a popular Headmaster with his pupils and he maintained good discipline. J. T. Owen was a master of the Welsh language and he was a very fine speaker in the language.

The new Headmaster, G. G. Davies, knew the School well because he had frequently attended the Governors' meetings as Deputy Director of Education. Born in Hirwaun, Glamorganshire, Griff Davies had graduated from the University College of Wales with First Class Honours in German. A year as an exchange teacher in Germany was followed by a degree in French at Aberystwyth. His first teaching post was at Cardiff where he taught modern languages from 1937 to 1939. Davies entered the Army in 1939 and served from 1941 in the Far East where he spent over three years in the harrowing conditions of a Japanese Prisoner of War camp. After the War, he returned to Cardiff for four years before he became the Further Education Officer for Cardiganshire. In 1959, he was appointed Deputy Director of Education which placed him in a close relationship with the County's schools. Griff Davies was instrumental in creating the Secondary Schools Amateur Athletic Association in the county and in forming the Cardiganshire County Youth Orchestra.

The new Headmaster's first task was to re-arrange the School's accommodation following the completion of the new Crafts block. The old Agricultural Science Laboratory was converted into an advanced Chemistry Laboratory and a new Agricultural and General Science Laboratory was added to the Science Wing. The Head of Science, John Evans, only enjoyed these new facilities for one year. John Evans had been appointed to teach agriculture in 1933 and he had seen the subject develop rapidly after the War until the one acre of land he had available in 1939 for practical work had become 20 acres with a flock of 35 ewes. For thirty years, he was known to his pupils, with affection, as 'Carbon'.

The main task facing the new Headmaster was preparing the School for the raising of the school-leaving age to 16 in 1970. More accommodation was required in the form of four new classrooms and Davies persuaded the Governors to approve, as well as the four new classrooms, the conversion of the gymnasium to a swimming pool, the building of a new gymnasium, a new kitchen and dining room and a language laboratory. This ambitious plan was placed in the Major Building Programme for 1969. Little progress had been made on these plans by 1969 and the County Buildings Committee recommended that a mobile classroom be provided to meet the School's needs in 1970-71. The County Architect reported in 1968 that the School's accommodation was suitable for 530 pupils while the School had 585 pupils. One reason for the slowness of the Local Education Authority in dealing with this problem was the falling number of pupils in the School; the number of pupils in September 1969 had fallen to 547 and the Governors urged the Authority to look at the catchment areas of the County's secondary schools. A new pottery room to replace the old Nissen Hut was approved, but this was not built for four years. A language laboratory was approved in 1971 and it was installed in the old Crafts Room. With his academic background in languages, this was a favourite project of the Headmaster. He introduced the teaching of German to the School and took some classes himself. Davies also encouraged the further development of Welsh language teaching and the minutes of the Governors' meetings were kept in Welsh from 1968.

By 1969, the number of pupils in the School had risen to 619 and there was considerable pressure on accommodation. An application for a mobile classroom was turned down by the Buildings Committee because of a lack of funds. The mobile classroom was finally installed in August 1972. Discussions on the provision of extra classrooms continued as the number of pupils increased to 644 in 1972. A local committee had been formed to forward the plan of a swimming pool for the School and the district. The County Architect wanted to investigate a scheme for converting the old canteen into a pool, but the Governors accepted the Committee's argument that this was too small.

Two major changes took place in the staffing of the School during Griff Davies' headmastership. Miss Elaine Lewis retired in 1969 after forty years service to the School as Domestic Science Mistress. Miss Lewis had entered the School as a pupil in 1919 and her connection with the School covered half a century. While most of the pupils in the post-war period remembered her as a Domestic Science mistress, she had taught Physical Training, English, Welsh, and Music in earlier years. She had supervised the School Club and she had been an enthusiastic participant in every School Eisteddfod. In the following year, W. A Jones retired after forty years as English master at the School. He was a familiar figure to all pupils as he cycled to School every day and pursued any boy walking up the School hill without a school cap. A fine scholar, he devoted much time to the development of the School Library. During the 1950s, Jones introduced the teaching of italic handwriting and two of his pupils achieved remarkable success at calligraphy exhibitions. From 1932 to 1970, he was the Staff Editor of *The Link* and the issues prepared during these years are an elegant testimony to his care for the School. He gave up every Friday evening during the winter terms, from 1945 to 1970, to the School Club. After his retirement, W. A. Jones decided to embark on the difficult task of a doctorate in English literature, which he achieved with distinction. He was a man who loved learning and who delighted in teaching. Miss Maria Evans succeeded Miss Elaine Lewis as deputy headmistress and Mr. Alcwyn Evans succeeded W. A. Jones as deputy headmaster.

W. A. Jones served as acting Headmaster when J. T. Owen and Griff Davies were ill. With reluctance, Griff Davies decided that he had to resign prematurely in 1973. He had a clear vision of the way in which he wished the School to develop and it was regrettable that economic conditions and ill health prevented him from bringing his plans to fruition. Before he retired, the County Council had agreed to build a swimming pool in the School's grounds. Griff Davies had established a happy relationship with his pupils and his staff and he took an affectionate interest in the history of the School. He wrote, but did not publish, an admiring sketch of the career of J. M. Howell, one of the great pioneers of the School. At the last meeting of the Governors attended by Griff Davies, the Governors received with regret the resignation of Mrs. Nesta Poulgrain who, like her father J. M. Howell, served the School for many years.

This was the last year of the School as Aberaeron County School. From September 1973, the School, under the new Headmaster, D. J. Thomas, would be known as Aberaeron Comprehensive School and it would be administered, from 1974, by Dyfed County Council. The new arrangements required a new constitution for the Governing Body and new Governors. Mrs. Theodora Lloyd of Llanon who had served as a Governor for over thirty years left the Board; Mrs. Lloyd had succeeded her mother, Mrs. Jones of Roseland, Llanon, and she was the last link with the founders of the School.

Note

The main source for this chapter was the log-books of the School's Governors which survive for the period 1896-1949, kept in part at the Aberystwyth Office of the Dyfed Record Office and in part at the School. After 1949, the Governors' meetings are recorded in the official minutes of the Cardiganshire County Council. Further material may be found in the files on the School, up to 1944, kept by the Board of Education and which are now held by the Public Record Office (Class ED 35). The Ministry of Education's files for the School in the late 1940s and the 1950s were destroyed in a flood during the early 1960s. The papers of Howell Evans are kept in the National Library of Wales. The School's magazine, *The Link*, is an important source and a complete set is held by the School. Incomplete sets of this magazine are held by the National Library of Wales (lacking 1962-64 and 1973); the Public Library in Aberystwyth (a collection of 19 issues); and the British Library in London (1909-11, 1922-52, 1954). The final source was the memories of family and friends.

G. G. Davies, B.A., Prifathro 1965-1973

"Arms and the Man" - 1967
Richard Stead, Corrine Shaw, Alan Thomas, Hawys Edwards, Loveday Thomas, Alan Robinson, Jonathan Jones, Mr. Tudor Jones.

"Helynt yn yr Hafdy" - 1969

Lyn Jones, Yolande Jones, John Jenkins, Bethan Lloyd, Ann Williams.

"The Winslow Boy" - 1971

Mr. W. J. Lewis (Producer), Brian Evans-Jones, Trevor Pritchard, Richard Phillips, Wallis Jones, Graham Hope, John Jenkins, Mr. Tudor Jones, Monica Davies, Yolande Jones, Joy Keyworth, Mandy Petty.

Dosbarth Chwech / Sixth Form - 1973

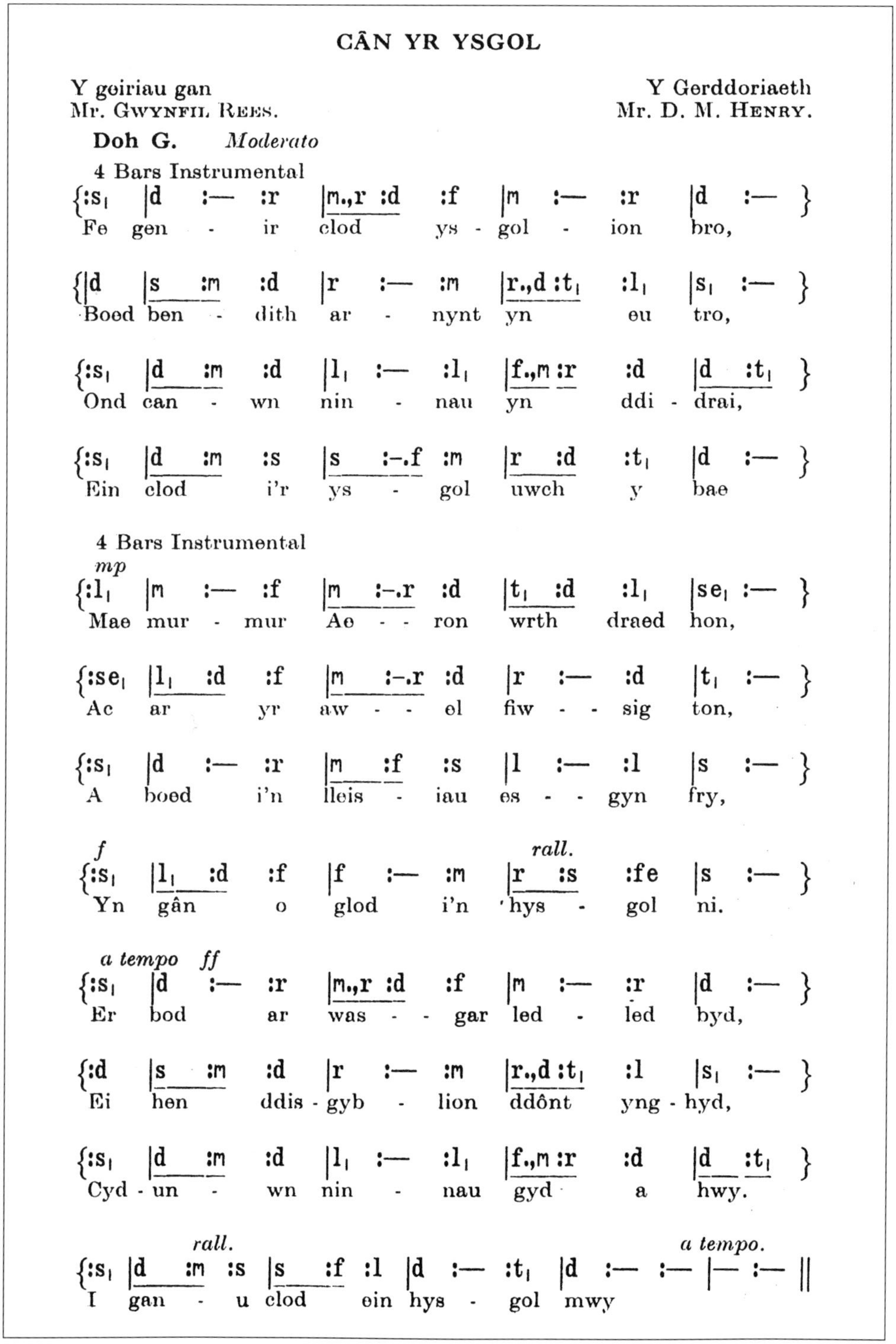
CÂN YR YSGOL
Y geiriau gan
Mr. GWYNFIL REES.
Y Gerddoriaeth
Mr. D. M. HENRY.
Doh G. Moderato
4 Bars Instrumental
{:s, |d :— :r |m.,r :d :f |m :— :r |d :— }
Fe gen - ir clod ys - gol - ion bro,
{|d |s :m :d |r :— :m |r.,d :t, :l, |s, :— }
Bood ben - dith ar - nynt yn eu tro,
{:s, |d :m :d |l, :— :l, |f.,m :r :d |d :t, }
Ond can - wn nin - nau yn ddi - drai,
{:s, |d :m :s |s :-.f :m |r :d :t, |d :— }
Ein clod i'r ys - gol uwch y bae
4 Bars Instrumental
mp
{:l, |m :— :f |m :-.r :d |t, :d :l, |se, :— }
Mae mur - mur Ae - - ron wrth draed hon,
{:se, |l, :d :f |m :-.r :d |r :— :d |t, :— }
Ac ar yr aw - - el fiw - - sig ton,
{:s, |d :— :r |m :f :s |l :— :l |s :— }
A bood i'n lleis - iau es - - gyn fry,
f
rall.
{:s, |l, :d :f |f :— :m |r :s :fe |s :— }
Yn gân o glod i'n 'hys - gol ni.
a tempo ff
{:s, |d :— :r |m.,r :d :f |m :— :r |d :— }
Er bod ar was - - gar led - led byd,
{:d |s :m :d |r :— :m |r.,d :t, :l |s, :— }
Ei hen ddis - gyb - lion ddônt yng - hyd,
{:s, |d :m :d |l, :— :l, |f.,m :r :d |d :t, }
Cyd - un - wn nin - nau gyd a hwy.
rall.
a tempo.
{:s, |d :m :s |s :f :l |d :— :t, |d :— :— |— :— ||
I gan - u clod ein hys - gol mwy

Cân yr Ysgol

Tîm Gwyddbwyll / Chess Team - 1962
(Sitting) Gareth Harry, Barry Williams, Alan Rogerson (Capt)
(Standing) Tony Price, Michael Young, Goronwy Jones, Timothy Thomas.

Staff yr Ysgol / School Staff
1973

D. J. Thomas B.Sc. G. G. Davies B.A. J. T. Owen O.B.E., M.A.

PRO PATRIA

Old pupils of the school who lost their lives in the Great War.

Taken from the 1922 "Link".

Lt. ALBERT GORDON DAVIES, M.C., of "Tanyfron Villa", Aberayron, entered school September 17th, 1901, and in 1902 left for the Bank. Became clerk at the N.P. Bank, Head Office, London. Enlisted in the 5th Regiment of the Royal Welsh Fusiliers, and was killed at Messines Ridge.

D. ERNEST DAVIES died on service, whilst stationed at the Crystal Palace, London.

DANIEL MEURIG DAVIES, M.M., of "Taincwm", Gartheli, Felinfach, entered school on 20th September, 1911, then entered St. John's College School, Ystrad Meurig (Senior School). In 1917 he enlisted in the Pembrokeshire Yeomanry and in 1918 was transferred to the Durham Light Infantry. Won the Military Medal for very great bravery on May 27th, 1918. Died of wounds on October 6th, 1918, at Angeles Wood, and was buried at Combles, France.

Lt. EVAN JAMES DAVIES, of "Park House", Felinfach, entered school on January 12th, 1902, and left for the Ystrad Meurig School. Qualified for the L.P. Bank in 1905, and was two years at Essex Road Branch, London, three years at Penge (London), and six years as cashier at Dartford, Kent. Entered O.T.C. in 1916. Joined 1st Batt. Welsh Guards and was killed at Boiry Bequerelle, France on March 28th, 1918.

2nd Lt. EVAN WALTER DAVIES, of Pontmarchog, Cribyn, entered school on 17th September, 1906. He left school at the junior stage to enter the Bank. Enlisted in the forces and received a commission. He was killed at Gaza, March 26th, 1917.

J. PENRY DAVIES, of "Emrys House", New Quay, entered school September 14th, 1908 and left to take up apprenticeship as Marine Engineer at Cardigan. Enlisted as a private in the Welsh Regiment and died of wounds at Bray-sur-Somme on April 21st, 1917.

TOM DAVIES, of Penbryn, Cribyn, entered school September 22nd, 1902. Left school in 1906, and obtained a lucrative post at the L.P. Bank, Brecon. Joined the forces on the outbreak of the Great War and was killed on the Somme, October 27th, 1916.

T. H. DAVIES, of the Post Office, Felinfach, entered school in 1901. Before enlisting he was on the reporters' staff of the "Welsh Gazette". He joined the 15th R.W. Fusiliers in October, 1914, left for France in 1915, and was killed at Mametz Wood, in the Somme Battle, on the 10th of July, 1916.

JOHN LLOYD EVANS, of Morfagwyn, New Quay. Entered school in 1905, and left in 1908, to prepare himself for the vocation of Engineer (Marine). Early in 1917 he qualified as Chief Engineer and was killed on the high seas by enemy action on September 16th, 1917.

DANIEL HAROLD JENKINS, of "Clarovine", Millet Park, Llanon. Joined the 1st Batt. Welsh Guards May 19th, 1915. He was killed in France on the 27th of May, 1918, and was buried at Bienvilliers Cemetery, near Arras.

2nd Lt. DAVID JONES, of Dolau, Dihewid, entered school 17th September, 1906. On leaving school he took up duties of assistant master at Llangybi Council School and in September, 1914, entered Carmarthen Training College, where he took a great part in the social life of the institution. He enlisted as a private in the R.W. Fusiliers in 1915, and in 1916, was drafted to France. Within a few weeks almost, he was severely wounded, but recovered and went to France again. Not long after, he received his commission in the Shropshire Light Infantry. He fell near Ypres on the 25th July, 1918, and was buried nearby.

Capt. EDGAR JONES, C.F., of "Garth", South Road, Aberayron, entered school on 17th January, 1902. Took up teaching in his native town, then entered Ystrad Meurig School, and finally graduated B.A., Lampeter College. Became Curate of St. Timothy Church, Sheffield, and joined as Chaplain to the Forces. He died of wounds at Roisel, France, October 24th, 1918.

2nd Lt. EVAN LEWIS JONES, of Gofynnachfawr, Llanarth, entered school September 11th, 1905. Passed the Senior and Marticulation, C.W.B., and in 1910 entered the University of Wales, Aberystwyth, where he graduated B.A., with 1st class Honours in Botany, in 1914. Received a commission in the North Staffordshire Regiment in 1915, and was then transferred to the Machine Gun Corps. He was killed at Serre, in the Battle of Ancre, November 13th, 1916, and was buried at Bertram Court Cemetery, France.

IVOR JENKIN JONES, of Penwern, Cilcennin, entered school on 19th of September, 1910. In 1913 he qualified for the N.P. Bank, and was stationed at Towyn. After being about two years with the Bank he joined the R.W. Fusiliers. A year later he was severly wounded, but recovered, and returned to the same regiment, R.W. Fusiliers, and was killed on the 3rd September, 1918, at Salisel.

Lt. J. HAROLD JONES, of Alban Square, Aberayron, entered school in November, 1901. He left in 1905 for the Bank and became Chief Clerk at the N.P. Bank, Brecon. Enlisted in the Royal Fusiliers and died on October 1st, 1917, at Zonnebeke, France.

J. SIDNEY JONES, of "Garth", South Road, Aberayron, entered school on 21st January, 1901. Left in July, 1904 to enter the University, Cardiff, then joined the staff of Silwood Street School, London. Joined the R.A.M.C. and made Corporal. Contracted illness after service and died in London, April 5th, 1919.

LEWIS ROBERTS JONES, of 2, Tabernacle Street, Aberayron, enterd school on the 15th of September, 1909. Left school to take up apprenticeship of Ironmonger in his native town, then at New Quay and Swansea. He was killed at the Battle of Gaza, March 26th, 1917.

THOMAS ENOCH JONES, of "Rock Villa", Aberarth. Served as Second Officer on the S.S. Goathland, and lost his life on the way from Nazaire to America, July 4th, 1917.

Sergeant T. IRENEAUS JONES, of "Gwmryn", New Quay, entered the school in September, 1906, and left in July, 1909, to take up a post at New Tredegar. Entered Carmarthen Training College, September, 1915, and in October joined the 1/7th Welsh Cyclists. Was promoted to Sergeant, but contracted illness while on service, and died at his home, October 28th, 1919.

W. GWYNNE JONES, of Penlon, Pennant, entered school on the 13th of September, 1910. Passed the Junior, Senior and Higher examinations of the C.W.B. and in 1915 entered the University of Wales, Aberystwyth. In 1916 he went to sea in the S.S. "Mersario" and was drowned off the North Coast of Africa as a result of enemy action on October 1st, 1917.

CHARLES GUY PATRICK, of Black Lion, New Quay. One of the earliest pupils of the school. Whilst a Third Engineer on the S.S. "Canilla", he lost his life owing to enemy action, November 27th, 1917.

2nd Lt. HENRY L. PUGH, of Paris House, Aberayron, entered school on the 14th of January, 1901. When the war broke out he joined the South Wales Borderers, and was killed at Highwood, on the Somme, September 11th, 1916.

GWILYM REES (2nd Engineer), of "Louisa House", Belle Vue Terrace, Aberayron, entered school on January, 17th, 1899. He left school to go to sea as an engineer. As a result of enemy action whilst on his way from Genoa to Glasgow was drowned off the Irish Coast in the S.S. "Paddington", on the 21st July, 1917.

EVAN LEWIS WILLIAMS, 1st Battalion of the Welsh Guards. In March, 1915, he enlisted in this battalion at Neath. After undergoing training in London he went to France in August. He was wounded near Poperinghe on July 27th, 1917, and died the following day.

❖

THE 1914-18 WAR MEMORIAL

Wynford Edwards

During 1921 the committee of the Old Pupils' Association had pondered the form that the War Memorial should take. There had been agreement that a fitting memorial should be established and £80 had been raised following various collections. Mr. Howell T. Evans, the Headmaster, and Mr. T. Arnold Lewis were keen to establish a Scholarship Fund. The money should be invested and the interest used to pay for an annual Scholarship. However, as the sum collected during the year was small, it was felt by some that the Scholarship would not be very large and, therefore, would not reflect well as a War Memorial effort.

At the General Meeting on Boxing Day 1921, Dr. D. M. Davies proposed that the War Memorial should take the form of a tablet which would be erected in the library of the School. This suggestion was put to a vote and carried by a large majority. A War Memorial committee was entrusted to seek designs for a suitable tablet.

During this period a Belgian refugee, Mr. Joseph Reubens was based at Highmead mansion in Llanybydder. He was retained and supported by the Davies Evans family who, for their part, used Reubens' expert woodworking and carving skills to improve and enhance various fixtures and furniture in the mansion and around the estate property.

The Highmead family worshipped at Llanwenog Church. When the interior pews and other woodwork were seen to be in need of refurbishment it was to Reubens that the Davies Evans family turned and the examples of his expert hand can still be seen there today. Also at the mansion, there is a magnificent fire surround and mantle shelf and a wonderful main staircase which has survived the succeeding occupations of the American Forces during the second World War and generations of school pupils since then.

It was to the same Reubens that the memorial committee turned to design and make the Aberaeron School War Memorial in 1921-22. The committee considered other designs in metal, but it was Reubens' design which they favoured and after minor alterations regarding the school crest and inscription at the foot "Gwell Angau na Chywilydd", he was asked to undertake the task of making and fixing the War Memorial in the school library. It was unveiled on Boxing Day 1922. The following account of the unveiling ceremony appeared in the local press at the time:

"ABERAERON COUNTY SCHOOL WAR MEMORIAL

UNVEILING CEREMONY

The tablet erected in memory of the old pupils of the Aberayron County School who gave their lives in the Great War was unveiled on Tuesday (Boxing Day, 1922). It is a massive oak tablet, beautifully carved, and was executed by Mr. Reubens, of Bruges, a Belgian artist who was a refugee in this country during the war. Today the school feels proud that this beautiful memorial stands as a tribute to those who spent many bright hours within the school walls, who heard their country's call, and who made the supreme sacrifice. Some joined up on the threshold of professional and commercial careers, others left lucrative positions to face privations for many years, and ultimately to become the victims to the onslaughts of the enemy. While the County School lasts, the names of these brave boys will be cherished. Engraved on the tablet are the names of Albert Gordon Davies, D. Ernest Davies, Daniel Meurig Davies, Evan James Davies, Evan Walter Davies, J. Penry Davies, Tom Davies, T. H. Davies, John Lloyd Evans, Daniel Harold Jenkins, David Jones, Edgar Jones, Evan Lewis Jones, Ivor Jenkin Jones, J. Harold Jones, J. Sidney Jones, Lewis Roberts Jones, Thomas Enoch Jones, T. Ireneaus Jones, W. Gwynne Jones, Charles Guy Patrick, Henry Loyn Pugh, Gwilym Rees, Evan Lewis Williams.

The unveiling ceremony was performed by Mrs. Price Lewes, Tyglyn, whose late husband (Major Price Lewes), was first Chairman of the Governors, while the dedication was performed by the Rev. J. C. Hughes, M.A., Ph.D., son of the late headmaster, Mr. C. J. Hughes. The proceedings were presided over by Mr. D. M. Davies. Dr. J. C. Hughes, in a few well chosen words, stated that he accepted the invitation with great feeling. Although not an old pupil, the school had associations which were near and dear to him. He pronounced the dedication and the audience sang "O Fryniau Caersalem".

Addressing the audience, the Chairman said: "The old pupils of the school responded nobly to the call of duty, and thank God the majority of them who served on land, sea and in the air have returned to us. We owe them all a deep debt of gratitude, a debt which we can never repay: but our thoughts today are directed towards those who, unfortunately, lost their lives in the great cause. The war may seem a long time ago, and many deeds of valour may have been forgotten; but as old pupils we feel that some fitting memorial should be erected in the school as a tribute to and a token of respect for our gallant dead. Their names have been engraved on the tablet so that the present and future pupils may think with reverence, of those who gave all for their country; and that, though dead, their memories may ever remain green, and their names kept in remembrance, as long as this school exists. Though no memorial, whatever it may cost, or whatever form it may take, can ever be worthy of such a sacrifice, yet the committee appointed to carry out the arrangements have endeavoured, with the means at their disposal, to erect as fitting a memorial as they could. They were very fortunate in securing the services of Mr. Reubens, a Belgian sculptor, well known in his own country. Many of his carvings are to be seen in the neighbourhood of Lampeter. I may mention especially Llanwenog Church, and those of us who saw some of his work were satisfied that the execution of the tablet was left in competent hands. He has presented us with a beautiful carving in solid oak, and when you have seen it you will agree with me, that our choice of an artist was justified. He had put in the work his artistic soul. Col. Lewes, of Tyglyn Aeron, an officer of high rank, who rendered distinguished service in the war, the son of the late Major Lewes, was the one who was to unveil the memorial today. Unfortunately and much to his regret, his military duties prevented him from honouring us with his presence. His mother, Mrs. Lewes, who has always taken a keen interest in the school, however, kindly consented to act in his stead."

Mr. J.M. Howell said that it was his great privilege on behalf of the Governors to receive into their custody that beautiful memorial as a sacred trust. It commemorated the heroism and sacrifice of 24 lads who met death face to face without flinching in the heyday of their youth. They stood, so to speak, that day at their graves, although their dust lay in hidden places. They did so not with sadness, but with pride. It added to the weirdness of their thoughts that four of them were lost at sea, while two were in Gaza, and fourteen in France. That memorial would be a shrine to which people from a wide district would come. And how strikingly representative of the district which the school served was the roll of the dead. (Two were from Aberarth, eight from Aberayron, one from Cilcennin, three from Ystrad, one from Dihewyd, one from Pennant, one from Llanarth, one from Llanon, four from New Quay, and two from Cribyn.) Mural monuments in their graveyards were allowed after a time to crumble and fall. The family died out, their deeds and names were forgotten. But those whose memorial they were now unveiling were among the immortal dead. The generations of the future would also be the trustees of their fame and memory. The County Education Authority, however careful it might be in saving the rates, would not grudge the upkeep of that panel. For they were men who did not wait for death. They went out and met death. God gave no anaesthetics, and duty to them was God. Carlyle in his life of Stirling spoke of someone who died young, and applied it to Stirling, saying "I am glad he died young for I shall now know him as a youth for ever". That was a heritage given to those whose longing had been once more accentuated by the unveiling of that memorial.

On behalf of the school, the Headmaster, Mr. Howell T. Evans, M.A., thanked the old pupils for the generous and elegant gift they had made as a tribute to the memory and heroism of their fallen comrades. The tablet would remind successive generations of pupils not only of the self-sacrifice of the dead heroes, whose names were engraved thereon, but also of the liberality of the present generation of old pupils, and their affection for their old school. (Hear, hear). He spoke that day under a great disadvantage. He had not had a share in the education and training of any of those brave men. He had not even a personal acquaintance with any of them. At the same time it was his privilege to be the guardian, for the time being, of the honour and tradition of the school. Whatever the past traditions of the school: whatever its achievements in the future, all past records paled before the noble self-sacrifice of these men. (Cheers). And it was to be hoped that the future would never make such a demand of its children as was expected from those commemorated that day. What did these men die for? They died for the security of this Empire. That did not mean the material welfare of the Empire. The greatest empires of the past had vanished: those of the present and the future would follow them to their doom. He spoke rather of the spiritual and everlasting principles for which this Empire stood, the principle of humanity and universal justice. (Cheers). It used to be said of the Roman Empire that, wherever the Roman eagle flew, there was guaranteed freedom from oppression. The British Empire had a wider conception of humanity. Wherever the Union Jack was planted, there it could be said with truth that all men, not Britons only, were equal before the law. (Cheers). Deeds of injustice, of cruelty, even of perfidy had been perpetrated by ambitions and dishonourable men in the name of this Empire, but the better conscience of the nation had ultimately revolted against them and eventually made amends, and no country had stood so consistently for the principles of justice, and the freedom of man. There were mighty monuments of our power which would make us wonder of this and succeeding ages; there were still mightier monuments of our reverence for justice and freedom both in our laws, and in our self-governing colonies. For those principles these heroes fought and died. And this Empire had been built up with a courage gained by habit, and not enforced by law. There is a courage born of the devotion of a slave to his master. There is a courage born of the devotion of a soldier to his country. But there is a higher and mightier courage than either of these - the courage gained by habit. No soldier in the Great War was more devoted to his Fatherland than the German soldier; and the courage bred of that devotion stood the strain of years of anxiety and suffering. But a limit was reached beyond which it would endure no more; and that was the beginning of the end of the war. But the courage of these men was the cheerful courage that had become a habit of life, and which lasts while life lasts. It has been inherited from a long line of ancestors. It has been nurtured in our schools and on our playing fields, and strengthened in life's battle. The sacrifices which these men collectively made was individually repaid to them. They received each one for himself, a praise which grows not old and the noblest of sepulchres. He did not mean the sepulchre in which their remains are laid, but that sepulchre in which their glory survives and is always proclaimed in word and deed. For the whole earth is a sepulchre of famous men; not only are they commemorated by columns and inscriptions in their own country, but in foreign lands there dwells an unwritten memorial of them, graven not on stone but in the hearts of men. We should make them our examples.

The meeting was closed with the singing of the National Anthem, Mrs. Dr. W. J. Davies, Balmain, taking the solo. Bugler E. Davies Jones, Lampeter, sounded the "Last Post" and the "Reveille". After the ceremony, the relatives of all those present and the Managers were the guests of Dr. D. M. Davies to tea in the school buildings."

It is gratifying to note that the memorial is still in its original place in the school library. The oak from which it was so expertly carved has mellowed over the years but it still casts a majestic presence over the library. Recently the War Memorial was cleaned and refurbished and I'm sure that those who were involved in its inception and unveiling would be pleased that the sentiment expressed at the time regarding its solemn purpose have been largely adhered to.

❖

EXTRACTS FROM REMINISCENCES WHICH APPEARED IN THE JUBILEE PROGRAMME IN 1946

❖

LOOKING BACK

Miss Olive M. Jones, Aberaeron.

She was the first pupil to register at the County School in 1896.

The school where I had my first glimpse of secondary Education was very different from the one I see today. The only building available in Aberaeron and approved by the Charity Commissioners was the Assembly Room in what was then called the Town Hall. Outwardly the four walls of the County Hall remain as in 1896; there the similarity ends. The windows on the ground floor were open arches, iron-barred but with a central iron gate-way leading into a be-flagged market place of many booths for the tradesmen and farmers of the neighbourhood to transact business.

Behind this busy hive of activity and partitioned from it by a sliding door was one long room. This was the Assembly Room, famous for debate and meeting place for town activities, social and political. In the day time it was the Grammar School - for Boys only. Education of a similar type was provided for Girls in a private school by Mrs. T. Z. Jones, who became a Foundation Governor of the new school.

It is difficult to realise today what an epoch-making event was the passing of the Welsh Education Act. The first batch of pupils knew little and cared less for its significance. When the girls invaded the Assembly Room, a new room - "Magistrates' Room" had to be requisitioned up a very steep flight of stairs. These two rooms housed the new Intermediate School. What was of far greater importance to those early pupils was the thrill of sliding down the slippery banister of those steep stairs in reckless pursuit of one another into the flagged "pashet" below, heedless of the exasperated threats of the then "Mrs. Mop" with her broom and unique vocabulary! A heavy curtain thick with dust, source of intense annoyance to the Staff but of endless pleasure to those on mischief bent, officially divided the Assembly Room into two classrooms. At the far end was the solitary fire-place, open and smoky - a cupboard each side of the fire-place stored the entire equipment then available for teaching purposes both in Science and Art.

The staff consisted of three: The Head, one Assistant Mistress and one Master. What a debt we owe them for their patient industry and their ready adaptability under such adverse conditions to teach practically every subject except Domestic Science, Physical Training and Games! It is interesting to recall that for a decade or so no Welsh-speaking Assistant was appointed on the staff.

In the first entrance examination the Girls gave a good account of themselves by wresting first place from the Boys.

Some of the original pupils were Maggie B. Jones (Mrs. Williams, Bungalow), Beatrice Jones, Winnie V. Jones (Mrs. Davies, Killara), Katie Williams (Mrs. Thomas, Aberystwyth), Emma Evans, Tynant (Mrs. Hughes Davies, Bridgwater), Sarah A. Jones (Garth), Jane Evans (Esgairwen), Dannie W. James, Willie H. Lewis (Llanarth), David M. Davies, Morgan E. Davies, Lee Davies, D. Emrys Williams. No pupils ever experienced a greater thrill than they did when they left their two rooms in the Old Town Hall to take possession of the "School on the Hill".

These are memories of past days. Generations of pupils come and go: the school lives on. May its future be bright and fragrant, rich in learning and giving to its pupils the "Good name which is better than precious ointment."

❖

MY SCHOOLDAYS

Mr. D. T. Jones M.A., Ll.B. (Director of Education for Pembrokeshire)

When I first went to school in September 1904, the way to higher education in Wales was along a narrow track hardly ten years old. It was for many the only way through the jungle of inopportunity. It was still somewhat hedged in. Today it is a broad highway, well paved, and well posted with signs and directions.

In 1904, the school was still a-throb with the ardour of adventure. After nearly a decade, it was becoming more and more conscious that the road through the jungle was not wide enough, and might still be obliterated if the people failed to send enough boys and girls to keep the grass down and the undergrowth from re-spreading. In September 1904 we were, I think, some 80 pupils. We were looked after by a staff of six. We were supplied with an assembly hall, three classrooms, two laboratories and a cookery room. We had a terrace in front, where for a few minutes a day, we relieved our feelings. Below it was a level piece of ground which was called "the headmaster's garden", as forbidden ground as the garden of Eden after the Fall. We found that it was the apple of the headmaster's eye. Mr. Charles J. Hughes, B.A. was then the word, and the word was ultimately with him.

Woodwork was not on the curriculum. It was the staff alone that did some woodwork, ourselves being the material on which they worked. I also miss still the neglect of the literature and history of my own race. Don't misunderstand me. I have never ceased to be grateful for the entry given me into the literature and history of other peoples, among them the greatest literature in the world. During the last term I was introduced into the world of the Welsh lyric, and had glimpses of the nervous political prose of the Welsh pamphleteers and journalists of the 19th century. Owing to an escapade at Tregaron, after playing the local school at football, Mr. E. O. James, B.A. gave us the story of Henry Richards' imperishable record, just a decade before many of us were drawn to see the face of the thing he detested and abhorred. I saw the things of my own race, the best things it did, and the greatest thoughts it expressed, through the keyhole, as it were, of an annexe next to the main structure of the syllabus in English and History.

Games? We played football only, but that we did play. Most of the boys of Aberaeron seem to have been born with a ball at their toes. They could toy with it as their fathers, many of them, toyed with the globe in the humble barques and schooners. We had one school field "Cae Môr". Much of its grass was salty, and its surface was as uneven as the nearby sea in a gentle swell when the tide is flowing on a calm evening. We would graduate into match play on "Cae Sgwâr", that magic carpet of grass which was the sports forum of the town. From the tips of the grass oozed into our feet the spirit of some great eternal footballer from some prehistoric age. Whatever we came from, we learnt to kick a ball in a certain way, and wherever we went we never found better. We were, despite all this, sometimes beaten in match play, but in conflict of styles, we had no masters within the quadrilateral of schools which formed our unofficial league. The game as it was played at Aberaeron had a genius of its own.

There are so many things collected higgledy-piggledy about me as I write - our seven-mile journey from and to New Quay at weekends...our lodgings at 1/6 a week and 1/9 on Sundays...the awful responsibility on the boy who was to keep the football right through the season...sitting at prize-day with the staff in front and our parents behind...shooting with an air-gun at Mr. Munro Hughes' croaking parrot in the apple tree...trying to get into petty sessions by wearing long trousers...stretching a threepenny bit (pocket money) to last a week...devising how to get into the horticultural show by an exercise of wits on "Cae Môr" in the moonlight...doing and devising all things that were possible and some that were prohibited in our happy secure world, as it was before the storm broke upon us.

These and the sudden flashes of light that came heaven knew how and when, from an inspired moment within those walls, have helped to make us what we are. Using another figure of speech they were the tributaries of our own and others' experiences which flooded the early meandering course of our fluent lives, and helped to broaden and straighten them by the time we began to glimpse the sea.

The personalities I remember best among the Staff were, "Williams Bach", who stamped history on our minds, indeed on our very bones. We had no difficulty in understanding how Calais might well be carved on the heart of an English queen. Because I dared suggest to him once that I did not like notes, he called me "a stuffed booky." I did not quarrel with the verdict, only with the way in which it was made public. But when he realised that I was interested in the subject, he began talking to me about it in a highly confidential manner which I found most interesting. To my great pride he lent me books, in that generous way in which men lend books when they do not care how and in what condition they will return, if at all.

And there was Miss Bennison, a tall dignified lady who spoke to me in French from the very first day she saw me. I only know that her first and last word was in French, and that I lay linguistically wallowing broadside on, in between those two waves of greeting and farewell. She was not there long enough to realise that I had words in Welsh I dare not utter, and words in English I could not, that our lips were shaped for pea-shooters, and not for the French "u". But to me she looked every inch a lady, whom I now liken to Queen Alexandra.

E. O. James was a born teacher. He moved slowly and with circumspection. Brick by brick he built his structure, and now and then took us away from the immediate task in hand, and turned our eyes to the scene around. He was concerned that we should see the site in its setting. It was he who first suggested to me what was the difference between mere writing and literature. And though we understood Lamb when he said to the name on the tombstone: "I am worth twenty of thee, I live, I breathe", E. O. made not only Cicero interesting, but Cicero when he was speaking of Old Age.

Space forbids what time would allow...Miss Owen, Miss Maddocks, Mr. Robson, Mr. Barnes, Mr. Ellis... So they moved through the school in my time, and each played hopefully on the keys, while the strings were new, and full, and vibrant. For them we hope the erosion of time has not banished the tunefulness which youth possesses and which they must have heard occasionally with some one or other of us.

❖

THE GOOD OLD DAYS

Mr. G.M. Howell B.A. (71 Haymarket, S.W.1.)

My first impulse on being asked by Mr. J. T. Owen to write a screed on my memories of the Old School was to refuse as my school days were so far away, but recently while tearing up some old papers I discovered a photograph of Form IV, still fresh and new and the memories surged up, clamouring to be put on paper. Aberaeron County School! Well do I recall that morning of September 1907 - the first walk up the school path, with a sinking feeling in the pit of the stomach, mingled with an eagerness to face the new and strange life in front.

The first days were humiliating. Shall I ever forget the shame of replying "Yes, Sir" instead of "Adsum" at the first roll call? How I remember the first term, with a Cwmere and Tanyfron child almost in every form; the forming of new friendships; the first acquaintance with strange new subjects! The staff then consisted of the Headmaster - Mr. C. J. Hughes, Mr. E. O. James, Miss Maggie Owen, Mr. Barnes and Miss Maddocks, the last two soon to be replaced by Mr. W. J. Jones and Miss Ethel Thomas, whose immaculately laundered white blouses with wide mauve stripes soon became the envy of all the girl pupils. There were three Honours pupils - the lordly ones - Catherine Anne Jenkins, Albert Lewis and Walter B. Williams. The first thrill of the term was the news that the great Beckett, a legendary figure was now Captain of the first eleven at Cardiff University.

Then the weeks slipped away with the exciting Saturday Hockey matches on Cae Prince nearly always ending in a fight between Kathleen and Arnold; the trip to Aberystwyth in the char-a-banc when every hill had to be trudged up; the welcome break on a cold winter's morning at the Red Lion, Llanrhystyd, for a steaming hot cup of tea; the welcome return visit of the Aberystwyth teams whom we liked.

Then came the delighful anticipation of Prize Day: the first singing lesson in the Central Hall for the autumn chorus, always "Hail Smiling Morn", or "Comrades in Arms"; the headmaster striking his tuning fork and giving the pitch in a melodious bellow. Then the hunt for ivy and holly for decoration, and the great day came. First, the tea organised by the Headmaster's wife sided by genial red-faced Mari Hughes - then, the concert, and who can forget Dora Roseland and her tender interpretation of Thomas Hood's "Bridge of Sighs"? And the great day was over. But hush! did I almost forget the stately arrival of a carriage at the Alltygraig gates and the solemn descent of Mrs. Munro Hughes, one of the Governors, followed by maid - bearing rugs and the inevitable Will Jones, looking and I know thinking herself as important as Queen Victoria arriving at Osborne?

The next year in Form III was bright and notable only for one great escapade to "Allt-y-Cwmmins" where we spent a long afternoon regardless of the insistent call of the bell and reckless of consequences.

Next year, Form IV, named half in despair, half in reluctant approbation "Pandemonium" by Mr. E. O. James. What a glorious happy year! It was the year of Halley's Comet and Ernest and myself with diabolical cunning at the beginning of every Arithmetic lesson would ask Mr. Jones about the comet, with the result that the lesson passed without even one hated sum being put on the blackboard. My reward came the following Prize Day with the presentation of Sir Robert Ball's "Other Suns than Ours" to my disgust and rage - a book never opened then or since.

How vivid they still are, those long golden summer days, with the sound of the reaping machine in the waving Feathers field, the smell of the new mown hay wafted in through the open windows, with the chant of the corn-crake, - a bird now almost extinct, according to Miss Frances Pitt: the early liberation on Thursdays, the walk home through the deserted town with every shop window veiled by a blue blind, giving a queer sense of unhappiness enhanced by the thought of the looming "Seiat" and the unlearnt verse. This sense of unhappiness persisted so strongly that even twenty years later in Paris or Monte Carlo, Thursdays gave me a queer feeling of guilt and unrest. Pandemonium!

At the risk of wearying generations that knew not Joseph, I must quote from the photograph I hold, the old familiar names - Penrhiw, Grace Gwallt Gwyn, Lillian, Annie Williams, New Quay, Hedwidge - all five passed on in their youth. Beaufort in the centre striking the pose of a Roman Senator, Perry, Ernest, myself, Meia Mydroilyn, Dai Davies Cribyn, Jane Bodrhyddan, Maggie Bryncerni and Simon. The only one missing is the brilliant Kathleen who was ill at the time. Kathleen! the Head Librarian for the "Magnet" and the "Gem", the perusal of which, living as we did in the aftermath of what I can only call the dreadful Welsh Religious Revival, was a deadly sin, the same stern spirit which brought forth the thundering denunciations of a John Elias from Mr. E. O. James, on poor Ernest who tore down the school path and back during morning recreation to get the result of the Jack Johnson-Jeffries fight from the "Western Mail".

We were so talented that from our ranks alone was recruited the School Dramatic Society. Then followed the hilarious series of farces - "Freezing a Mother-in -Law", "The Birthplace of Podgers." The greatest thrill was to steal up to school, enter through a window and play hide-and-seek until the arrival of the teachers, distributed only by a clanking of buckets and the appearance in the gloom of an eldritch figure - "Rachel R'orion" (or was it "Anne Post?") muttering dire threats of what the headmaster would do when she told him next day. The school year ended with the Junior C.W.B. examination. Is it the rose coloured spectacles of distance that makes that one year so golden and blessed? Here I must quote my favourite of all poems - Charles Kingsley's:

"When all the world is young, lad,
And all the trees are green;
And every goose a swan, lad,
And every lass a queen;
Then hey for boot and horse, lad,
And round the world away;
Young blood must have its course, lad,
And every dog his day.
When all the world is old, lad,
And all the trees are brown;
And all the sport is stale, lad,
And all the wheels run down;

Creep home, and take your place there,

The spent and maimed among:

God grant you find one face there

You loved when you were young."

The next year was unhappy. We were merged into Form V and the old magic was gone. The last year was more sober, but none the less happy. Lessons had now become talks and the teachers friends and hated subjects done with for ever. I still remember my dread of the approach of the very last lesson with all the poignancy of Alphonse Daudet's "La Derniere Classe". 1913! the threshold of dire events; the last year when the world was a world worth living in. So we left, and our departure marked the closing of an epoch.

My outstanding impressions are of two noble virtues: "Innocence" - the innocence of a happy band of boys and girls, with the nearest railway station thirteen miles away, with no theatres, cinemas, wireless, jazz or lipstick: the other salient virtue "Courage" - that lovely virtue as immortalised by J. M. Barrie; the courage of the boys and girls who walked in every Monday, summer and winter from New Quay, Llanon and poor Olwen from Talgarreg and again home on Friday evenings; the Courage of a tired and overworked staff without one free period, who after a hard day's work had to face the long hours of coaching the Honours pupils and correcting mountainous stacks of homework, and finally the courage of those classic landladies - Miss Lampshire, Eleanor Jenkins, Miss Jones Maglona, and "Jane Llaeth", who looked after, fed and mothered anything from three to eight turbulent youngsters at one time. Verily theirs is the Kingdom of Heaven!

Finally, the question - "What did the School do for us?" To each one his own answer. At the risk of appearing vain-glorious I must apply my own answer in my own particular case. This very month I travelled back from Marsellies to Paris with three French soldiers. After some time spent in conversation they discovered I was English - or should I say British - and when one of them asked me "How did you learn to speak French so beautifully?" I felt tempted to reply, "Oh, just ask Maggie Owen, Aberdovey!"

Well, that's just it; that is what the school did for me.

❖

REFLECTIONS

Mr J. Llefelys Davies, M.Sc. (Assistant Manager, Milk Marketing Board)

For good reasons, advancing age in a school is reckoned to be an asset, whereas for equally good and obvious reasons, it is not so with human beings. Not that I am quite so old as the School - although, when I look back, there seems a fair stretch to the days of Form II in 1916. But first, let me congratulate the school, its Governors, administrators and teachers - those who have gone and those who are happliy still with us, carrying on the excellent work. Much has been achieved and many have striven successfully to bring the school to its present position. There have been pioneers in education in our own country; I wish those men and women could see the School today. After years of struggle it is finding its place. It will now make a reputation - perhaps build a tradition: it will certainly continue to serve the children of this district and give to them their start in life. For this part of Cardiganshire it is perhaps the most important institution; it deserves our unflagging interest and support.

This is a time for celebration for what has been achieved and, in thinking of the School today, I cannot help contrasting the present conditions with those which existed thirty years ago. Sometimes we doubt if progress is being made - indeed some doubt the conception of progress. So far as the School is concerned the improvement in facilities for training, and I am sure in the education provided, is tremendous - even over this short span of years. I happened to be at the School during the First World War when Mr. Hughes was Headmaster and later when Mr. Howell T. Evans came. This was a bad time and I ask the present pupils to believe that the facilities were extremely restricted. At this time the total number of pupils did not exceed about 160 - drawn mainly from the accessible towns and villages. The remote countryside had hardly made contact with the School and the rough country boys could easily be distinguished from the more sophisticated lads from Aberaeron and New Quay - or so we thought. We spoke Welsh and they were fond of English, even at that time.

However, life at school soon brought us together and, if I remember rightly we started the School Club in my period. Our first meetings were held in the rather inhospitable rooms of the Town Hall; Mr. W. J. Jones looked after our nights out then as he did for many years afterwards. I shall never forget the first attempt at a dance in the Club - something which, being a country boy, I had vaguely heard of but never seen. Needless to say we stood around the walls watching those who ventured into this mystery. Many have stood around in dances ever since, and what a pity. I never learnt to swim while at school. I wonder how many other boys have had similar experience? These are elementary but important parts in education for life.

Things are better now. The country boys and girls expect to come to the School. They ride in buses and go home each night. The system of lodging from Monday to Friday was thoroughly bad and I hope that future generations will not have to suffer it. Looking ahead, there seems every opportunity for the School to educate the children of mid-Cardigan in the fullest sense.

I would be the last to claim that the education which many of us received at Aberaeron was the best available or that it was up to the standard of many good schools at that time. No, let us face it squarely: it was not good, although it was the best perhaps that could be afforded at that time. Why the poorer areas and the poorer people have to suffer the worst education when they need the best so much I can never understand.

Are the opportunities here now to make up for past deficiencies? I hope so. The school buildings are modern with very good facilities for work and play. The County Authority and the Ministry of Education have the funds and, I believe, good intentions. Will they make a school of character? Will they create a tradition which will be important in the lives of the scholars and in the life of mid-Cardiganshire? I am told that the school is to be multilateral under the new arrangements. I sincerely hope that it will not miss its single purpose of developing character in its pupils. Frankly, I am not happy about these centralised systems, particularly in matters of education. I feel somehow that the School itself must develop individuality before it can really educate the pupils of the current and future generations. When the Governors act for higher authorities which provide the funds it is difficult to see how the school can develop its character. At this celebration of fifty years I feel that the School has left behind a struggling past and is at a turning point. The direction we now take will affect the next fifty years. Can the old pupils help? They have no voice in school matters. Can they help the Governors? Will they be allowed to help? Can we get the best out of centralised control and direction whilst leaving a big and sufficient field for local endeavour and enterprise? These matters are being discussed, I hope, and in reaching decisions, I pray that we should not standardise more than is absolutely necessary in our own Secondary Schools.

❖

RHWNG DAU GYFNOD

Y Parch. L. Haydn Lewis M.A.

Barnaf fod y pennawd yn un digon teg oblegid mai ym mlynyddoedd olaf oll Mr. C. J. Hughes, a rhai cyntaf Mr. Howell T. Evans y cefais y fraint o fod yn yr "Hen Ysgol".

Gallaf addef na wyddwn yn iawn y pryd hwnnw beth oedd arwyddocâd dyddiau ysgol fy nghenhedlaeth i yn hanes a thref datblygiad yr ysgol ei hun. Gwelaf bethau ychydig yn gliriach erbyn hyn. Ymddengys bod cyfnod cyntaf yr ysgol yn dirwyn i ben a'i hail gyfnod yn ymagor. Ar lawer cyfrif, i'r hen fyd y perthynai'r naill er mai peth annwyl iawn ydoedd, tra mai gwaddol y "daeargryn", - yn Rhyfel ac yn bopeth arall, ydyw y llall. Arall yn ddiau a ddywed am Mr. C. J. Hughes, - yn well ac yn helaethach na mi. Cadwodd ei urddas, ei burdeb, a'i dynerwch cuddiedig, hyd y diwedd, a pherchid ef gan bawb. Hen ddulliau addysg, unigol a gwahaniaethol, oedd ei ddulliau o bosibl, ac ystrywiau digon hen ffasiwn ac atgas ar gosbedigaeth i'r sawl a'i haeddai hi. Nid oedd ystwythder mawr i'n gwaith-llafur a phrin efallai oedd y gweddau cymdeithasol. Pan euthum iddi yn 1915 yr oedd E. O. James a W. J. Jones, Miss Wild, Miss D. M. Davies, Miss Thomas a'r Gogyddes Miss Jones, yn brif lafurwyr. Coffa da a diolchgar odiaeth sydd gennyf am bob un ohonynt er mai ychydig iawn o waith a wnaeth llawer ohonom iddynt yn y blynyddoedd cyntaf, - rhyw ymladd at farw a "Elementa Latina" a'r "Nesfield", peryglu bywyd beunydd yn y "Lab", a gwneud pethau erchyll iawn yn "Ystafell y Coed". Prennau oeddem yn wir i bob golwg, heb un gobaith am dwf byth! Daw atgof melys iawn yn ôl bellach o'r blynyddoedd cynnar hyn, rhywbeth efallai nad oes iddo enw arall heblaw atgof yr "Hen Fyd". Helyntion rhyfeddol gyda'r chwarae a'r teithio, mewn dyddiau pan nad oedd cyfleusterau ac offer yn rhy dda, deuant yn ôl fel ffilm ddistaw y cynfyd megis, ac nid heb ei bloedd yr un pryd. Yn y blynyddoedd cyntaf hyn, mi dybiaf y cydiodd traddodiad yr Ysgol ynom. Teimlwyd ei chyfaredd yn fuan iawn wedi'r dydd cyntaf, ac yr oedd hwnnw ei hun yn un go fawr. Ni wyddem ddim am "fore pethau", i lawr yn Neuadd y Dref, ond tybiem fod urddas a pharchedigaeth anghyffredin yn perthyn i'r "Reunion" a'r "Link" a phethau o'r fath. Yn raddol, symudem ymlaen o ddosbarth i ddosbarth, a deuai cysgod rhyw gyfrifoldeb mwy arnom. Helyntus braidd ydoedd y blynyddoedd 1916 a 1917 oblegid difrifwch y Rhyfel; gwnaed cyfnewidiadau sydyn a dieithr ymhlith yr athrawon, ac anniben iawn, ambell adeg, oedd y sefyllfa. Tua diwedd 1917, yn ôl y tabledau hanes, fe newidiwyd y drefn i gyd oblegid apwyntio prifathro newydd, ond ni charwn ffarwelio â'r cyfnod blaenorol heb dalu gwrogaeth dda i'w swynion a'i hudoliaeth pell.

Teimlais gyfaredd a newydd-deb gwaith Mr. E. O. James yn fawr iawn, oblegid mai fy iaith fy hun i gryn fesur a ddefnyddiai, ac heb yn wybod i mi deffrodd gefndir na wyddwn fawr amdano cyn hynny. Gwnaeth Mr. W. J. Jones a'r athrawesau eu cymwynasau amlwg, a llawer o ddedwyddwch a gofiaf o'r dyddiau boreol hyn.

Awgrymais eisoes y newid a ddaeth pan apwyntiwyd Mr. Howell T. Evans yn bennaeth yr ysgol. Tybiaf fod hwn yn ddigwyddiad tra phwysig yn ei hanes hi. Rhoddodd ef ffrâm a chynllun mewnol newydd i fywyd yr ysgol. Ni allaf nodi'r cwbl yn fanwl, ond yn unig y "tai" a sefydlwyd, y Preffectau, a'r Dyddlyfrau, a'r drefn addoliad. Bu cryn dipyn o wrthryfel yn erbyn yr holl bethau hyn, ond setlo i lawr a wnaeth pawb heb fod yn hir i'r drefn. Yr oedd yr hen amseroedd yn dirwyn yn gyflym i ben ac ysbryd modern eisioes wedi ymddangos yn y byd i gyd. Diflannodd yr hen felly, a daeth y newydd i fod. Y blynyddoedd hyn oedd blynyddoedd llencyndod llawn fy nghenedlaeth i a thrwy wydrau'r terfysg hwnnw y gwelais i hwy ac mewn rhyw ystyr y gwelaf hwynt o hyd. Yr oedd rhyw fath ar "ddadeni-ysbryd" yn ymhel â ni a rhaid oedd cael mynegiant iddo yn rhywle. Dyna paham y cychwynwyd "Clwb" tua 1920. Ysfa am adloniant cymdeithasol a diwylliant mwy agored oedd tu ôl y peth, ac allan o'r ysgol, yn Neuadd y Dref, y dechreuwyd y gwaith. Rhagwelodd y prifathro y perygl, a throwyd pen y ffrwd afiaethus yn ôl ac i fyny i'r ysgol. Cefais ran gweddol flaenllaw o bosibl yn hyn ac nid yw yn edifar gennyf os bu o ryw les i dwf cymdeithasol yr Hen Ysgol. Ceisiodd rhai ohonom yn ddiweddarach gychwyn "Cylchgrawn-ysgol", neu gylchgrawn-tŷ, a bod yn fanwl. Llwyddwyd i gael rhai rhifynnau allan, yn rhodresgar ddigon o bosibl, ond nid heb lwyddo i ryw fesur o leiaf. Efallai mai geiriau Wordsworth yn unig sy'n llanw ystyr profiad yr holl ddyddiau cyffrous hyn:-

"Bliss was it in that dawn to be alive,

But to be young was very heaven."

Wrth edrych yn ôl ar flynyddoedd yr ail gyfnod nid wyf yn ffeindio bod diffinio'r peth drwyddo yn hawdd iawn. Chwilio yr oedd llawer ohonom erbyn hyn am rywbeth na wyddem yn iawn beth ydoedd ynddo ei hun, chwilio am enaid ac am ddeall, ac am gelfyddyd i fyw efallai! Prif ddiffyg addysg yr ysgol yn y ddau gyfnod oedd ei fod yn anwybyddu ffynonellau cynhenid ymwybod y disgyblion. Ond dyna ni, yma y gorwedd melltith addysg Cymru benbaladr. Tybiaf i'r prifathro newydd roddi mwy o le o lawer i hyn, ond eto yr oedd mwy lawer yn aros heb ei wneuthur. Pwysleisiodd ef yn wir y ffaith mai cyfanwaith llwyr a llydanwaith cyfoethog yw addysg a thalaf deyrnged iddo am hynny. Erbyn heddiw y mae "Deddf Addysg" newydd ar lyfrau'r wlad. Deddf ydyw hon a ddylasai fod ar y llyfrau gan mlynedd yn ôl petai modd gyda'i phwyslais gwell ar Fro, Cenedl, a Byd. Sut bynnag, Mr. Howell T. Evans oedd pensaer yr ail gyfnod a welais i, a chlod fyddo iddo ef a'r gweddill ymdrechgar ohonynt, am hynny.

"Bellach f'ysbryd a ballawdd"; o ran hynny ni chaniata gofod i mi ymhelaethu dim. Pwy a draetha rin a hoen y dyddiau oll, yr hen gyfoedion mwyn, a'r ysgarmesoedd a'r helyntion oll? Rhamant y genhedlaeth ydyw, na thraethir byth mohono, fe ddichon, ond daw yn ôl o hyd yn ei dull ei hun fel hudoliaeth nas diddymir. Bu'r "Hen Ysgol" yn help i mi fy adnabod fy hun - os gwnaf hynny byth: dangosodd i mi ben y ffordd sydd yn mawrhau'r byd llydan a chyfoethog hwn. Gwn y dymuna fy nghenedlaeth i y gorau posibl iddi, canys y mae dyddiau'r "Jiwbili" yn rhai go bwysig. Uwch a gwell y byddo'r "Hen Ysgol" o hyd!

"Yno, mae cynnydd uchel amcanion;

Ni ddaw fyth i ddeifio hon golli ffydd,

Na thro cywilydd, na thorri calon."

❖

Gorau Ymgais Gwybodaeth

ATGOFION

Mr. Jac L. Williams B.A., B.Sc. (Coleg y Drindod, Caerfyrddin)

Nid oeddwn i'n un o ddisgyblion cyntaf yr ysgol ac nid wyf ychwaith yn un o'r rhai sydd newydd ymadael â hi. Ni allaf felly edrych yn ôl dros hanner can mlynedd ar gyfnod rhamantus bore oes, a thybio ei fod yn llawer iawn gwell nag yr ydoedd, fel y gwna'r rhan fwyaf o bobl sydd wedi croesi'r trigain. Nid wyf wedi ymadael yn ddigon diweddar ychwaith i fod â chof byw gennyf am bawb a phopeth. Nid oedd yr ysgol yn ei ffurf gyntaf yn yr amser y bum i yno nac ychwaith yn ei ffurf bresennol. Yr oedd ystafell newydd wedi ei hadeiladu ar y chwith ychydig cyn i mi fynd yno ac yn eiddo i'r pumed dosbarth. O'r braidd na ellid dweud ei bod wedi'i sancteiddio i'r dosbarth hwnnw, oherwydd ni oddefid ei halogi gan neb o'r dosbarthiadau is. Nid oedd yr adeilad hardd sydd erbyn hyn yn gartref i'r ymarfer corff wedi ei ddechrau. Ymledodd y prif adeilad yntau i'r ddau gyfeiriad wedi'r dyddiau hynny. Ni bum erioed y tu mewn i'r adeiladau newyddion, a rywsut nid oes arnaf fawr o awydd mynd. Caraf feddwl a breuddwydio am yr ysgol fel yr oedd yn 1936 pan ymadewais â hi.

Dylwn gyfaddef er hynny i mi fod un min nos y tu mewn i'r glwyd yn cerdded o gwmpas yr adeilad newydd gyda chyfaill i mi. Buom yn syllu o ben ysgwyddau'n gilydd trwy rai o ffenestri'r hen adeilad yntau, ac yn cael llu o atgofion melys am yr hyn a ddigwyddodd yn y lle a'r lle. Chwiliais yn hir am garreg y torrais fy enw arni yn y wal wrth ochr yr ysgol. Ni ddeuthum o hyd iddi. Yr oedd hithau fel finnau erbyn hyn wedi ei symud o'i chynefin fro, ac ni synnwn glywed iddi gael ei chladdu a'i chuddio am byth yn y ddaear pan dorrwyd sylfaen yr ystafelloedd newydd.

Diwrnod mawr yn fy mywyd oedd fy niwrnod cyntaf yn Ysgol Sir Aberaeron. Nid oedd mynd yno'n llawn cymaint o antur efallai â mynd i'r ysgol elfennol. Y tro hwnnw ehangodd fy mhrofiad o'r fferm fechan ar Fanc Llanddewi Aberarth i fywyd y pentref. Collais ryw gymaint o'm diddordeb yn yr ieir a'r anifeiliaid a fuasai'n gymdeithion difyr a diddorol yn fy chwaraeon ar y buarth, a dechreuais gymysgu a chyd-chwarae â phlant eraill, a chymryd diddordeb mewn cyfeillion. Clywswn dipyn am ysgol y pentref oddi wrth fy rhieni cyn i mi erioed weled ei thu mewn, ond ni chawswn dystiolaeth uniongyrchol ganddynt hwy fel yr hyn a gawswn beunydd bron am yr Ysgol Sir gan rai a aethai yno flwyddyn neu ddwy o'm blaen. Gwyddwn enwau a ffug-enwau pawb o'r athrawon fisoedd cyn i mi fynd yno. Gwyddwn am eu neilltuolion oll, a gwyddwn ym mha wersi y gellid cael tipyn o hwyl ac ym mha rai y byddai fy nhrwyn o hyd ar y maen. Gwyddwn y rhoid fy mhen o dan y tap rywbryd yn ystod yr wythnos gyntaf, a gwyddwn fod yno Eisteddfod ar Ddydd Gŵyl Dewi.

Cofiaf yn dda amdanaf yn mynd i mewn trwy'r drws am y tro cyntaf. Yr oedd nifer o'r bechgyn a fuasai yno o'r blaen yn sefyll yn awdurdodol bwysig gyda'r wal yn ddwy res hir o'r drws i'r "corridor" lle y crogem ein cotiau, a gwthiai'r ddwy res yma ni'r newydd ddyfodiaid o'r naill i'r llall wrth i ni fynd yn ein blaenau. Wedi cyrraedd yn ddiogel a di-anaf, a chrogi'r bag lledr a'r cap newydd coch a glas ar y bach, ni bum yn hir cyn cael gafael ar y tri arall a ddaethai yno o'r un ysgol elfennol am y tro cyntaf. Cymerodd cyfaill caredig a âi i'r un ysgol Sul â ni y pedwar ohonom a dan ei adain a dangos i ni ryfeddodau'r ysgol.

Coffa da amdanom yn syllu i mewn i'r "lab" am y tro cyntaf. O'r braidd yr oeddwn yn ddigon tal i gyrraedd y gwydr a oedd yn rhan uchaf y drws ac edrych i mewn. Nid oedd gennyf fawr o syniad beth oedd "lab" yr amser hwnnw. Yr oedd hyd yn oed y gair yn ddieithr ac yn llawn dirgelion. Yr oedd rhyw swyn rhyfedd ac atyniadol yn y rhesi o boteli amryliw a welwn ar y meinciau ac yn y cypyrddau. Troi wedyn i'r ystafell gwaith saer a gweld pob offeryn yn ddestlus yn ei le, yn union lle mynnai Mr. W. J. Jones iddo fod.

Ond dyna'r gloch yn canu a phawb yn tyrru i'r neuadd. Y mae llu o atgofion melys gan bawb a fu'n ddisgybl yn ysgol Aberaeron am y neuadd hon. Erys yn fyw o flaen ein llygaid tra bo gennym gof a dychymyg, y gofeb yn y pen blaen, y cwpanau arian a'r tariannau ar y ddwy ochr, a rhestr y graddedigion yn ei phen ôl. Cofiaf yn dda am athro a ddywedai wrthym dro ar ol tro, flwyddyn ar ôl blwyddyn, mai cael ein henwau ar y bwrdd hwn a ddylai fod yn nod gennym yn yr ysgol ac nid torri ein henwau â chyllell boced ar ddesg neu garreg. Nid yw'n edifar gennyf i mi geisio cael y ddau. Yn y neuadd hon y dechreuem ein diwrnod gwaith o'r diwrnod cyntaf yn yr ysgol hyd yr olaf. Yn y neuadd yma y cynhelid pob cyfarfod o bwys ym mywyd yr ysgol. Yma cynhelid rhagbrofion yr Eisteddfod, ac y penderfynid a gaem ymddangos o flaen y dorf yn neuadd y dref. Yma y cynhelid y cyfarfod gwobrwyo o flwyddyn i flwyddyn. Yma hefyd y cyfarfyddai'r Clwb ac y mae gan lu ohonom atgofion melys am y sefydliad gwerthfawr hwnnw. Ni fedraf er hynny beidio â mynegi'r farn y buasai'n anhraethol gwell, yn enwedig i ni blant cefn gwlad, pe cedwid o leiaf hanner ei gyfarfodydd yn Gymraeg, a phe gwneid ymgais i ddatblygu tipyn o dalent y noson lawen Gymreig yn yr ail ran. Y mae'r ddawn i siarad yn gyhoeddus yn y ddwy iaith yn ddigon prin o hyd, ac ofnaf fod perygl i'r sinema a'r ddawns ddisodli pob adloniant gwreiddiol a Chymreig hyd yn oed yn ei hardaloedd gwledig oni ddaw arweiniad o rywle.

Ofer i mi geisio gwneud rhestr o'r atgofion a red trwy'r meddwl wrth i mi ysgrifennu hyn o erthygl. Ni ellid eu cynnwys i gyd mewn un llyfr. Cofiaf am y bachgen hwnnw'n rhoi sgrech sydyn ac erchyll ar ganol y cwrt tenis pan ddisgynnodd ŵy wedi ei ddwyn o rywle ar ei wegil. Cofiaf am athro annwyl yn treulio awr gyfan i geisio egluro i rywun yn y pedwerydd dosbarth beth oedd berf, ac yntau gydag ystyfnigrwydd diarhebol yn gwrthod gweld y goleuni. Nid oedd pall ar amynedd a goddefgarwch yr athrawon gyda rhai ohonom. Cofiaf am ambell anrhydedd a gefais, megis chwarae pêl droed dros Danyfron pan oeddwn yn y dosbarth chwech. Sylweddolaf erbyn hyn mai fy maint yn unig a roes i mi'r anrhydedd o fod yn "full back" am unwaith yn fy mywyd. Cofiaf hefyd am lu o bethau na feiddiaf hyd yn oed yn awr eu crybwyll yn gyhoeddus na'u cyfaddef wrth un o'r athrawon.

Mawr yw fy nyled i Ysgol Sir Aberaeron. Ynddi hi y lluniwyd llawer o'm cymeriad, a heb ei chyfraniad hi ni buaswn yn ddim tebyg i'r hyn ydwyf. Blynyddoedd gwerthfawr odiaeth oedd fy nwy flynedd olaf yno, pan oeddwn yn y dosbarth chwech. Da gennyf feddwl fod y tri athro a roes i mi gymaint o'u llafur a'u gofal yn aros yno o hyd i wasanaethu'r rhai a'm dilynodd. Diolchaf i Mr. J. T. Owen a Mr. W. A. Jones am fy nysgu i hoffi'r cain a'r prydferth mewn llenyddiaeth yn y ddwy iaith. Credaf i hadau fy nghariad at Gymru fel gwlad ac fel cenedl gael eu hau yng ngwersi Cymraeg y dosbarth chwech. Mawr yw fy nyled i Mr. T. H. Fox am roi i mi gystal golwg ar ogoniant yr hen fyd clasurol ac yn arbennig am fy nysgu i weithio a pheidio â disgwyl llwyddiant heb ymdrech. Bu fy nghais i osod fy enw am byth ar garreg yn yr ysgol yn ofer. Diflannodd y garreg erbyn hyn. Efallai ei bod wedi ei malurio, a'r tair llythyren a dorrais arni wedi eu dileu. Ni ddileir byth mo ddelw'r ysgol ar fy nghymeriad i.

Teimlaf ryw agosatrwydd at bawb a fu'n dysgu neu hyd yn oed yn methu dysgu y tu mewn i furiau'r hen ysgol. Weithiau byddaf yn cyfarfod â hen ddisgybl nad adwaenaf. Cyn gynted ag y dof i wybod iddo fod yn Ysgol Sir Aberaeron, teimlaf yn gyfeillgar yn ei gwmni. Nid oes pall ar sgwrs wedyn. Onid un teulu ydym oll wedi ein magu ar yr un aelwyd, a honno'n aelwyd hynod gynnes a chysurus? Er gwasgaru i bedwar ban y byd y mae'r atgofion cyffelyb sydd gennym yn ein clymu wrth ein gilydd. Boed i'r teulu gynyddu a hir oes i'r ysgol i wasanaethu cenhedlaeth ar ôl cenhedlaeth o ieuenctid y sir. Boed i ninnau, ei disgyblion, o bob cyfnod yn ei hanes, adlewyrchu ei phethau gorau lle bynnag y bôm.

❖

EDRYCH YN ÔL / LOOKING BACK

Miss Maria Evans (cyn-ddisgybl 1924-1929)

Athrawes a Dirprwy Brifathrawes 1942 - 1976.

Deuthum yn blentyn i Ysgol Sir Aberaeron ym 1924. Yr adeilad gwreiddiol oedd yma y pryd hynny, ac mae y rhan yma yn dal o hyd er bod llawer wedi ei ychwanegu ato. Wedi dod o Ysgol Elfennol Mydroilyn edrychai'r adeilad yn anferth, yn ddigon i roi braw i mi. Cymharol fychan oedd yr ysgol yr adeg honno, tua 120 o blant, chwech o athrawon a'r Prifathro, Mr. Howell T. Evans, fel pen teulu, yn adnabod y plant i gyd. Os byddem mewn unrhyw anhawster gallem fynd ato a chael croeso â breichiau agored. Yr oeddem yn lwcus i gael Prifathro mor ddynol. Mr. W. J. Jones a ddysgai Gemeg a Gwyddoniaeth, Mr. W. E. Roberts Saesneg a Lladin, Mr. J. T. Owen Cymraeg a Hanes, Miss Thomas Ffrangeg, Miss Williams Daearyddiaeth a Bywydeg a Miss Enid Owen Gwyddor Tŷ. Wedi i Mr. W. E. Roberts adael i Ysgol Ramadeg, Aberdâr, daeth Mr. W. A. Jones i ddysgu Saesneg a Mr. T. H. Fox i ddysgu Lladin. Er hynny, disgwylid i'r holl athrawon ddysgu testunau eraill heblaw eu prif bwnc.

Gŵr amryddawn oedd y Prifathro, heblaw rhedeg yr ysgol yn ddeheuig, dysgai Fathemateg, Hanes a Cherddoriaeth. Yr oedd yn athro gwych mewn Mathemateg, yn ddiddorol iawn yn y dosbarthiadau Hanes, a byddai'n siŵr o sôn am y Bedyddwyr ymhob gwers. Doniwyd ef yn helaeth â'r ddawn o ddysgu. Yr oedd yn gerddorol, ef oedd arweinydd Côr yr Ysgol a byddai'n cynhyrchu operau. Yr oedd Eisteddfod bob blwyddyn a'r Tai - Portland, Tanyfron a Thyglyn - yn cystadlu mewn eitemau cerddorol a llenyddol. Yr oedd Clwb yr Ysgol yn cynnwys y plant hynaf yn cwrdd bob nos Wener yn y Neuadd. Caent ddadleuon, darlithiau ac ati yn y rhan gyntaf, a dawnsio yn yr ail ran. Yn yr amser yma y plant yn unig a redai'r Clwb. Credai'r Prifathro bod hynny yn hyfforddiant da a chymdeithasol. Wedi ei ymddeoliad yr oedd dau athro hefyd, yn gyfrifol am y Clwb. Cafodd y Prifathro lawer o ddylanwad arnom fel plant, mor bwysig oedd ei waith yn ein paratoi i wynebu bywyd. Yr oedd yn ysbrydoliaeth i bawb.

Yr oedd Mr. W. J. Jones yn ofalus iawn am y plant. Byddai yn yr ysgol yn gynnar iawn bob bore ac arhosai yn y ffenestr yn y Neuadd yn gwylio'r plant yn dod i fyny i'r ysgol. Ar y pryd hyn yr oedd y merched i ddod i fyny'r llwybr a'r bechgyn y ffordd hirach heibio Afallon a'r ffordd tua Cefntyncoed. Byddai'r bechgyn yn dod i fyny'r llwybr weithiau a byddai W. J. yn eu gwylio hyd iddynt gyrraedd yr ysgol ac yna mynd allan atynt a'u danfon yn ôl i ddod i fyny ffordd y bechgyn.

Pan ddechreuais yr ysgol yr oedd y rhan fwyaf o'r disgyblion a ddeuai o'r tu allan i'r dref yn aros am yr wythnos yn Aberaeron. Yr oeddwn i yn byw rhyw ddwy filltir tu allan i Lanarth. Cerddem bob bore Llun i ddal y bws i ddod i Aberaeron a mynd yn ôl gyda'r bws nos Wener. Yr oeddem yn aros am yr wythnos gyda Mr. a Mrs. John Davies yn Albert Street. Yr oedd pedair ohonom yno a chawsom lawer iawn o hwyl. Yr oedd rheol yr amser hwnnw bod rhaid i'r disgyblion fod i fewn yn y tŷ erbyn chwech o'r gloch. Byddai'r athrawon a'r "Prefects" yn cerdded y dre i weld os oedd rhywun allan. Nid oedd rhaid iddynt ofidio amdanom ni. Os na fyddem i mewn cyn chwech, gwae ni, yr oedd Mr. Davies yn gwylio ac yn edrych ar y cloc, ni fentrem fod yn hwyr. Eisteddai yn yr ystafell yn darllen ei bapur pan oeddem yn gwneud ein gwaith cartref o gylch y bwrdd ac ni chaem ddweud gair - yr oedd yn waeth na bod mewn dosbarth yn yr ysgol. 'Roedd y plant i gyd yn gwybod am Mr. Davies, ac er mwyn cael sbri, byddent yn dod i gnocio'r drws a rhedeg i ffwrdd. Yr oedd yn wallgo ac yn rhedeg ar eu hôl. Ni chlywais iddo ddal yr un, ond gwn iddo unwaith golli ei slipers yn y Cae Sgwâr! Er hyn i gyd, yr oeddem yn eithaf cysurus yn y llety am fod Mrs. Davies yn garedig iawn. Bum yn aros yma am dair blynedd, hyd nes i Mam ddod i fyw i Aberaeron.

Pan ddeuthum i'r ysgol, dechreuem yn Form III, wedyn Form IV, Form Shell a Form V. Ar ddiwedd y flwyddyn yma eisteddem "Senior", fel y'i gelwid y pryd hynny, a thrwy hyn, os gwnaem yn ddigon da, gael "Matric" a'n galluogai ni i fynd i Brifysgol. Yn yr amser yma yr oedd pob dosbarth yn aros yn ei ystafell a'r athrawon yn symud o un dosbarth i'r llall.

Ar ôl blwyddyn yn Form VI, euthum i Brifysgol Aberystwyth a graddio mewn Bywydeg ac yna i Goleg Maria Gray yn Llundain i ymarfer dysgu. Wedi bod yn dysgu yn Ysgol Ramadeg Towyn, Meirionydd, deuthum yn ôl ym 1942 i ddysgu Bywydeg ac Amaethyddiaeth, i gymryd lle Mr. John Evans, a aeth i weithio gyda Phwyllgor Amaethyddiaeth y Rhyfel. Bum yma hyd nes i mi ymddeol ym 1976 fel Pennaeth Adran Bywydeg a dirprwy Brifathrawes.

Erbyn i mi ddod yn ôl, yr oedd yr ysgol wedi ehangu. Yr oedd deg athro a thua 200 o blant, llawer ohonynt yn blant noddedig o Lundain a Lerpwl. Yr oedd yr adeilad yn fwy gyda rhagor o ystafelloedd, yn eu mysg labordy lle dysgwyd Bywydeg, Amaethyddiaeth a Ffiseg. Fel aeth yr amser ymlaen codwyd rhan newydd o'r ysgol y tu arall i'r llwybr, yn cynnwys Neuadd fawr, ystafelloedd dysgu a labordai. Agorwyd y rhan yma ym 1950. Ar ôl hyn yr oedd pob athro â'i ystafell ei hun a'r plant yn mynd o amgylch. Mor braf oedd cael labordy Bywydeg i mi fy hun!

Yn ei blaen aeth yr ysgol, adeiladwyd llawer o ystafelloedd eraill i wahanol bynciau. Cynyddu oedd nifer y plant a phan adewais ym 1976, yr oedd tua 800 o blant a 45 o athrawon yn yr ysgol, ac erbyn hyn yr oedd yn Ysgol Gyfun.

Pan ddethum yn ôl fel athrawes, Mr. Howell T. Evans oedd y Prifathro hyd ei ymddeoliad ym 1944. Bum gyda thri Prifathro arall, Mr. J. T. Owen, Mr. G. G. Davies a Mr. D. J. Thomas, a phob un â'i bersonoliaeth ei hun.

Treuliais amser hapus iawn yn yr ysgol, yn blentyn ac yn athrawes. Cefais bleser a boddhad.

Dymunaf lewyrch parhaol i'r ysgol yn ei hail ganrif.

The Aberaeron Intermediate School - 1930-34

Memories of an old pupil

In the early years of the century, the Victorian influence in everyday life had changed very little, and so it was with the Aberaeron Intermediate School. While its educational facilities were slow in developing, the structure remained unchanged until the end of the 1930s. The sole addition during that period was a single classroom built at the south end in 1929.

Those of us who had our education at the school in the early 1930s, cannot help but remember the social conditions in that period. Communications were slow and cumbersome; a journey by rail to Carmarthen took two and a quarter hours. Electricity was only beginning to be installed in the home and on the streets. The cart and horse was very evident on the roads and was the means of delivering most of the heavy goods. Also, with very few radios installed in the town, the world news only came through on the following day with the delivery of the daily newspapers. The upper classes owned the only cars seen on the roads and housework was very laborious with none of today's modern equipment to ease the work. Above all, the low incomes made it extremely difficult for parents to meet everyday expenses and pay the fees, and other costs, to give their children an education, as in those days, you had to pay for your education.

In order to become a pupil at Aberaeron Intermediate School, a child had to pass a scholarship exam. This was held in May, on a Saturday, when pupils from all the primary schools in the catchment area assembled in the school hall and sat an Arithmetic exam in the morning and a Welsh/English exam in the afternoon. You had to gain 100 marks to pass, and individual schools were informed a month or so later who had qualified.

New pupils arrived in September, on the second day of term, already fitted out with the uniforms supplied by the sole distributor of school uniforms - City House. Boys had to wear navy blazers, complete with A. C. S. badge and caps which had navy, red and white panels. The girls wore navy, red and white striped blazers; navy gymslips and navy nurse-type caps. Strict instructions were given for caps to be worn at all times outdoors on school days.

After being shown to your classroom you were given a timetable. At 9.30 a.m. it was assembly for prayers and readings. There were four lessons in the morning and three in the afternoon. The teachers also gave instructions about which textbooks were needed. These had to be purchased from a pupil from a previous year or bought from a second hand book shop such as Foyles of London or Galloways of Aberystwyth. The teacher priced the book if bought from a pupil and that price had to be paid.

In 1930, forms 2 and 3 were for first year pupils. Their rooms were situated on the right side of the boys' corridor. Forms 4a and 4b, for second year pupils, were located behind the hall (the present day Memorial Library). Third year pupils were in a form called "SHELL" which was situated in the hall at the rear. Shell was rather an unusual name - no one has ever offered a reason why it was so called and it ceased to exist after 1932. The seniors, or fourth year pupils, taking their C.W.B. exams, were in the new classrooms at the south end of the school. Other rooms included the laboratory, woodwork and cookery rooms and of course the Headmaster, and the masters' and mistresses' rooms.

Discipline in those days was very strict. The cane was used by the Headmaster - while the masters were not loath to give rough treatment to those pupils who deserved it. A pupil who did not doff his cap to a passing teacher in the street would be hauled before the teacher concerned the following morning to receive punishment - usually 100 lines. There was also a "curfew" in force on school days when all pupils were not allowed on the streets after 6.30 p.m. without the permission of the staff. Detention was another form of punishment when pupils were kept in after school hours, if homework had not been completed satisfactorily, or any other misbehaviour in class.

At the end of the 1920s, approximately 180 pupils attended the school and by 1930, the staff consisted of the Headmaster, Mr. Howell T. Evans and four masters - Mr. W. J. Jones, Mr. J. T. Owen, Mr. W. A. Jones and Mr. T. H. Fox and four mistresses - Miss Jones, Miss Timothy, Miss Treharne and Miss Elaine Lewis.

Mr. Howell Evans was a historian of repute and author of the book "History of England and Wales", which was our standard history textbook throughout our school years. He was also an accomplished musician and conductor.

Mr. W. J. Jones was senior master and taught Chemistry. He was the accepted Sports master of the period and also the Woodwork master.

Mr J. T. Owen was a very respected Welsh teacher, a person of many talents and an actor who took the lead role in many successful Welsh dramas performed in the 1920s.

Mr. W. A. Jones, who succeeded Mr. W. E. Roberts in 1927, was the English master.

Mr. T. H. Fox, the youngest staff member, came to school in 1930. He was a strict disciplinarian and an excellent Latin Master. He married the French teacher, Miss Ethel Davies after the war and left to join the staff at Cardiff High School in 1963. He had the unusual habit in those days of 1930 of calling all pupils by their surnames.

Miss N. Timothy taught French and left in the mid 1930s to live in Cairo.

Miss Treharne, from the Midlands, taught Mathematics and Miss Elaine Lewis, a former pupil of the school taught Cookery.

In direct contrast to the transport facilities available today, everybody walked to school, including the staff. The path leading from the main road to the school could hardly take two abreast. It proceeded between wire fences with open fields on either side right up to the school gate. Deliveries to the school were made via the Alltygraig road and cars were seldom driven up to the school grounds. The Alltygraig road was also used by those pupils who travelled daily by rail. Many pupils walked miles from the outlying areas each morning to attend school and returned home in the evening. Those who came from areas where no rail or bus services were available, stayed during the week in lodgings in the town and there were many houses which kept such pupils.

An irritating custom for the new first year boy pupil took the form of an initiation. The senior boys seized a new pupil and put his head either under the tap in the boys' corridor wash basin or under the water pump at the rear of the school. This was called "tapping". The poor fellow at the receiving end sat in class throughout the day with his upper clothing soaked! Strangely enough, no one was ever reprimanded for this senseless act.

The end of term exams were called terminals. Pupils would be moved into various classrooms so that no pupil of the same form sat next to each other. The exam results were put up on a baize board in the hall, and at the end of each term, a report was sent by post to each home, so that parents could know how their child was progressing.

As in every period, a pupil emerges as an outstanding scholar and goes on to fulfil a brilliant career in later life. In this respect, 1930-34 was no exception. The outstanding pupil throughout this period was Jac Lewis Williams, who became a Professor at Aberystwyth University and a leading figure in Welsh educational circles. Other notable old pupils of this era were Garrod Thomas and Enoch Thomas. The majority of pupils split their efforts between work and enjoyment - some biased more towards studies while others were more interested in sports.

Games periods were held on Thursday afternoon for the whole school. Soccer was the dominant sport for boys in winter and hockey for girls. Soccer for the seniors was played on the Square field, while the juniors went to the small playing field approaching the beach, which was also where the girls played hockey. A trial rugby game was once tried in the Square field with long poles attached to the uprights of the soccer goal posts. Mr. Fox was in charge, but he gave it up after the first attempt. There was no radio or television in those days to offer guidelines - nobody had seen a rugby match and were totally ignorant of the rules! Rugby was eventually introduced after the war years when a number of masters from South Wales were appointed to the staff. In the summer, cricket and tennis were the main games and one can remember the few cricket matches which were played against visiting teams with the two masters - Mr. W. A. Jones and Mr. T. H. Fox - as opening batsmen.

The highlights of the year, which evoked keen rivalry between the houses - Portland, Tyglyn and Tanyfron - were the School Eisteddfod and Sports day.

The Eisteddfod was held every year in the Memorial Hall on the evening of St. David's Day - the prelims having been held in the school hall during the morning. 1932 was the exception, when, owing to a heavy snowstorm and raging blizzard which isolated the town for many days, the Eisteddfod was postponed for just over a week. An amusing incident in one particular Eisteddfod occurred when, due to lack of singers, one of the Tanyfron boys was forced to sing bass in the quartet competition. The adjudicator commented in his adjudication that the bass was "like a wandering Jew". This caused much embarrassment and leg pulling to the boy concerned.

The Sports day was held in the playing field on the way to the beach. The playing field in those days was much smaller, comprising of one hockey pitch and an undersized soccer

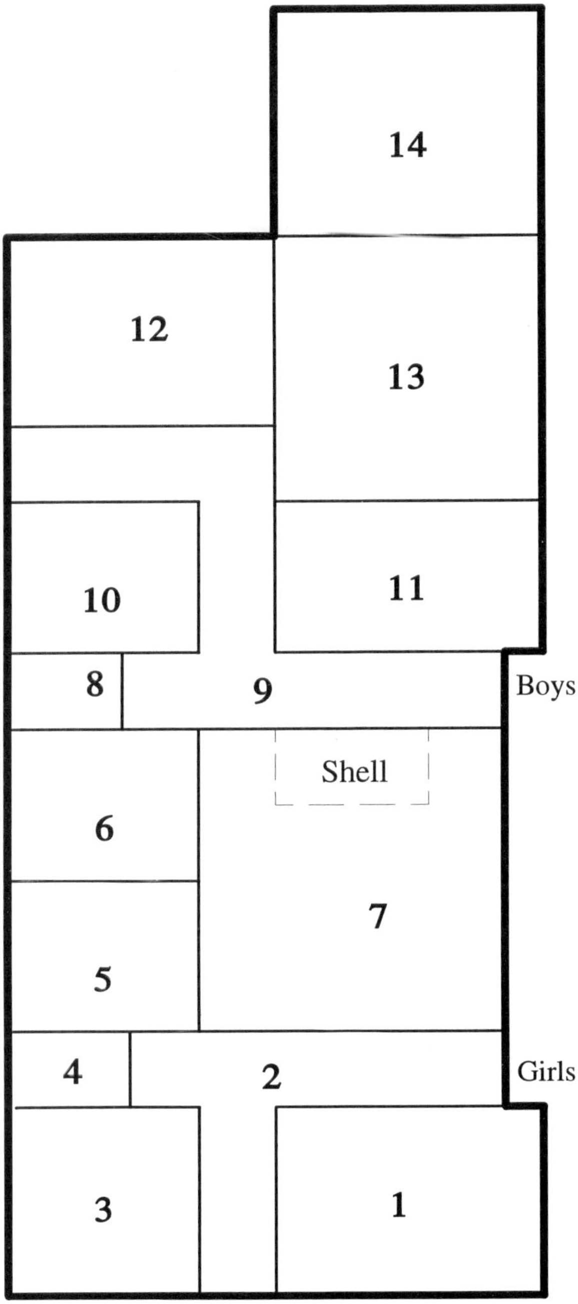

Rooms:

1. Headmaster
2. Girls' corridor cloaks
3. Cookery
4. Mistresses' Room
5. Form 4b
6. Form 4a
7. Hall / Shell
8. Masters' Room
9. Boys' corridor cloaks
10. Form 3
11. Form 2
12. Woodwork
13. Laboratory
14. New Classroom (1929)
    Form 5

ABERAERON INTERMEDIATE SCHOOL - 1930.

pitch. Sports day attracted a large crowd and the races included many events which are out of fashion today - such as the sack race, three legged race, egg and spoon race and the slow bicycle race, where the last competitor won the race! One can also remember the blackboard and easel in the centre of the field, with Mr. W. J. Jones recording the events and winners on the board with chalk in his copperplate printing.

Another event which I recall with mixed feelings was the occasion when the Headmaster - a keen musician - would order all the pupils to assemble in the main hall for a musical afternoon of classical instrumental music provided by three ladies - the Dorian Trio. This was appreciated by the musically minded, but for the majority of pupils, it was a very boring afternoon and some of the boy pupils would take the risk of escaping up "Woodbine Lane" to avoid the boredom. Woe betide them if they were caught!

To end on a lighter note, one has memories of the "tuck shops" frequented by schoolchildren in those days. There was "Siop y Bont", a thatched cottage, near the main road bridge approaching the railway station (said to have been one of Twm Sion Cati's haunts). Miss Davies kept bottles of sweets in her small room. Another shop was in a house in Lower Regent Street near the playing fields, where Mrs. Thomas sold home made rock. The shop was often visited after a game of football. The third was in Chalybeate Street, where Mrs. James, "Siop Madlen" was the favourite for County School children. She sold home made "pop" for 1d a glass and liquorice strips and pipes together with sherbert fountains and gobstoppers at 4 for a 1d. These tuck shops were places where one would have real value for money to make the most of the small amount of pocket money allowed children at that time. Sadly the three ceased to exist by the end of the thirties, and on the day Miss Davies, y Bont, was buried, the thatched roof of her cottage fell in.

Many of those who were pupils in the 1930s have now passed on; among them those pupils we remember so well, whose young lives were cut short by the horrors of war. Those of us who remain have witnessed immense changes in the school during the passing years. Thousands of pupils have passed through the corridors of Aberaeron Intermediate School, and many have gone on to fulfil brilliant careers; while most can be grateful for an education received which equipped them for their future needs after leaving school. Aberaeron Intermediate School can be justly proud of its one hundred year existance.

❖

Atgofion

Joan Davies

Newydd gael fy unarddeg oed oeddwn i pan es i i Ysgol Aberaeron, i'r Cownti Sgŵl, neu'n hytrach i'r Cownti, ar lafar. Roeddwn i wedi cael beic newydd sbon, un gyda handl bars uchel, yr hen "sit up and beg", i'm cario yno y ddwy filltir o daith o Gaebislan. Roeddwn i'n cael gorchymyn bob dydd gan fy mam i ofalu peidio â reidio ar y ddau oriwaered mawr ar dop ac ar waelod rhiw'r eglwys, ond mae'n ddrwg gen i orfod cyfaddef mai anaml iawn y byddwn i'n gwrando. Byddai amser yn brin yn y bore, a reidio'r holl ffordd fyddwn i yn amlach na pheidio. Dim ond unwaith y llithrodd y beic a minnau bendramwnwgl dros ein gilydd, a hynny ar sglefren o rew ar fore iasoer o Ionawr, ond doeddwn i fawr gwaeth wedi'r godwm, diolch am hynny.

Bob rhyw dair wythnos, byddwn yn galw yn y bwthyn bach ar dop y rhiw, wrth ymyl yr eglwys, i werthu cwningen i Sali, "cymeriad" o hen wraig ffraeth, bob amser yn eistedd ar y sgiw wrth y tân, ei hewinedd yn hirion las, a chap dyn ar ei phen. Fi fy hunan fyddai wedi dal y gwningen, ac ar handl y beic y byddwn yn ei chario, yn hongian gerfydd ei choesau ôl. Chwe cheiniog fyddai'r pris - (pump os mai bwch fyddai gen i!). Byddai Sali'n mynnu mai bwch fyddai pob un, - a wyddwn i ddim mo'r gwahaniaeth! Ond roedd pum ceiniog yn bum ceiniog bryd hynny, ac yn arian poced da mewn poced wag. Beth fuaswn i'n wneud pe bai Sali yn gwrthod prynu, wn i ddim, - cynnig y gwningen i ryw gi llwglyd a welwn ar y ffordd mae'n debyg. Beth bynnag, ni chododd y broblem !

Wedi cyrraedd Aberaeron, parcio'r beic, ochr yn ochr a rhes o rai eraill, yn un o hen stablau gwesty'r "Feathers" (gwesty'r "Plu" heddiw), a cherdded hyd un o strydoedd y dref, ac y fyny'r llwybr (<u>cul</u> bryd hynny) at yr ysgol. Byddai'r daith droediog honno yn cymryd bron cymaint o amser â'r daith ar y beic, ac ar y llwybr hwnnw y cefais i aml wlychfa, bron hyd at fy nghroen, mewn tywydd gerwin, fy nhraed yn wlyb diferol, a'r hen sanau duon, hirion hynny (coffa da amdanynt!) yn cordeddu am fy nghoesau, ac yn glynu fel lastig weddill y dydd. Ie, yr hen lwybr, a dim ond lle i <u>un</u> ar y tro i gerdded yn hwylus arno, ond esgus iawn bryd arall hefyd i glosio at gariadon wrth fynd a dod i'r ysgol!

Na, ni fu fy wythnos gyntaf yn yr ysgol yn un bleserus iawn. Roeddwn i wedi mynd yno o ysgol fach Aberarth, - ysgol o ddwy ystafell, a thri athro, yn amlach na pheidio, ysgol lle roeddwn i'n adnabod pawb, ac yn adnabod eu teuluoedd. Ond yn Aberaeron, doeddwn i'n adnabod fawr neb. Doeddwn i ddim wedi arfer â gwersi o hyd penodol; roeddwn i'n cymysgu enwau'r athrawon; 'roedd cynifer o'r pynciau yn ddieithr i mi, ac 'roedd yr holl ystafelloedd yn un rhwydwaith o ddryswch. Cyn diwedd yr wythnos roeddwn i'n dyheu am gael mynd yn ôl i ysgol fach Aberarth.

Yna, fe ddois ar draws partner tebyg i mi fy hun, gyda'r un diddordebau a'r un synnwyr digrifwch - Mair o Abermeurig, bro mebyd fy nhad, - Mair Gwastod. Gweddnewidiwyd fy mywyd ysgol, a dechreuais fwynhau pob munud o bob dydd. Rwy'n cyfaddef i ni fod yn ddireidus, yn bryfoclyd o ddireidus at rai athrawon ar brydiau, ond rhyw hwyl diniwed fyddai'r cyfan.

Dwy o'r gwersi yr wyf yn edifar iawn i mi beidio â gwneud fy ngorau ynddynt oedd y wers goginio a'r wers wnïo, a 'does gen i fawr o glem ar wneud yr un o'r ddau beth hyd heddiw. Doedd dim ystafell ddosbarth iawn i ddysgu'r pynciau hynny, dim ond yr ystafell lle caem ein cinio ysgol. Un bwrdd hirfain oedd yno, a phawb i eistedd wrtho. Eisteddai'r plant da yn y pen nesaf at yr athrawes. Byddai Mair a minnau wedi rhedeg yno i fachu dwy sedd yn y pen pellaf oddi wrthi, ac oherwydd fyddem ni ddim yn clywed popeth bob amser, (neu ddim yn dewis clywed!) yr unig gacennau y medrem ni eu gwneud yn llwyddiannus fyddai "rock cakes". Byddai, fe fyddai rheiny fel craig - yr union fel y dylen nhw fod! A waeth i mi gyfaddef, fe gedwais ambell ddilledyn di-siap, annwisgadwy am rai blynyddoedd wedi i mi adael yr ysgol, dim ond yn goffadwriaeth am y gwersi gwnïo aflwyddiannus! Rwy'n prysuro i ddweud nad ar yr athrawes yr oedd y bai, ac yn fuan iawn yn fy ngyrfa addysgol, roeddwn i wedi "gollwng" y ddau bwnc bondigrybwyll!

Y cae hoci wedyn, - dyna le arall lle profais i'n fethiant llwyr. Roeddwn i wedi cael ffon hoci newydd sbon, ond fu fy nghoesau i'n ddim ond targed i bob ffon a phêl ar y cae o'r cychwyn cyntaf. Bob prynhawn Iau, byddwn yn mynd adref yn ddrwg fy hwyl, yn gleisiau i gyd, ac yn melltithio'r gêm. Yn fuan iawn dechreuais ffugio bod gennyf ben tost un wythnos, poen yn fy mol yr wythnos wedyn, cric yn fy nghefn wedyn, a phob math o esgusodion dychmygol cyffelyb. Dewisais fynd i'r "detention", ac aros yn yr ysgol bob prynhawn Iau, i wneud gwaith digon di-fudd yn aml, ond byddai'n well na rhynnu'n gleisiog ar y cae chwarae - a dydw i ddim yn meddwl bod Cymru wedi colli seren ym myd hoci!

Diwrnod y mabolgampau wedyn. Tair ras oedd eithaf fy nghyrhaeddiadau i - y ras cario ŵy (tseina) ar lwy, y ras ffetau, a'r ras dair troed - "rasus ffyliaid" yn ôl y sawl a gymerai'r mabolgampau ormod o ddifri, ond dyna fe, i'r categori hwnnw y disgynnwn i, a hynny'n ddigon teg! Ond yno hefyd yr oedd yr hwyl.

Achlysur arall a roddai gyfle i ni gael ein sbort diniwed fyddai ymweliad y triawd llinynnol a'r ysgol, triawd a ddôi ar eu rhawd unwaith y flwyddyn. Tair merch tua chanol oed, yn broffesiynol iawn eu crefft a'u dawn, - ond dyna oedd y drwg wrth gwrs. Roedden nhw'n rhy broffesiynol i rywun wedi'i fagu ar gerddoriaeth cyfarfodydd cystadleuol pentref bach Aberarth, a doeddwn i, na fawr o neb arall, yn gallu gwerthfawrogi fel y dylem ni. Felly, bachu sedd gefn amdani, a gwneud ein hwyl ein hunain. Cyfle arall a gollwyd!

Cinio ysgol wedyn. Hanner coron oedd ei bris am wythnos gyfan, a chinio da fyddai hefyd, rhywbeth gwahanol bob dydd, ond pinacl y wythnos, y cinio rhost ar Ddydd Mawrth. Byddai disgwyl i ni'r merched helpu gyda'r clirio lan a'r golchi llestri, pawb i wneud ei ran yn ei dro. Ysgwyd y lliain fyddai'r gwaith yr anelai Mair a minnau amdano bob amser. Byddai hynny'n golygu cael mynd allan, diflannu o'r golwg rownd y gornel, ac wrth ysgwyd, taflu'r lliain am ben y bechgyn, - a thalu'n ddrud am hynny! Am hwyl! Erbyn i ni orffen gyda'r lliain, byddai'r golchi llestri wedi'i wneud!

Ond yr oedd yno un peth yn yr ysgol y byddwn i wrth fy modd gydag ef - y 'Steddfod. Fe rois fy ngorau i'r 'Steddfod, nid ym myd canu ac adrodd (am na allwn i wneud un o'r ddau beth) ond ym mhob agwedd arall arni. Byddai'n 'steddfod dda, a'r cystadlaethau yn amrywiol iawn, yn rhoi cyfle i bawb, beth bynnag eu talent. I dŷ Tanyfron y perthynwn i, a gallwn lafarganu'r hen gri (digon di-ystyr, hyd y gwn i) -

"Swm, Swm, Saca,

Swm, Swm, Se,

Bwshaba, Bwshaba,

Bwshaba, Be........."

gystal â neb heddiw. 'Rwyf wedi bod yn rhan o lawer 'steddfod ysgol ers hynny, ond welais i erioed y fath frwdfrydedd heintus ag oedd yn 'steddfod ysgol Aberaeron yn fy amser i, a'r tri goliwog, - glas, melyn a phiws, gwyn a gwyrdd, yn crafangu eu ffordd fesul deg marc i fyny'r ffrâm bren yn Neuadd Goffa'r dre i sŵn bonllefau gwallgo..., a'r marciau am ennill y gadair, a'r gystadleuaeth gorawl, fel arfer yn penderfynu tynged y tai ar diwedd y noson. Methu'n lân ag ymlacio. Na chysgu noson y 'steddfod, a'r llais yn gryg fore trannoeth!

Un cyfaddefiad bach arall. Mae yna goeden yn ymyl yr ysgol, a phedair llythyren wedi'u cerfio yn ddwfn i'w bôn (wedi'u cerfio ryw brynhawn Iau pan ddylai Mair a minnau fod ar y cae hoci, neu yn y "detention"!). Maent wedi'u cerfio fel eu bod yn edrych yr un fath ar draws ac ar hyd, fel hyn -

M. J. (Mair Jones)

J. W. (Joan Williams)

Roedd y peth yn hollol anfwriadol. Digwyddiad oedd y cyfan, ond ar y pryd, meddyliem ni ein bod wedi cyflawni camp fathemategol fawr! Rydw i'n gwybod yn iawn ble mae'r goeden. Dd'weda i ddim wrth neb chwaith, ond os caf gyfle i fynd i un o gyfarfodydd dathlu'r canmlwyddiant, fe af i edrych amdani, dim ond i weld faint mae'r llythrennau wedi pylu, neu a ydynt wedi diflannu'n llwyr bellach. Wedi'r cyfan maen nhw yno ers dros hanner can mlynedd! Rhyw ymgais at anfarwolaeth plentynaidd oedd y cymhelliad wrth gwrs.

Ydy, mae'r hen ysgol wedi newid. Mae hi'n llawer mwy o faint nag oedd hi yn fy amser i; mae'r cyfleusterau yn well, mae'n siwr; fe ddysgir llawer mwy o bynciau ynddi, - ond do, cefais innau addysg dda yno, gan athrawon ymroddedig, cydwybodol, heb i ryw dermau dyrys fel cwricwlwm, asesu, proffiliau, gwerthuso, a chant a mil o rai tebyg, hofran uwch fy mhen. Cefais lawer o hwyl a sbri yno hefyd, ac mae'r cofion yn felys.

Rhwydd hynt i'r hen ysgol, ei staff, a'i disgyblion i'r dyfodol.

❖

Diwrnod yr agorwyd y rheilffordd yn Aberaeron
Opening of the railway at Aberaeron
Mis Mai / May 1911

Gorsaf Felinfach / Felinfach Station

Plant y Trên

Morfudd Davies

Daw atgofion di-ri yn ôl i mi wrth feddwl am fy nyddiau ysgol. Cyn amser y trên bach a redai o Aberaeron i Lambed, arhosai'r rhan fwyaf o'r plant a ddeuai o'r ardaloedd rai milltiroedd o'r dre mewn "lodgings" ar hyd yr wythnos, ac yna mynd adref ar Nos Wener. A dyna'r patrwm i lawer, hyd yn oed yn y tridegau. Ond 'roedd gennym ni, y plant a oedd yn byw ar hyd Ddyffryn Aeron, ac ymhellach i fyny mor bell â Llambed, y trên bach i'n cludo. Dyna'r darlun a ddaw gyntaf i'm cof.

'Roedd y "bach" yn cyfleu ei faint, a'r anwyldeb a deimlem tuag ato, gan ei hawlio fel rhywbeth a berthynai i "ni" yn unig. Dau gerbyd a oedd iddo, injan i'w dynnu a fan y gard o'r tu ôl. Byddai iddo ddreifer wrth gwrs, taniwr i luchio'r glo i'r ffwrnais er mwyn creu stêm, a gard. Dyma enwau rhai o'r gweithwyr a oedd yn cael eu hadnabod wrth eu galwedigaeth neu enw eu cartrefi. Mae gen i gof da am Dai Griffiths y dreifer (a thad Stewart a Gordon), Jones Orenza a John Evans (tanwyr), Williams y Gard a Roach.

'Roedd yna "halt" neu "holt", fel y byddem yn ei galw, bob rhyw ddwy neu dair milltir rhwng y ddwy dref. Safai Trewynt lle 'roeddwn i'n byw rhyw dri lled cae yn uwch na phentref Felinfach, a byddai Mam yn gweiddi arnaf i, i frysio pan welai hi'r trên yn Hendrelas â'i fwg gwyn yn esgyn i'r entrychion ac ymledu i lawr y dyffryn i Ystrad a chymysgu â'r tarth a godai o'r afon.

Ar fore oer a'r barrug gwyn dros y caeau, y coed yn sgleinio a'n bysedd yn rhewi, caem loches gynnes yn swyddfa fechan Bill Richards a oedd â gofal y stesion. Bu Richards (fel y galwem ef) mor garedig i ni a'n gadael i heidio o amgylch y stôf haearn ar ganol y llawr. Bu i ddireidi heintus beri i ni chwarae triciau ar Richards ond yr oedd ef wedi codi'n ddigon bore, a gofalai dalu'r hen geiniog yn ôl! Byddem yn cuddio ei fflag werdd neu hongian hysbyseb neu farddoniaeth ddwl ar y wal. Ond un bore, pan ddaeth y trên i fewn i stesion Ystrad (nid "holt" 'mo hon) 'roedd fy mag ysgol a'm holl lyfrau ar goll! Er chwilio'n wyllt, 'doedd dim ohonynt i'w gweld. Rhaid oedd cychwyn ar y trên yn ddigon diflas. Ond wrth droi'r tro, dyma'r trên yn arafu a chychwyn yn ôl yn araf - neu "shynto" fel y dywedem. Wrth gyrraedd yn ôl yn y stesion, dyna lle'r oedd Richards a'r fflag werdd yn ei law, yn dal fy mag ysgol uwch ei ben!

Nid dyna'r tro cyntaf na'r tro olaf i'r trên bach wneud hyn, oherwydd byddai ambell blentyn neu'i gilydd wedi cysgu'n hwyr a chyrraedd rhyw eiliad neu ddwy ar ôl i'r trên gychwyn am Aberaeron. Gwnai aros hefyd i ambell wraig luddedig a gariai fasgedaid o fenyn ar ei braich ar ei ffordd i'r dre. Diolch am garedigrwydd y gweithwyr yn y tridegau. Nid yr un rheolau oedd yn bodoli â rhai B.R.! 'Doedd dim trên yn cychwyn yn ôl i Lambed tan 5.25 y prynhawn. Sut fyddem ni yn treulio'n hamser o 4 o'r gloch? O, nage, nid yn gwneud ein gwaith cartref, gallwch fentro! Dyna hwyl oedd chwarae o gwmpas yr ystafelloedd, yn dawnsio yn y neuadd (y llyfrgell yn awr) a'r bechgyn yn rhedeg o gwmpas fel ceffylau. O bryd i'w gilydd byddai'r glanhawyr, wrth reswm, yn cael digon o'r ffwlbri ac yn cwyno wrth y Prifathro, Mr. Howell T. Evans. Bore trannoeth byddem yn cael siars gan Mr. Evans i ymddwyn yn well neu.....

Pan ddeuai tywydd oer a gwlyb y Gaeaf, trefnai fy rhieni i mi aros am ryw ddau neu dri mis gyda ffrindiau i'r teulu yn y dre gan fod rhyw hanner milltir gen i gerdded yn y tywyllwch i'm cartref. Ar fore Llun, byddai mam yn llanw basgedaid o fwyd - digon i barhau hyd ddiwedd yr wythnos. 'Roedd cymaint ohonom yn y dref fel bod cryn hwyl i'w gael. Byddem yn clymu edau ddu wrth gnociwr aml i ddrws a thynnu'r edau, yna rhedeg i ffwrdd cyn i neb ateb. Hen dric! Mae'n dda gen i ddweud i ni ymddwyn yn fwy gweddus fel y tyfem i fyny.

Daeth tro ar fyd, a newid mawr ym mhatrwm teithio gyda dyfodiad y bws. Cyrhaeddem ein cartrefi rhyw awr yng nghynt a chael pryd o fwyd yn gynnar ar ôl diwrnod hir. Ond rywfodd ac i raddau, fe gollwyd y gymdeithas glos a fu'n gymaint rhan o'n bywydau ar y trên bach.

Nid dyna'r cof olaf sydd gen i am y trên. Fe wnaeth chwibanu yr holl ffordd trwy'r dyffryn i'm cyfarch ar y diwrnod y priodais y gŵr a ddaeth, yn ddiweddarach, yn Brifathro ar ysgol Aberaeron.

Melys y cof.

THE EVACUEES

Tecwyn Jones (1941-45)

An evacuee:- "*a person transferred from a vulnerable to a safe area on account of air-raids.*" Everyday English Dictionary.

The evacuation of 1939 was a unique event in the history of Britain, and is ever likely to remain so, and the sudden arrival and involvement of evacuees from big cities in rural schools, was an experience, duly shared by Aberaeron County School. Whilst the evacuation is well documented in public records, few, if any, of the younger readers of this chapter will know anything about the exercise, or its participants whose own memories of it are fading fast. If only, therefore, to put it in proper context, it behoves me to give some background to my subject, which might, incidentally, help to secure for both the evacuees and the kind people of Ceredigion who took them in, some place in the annals of the School to which so many of us are grateful.

The Evacuation

The mass dispersal of civilians from London and Liverpool, and some other English cities, to more rural localities, including the countryside of Ceredigion, which officially began on 1st September 1939, was the largest, single organised relocation of people in the history of Britain. Together with the privately arranged evacuations of earlier summer months, it accounted for the movement of some three million people from areas thought to be prime targets for German bomber-raids. By the end of September, a quarter of the population of Great Britain had relocated, including 825,000 school children, 624,000 mothers with children under school age, 13,000 expectant mothers, 7,000 blind persons, and 113,000 school teachers.

It was an exercise of epic proportions, first conceived shortly after the end of World War I (1914-1918), when analyses of 103 German air-raids on London in 1918 showed, that the 300 tons of high explosives dropped on the city resulted in some 5,000 casualties and 1,400 deaths. Given Air-Ministry estimates that in a future war, enemy planes would drop 100 tons of high explosives on London on the first day, 75 tons on the second, and 50 tons per day for a further month, and with the further threat of horrendous poison-gas attacks, the defence of the country's population became a matter of paramount concern. The Government's Sub-Committee on Air Raid Precautions (ARP) was convened, in 1924, specifically to address this issue, using London as a model for all other vulnerable cities.

The Committee was pragmatic rather than altruistic. It recognised that in the event of war, London would be required to continue to supply the country's needs, and that anyone residing within it, whose presence might hinder the achievement of that objective, should be moved out, prior to the commencement of hostilities, so as to reduce the risks of casualties and confusion. Panic amongst the civilian population during air-raids was seen as a potentially serious problem, with the poorer people of East London (quite wrongly as events were to show) being seen as particularly likely to "flock from their houses" at the sound of sirens, and to be "driven mad with fright", on account of the emotionally unstable nature of their multi-ethnic communities! Looting of wealthier areas of London by the poor was another potential problem. It strengthened the view that in the event of war all residents of poorer areas should be evacuated - children and parents alike.

Nevertheless, evacuation priority was accorded to schoolchildren, not least because their schools would need to be commandeered for use as mobilisation centres for the armed forces and other services. But the logistical problem and costs of evacuating 1.2 million school children presented serious problems, and the Committee therefore recommended that only those from the poorer districts should be accommodated under the Government's evacuation programme. Those of wealthier areas were thought to have the means to arrange their own relocation. The view of the then Chief Inspector of Elementary Schools (H. H. Richards), was that children should remain in London in the event of war and face it out with the rest! Some concern was expressed about how children from the poorest areas might be received in country homes.

The Government's evacuation plan which ultimately embraced women, children, the aged and the helpless, was first made public in 1933, and under the auspices of the House of Commons Committee on Evacuation, convened in May 1938, an acceptable plan for the movement of all non-essential personnel from designated danger zones of London was finalised. This, using the railways, was thought to be capable of moving 4 million people out of the capital in 72 hours, and in order to ensure that the main railway termini were available and operational, the evacuation was to begin 72 hours before the start of hostilities. So it was, that the evacuation of schoolchildren from London and Liverpool began on 1st September. The Liverpudlian evacuees who arrived in Aberaeron and its environs on that day and the next, heard of the outbreak of World War II in the safety and strangeness of their foster homes.

The Evacuees

Those to be found in the catchment area of Aberaeron County School in September 1939 were mostly official evacuees from Liverpool, but there were a much smaller number of private evacuees, predominantly from London and the South-East. Most of these private individuals had been on holiday in the area during the summer, and with the outbreak of war had stayed on with relatives or, as in my case, with the unrelated families with whom they happened to be staying at the time. All of them had some knowledge of local culture and customs and were familiar, to varying degrees, with their surroundings and communities. They did not suffer critical cultural shock. Those who through blood-relatives had roots in the area, may have had some help in alleviating their "hiraeth", but without ever losing it or their anxiety over loved ones left in the danger zones of home cities. Other children who came as part of families, brought their home family environment with them, and they in common with all private evacuees, had some sense of security whilst they sought to integrate with, and were assimilated into, local communities.

This was not so, in the case of the official evacuees from Liverpool, who arrived late at night in local village schools and halls after a long and tiring journey into the unknown. As they huddled in small groups for mutual comfort, complete with their baggage-label name-tags tied to their jackets, their gas-masks in cardboard boxes strung around their necks, and clutching a small case of clothes and a few treasured possessions, they were bemused, bewildered and bereft of any sense of belonging. They were allocated to, or chosen by their future foster-parents, on the basis of age, gender, appearance, demeanour, and an instinctive assessment of compatibility which fortunately proved to be well-founded more often than not. However warm the welcome, their lot was a sad one!

Many of them came from that kind of abject poverty that is only to be found in the slums of major cities, and as Glynne Jones of Glynaeron (1943-49) reminds us, "We thought that after the 1930s depression we could recognise poverty, but the arrival of those children from Liverpool opened our eyes to a new dimension of deprivation."

Most of them moved into foster homes with far better amenities, comfort and care than had been available to them at home. They enjoyed a better standard of living, were better clothed and fed, and led more wholesome lives. The majority flourished, and greatly enjoyed their new homes, lives and adventures, and responded well to the "croeso" of caring Ceredigion people, whose unspoken message to these small children, in the words of the musical "Oliver", were to "consider yourself at home, consider yourself part of the family."

Nevertheless, they suffered a severe cultural shock. They missed city amenities such as electric light, public transport, Saturday morning cinema, radio entertainment, tinned food and, of course, their native tongue. But, despite all attempts to replace it, what they missed above all else was their mother's love. Only those who experienced this loss can know the depth of despair and heartache it brought.

The vast majority of evacuees in the Aberaeron area in 1939, both official and private, were of primary school age, and very few qualified then for secondary education. Most, therefore, spent a year or so at local village schools and it is my impression that evacuees did not become a significant proportion of the pupil population of Aberaeron County until 1941. It was only in September of that year that the School had to take action to accommodate a sizeable, English-speaking, monolingual contingent, unwilling, for understandable reasons, to study Welsh as a second language. It was this that led to the replacement of Forms 2A and 2B, with 2W (Welsh) and 2F (French) in 1941 - a fashion that lasted less than two years.

What was particularly significant was that by the time these evacuees enrolled at Aberaeron, they had already spent a considerable time in very Welsh village schools, and had absorbed a great deal of Welsh culture. Their impact at Aberaeron County, as representatives of a foreign (English) culture, was therefore far less than might otherwise have been expected. They came with a somewhat diluted version of their native background. Their effect on the School was further reduced by the fact that, those with strongest English cultural backgrounds, i.e. the official evacuees from Liverpool, stayed only briefly at Aberaeron. To the best of my knowledge, virtually all Liverpudlian evacuees who enrolled in 1941, or earlier, returned home in 1942/43, like so many others, at the time when their home cities were free from air-raids. Only the private evacuees stayed on until 1945 or later, and it is only from within their number that contributions to this chapter have been forthcoming.

First Impressions

Christopher Sewell, who came to Aberaeron County from a boys only public school (Bedford), recalls how he was at first repelled by the strangeness and Welshness of it all. Such was his unhappiness in those early days, that he resorted to dipping his clinical thermometer in hot water to feign fever, and having done so frequently enough, he succeeded in getting himself withdrawn from School for private tutoring. Boredom, however, caused him to return, and as the strangeness faded, and the welcome and confidence of fellow pupils grew, peer friendships and camaraderie brought him great joy and happiness.

My first day at Aberaeron County was an unmitigated disaster! I set off on my bicycle on the five-mile journey from Rhiwbren Fawr, on that sunny September morn in 1941, crowned with my new blue and red-ringed school cap, which cost 5s.4d, and was my pride and joy. Four hundred yards later it was reduced to ribbons! I had foolishly used my cap to protect my hands whilst releasing a terrified, white and tabby tom-cat from a gin trap in a hedgerow of Cae Cabbage. The poor animal had torn my cap to shreds with the claws of its three free feet, and as it scurried three-leggedly away, I cried.

When I arrived at school I was accosted by a formidable be-spectacled lady, who I later came to know as Miss Elaine Lewis, who, having ascertained that I was a "new" boy, said, "Where's your cap?" "In my satchel", I replied. "Then wear it," she said as she walked off. I didn't wear it then, and I never wore it ever again. Home repairs that night reduced my cap to a shapeless mass, not unlike a patch-work quilt with a peak, and I burnt it.

From the front row at Morning Prayers in the Hall, to a background of "Efengyl tangnefedd" I stared in awe at a gown-clad row of stern-faced teachers, and with a logic that defies analysis, I decided I liked the good-looking ladies (Miss Davies and Joan Evans), and didn't like the master with a green gown (J. T. Owen) nor the big bald man who looked like a policeman (W. J. Jones) and the pianist (Elaine Lewis) was someone to be avoided at all costs!! Suddenly Howell Evans, the headmaster, dismissed all pupils except we newcomers, and then by calling out names from a list, and shouting either "2F" or "2W", he despatched all, except four of us, to the care of Prefects. We four who remained, were told that as our home Education Authorities did not recognise us as official evacuees, we could only enrol on payment of fees of £2.13s.4d per term (an absolute fortune it seemed) but, on the promise of payment, we were despatched to Form 2F in the wood-work room.

During the exceptionally long morning break, my aimless playground wanderings brought me close to a group of young men and women of Forms V and VI. The "boys" were giants in long trousers (fel cewri) and the "girls" were bosomed (fel menywod) and I never imagined then, that I would ever become a member of such a sophisticated and mature group. (When indeed I did reach Form V, the boys had all shrunk, the girls' bosoms had diminished, and we seemed totally devoid of any trace of sophistication and maturity! We were just Form V). I listened attentively to loud and learned, but totally unintelligible, conversations. Some claimed to be "sitting higher this year", but no-one apparently was doing the opposite! Some, obviously from farming backgrounds, talked of "sheep and goats" and of "ploughing physics". A small group of budding Einsteins were busily using half-pennies to elucidate the mysteries of the laws of chance in the form of "odds and evens". Others, presumably with seafaring connections, talked of "pitch and toss", and one small group departed for some mystical destination referred to as "up woodbine lane."

At school lunch I had some "cawl" with a slug in it, followed by a meal of partially cooked potatoes and detestable cabbage, the taste of which even cold, hard prunes and custard failed to dispel. I dashed down to town to buy a bottle of radiant blue ink, and for Geography a 2s.6d box of crayons, only to have the latter stolen later in the day by a fellow evacuee, who was quick enough to write his name on the box and so deny my ownership of it during an inquest convened by Miss Clayton. I then went to buy books, priced by staff, from older pupils, and was persuaded by Glyn Jenkins to buy his empty stamp album for 8d. I resold it within minutes to Sydney Little for 1s.4d. This transaction resulted in a very angry Glyn Jenkins, and a profit to me of either a copy of Treasure Island, or a bottle of dandelion and burdock and a packet of Osbourne biscuits available at "Siop Botel Ink" at the top of Vicarage Hill. I chose the latter.

I was caught by the Form IV press gang and ducked under a cold tap in the gym, which left me with a soaking wet collar for the rest of the day and caused me to lose my voice! All in all, I was not pleased with the day's events, and after school, as I pushed my bike up that interminable hill at Neuaddlwyd, I slowly collected my thoughts.

I was elated by the novelty of learning, Chemistry, Biology, Geometry, French and Latin, and excited by the prospects at Aberaeron. But what struck me above all else about my new school, was the Englishness of it all. No-one, within my hearing at least, had uttered a word of Welsh since the dying strains of "Efengyl tangnefedd". I had been instructed, taught and otherwise addressed exclusively in English all day, and my inadvertent lapses into Welsh had been steadfastly ignored as if to indicate that Welsh had gone out of fashion! I had no problem with English as such, it was the first language, but I missed the companionship which the more familiar and warmer words of Welsh seemed to engender. After two years at Mydroilyn Council School I was wrongly attuned to the Aberaeron medium of communication. 'Roedd hiraeth arnaf am yr Ysgol ym Mydroilyn a'r hen iaith roeddwn i newydd ei dysgu! Tomorrow I thought might be a better day — and it and all the other tomorrows for the next four years, were indeed much better.

Lasting Impressions

Margaret Cockburn (née Jones) whose first experience of a co-ed school was Aberaeron (and caused her some early apprehensions) was proud like many others to follow in her parents' footsteps and, like them, to be taught by W. J. Jones (Bottle). She, like all of us, did not welcome the school-imposed curfew, which required us to be indoors by a given time each evening. She loved the Club, and her general impression of her days at School are "of a very happy time", and are strongly echoed by Thirza Laloo (née Lewis). To Milwen Evans (née Davies), Aberaeron County was a haven of security and stability, at a time when her life, like that of all other evacuees, had been turned upside-down. She got in by the back-door when the School was full, and is eternally grateful as Aberaeron, she believes, stood her in good stead for launching out into the world after the war. It is her view that her "years at Aberaeron were invaluable for instilling in me a sense of value, sense of fun and generally giving me an optimistic view of the future." Like a lot of others, Milwen acknowledges the quality of W. A. Jones' teaching, and attributes her enduring love of poetry to him. Alun Morgan (David Alun Jenkin in full) echoes these sentiments, and recalls how his "sense of joy and happiness at school helped him to forget his evacuee anxieties for the family in London, and his hiraeth for home." He particularly enjoyed the "great sense of belonging which the School engendered — belonging to a harmonious unit exemplified especially by the Club and reflected to this very day by the success of the 1939/45 Reunions." He has vivid memories of Aberaeron's own Mr . Chips (W. J. Jones), that teacher supreme (W. A. Jones) and Mr Fox "who taught us our Amo, Amas, Amat without ever conveying any sense of love, especially to the boys." Alun refers with deep affection to his "partner-in-crime and all else", the late Tom James, beloved of so many, and who contributed so much to the sense of fun which pervades Alun's reflections, "without ever diminishing our dedication to lessons and to upholding the proud academic record of our School." Memories of the Club are prominent in Alun's reminiscences with its mock trials, charades and staff impersonations led by John Raymond Jenkins, and it seems that "extra-curricular amorous assignations in the Memorial Hall Cinema, under constant threat of discovery by Bottle sitting in the elevated rear seats", have not yet been forgotten.

Glenys Pashley (née Ball), who joined 2B in 1940, remembers with affection the School choirs, especially male voice renditions of the "Soldiers' Chorus" and even more vividly, the poetry and recitation for which the School was renowned, and to which she in her native English, contributed. She, like many of us, regretted the subject options (presumably a result of staff shortages) which obliged us to choose between History and Physics, Biology and Chemistry, and in the case of girls between Maths and Domestic Science, when many of us had equal interests in both options of the above pairs. Glenys recalls a confused lesson on the flora of Australia given by Miss Clayton which led an unnamed class-mate to write in his note-book, "The eucalyptus tree, instead of losing its leaves in Winter, it barks."

She refers to Bottle's punctuality - which Jones Bach, at Bottle's farewell party, strenuously denied, saying that being 20 minutes early, as Bottle inevitably was, was not being punctual! Glenys loved the Club, but like me, hated the School dinners. She wrote a clever disparaging poem to make her point.

This is the dinner the children hate
And so do I,
When they lose their place, if they get in late,
And the bread is dry;
And the teachers in charge do nothing but scold,
And the dinner by then is almost cold,
And the boys put the tables away as they're told,
And all the girls have the cloths to fold,
And so do I.

On her return to school in Surrey, she apparently told the staff there, that whilst the teaching at her new Surrey school was excellent, "the staff are not as friendly and it isn't nearly as much fun as my old school in Aberaeron."

If anyone had fun at Aberaeron, despite for ever bring in some kind of trouble, it was the late Geofrey Hughes (who died this June) better known by the name of "Sunshine", bestowed on him by Joan Evans. Harold Robinson recalls the occasion when the Form was discussing the "Passing of Arthur", and when W. A. Jones asked the class to explain how Arthur (who had been betrayed in battle) "lay like a shattered column", Geof's prompt response was "The Fifth Column, Sir!" (a war-time threat of infiltrated German spies).

Christopher Sewell's lasting memories include camaraderie in an atmosphere which was devoid of bullying, fostered friendship, and taught us how to get on together. He recalls the lunch-time sing-songs while standing on desks in classrooms, the Club, in which of course he played a major role, if only as a vigorous advocate in mock-trials. He is unequivocal in his judgement that his time at Aberaeron were "the happiest days of my life", and he attributes his subsequent success as a specialist teacher to the "teenage peer group cooperation that was so prominent at Aberaeron."

As for me, Aberaeron County was the focus of my life for the whole time I was there. Splendid as my life was in many ways on an isolated large farm in Mydroilyn, it was only at school that I had the companionship of peer groups and contemporary friends with whom I could share pleasure and pain, and in whom I could confide my innermost thoughts, my mischief and make-believe. Aberaeron County was the focus of my social life and, except on Fridays which began with a double Maths period, I couldn't wait to get to School, to learn, to love and to have fun. Like Alun and the rest, I had a great sense of belonging, and the School was small enough and so closely knit, as to create and sustain a strong family feeling. This grew as one progressed, not only between classmates but also between pupils and those members of staff including Mair Fach, Joan Evans, Olive John, Nesta Lewis, Miss Clayton, Bottle and Jones Bach, who were endowed with empathy which shone through even their sternest exterior. There was a warmth which I welcomed, and a caring which I cherished, and now fifty years on, I can confirm my earlier conclusion that Aberaeron County greatly enriched my life. It was to me, as an evacuee, a surrogate family which brought me greatly valued happiness.

Our Contributions to the School

Did we evacuees give anything in return? I believe that individually, rather than as a discrete group, we did contribute something of value. We brought our own peculiar views and, unconsciously perhaps, our own philosophies. We had an independence, albeit enforced, and our own interpretations - so often appreciated by Jones Bach, and we had our talents. Ivor and Glyn Jenkins were, with others, forever academically prominent, Sidney Little (ex Liverpool and New Quay), whose father was said to have been the first merchant seaman to be killed by enemy action in World War II, was a talented footballer as well as a scholar. Bridgette Webb, Glenys Ball and Christopher Sewell were accomplished poets. Alun and others excelled at sport, and one evacuee sang well enough at least to win the junior and senior boys' solos at the School Eisteddfod for Tanyfron!! Who can forget Ivor Jenkins' winning short address on the "Ideal School" at the Eisteddfod, or Christopher's vigorous rendering of Gunga Din especially when he unconsciously transcribed the "u" and the "e" in that wonderful sentence, "Here's a beggar with a bullet through his spleen." One evacuee, Freddie Nolan (ex Liverpool and Mydroilyn) even brought the wonderment of a physical freak! He could, as a result of being double-jointed we were told, bring his arms with his hands tightly clenched over his head from back to front and vice-versa. We also did our bit for Flight 1511 of the Air Training Corps, when Evan Watkin of Ceri House, Ffos-y-Ffin, was judged to be the best morse operator, and I was selected as a member of the boxing team to meet the Swansea Grammar ATC (a contest which, I'm pleased to say, was cancelled - iach yw wyneb cachgi!!).

I can claim to have made one other valuable contribution to the local community, in the form of a scapegoat, when I and others were called to task for mischief! Without anyone to speak in my defence, certain over-protective parents all too frequently succeeded in branding me as the "root of the evil", and I suffered the caning consequences. Following one such occasion, when my spirits were exceptionally low, and as I, with Aberaeron-instilled courtesy said "Prynhawn da" to the Reverend Thomas of Arfryn, Llwyncelyn, it all came to a head. "Prynhawn da, 'machgen i", dywedodd ef, "ac o ble ydych chwi'n dod?" "O Rhiwbren Fawr", ddywedes i. "O, da iawn", dywedodd Thomas, "a beth yw'ch enw?" "Tecwyn", ddywedes i. "Tecwyn beth?", gofynnodd yr hen bregethwr. "Tecwyn gwreiddyn y drwg, by all accounts!", oedd fy ateb wrth frysio bant.

Two evacuees who came sadly remain forever. Walter Ainsley, a class-mate from London, who died from meningitis in 1943, was put to rest after a School funeral at Henfynyw, and James Minney, who came as a youngster and stayed on after the war and attended Aberaeron County in the late 1940s, and was accidentally drowned in the Aeron in 1951, was buried following another school funeral at Cilcennin.

Local Impressions of Us

But what did the locals think of us? I leave it to Aneurin Jones, then of Aberarth, who joined the School in September 1939, (proudly wearing his blue and red-ringed cap), to comment in his own generous and inimitable way. Following a poetic account of his first day at School and the joys and tribulations of the months that follow, which deserves exposure elsewhere in the annals of our School, he has the following to say about the "Newydd-Ddyfodiaid" (Newcomers).

"Plant o bant oedd rhain; y mwyafrif o'r dref ac o ddiddorbeb mawr i ni'r brodorion. Rhai oeddynt o brofiad a chefndir gwahanol ond eto â'u gwreiddiau'n gadarn ym mhridd Ceredigion. Rhieni llawer ohonynt wedi ymfudo i'r trefi mawr, ac agor busnes, ond yn parhau i ddod nôl yn gyson am dro bach a gwyliau yn aml. 'Roedd y Gymraeg yn gryf ar eu gwefusau.

Efallai fod arwyddocâd yn yr enwau. Pwy fentrai olrhain yr achau a gwahaniaethu rhwng Alun, Ifor, Emrys, Tecwyn, Gwen, a Milwen, Rhiannon, Hywel, Siencyn ac Aneurin?

Beth bynnag, cwrdd a chymysgu'n ebrwydd a wnaethpwyd. Lledaenwyd ein gorwelion ni, a llyfnwyd tueddiadau trefol ein cyfeillion newydd. O fewn dim, disgyblion ysgol Aberaeron oeddem oll - pa waeth o ble daethom! Crewyd a chadarnhawyd cyfeillgarwch sydd wedi goroesi hyd heddiw. Pan gwrddwn nawr yn ein haduniad flynyddol daw ddoe 'nôl ar unwaith. "Ti a tithe" yw hi, a daw'r un atgofion gwerthfawr i gof pawb.

Cyrhaeddodd sawl carfan arall y cylch, ond fe'u cadwyd ar wahân. Daeth y "Nautical School" i'r Cei, a mawr fu'r cystadlu ar y cae chwarae a'r maes caru. Prin fu'r cysylltiadau parhaol, er fod un o'r bechgyn heddiw yn gyfaill mynwesol. Cyrhaeddodd Catholigion o Lerpwl, ond gan nad oeddynt yn mynychu'r un tŷ cwrdd na'r un ysgol â ni, does fawr o gof amdanynt. Tipyn o gecran, cyfnewid ambell begen a dyna'i gyd.

Ond am y gweddill! Gwacach o lawer fyddai 'mywyd i wedi bod hebddynt. Anodd meddwl am fod heb adnabod Harold ac Emrys, Thirza a llu eraill. Braint oedd cael blas eich cwmni - ddoe a heddiw. Diolch am gyfoethogi 'mywyd, lledu 'ngorwelion ac am gyfeillgarwch trylwyr a theyrngar. Diolch hefyd am lu o atgofion gwerthfawr."

Aneurin's sentiments are most sincerely reciprocated by we, the evacuees. We were grateful to be so warmly welcomed, and privileged to be accepted as integral members of the School community. We were indebted for the company and friendship we then enjoyed, and we remain so as these friendships endure. Our horizons were widened, our experiences enhanced, and our lives enriched, and as a result, perhaps we, in our own modest way, contributed with hundreds of thousands of other evacuees, on our return home, to changing the face of the nation. It is claimed that the enlightening experiences of armed forces personnel were the major cause of social change in post-war Britain. If this is so, then how much did the new visions of wealth and well-being experienced by the deprived and poor "have not" evacuees of Liverpool and London also contribute to the changing Britain of post-war years?

The social effects of the evacuation on the evacuees and those who took them in is incalculable. How many of us would have pursued our chosen careers had we not spent our formative years at Aberaeron? Would I have become a biologist, had I not been removed from the barren city to the fascination and delights of the countryside? I doubt it!

Epitaph

All this reminiscing has brought a host of ghosts of the past walking through my mind. I see a big man wearing a high-crowned, broad-brimmed trilby and a calf-length buttoned-up raincoat closely fitted over sloping shoulders, whose silhouette, when so attired, led to his nickname "Bottle" (but which would surely otherwise have been "Gentleman Jones.") I hear that teacher *par excellence* telling me that "There is no such word in the English language as "Byyer." I see the long-limbed Miss Hughes who could deliver a resounding "bonclust" with unerring accuracy even to those sitting at desks close to the class-room walls, whilst maintaining that "I've never heard anything like it in all my born days" (on what other days could she possibly have heard anything I wondered?). I am aware of the hunched over figure of John Ten, with his hands deep in his trouser pockets and his face pushed into mine, telling me yet again "Bachgen, 'rwyt ti'n llosgi o felltith!"

But let those and other ghosts prevail. Whilst bringing me heartache as I try in vain to recapture my youth, they also cause me to smile, and I welcome them, as I recall so vividly fond memories of a School to which all of us evacuees owe so much and say **Diolch yn fawr iawn**.

❖

A.T.C. Football Team 1942-1943
Gethin Williams, Tommy Lloyd, Iorwerth Roberts, Owen Lewis, Dewi O. Evans, Gomer Jones, John Merrell, Griff Jones, Maldwyn Price, Freddie Davies, Victor Hubbard, Aneurin Hopkins. (Absent - Stuart Griffiths)

1511 Squadron A.T.C.

1511 Squadron A.T.C.

Dosbarth Chwech / Sixth Form
c. 1945

Cyfnod y Rhyfel / Wartime

COFIA

Aneurin Jones (Aberarth) 1939 - 45

Cychwyn

Hynod o fyw yw f'atgofion am fore o hwyr Fedi yn 1939 - un o'r boreau lleddf a llaith hynny sy'n argoeli Hydref. Roedd byd natur fel petai'n herio gorthrwm y gaeaf a phobl Prydain gyfan yn paratoi i wrthsefyll her Hitler.

Safem ar y bont yn Aberarth. Gorchuddiai carthen o darth y cwm cul gydag ambell goeden yn mentro'i brig i'r awyr gan golli'i dail olaf yn yr ymdrech. Roedd pawb a phopeth yn stond yn disgwyl yr annisgwyliadwy.

Disgwyl y bws, oeddwn i, ar fy more cyntaf yn yr "ysgol fawr". Roedd 'na dwr bach ohonom - y rhai newydd yn amlwg dawel. Gwisgwn gap coch a glas cylchog, newydd sbon - satchel newydd ar un ysgwydd a'r mwgwd nwy, mewn bocs papur caled, ar y llall. Yn glos atom 'oedd aelodau'r ail flwyddyn, i gyd yn brofiadol gegog a llawn chwerthin wrth ddatgan yn uchel fod "uffern o dapio yn ein haros." Ychydig i'r naill ochr, safai'r bechgyn a'r merched hŷn yn trafod pethau pwysig yn awdurdodol dros ben. Roeddem ni'r moch bach a'r clustiau mawr, yn clywed sôn am athrawon ag enwau od megis "Bottle", "Carbon" a "John Ten". Gwae ni rhag croesi "Fox". Siaradent yn ddoeth am brisio llyfrau, pwy fyddai yn Nhyglyn, neu un o'r tai eraill, ac am orfod bod yn tŷ erbyn saith o'r gloch neu gael "Report" gan un o'r bodau pwysig hynny - y Prefects.

Bu'n haf hirfelyn heulog a hynod. Cafwyd gwyliau hwy nag arfer am nad oedd adeiladau newydd yr ysgol yn barod. Roedd "yr ysgol fawr" 'nawr yn fwy - wedi dyblu ei maint ers pan y bum ynddi - oes yn ôl - yn sefyll arholiad yr ysgoloriaeth. 'Nawr, cynhwysai rywbeth rhyfedd o'r enw "y gym". Yn mynnu tarfu ar ein meddyliau - hyd yn oed heddiw - oedd y ffaith ddiflas, ond gwefreiddiol, ein bod yn rhyfela. Er mai cilddwr Ceredigion oedd ein cartref a'n bod ymhellach na neb arall o fygythiad yr Almaenwyr, roedd cwmwl pygddu, parhaol, yn gwgu arnom o'r gorwel.

Yn ystod y gwyliau, gwelwyd "y Territorials" yn gwibio'u gynnau o gyrchfan i gae neu glôs gerllaw. Roedd cadw sglein arnynt yn bwysicach na'u tanio. Fin nos, gwelid golau llachar "y searchlights" yn llwybro'r awyr, gan chwilio am reswm dros eu bodolaeth yn hytrach na gelyn. Llanwyd sachau â thywod i warchod ffenestri adeiladau cyhoeddus a disgynnodd blanced y "blacowt" i ddiffodd pob fflach o olau nosol. Prin oedd ein profiadau ni'r pryd hynny a 'doedd dim un o'r disgyblion, ar y bont yn Aberarth, yn sylweddoli y deuai i'w plith, yn go fuan, gyfeillion fyddai wedi clywed cyfarth y gynnau a gweld effaith eu cnoi. Mwg y magnelau fyddai eu niwl hwy ac adfeilion eu cartrefi fyddai'n gwthio trwy'r tarth gwenwynig.

Ond, pa ots am hynny heddiw! "Co'r bws yn dod!" - bws Crosville coch, gorlawn, i'n cludo i'n canolfan newydd. Wrth esgyn iddo, fe'n trawsnewidiwyd o fod yn "fois mawr" Aberarth i benbyliaid Aberaeron. 'Roedd awyrgylch y bws yn llethol - yn llawn sŵn, sawr ac ansicrwydd. Talu ceiniog i'r "conductor", clywed rhagor o sôn slei am erchyllderau oedd yn ein haros ac yna disgyn o flaen y "Feathers" yn Aberaeron. Wedyn, ymdoddi'n rhan anhysbys o'r neidr Navy Blue oedd yn igamogamu'i ffordd i fyny'r "Path" i grombil yr adeilad dieithr ac enfawr oedd ar fron y bryn.

I mewn trwy'r drws cadarn â ni, i ganol dwndwr anesmwyth y rhai hyderus o'r Cei ac Aberaeron. Rheiny'n adnabod llawer a ninnau'n nabod nemor neb 'nawr, am fod plant mwy, a mwyaf Aberarth, wedi eu cornelu gan eu cyfeillion ac yn clebran gymaint byth am bethau cwbl ddieithr i ni'r newydd-ddyfodiaid. Cofiaf un crwt o'r Cei yn cyhoeddi'n groch fod mwstas gan un o'r athrawon newydd a bod yr athrawes Ddaearyddiaeth newydd yn "smasher". Deallais, yn glau, ei fod yn gywir.

Sylwais ar ddyn tal, llwyd ei wedd, mewn clogyn du, yn sefyll yn y "corridor". Roedd golwg ddifrifol garedig arno gyda hanner gwên fel petai'n ceisio gwawrio ar ei wyneb a chuddio'i ddannedd ar yr un pryd. Cyfarchai hwn a'r llall ac, er syndod i mi, gwyddai enw bedydd pob un o'r ugeiniau oedd yn tyrru o'i gylch. Amlwg hefyd oedd y parch tuag ato. Feddylies i erioed y byddai hwn mor flaenllaw yn f'atgofion dros hanner canrif yn y dyfodol. Dyma Mr. Chips Ysgol Aberaeron; wedi buddsoddi ei fywyd iddi ac, am byth, yn rhan anhepgor ohoni i bob un fu'n ddigon ffodus i'w adnabod. Mae pob athro da yn haeddu llysenw. Roedd gan hwn dri a does dim angen atgoffa neb beth oeddynt. Iddo ef, roedd dau beth, digon diniwed, yn gwbl atgas - dwylo mewn pocedi a rhedeg ar hyd yr ysgol. Cofiaf, am byth, y diwrnod oer pan welodd fi'n rhedeg, a'm dwylo'n ddwfn ym mhocedi'r trowsus byr oedd, y pryd hynny, yn dderbyniol wisg i fechgyn iau'r ysgol. Roedd hi'n oer a rhaid oedd croesi'r cwrt tennis, yn llygad y gwynt, cyn cyrraedd y toiledau yn "y gym". Wel, cefais gerydd un cymal nas anghofiaf byth. "You're no gentleman my boy!" Os nad oeddwn i, roedd e' - o'i goryn moel i sodlau'i 'sgidie sgleiniog.

Yn arswydus o sydyn, torrodd gorchymyn y gloch ar draws y dwndwr. A bu distawrwydd! Cloriannwyd ni i'r neuadd - ystafell oedd, i mi, yn enfawr. Yn wir, roedd hi bron cymaint ag ysgol gyfan Aberarth. Distawrwydd llethol 'nawr a sawl un mewn clogyn du yn swshian pob sibrwd a symud. Dacw'r drws pren cadarn yn agor a'r pwysicaf oll yn ymddangos - Y PRIFATHRO. Dilynodd ei glogyn du ef trwy'r drws. Safodd ar y llwyfan isel a syllodd arnom. Y tu ôl iddo 'roedd cerflun pren hardd, i gofio am aberth y Rhyfel Byd. Roedd f'ewythr Dai arno. O'i flaen, roeddem ni â gofid rhyfel byd arall. Rhoddwyd tonc ar y piano gan ddynes awdurdodol yr olwg mewn sbectol, a chanwyd emyn. Yna, gwasanaeth byr ac eglurhad hir am hyd anarferol y gwyliau. Minnau'n methu deall o hyd beth oedd "y gym" yna oedd ar dafod pawb. Roedd hyd yn oed y pwysicaf oll yn sôn amdano. Bant aeth pawb 'nawr, ond ni'r newydd-ddyfodiaid! Detholwyd ni i ddosbarthiadau 2A a 2B yn ôl ein perfformiad yn arholiad yr ysgoloriaeth. Beth ddigwyddodd i 1A a 1B tybed?

Pleth o atgofion yw gweddill y dydd - dysgu sut i godi cap a chyfarch athrawon yn barchus ar bob achlysur; deall bod rhaid newid 'sgidie bob tro y byddem yn gadael, neu'n dychwelyd, i'r adeilad; diodde'r tapio, digon diniwed, yn ystod y "break"......! Athro newydd, o'r enw W. M. Meredith, fu'n ein tywys trwy'r bore. Dyn tal, gosgeiddig, eisioes yn boblogaidd gan y merched, oedd W. M. M. Daethom oll i'w barchu a'i hoffi. Dirfawr ein siom pan ddaeth y newydd trist ei fod wedi'i ladd ar un o'r "Malta Convoys" erchyll hynny oedd yn rhan o'r newyddion dyddiol ar y pryd.

Llusgodd bore blinedig o hir heibio cyn mynd i lawr i'r Compton - ar ôl newid 'sgidie wrth gwrs - i gael cinio. Roedd criw bach ohonom yno yn ceisio sicrhau'n siâr o'r bara menyn a'r "prune jam" oedd o'n blaen. Cyn hir, caem gynnig cawl, digon diflas, yn yr ysgol ac yna, ginio llawn wedi ei baratoi dan law a gofal Mrs. Lloyd. Sut y llwyddodd hi a'i "helpers" i gynhyrchu cystal bwyd - yn enwedig y pwdin reis - mewn cegin cyn lleied ac ar "range" coed tân a glo, wn i ddim!

Bwytawyd yn y neuadd ac roedd gofyn codi byrddau, a'u harlwyo, bob awr ginio. Eisteddai athro, neu Prefect, ar ben pob bwrdd. Gwae chi os mai "Carbon" oedd yn eich gwarchod. Mynnai ef gnoi pob cegaid ddeuddeg gwaith cyn llyncu. Felly, ei ford ef fyddai'r olaf i orffen gan fyrhau amser chwarae yr awr ginio yn ofnadwy.

Treuliwyd gweddill dydd y newydd-ddyfodiaid yn dysgu sut i brynu llyfrau plant y flwyddyn uwch. Oeddem, roeddem ni'n gorfod talu am lyfrau ysgol. Daeth "Holliday's Latin Primer" a "Palmer and Parr's Geometry for Schools" yn rhan o'n geirfa ddyddiol. Derbyniwyd dyddiadur gwaith nos oedd i'w arwyddo, gan riant ac athro dosbarth, erbyn bob Dydd Llun. Os wedi troseddu, yn hwn y rhoddid y "Report" a godai ofn yn esgyrn pawb, ond y mwyaf haerllug, ac a olygai golli pum marc, o'ch cyfanswm, ar ddiwedd tymor. Cawsom lyfrau ysgrifennu gydag enw'r ysgol yn amlwg ar y clawr - yn Saesneg. Roedd clawr caled i lyfrau ysgrifennu W. J. - arwydd o'i safle yn yr ysgol efallai. Dangoswyd sut i helaethu pob tudalen trwy dynnu llinellau ychwanegol ar y top a'r gwaelod. Roedd hi'n amser rhyfel a deuai prinder papur yn go fuan. Cofier nad oedd Mr. Biro wedi ei ysbrydoli eto. Pen ac inc o'r llestr yn eich desg oedd yr offer neu, os yn "Well to do", fountain pen. Lledaenodd llawer i "flot" o fin y "ruler", ar y tudalennau glân, o big y "Parkers" a'r "Waterman", y diwrnod hwnnw - arwydd o ofn ac ansicrwydd y glas-ddisgyblion mae'n siwr.

Wel, diwedd ddaeth i ddiwrnod blinedig a blinderus. Troedio'r "path" unwaith eto - gwaherddid rhedeg - ac wedi dysgu gwisgo'r satchel fel cyfrwy yn groes i'r ysgwyddau gan roi'r bys bawd yn y strapen, fel byddai ffermwr go iawn yn bodio'i wasgod. Lawr, heibio'r Compton, a sylwi'n swil ar ffenestri wynebog bysiau dieithr y Western Welsh. 'Na gysur oedd esgyn i'r Crosville cyfarwydd a disgyn, yn dra diolchgar, ar bont groesawgar Aberarth.

Cynefino

Herc cam a naid 'nawr dros chwe mlynedd ddedwyddaf a mwyaf ffrwythlon fy mywyd.

Herc trwy ansicrwydd y cyfnod cynnar. Cofiaf lawer o fynd a dod ymhlith yr athrawon - Griffiths, gormeswr y gampfa, yn ein gadael a'r rhingyll Robertson, o wersyll y milwyr yn Cilcert, yn cymryd ei le'n rhan amser. Paffiwr proffesiynol oedd ef, a mawr yr edmygwyd ei lygad du pan ddychwelodd yn fuddugol o un ornest. Bu sibrwd iddo roi plwc bach i galon ambell athrawes ifanc hefyd. Wrth ffug-baffio yn y "gym", chwythai trwy'i drwyn gan greu rhyw sŵn tebyg i farch Bryn-Dewi pan synhwyrai fod caseg yn y cyffuniau. Efelychwyd ef yn frwd gan lwyth o fechgyn yr ysgol oedd yn brysur chwilio am arwr milwrol yn ystod y dyddiau diflas hynny.

Cofiaf yr oerfel boreol ac ansicrwydd y gwres canolog - oherwydd prinder tanwydd, ac nid bai Mr. Lloyd o gwbl. Oedd, roedd prinder popeth ond amynedd yr athrawon. Cynhaliwyd ymarferion gochel ymosodiad o'r awyr yn gyson. Clywed chwibanu uchel! Yna gadael popeth a gwasgaru i'r pedwar ban i gysgodi tan goeden, neu lwyn eithin, neu dwmpath rhedyn. Galwyd ni'n ôl trwy ganu'r gloch ysgol. Roeddem ni'r ifainc, yn methu'n lân a deall paham fod y bechgyn a'r merched hŷn hwyred yn dychwelyd o'r ymarferion hyn. Tyfodd eglurhad gydag amser ac aeddfedrwydd.

Cofiaf, gydag ias, gael llond bol o ofn yn ystod un o'r ymarferion hyn. O dan nawdd yr A.T.C. ac F. O. Fox, roedd awyren Tiger Moth wedi ei gosod ar y clôs o flaen y gampfa. Gwefr gyson i ni'r bechgyn oedd cael eistedd yn hon. Trawsnewidiwyd hi'n ddyddiol i Spitfire, neu Hurricane, a difethwyd cannoedd o awyrennau'r Almaen ganddi. Wel, un diwrnod, roeddwn i'r arwr dewr, di-ofn - cymeriad Rockfist Rogan - yn eistedd yn y cock-pit pan ganodd y corn-rhybudd oedd ar do'r orsaf heddlu, yn y dref. Os oedd y gelyn ar daro, fe fyddai'n sicr o weld yr awyren ac ymosod arni hi yn gyntaf. Gyflymed fu'm dianc o'r fan, 'rwy'n siŵr fod mwg a thân yn fy nilyn lan i Woodbine Lane. Ni ddaeth gelyn y pryd hynny nac unrhyw achlysur arall, hyd y gwn i.

Ar wahân i gyfarth y gynnau o gyfeiriad Cilcert a sŵn cachgibwm yr awyren a dywysai'r targed coch a gwyn, lawr ei phenôl, bob dydd, benbwygilydd, digon heddychlon fu'n rhyfel ni. Rhan o'n diddordeb dyddiol oedd casglu darnau o'r targedi a syrthiai mewn gardd neu gae gan ddynodi llwyddiant yr anelwyr. Weithiau, syrthiai targed cyfan. 'Na gyffro wedyn! Roedd y defnydd yn ddefnyddiol i bob math o bethau pan oedd popeth yn brin. Bu tipyn o sôn a siarad fod dillad isa' ambell ferch yn goch a gwyn, ond methwyd yn lân cadarnhau hynny!

Yn tarfu ar y tawelwch oedd newyddion diflas fod hwn a'r llall wedi'i ladd ar y môr, ym Madagascar neu fannau anghysbell cyffelyb. Dysgasom ein Daearyddiaeth trwy gyfarwyddo ag enwau megis Tobruk, Benghazi, Stalingrad a Singapore. Marciwyd mannau fel Mannheim, Cologne, Berlin a Dusseldorf yn glir iawn ar ein meddyliau, ond enwau awyrennau oedd Wellington, Halifax a Lancaster.

Cyfarwyddo

Cam trwy'r cyfnod canol a dechrau cymryd rhan yn y gemau pêl-droed dyddiol a di-ddiwedd rhwng y Western Welsh a'r Crosville. Os yn ffodus - gan fod prinder peli - byddai rhywun wedi cael gafael mewn pêl fach. Gan fod tua deugain ar bob ochr, byr fyddai hoedl honno. Os nad oedd pêl, gwnai darn o bren, neu garreg, y tro. I gychwyn, pobl yr ymylon oeddem ni yn sefyll naill ochr a mentro ambell gic os digwyddai'r bêl ddod i'n cyfeiriad. Yna, yn ara' bach, mentro i ganol y "pitch" a magu digon o hyder i erfyn "pass". Cyn hir, dechreuodd y "bois mawr" - arwyr y First XI - glywed ein gwaedd ac yna - yn wyrthiol bron - i ymateb. 'Nawr, roeddem wedi ein derbyn ac wedi ennill ein plwc yn yr ysgol. Yn nesaf, daeth y fraint o gael gwisgo crys pêl-droed tlws Tyglyn ac yna, yr acolêd uchaf - cael bracso trwy bwdel Cae Sgwâr mewn crys coch a gwyrdd, i gynrychioli'r ysgol yn erbyn Ardwyn ac eraill.

Datblygiad tra phwysig oedd bod yn deilwng - o ran oedran - o gael ein derbyn fel aelodau o'r Clwb. Nos Wener oedd y noswaith fawr. Ar y cychwyn, roeddem fel llygod bach ac yn bodloni eistedd ar sil lydan un o ffenestri'r neuadd tra'n edmygu nerf y bechgyn a fentrai ddawnsio gyda duwiesau Form VI yn eu gym tunics a'u blowsus Persil gwyn - ac yn cael gafael ynddynt hefyd! Bendith ar ben pwy bynnag a benderfynodd fod 'sane' duon yn deilwng ran o wisg ysgol merched Aberaeron am eu bod yn tynnu llai o sylw!!

Cwpla

Daeth, ac aeth, sialens y Senior, a wynebwyd y naid enfawr i'r chweched dosbarth. Roedd pump ohonom am herio'r Higher a dyna'r nifer mwyaf yn hanes yr ysgol, hyd hynny. Roedd dwy flynedd o'n blaen yn ein gwahodd i gyfnod dedwyddaf bywyd llawer ohonom - fawr o ofid, jyst digon o gyfrifoldeb a llawer o hwyl a sbri ymhlith cyfeillion clos o'r ddwy ryw. Un o ogoneddau ysgol Aberaeron oedd y ffordd y cymysgai bechgyn a merched yn gwbl naturiol. Roeddem yn medru bod yn ffrindiau!

Cyfnod y cyfnewid fu hwn. Do, cefnodd W. J. ar ei labordy a phwy na chofia araith anfarwol W. A. i'w hebrwng? Gadawodd Howell Evans a llanwyd ei le gan J. T. Owen. Ie, y sigaret yn disodli'r bibell a'r ysgol yn Cymreigeiddo, dros nos bron. Aeth Fox i'r Awyrlu a chyrhaeddodd Nansi Jones. Llaesodd poen Lladin ar unwaith. Ymunodd Mair Fach, o hoffus gof, â'r Adran Gymraeg a phan ymddangosodd Gwyneth Parry yn y cwmni, taenodd ysbryd newydd trwy'r ysgol. Roedd 'na ryw agosatrwydd anarferol a drodd barchus ofn o'r athrawon yn barchus gyfeillgarwch. Cafwyd cydweithio heb erioed i ni'r disgyblion groesi'r ffin a cheisio cymryd mantais. Yn bersonol, cefais i'r fraint o gael cydweithio gyda W. A. ar y "Link" a'r pleser o chwarae tennis yn erbyn Alcwyn. Cymerodd ef le Miss Clayton a adawodd i lanw'i lle fel Mrs. Thomas. Mwynheais sialens yr Eisteddfod a'r Mabolgampau - "y Sports" i ni. Bum yn chwarae Criced, Pêl-Droed, Tennis - a'r ffŵl, ambellwaith: wrth gwt yr olaf, dioddefais gerydd a digofaint ein

Prifathro newydd. Fe'm gwelodd, ar un nos Sadwrn braf o haf, yn mentro cyd-gerdded, a gwthio'i beic, gydag un o'r lluaws o ferched deniadol yr ysgol. Y cyhuddiad difrifol oedd y byddem yn "breichio" nesaf. "Bachgen, bachgen, rhag eich cywilydd chi!" medde fe. Fel mae pethau wedi newid!

Gwead o atgofion pleserus sydd gennyf heddiw - ambell ofid ond llawer o gyfathrachu clos a chyfeillgarwch cynnes gyda chyd-ddisgyblion ac athrawon.

Haf hirfelyn arall. Roedd y rhyfel bron wed''i hennill a ninnau wedi dathlu'n deilwng. Roedd y "blacowt" ar ben; y milwyr wedi cefnu ar Cilcert; ffair yn y Cae Sgwâr a nodau "Deep in the Heart of Texas" i'w clywed ar y cyrtiau tennis, lle treuliem oriau dedwydd ar ôl treialon yr Higher.

Daeth diwrnod y torri lan olaf i mi - diwrnod y rhwyg a'r gwasgaru. Twr bach tawel ohonom yn troedio'r "Path" am y tro olaf. Troi'n ôl ac edrych ar yr hen adeiladau cyfarwydd, cyfforddus, ie annwyl, ar fron y bryn. Cyfeillion clos o'r Cei ac Aberaeron yn cyd-gerdded, yn cysuro'n gilydd, ac yn addo cwrdd yn gyson. Anodd derbyn nad oeddem, bellach, yn perthyn i'r hen ysgol. O hyn ymlaen ymwelwyr fyddem, a'r awenau yn nwylo eraill.

Oedd, roedd hi'n nyth y dryw o ysgol a diflas dros ben fu'r daith yna 'nôl i Aberarth.

Ond dewch chi! Mae'r cyfeillgarwch yn fyw, y cyfathrachu'n parhau a'r atgofion eto'n llifo. Digwydd hyn oll yn ein haduniad flynyddol unigryw - yn y Tyglyn wrth gwrs! Parhau'n ifanc mae'r wynebau a diffuant y diolch gan bawb i'n hen ysgol. Penblwydd hapus iddi gan obeithio bod disgyblion heddiw 'run mor ffodus a diolchgar.

❖

1946 - AND ALL THAT

Glynne Jones (in school 1942-49)

"Llongyfarchiadau!" everyone was saying. Aberaeron County School was fifty years ancient!

Fifty? To a callow 16-year-old in Form 5, this meant looking afresh at grandparents and at dates on gravestones and at old sepia photos of bearded worthies in rumpled "brethyn cartref." 19th Century no less...

Yet, here we were, balancing classroom chairs on our backs, straggling down the school path to the Memorial Hall to celebrate this fiftieth birthday, to be presented with prizes, to half listen to speeches and, suddenly, to realise we were part of something special.

By then, four Headmasters had shaped our School's first half-century. Two of them were well known to us.

Howell T. Evans, a close neighbour and friend in Lampeter Road: historian and author, owner of Maesgwyn and the often erratically driven Armstrong Siddeley TG 1604, but, above all, in my eyes, an angler. Trilby-hatted, pipe firmly clenched in his mouth, head down, deep in thought, "Ianto" with rod in hand would pass our back door in Glynaeron heading for the river.

"Sewin bach i swper gyda'r wraig," he invariably would say.

And never did he return with an empty creel. His retirement in 1944, after twenty seven years of high achievement as Head, inspired an outpouring of affection from both school and the neighbourhood for this supremely gifted man.

J. T. Owen, his successor as Head, had already taught at the School for over twenty years. To listen to "J. T." in full, eloquent flow, eyes a-sparkle and enthusiasm lighting his face, was a memorable adventure into the richness, depth and the age-old mystery of the Welsh language. He was also a rod and line man as well as having a fine eye with a 12-bore, but neither he nor Howell Evans, I suspect, approved of my somewhat more efficient methods of relieving the Aeron of its salmon and sewin.

But, in the ration-booked greyness of 1946, we had much more than a 50th birthday to contend with. Grateful, but still fearful for the future, we had just emerged from a cataclysmic World War. The comparative safety of our little Cardigan Bay haven had spared us from its savageries. None the less, it touched us in many ways.

There were those who went away to war, never to return, including our friend and neighbour, Ifan y Felin. And in the School's upper yard at the gym's corner we had our own aeroplane, an old Tiger Moth, from which we sent radio messages to the rest of 1511 Air Training Corps Flight in what used to be the woodwork room next door to the boiler house.

Then there were perhaps the saddest of the war's casualties - the evacuees. Until they arrived in 1940, we thought that after the 1930s depression, we could recognise poverty. Tuberculosis, the old killer, was still a threat and several of our friends succumbed. But the arrival of those children from Liverpool opened our eyes to a new dimension of deprivation. We also had other newcomers at school, mainly from London and the Home Counties, who had local connections and who spent the war years with us.

There were also the small, silly things that remain in the mind, like a bunch of bananas - the first we had seen for three years - brought to school by a girl whose father was a sea captain. And our first sight of a ballpoint pen (the original "Biro") which was fat, badly balanced and prone to leave a greasy, splodgy trail on the page.

But if Aberaeron had been spared the battlefield's brutality, we certainly did not escape its clamour. For over four years, the headland just south of the town had been the site of the 13th Light Anti-aircraft Practice Training Camp. Day after day, Sundays excepted, Aberaeron shook to the thump of the high explosive shells of the Vickers 3.7 inch guns aimed at a target drogue towed relentlessly along the coastline by a low-wing monoplane. For variety, we had the chatter of the 2-pounder "pom-poms" at 100 rounds per minute, and whenever a target was downed overland, there was a mad rush to secure the valuable cloth section for "blackout" curtains and the net for shrimping and for the garden. To this camp came detachments from not only the Home Counties but also from the Commonwealth, and one year, memorably, a mighty presence from the U.S. of A. disbursing into our eager little hands largess in the form of chewing gum and candy, "K" rations and a culture hitherto alien to us.

All this was now in the past. After five years of darkness, the street lights shone again, and Aberaeron carefully hitched up her skirts and trod warily into the future.

But some things, like the timbers of the old "Allan", sunk like Aberaeron's maritime history into Pwll Cam's mud, had disappeared for ever. In the fields, the tractor, popularised by the local War Agricultural committee's depot at Pengarreg Farm, had supplanted the horse. The Crosville buses' livery had changed from maroon and blue to an environmentally gentler green and yellow. And the old-style Aberaeron "emporium" - the multi-purpose shops that stocked nearly all our wants, sadly knew their days were numbered. But the "trên bach", then unaware of its impending demise, daily made four passenger and one goods journey along the 13 mile line to Lampeter. For our first post-war inter-school cricket match, we caught the 9.15 train from Aberaeron, changed to the Tregaron line at Lampeter, lost to Tregaron for whom the brother of the present Archbishop of Wales was playing, and returned to Aberaeron at 9.30 that night.

The School "gym", unused during the war because we had nobody qualified to teach P. E. was opened in style by a team of Army P. T. instructors. Thorold Fox (Latin) and John Evans (Agriculture) returned to teach us after their war service and normality was cautiously resumed. The genteel rivalries of Tanyfron, Tyglyn and Portland at the School Eisteddfod and on the sports field quietly nudged away the barbarities that happened elsewhere during 1939-45. And an end-of-tunnel light of sorts appeared when we picked teams to play soccer at Cae County against the German prisoners of war housed in the hostel behind Aberaeron Hospital. A new Europe from the playing fields of Aberaeron?

Things, however, could never be the same again. Too much had happened: too many of our rural life's old traditions had been eroded by the tide of progress.

To my generation, Aberaeron County School had been a citadel, a place of stability as well as of learning; a bastion of hope and friendship during a time of uncertainty.

"Gore gadwyn gre gydiol

Ddaw i ni a ddoe yn ôl"

❖

A.T.C. Football Team
1946

RECOLLECTIONS

W. J. Jones (Teacher 1908-1944).

Extract from the "Link" 1946.

It was a glorious September day in 1908 when I stepped out of Lampeter Station to board a bus for Aberayron.

A simple detail met my eye and made me feel at home. A van was waiting there and facing me was the name Owen J. Jones, Aberayron - the name of my brother, who was with me. In later years this name was to mean much in our School Trips.

The journey to Aberayron gave promise of Nature's wonderful bounty - Falcondale Woods in early autumn dress were glorious and later on there was the perfect entry to Hengeraint Woods - to me a lasting picture of beauty - now alas, destroyed for others by road widening.

This first view of the Aeron Valley had given me real pleasure - pleasure that was maintained in the years to follow when cycling over all the surrounding country roads. The town of Aberaeron was prettier in those days than it is now - cement had not made its entry. Houses were plastered, and coloured with colours of various tints, giving the town a very clean appearance - warm and comforting. The pavements were all made of cobblestones from the beach, neat but uncomfortable to walk upon.

Many flower gardens flourished around the outside of Alban Square Field - these were removed at a later date by order of the Council because of increasing traffic.

South Road was a country lane, being merely a muddy cart track with grass verges. It contained four houses only, fields stretching from Hazeldene (newly built) to Dolaeron and "the Bont" - now in ruins. "Compton" was the Post Office and I was lucky to receive the first delivered letters in the morning - often before 9 o'clock, as I lived next door.

The present County Hall was then the Town Hall with the Market underneath. This building was judged by Mr. Fred Richards, the Newport artist, to be of rare beauty.

There was no railway in those days, and the nearby river bridge was narrow and humpbacked. There were no houses from this bridge to Llysaeron apart from the Vicarage and the Toll-gate, and no houses on the South side of Lampeter Road. Llyswen was a well known beauty spot; but the cottages have either been removed or altered and the whole scene has changed.

The County School overlooked a field - the Feathers Field, which was bounded by South Road. The School path was of earth, mud in wet weather, narrow all the way and ending at a turnstile gate at the lower end. There was a cottage at the end of the School Lane, where the entrance gate of "Gerallt" now stands - "Barbara's Cottage." The "Bont" was a sweet-shop and acted as the School Tuckshop during the morning "Break" and between sessions.

The County School was the original building erected in 1896 to the plans of Mr. Bankes-Price of Lampeter. It was excellently planned and excellently built. The timber work was of first-class quality and is excellent today. The school was coloured white on the outside making the building prominent at a distance.

It consisted of the Central Hall and eight rooms in addition, surrounding it. The present headmaster's room was then Form 4, the pleasantest room in school because of the splendid view over town and sea. Between this room and the kitchen was a short side passage with wash basins and serving as a cloakroom for the girls. Next to the kitchen and facing the entrance door was a small Staff-Room for the Mistresses. Form 3 was next with entrances from corridor and main hall, with Form 5 next door with similar entrances.

The Men's Staff Room was the present Stationery Room while the classroom adjoining had a stone floor and was fitted out for Elementary Science. The Boys' cloakroom corresponded to that of the Girls', and lastly there was a small Chemistry Laboratory with two benches ... in the present Form 6 and Library.

There was no Headmaster's Room. The Headmaster, Mr. C. J. Hughes occupying a desk on the platform in the Central Hall. From here, as now, the Morning Service was conducted and in addition the roll-call of all the pupils. The Hall also contained desks for two forms - Forms 2 - separated during the day by a curtain drawn across the room. At Prayers, taken by the Staff in turn, the pupils stood behind these desks.

The school desks were of many kinds, all ancient and cumbersome, accommodating from two to five. The interior of the school was far from inspiring. It had not been coloured for many years and the walls were now a faded green. The only "pictures" on the walls were the photographs of the hockey and football teams of past years and these were certainly not artistic, yet these were held in high esteem.

The Staff consisted of five members - the Headmaster, with four assistants - two ladies and two men, with a visiting Cookery Mistress from Aberystwyth once a week.

There were seventy pupils, and those from afar lodged in town from Monday until Friday in recognised lodgings. The New Quay contingent, a very strong one in every way, arrived on a Monday morning in their famous van drawn by an equally famous horse (this horse and van were later featured in a well known Welsh film).

When the local vans and buses reached Aberaeron just after tea, regular traffic with the outside world ceased - the last outward vehicle being the mail-van in the afternoon. This was horse drawn and had room for one passenger. There were no motor cars in town and only one ancient and unused motor cycle. These conditions soon improved; but it was some years before the fare to Aberystwyth was lowered by competition from 6/- to 2/9 at which figure it has remained ever since.

The school Hockey and Football teams were carried in the brakes of Mr. O. J. Jones and it was an education to sit behind the wonderful horses of "Owen the Van" and admire his control of the ribbons. He was on the road for nearly twenty-eight years - without a single

W. J. Jones B.Sc.

Yr hen adeilad / The old building

accident and he never failed to reach Lampeter in time with the mail.

Who will ever forget that drive to Tregaron across country to avoid the torrential downpours, our unexpected arrival and our victory? Our first winter trips in 1908 were to Llandysul, a journey of four hours each way, the return journey in each case being made in the pouring rain - in an open brake. Present pupils are pampered in comparison.

These and subsequent trips were made enjoyable because the bulk of the boys were members of the School Male Voice Choir trained by Mr. E. O. James, M.A. It was a case of singing the whole way home, many of the boys being first class soloists. In the case of the girls, we had an addition to music. A boy pupil with a splendid story and anecdote accompanied the hockey team and kept the company alive throughout the trip. This practice served him in good stead - he has since become a first class after-dinner speaker in London.

Washing after games in those early days was primitive. If lucky, the boys would obtain pans of warm water from the kitchen, and taking these to the corridors would create an awful mess endeavouring to remove the grime of the playing fields.

There were four C.W.B. Examinations - (1) Higher Honours; (2) Lower Honours; (3) Senior; (4) Junior; while some pupils sat for the Welsh and London Matriculation Examinations.

Soon there was a change. The two Honours Examinations were replaced by the Higher C.W.B. Examination, approximately intermediate in difficulty between the two Honours. The Junior Examination was abolished. I regard the dropping of the Junior to be a great mistake. It served a most useful purpose, being taken by Form 4 pupils and providing a splendid preparation for the Senior Exam (the present School Certificate Exam.). It avoided the rush and cram shown by many pupils in later years.

In 1910, two new rooms were added to the school - the new Chemistry Laboratory and a Woodwork Room - the present Form 5b room which then extended to the wall of the Laboratory - the through corridor being of a later date (1940-41). Being qualified in Manual Instruction, I volunteered for this pleasant and interesting subject.

Geography became established a little later, upon the appointment of a specialist from Dublin - Miss Watson, and I was relieved from taking it as a stop-gap subject. In spite of a special appeal at a Governors' meeting to introduce Physics into the syllabus it was not taught as a main subject for many years.

Lack of space prevents my rambling tale doing full justice to many aspects of school life; but I must pay tribute to the success of the Gilfach-yr-Halen Picnics, House Parties, Club Reunions and Old Pupils' Reunions, in which so much self sacrifice and real co-operation were shown. I also wish to express my thanks to all those who have shown great kindness and remained such friends throughout the years.

To the School and Pupils in general and the School Institute in particular I wish every success for the future.

❖

WORLD WAR II - ROLL OF HONOUR

They shall grow not old, as we that are left grow old:
Age shall not weary them, nor the years condemn;
At the going down of the sun and in the morning
We will remember them.

Sgt. PILOT WILLIAM CARTER, R.A.F., January 14, 1944 (missing).

A.C.1 EVAN LLOYD DAVIES, R.A.F., November 7, 1944.

Pte. EVAN TIMOTHY DAVIES, 6th Royal Welsh Paratroop Bn., Army Air Corps, September 9, 1943.

IDRIS DAVIES, 2nd Officer, M.N., November 5, 1942.

ISLWYN DAVIES, Chief Steward, M.N., November 5, 1943.

L.A.C. THOMAS IRWYN DAVIES, R.A.F., November 7, 1944.

L/Cpl. WILLIAM JAMES EDGAR DAVIES, Royal Welch Reg., October 1, 1944.

ALFRED WYNDHAM EVANS, 2nd Officer, M.N., May 3, 1944.

DAVID GORDON EVANS, 3rd Officer, M.N., August 1940.

EVAN EVANS, Able Seaman, M.N., March 5 1943.

Gnr. IEUAN TEGONWY EVANS, Royal Tank Reg., November 8, 1943.

Sgt. THOMAS ITHEL JAMES, Air Gunner, R.A.F., February 21, 1943 (missing).

Gnr. DAVID BASIL JAYNE, R.A., February 15, 1945.

Capt. TOM ELLIS JENKINS, M.N., about February 20, 1941.

W/O DAVID HORACE JONES, Fighter Pilot, R.A.F., November 12, 1944.

Sgt. ALLEN STANFORD JONES, R.A.F., March 9, 1941.

Sgt. EVAN ANCRE JONES, R.E., about April 29, 1941.

EVAN GILMOUR JONES, 3rd Engineer, M.N., October 19, 1941.

FRANCES JONES, Cadet, M.N., March 17, 1941 (missing).

Flt./Sgt. GWYNFOR JONES, Fighter Squadron, R.A.F., March 1945.

Flt./Sgt. JOHN ALBERT JONES, R.A.F., December 18, 1944.

Sgt. JOHN CEREDIG JONES, R.A.F.V.R., April 3, 1943.

Flt./Sgt. JOHN MORRIS JONES, Engineer, R.A.F., August 23, 1943 (missing).

JOHN ROGER SIMPSON JONES, Able Seaman, M.N., August 15, 1945.

Capt. CHRISTOPHER DAVID LEWIS, M.N., January 29, 1940.

JOHN HAROLD LEWIS, 2nd Officer, M.N., April 29, 1943.

Trooper THOMAS WILLIAM LLOYD, R.A.C., January 25, 1944.

WILLIAM MASKELL MEREDITH, Radio Location Officer, R.N., November, 1942. (On school staff October 1, 1939 - March 31, 1941).

EVAN SAMUEL MORGAN, Able Seaman, M.N., July 29, 1943.

JOHN TREVOR REES, Cadet, M.N., November 5, 1940.

Sgt. WILLIAM GWYNHAF THOMAS, R.W.F., May 6 1942.

IVAN COOPER WILLIAMS, Telegraphist, R.N., September 13, 1943.

Gadael gwaith a gadael gwŷdd - gadael ffridd
Gadael ffrwd y mynydd,
Gadael dôl a gadael dydd,
A gadael gwyrddion goedydd.

In Memoriam - William Maskell Meredith B.A. ("The Link" 1943)

Early in November last year (1942), a promising career was cut short and a charming personality was lost to us, when Mr. W. M. Meredith, at the age of twenty-six, was killed in action. Educated at Llandeilo County School and the University College of Wales, Aberystwyth, he graduated with First Class Honours in English Language and Literature. In addition, he was a trained teacher, holding the Diploma in Education of the University of Wales, and he had spent a year in post-graduate research. He joined the Staff of this school as English Master in October, 1939. At the end of March, 1941, to the regret of everyone, he left to enter the Wireless Section of the Royal Navy.

"They went with songs to battle; they were young,
Straight of limb, true of eye, steady and aglow."

How well do these lines by Laurence Binyon summon up remembrance of him! We see again his handsome, strong figure; the dark intelligent eyes; the expression, normally serious, but good-humoured and always ready to light up with boyish fun. "Steady and

W. M. Meredith, B.A.

aglow". There, surely, we have his personality. We remember his enthusiasm and thoroughness; we remember his zest in living, his wide interests - in literature, in music and in sport; we remember his modesty, his tact, his scrupulous consideration for the rights and feelings of others. He was indeed "Integer vitae sclerisque purus," and his influence on the school was wholly for good.

Small wonder then that Meredith, during the short time he was with us, gained the respect and affection both of his colleagues and of his pupils. I have beside me as I write two appreciations of him that make this clear. One is by a pupil and the other is by a member of the Staff. I am sure you would wish me to quote both. Here, then, first of all, is an extract from a letter written soon after the news of his death by a former pupil of this school. She writes:

> *"I was grieved and shocked at the sad news; for during my short stay at the school I sincerely appreciated his sterling qualities. I was there when he left to join the Navy, and his departure made me very sad. I know how well liked and respected he was by everyone at the school, and I am sure everyone who knew him mourns his loss. And though perhaps a wordy expression of sympathy from me may convey little to the reader, yet I assure you my heart is full of grief and sorrow for a life cut off so tragically. Perhaps I should never again have come into contact with him had he survived it all; but I should - and shall - always remember him with respect and admiration."*

This, I think, gives touching expression to the feelings of all his pupils. Let the following appreciation by Mr. W. J. Jones speak for his colleagues:

> *"It was with deep sorrow that the school heard of the death of Mr. W. Maskell Meredith - killed on active service in the Eastern Mediterranean. During his stay here, he had proved himself to be a worthy friend and colleague. he had entered into every phase of school life with the utmost enthusiasm; and when he left to join the Navy the pupils showed their respect for him in a very practical way - he had won their highest regard."*

He had kept in touch with the school right from the start, corresponding regularly during his training and subsequent voyages. His final letter came just two days before we received the sad news of his death. The school has suffered a grievous loss in his sacrifice.

After these admirable tributes there is, perhaps, only one thing I need do, and that is to record the great interest which Mr. Meredith always took in "The Link". He himself edited the 1940 number with great distinction. Even, I believe, in that final letter to which Mr. W. J. Jones referred, "The Link" was mentioned. This is but a special instance of his invariable loyalty to the school. By his death we have lost a young teacher of rare ability and a friend of the highest integrity and charm.

BYWYD

Awst 1926, J.M. Edwards

Daw y mêl o'r awelon - a mwyniant
I minnau yr awron;
A gwclaf wlad y galon,
Y tir sy deg tros y don.
O! wlad hardd, am olud hon
A hwyliau ei hawelon,
A thir brydferth oror
Daw hiraeth mud wrth y môr:
A gwybod fod bro gobaith
Dros su môr dyrys a maith.
Bro pob llanc mewn ifanc nwyd
A bro heddwch a breuddwyd;
Bro y mwynder tyneraf,
Bro llawn hud, bro llwyni haf:
Ni ddaw'r drin, ni ddaw ar dro
Haint na henaint i honno.
Ac yn y wlad mae cân lon
A bythol haf gobeithion;
A dihynt fy ngwaed o hyd
Heb ei hawel a'i bywyd.
Unig yn awr a gwan wyf,
O hyd hiraethu'r ydwyf;
Gwyra haul i'r gorwelion
Yn hir a dwys tua'r don:
Dyddiau hen diwedd einioes
Sy yn nesáu, a nos oes.

Ysgol Gyfun Aberaeron 1896 - 1996

Disgyn y glaw aflawen
A daeth nos i deithio nen.
Henaidd a gwael fy nydd gwyn,
Daw ei yrfa i derfyn:
Draw y mae yr hen dir mwyn
Einioes mewn cynnar wanwyn.
Draw y ccir pcll dir y gân
Ac hafau, wedi'r cyfan,
Nid oes yma ond siomiant
Heb gain hwyr ac heb gân nant.
Ag hwyr y gwin ger gwaneg,
Llawer dau dan y lloer deg
A ŵyr o hyd am oriau -
Munudau dwys dim ond dau.

❖

THE INSTITUTE / THE SCHOOL CLUB

Rhiannon Davies, 1995 - (President of the Club 1944/45)

No history of the school would be complete without special reference to the School Club. To me and so many others over the years it provided fun, informality, friendship, learning and purpose - all combining to produce a sense of well-being and direction. Its attraction lay in its complete contrast to the formal learning process, as well as its openness to all, from Form 4 and above, who, voluntarily, wished to participate in its wide range of activities. With hindsight, the establishment and continuity of The Club was a pioneering project, ahead of its time in concept and implementation. Many pupils over the years have been and remain indebted to the experiences it offered and felt it was a fitting seal to the overall school programme.

I want, within the terms of this reminiscence, to trace its origins from available records - admirably kept for the first forty-five years or so - to expand upon its organisation and varied activities, and reflect the testimony of others.

Late in 1919, Haydn Lewis was approached by several pupils with a view to arranging a Club for them. He writes:

"The desire was for games, reading of papers, debates as well as pugilistic displays (the latter being the vogue at the time). Different authorities were approached, and eventually, through the Monachty Estate Agent, a room was procured for a rent of 10/- (50p) a year. It was, therefore, an extra-mural institution thus ignoring the importance of the School's connection with it. For this reason, therefore, the Headmaster, Mr Howell T. Evans M.A. nipped in the bud this momentary aspiration. It was obvious by this time that there was a desire amongst the pupils themselves for a Club, and in view of this fact, the coming of the Institute was to some extent, inevitable. In 1920, a meeting room was provided, officers and a committee were elected and it was decided that an annual subscription of 2/6 (13p) should be paid by members."

These facts are further confirmed by Mr. Howell T. Evans on his retirement in 1944 when he wrote:

"The Christmas term of 1919 saw the first small beginnings of The Institute - Y Clwb. They met at the Council School. It was part of the original project to encourage "pugilistic displays" which was, presumably, the reason why boys and girls met separately, the girls to stay at home or in their lodgings to do their homework while the boys were at the Club. Then it moved to the Town Hall as a joint meeting. In 1921, it took up its abode in the school, its natural home, in its present form. The first Presidents were Haydn Lewis and Mary Catherine Lewis, and the first secretaries

Myrddin Evans and Nan Lloyd. There was much local prejudice against the social half of the proceedings, which manifested itself in some amusing incidents which must remain unrecorded. The chronicles of the Club have been faithfully kept to this day. They are the most valuable, and certainly the most interesting records in the school. The Club owes much to Mr W. J. Jones B.Sc. I value as one of my most cherished memories his untarnished loyalty to the school and to me personally; in particular, his devotion to the Club which he has piloted skilfully through many storms. He was on the staff when I came. He remains when I leave. One arm rests on the shoulder of my predecessor. The other he extends to my successor.

What of the thousand or more pupils who have left school during the last quarter of a century? I trust that all were given the opportunity to develop character and personality in an atmosphere of freedom and good comradeship."

It is fascinating to note the list of rules set out in 1920. They read as follows:

1. *No school work to be done in the Club.*
2. *While the girls are in the Club, the boys must be doing their homework, and vice versa.*
3. *Sliding down the bannisters is strictly prohibited.*
4. *Members arriving 15 minutes after the commencement of a meeting are liable to punishment.*
5. *Members are requested not to use the piano except with the consent of the Presidents.*
6. *The Officers are to have Supreme Power.*
7. *All breaches of the rules to be dealt with in the Law Courts.*

In the same year, the records show that under the chairmanship of Haydn Lewis and Mary Catherine Lewis, a school library was established, each member bringing a book or two. There was also a plentiful supply of games, such as chess, draughts etc. for those so disposed. Weekly and monthly journals, e.g. "Conquest", "John O'London" etc. were bought. Apparently, the town piano was hired and with its aid many enjoyable evenings were passed.

It can be justifiably claimed that some of the early activities of the Club influenced the development of many events associated with the school. I refer in particular to the School Reunion, the School Eisteddfod and Club Party. As far back as 1920, we are told that a full-sized lantern was hired from the Methodist Band of Hope Society. Entertainment was given in the School Hall and was open to friends and parents of pupils as well as the students themselves. The Hall was nearly full (a striking tribute) and the venture was, in every way a big success, so much that those responsible thought themselves justified in organising a similar meeting later on. Thus the School Reunion was born.

In 1921, the desire to organise an Eisteddfod reached fulfilment. Under the Officers of the Institute, a committee was formed and the St. David's Day Eisteddfod held that year proved an outstanding success.

I droi at iaith yr Eisteddfod - Capt. Evans "Hazeldene" oedd y Llywydd am y dydd a'r beirniaid oedd:

Cerdd - Miss Bessie Lewis R.A.M. a Mr D. James, Alban Square.

Llên - Mr E. O. James M.A. a Miss E .A. Roberts B.A.

Celf - Miss Richards B.A. a Mr W. J. Jones B.Sc.

Gwniadwaith - Miss Davies B.A. a Miss M. E. Thomas B.A.

Y cyfeilyddion oedd Mary Catherine Lewis a Della Owen. Rhoddwyd gwobrwyon arian ac enillwyd y Gadair am gân ar y testun "Dringo'r Mynydd" gan Jenkin M. Edwards a enillodd y wobr gyntaf hefyd am y Delyneg a'r Englyn.

Er llawenydd i bawb, cafwyd Eisteddfod lewyrchus a llwyddiannus tu hwnt i bob disgwyl, a dengys y cofnodion fod y "swm sylweddol" o £1.7s.3 1/2 (£1.37) oedd yn weddill, i'w gwario ar lyfrau ar gyfer y llyfrgell.

The first Club Party was held in December 1939, taking the place of the annual Reunion "because of the shortage of food." The M. C. for the occasion was Mr John Evans and "the party proved to be the most successful since Club was instituted." From then on, a Club Party for members and teachers has been held annually a few days before the end of the Christmas term.

I have received many examples of the scope of activities that were pursued. As well as Mock Elections, a classic illustration is the Mock Assizes conducted regularly on a systematic basis. The 1924 records note that Nesta Gillies brought forward a grievance against E. Ronald Luke, charging him with kissing against her wishes. After the cross-examination of the prisoner and the condemning evidence of witnesses, the Jury found Luke guilty of the serious crime of stealing a kiss from a young girl, namely Miss Gillies. After severe censure, the Judge, Sallie E. Davies, sentenced the prisoner "to return the kiss with costs."

Other charges brought included: "frequenting the Beach Hotel for the sake of playing billiards"; "entering the School by indirect means, to wit the window"; "climbing over the N.W. entrance to the Square Field and thereby causing the field to be closed to the school for football for a day."

The list of debates demonstrate how imaginatively and pertinently the minds of young people were encouraged to focus upon and analyse current issues. Some of the debate titles read:

"Surroundings have a greater effect than heredity on a person's character."

"Dylai Cymru gael Ymreolaeth."

"Women Imitate Men."

"Art has done more than science towards civilisation."

"Home or school has more influence over a child?"

"Fox-hunting should be abolished."

What is interesting about the above is the contemporary and up-to-date flavour of the issues discussed.

The Club was privileged to receive visits from outside and local guests whose memory still lingers with us. Ben Jones in 1930 writes of the time when Rev. Haydn Lewis B.A. past President of the Institute returned to the School to give a talk under the title "Travels Here and There".

"He described his first travels to Aberystwyth with "Owen y Fan" and his excitement on the opening of the Aberayron Express. He finished his talk by describing how he went to preach at Soar y Mynydd (ten miles from nowhere) - the Mecca of all adventurous preachers, and how Monday found him in bed, sore and weary after the previous day's exertions on horse-back. The lecture was not only interesting and instructive, but also exceedingly humorous."

Another memory is of Mr Roderick Bowen M.P., Q.C., who gave some of his time to talk on "The Common Market". He reviewed the arguments for and against entry and prompted much discussion and interest.

Eulanwy Jones wrote in 1956:

"For the 167 people present on November 23rd (and that surely is a record) that evening will long remain one of our most treasured memories of the Club. We were thrilled to welcome to our midst none other than the actors Richard Burton and Paul Schofield. They both gave their views on various aspects of stage and screen. The most popular item was the recitation of poems by both celebrities. It proved a gala occasion for the Club."

Local contributors also impressed. Mr W. A. Jones M.A. (our much revered English Teacher) was persuaded to lecture and to the horror of the members, he chose as his subject "The Life of Socrates". "There was an atmosphere of pending gloom in the Hall. Quite soon, however, everyone present was entranced listening attentively to a most thoughtful and penetrating presentation. A much dreaded hour passed so quickly."

Gareth and Gordon Parry presented slides of a Baltic Cruise aboard the ship "Dunera" taken by the pupils during August 1965. The journey took us to Sweden, Russia and Denmark. There were 110 persons present that evening all of whom were very complimentary of the photography of these Third Formers.

There was a social side to the Club which was significant for many. The number of girls and boys who turned out for dancing and games was proof that these so-called "childish pursuits" were quite popular.

"Quite a number of boys" writes John Glyn Roberts in 1926, "joined in the waltzes and fox-trots (I could not summon up enough courage)." The number of girls who hopped around the old hall showed no signs of diminishing. The old and somewhat stale games - Winks, Jolly Miller etc. and the dances - the Lancers and Sir Roger de Coverley, retained their popularity while a few new ones were introduced.

The importance of the Second Half of the Club is underlined in a recent letter from Henry W. Jones when he states "All eagerly looked forward to the dancing of the second half. Even those of a dromedary tendency among us lads experienced the mouth-drying thrill of actually having a girl in our arms - well almost. For this we would brave even the wide acres of the New Hall to lay claim to our chosen belles. What they thought of our clumsy toe-crushing I now shudder to think. How far away that kind of dance seems. The Club Party was always a special night with decorations, delicacies to eat, girls transformed in dresses and even the rebels with shoes polished and hair brylcreemed in anticipation."

As the years unfolded, there was no doubt that the Club was being regarded and respected as an essential ingredient of school life. In December 1925, the President of the Club, Evan Daniel Davies delivered an excellent address in Prize day in which he summarized the history of the Club, giving a description of its prospects during the coming Spring Term. "He came through the ordeal with flying colours and was complemented heartily upon his fine speech by many people including Prof. Gwynn Jones, distinguished guest of the day."

In 1927, Mr Hopkin Morris M.P., the guest speaker on Prize Day said he could easily perceive the way the School was run, if only by the work of the Club, and that it was a credit that the School possessed such a worthy institution.

Bridget Webb, an evacuee, delivered a speech in 1945 as the girl President. She stated:

> *"At a time when so much publicity is being given to the new Youth Clubs, it is pleasant to recall that the Aberayron School Club is now twenty-five years old and can almost be regarded as a pioneer of the movement for it has been run on what are now considered essentially modern lines ever since its inauguration. In fact, it is the only school organization I have ever heard of that is truly "of the pupils, by the pupils, for the pupils"."*

Even the war years did not affect the continuity of the Club. Sal Marsden's Presidential Speech in 1939, when all pupils were war-minded, was quite revealing:

> *"Very soon", she stated, "pupils were asking whether they would have a Club since it was impossible, because of the black-out, to have it in the evenings. The Headmaster, Mr Howell T. Evans, confirmed this, but kind and considerate as usual, promised an hour off each Friday afternoon for the Institute."*

Clwb yr Ysgol / School Club
1945

Clwb yr Ysgol / School Club
1956 - 57

This continued, it seems, for one term only. After that, the Hall was suitably blacked out and the Club held once again on Friday evenings. Sal Marsden continues: "without hesitation, therefore, I can conclude that the Institute this year is as successful as ever. May I say that although Hitler and his confederates may turn the world upside-down, while there is an Aberayron County School, the Institute will go on."

Reading through the personal comments received, the stability, attraction and continuity of the Club owed much to certain individuals whose vision and tenacity were quite remarkable. Many names could be mentioned, amongst whom would figure the Headmasters of School over the years, their Deputies, and other members of staff. Special reference, however, must be given to Mr W. J. Jones and Mr W. A. Jones. Bridget Webb recalls a Farewell Party to Mr W. J. Jones held on the evening of March 23rd 1945.

"Mr Jones was really the man who made the Club the success it is today, and in all the years he had missed only two sessions. In order to emphasize the importance of the occasion we decided to indulge in the formality of a supper-dance. As the party came to a close, Rhiannon Davies and Alun Morgan both made farewell speeches. Rhiannon presented Mr Jones with a cheque to which all members of Club had contributed. After singing "Auld Lang Syne" we all sang "For he's a jolly good fellow" and cheered Mr Jones heartily."

Until his retirement in 1970, Mr W. A. Jones had also been a faithful friend to the Club. Jonathan Evans-Jones paid a warm and sincere tribute to Mr Jones and claimed that his services to the Club had been invaluable - always at hand to advise, guide and help.

I have tried to recapture the flavour and significance of the Club, and focus upon its impact on the lives of students. Many past students have kindly written to me, expressing their personal memories and gratitude both to the School and the Club.

It was lovely to receive a comment from "one of the older surviving pupils" - C. Berys Lewis - who spoke so warmly of the influence of the School and the Club.

"I 'joined' as it were, in the early 1930s. Mr Howell T. Evans was the headmaster at the time and I can remember clearly his excellent staff of teachers, all of whom were kind but firm, and there was a high standard of discipline throughout the school. Our social activities were most enjoyable, especially the Club where we had debates and dancing, as I recall. We looked forward to Friday evenings with so much pleasure. We also had a good school choir, and, during one term, we gave an excellent performance of Gilbert and Sullivan's "H.M.S. Pinafore". I made some wonderful friends at school, and now, with the school celebrating its centenary, I feel proud and honoured to have been a small part of it all those years ago."

Seisnigaidd iawn fu'r Clwb erioed, yn enwedig felly pan 'roeddwn i yn yr ysgol yn ystod y rhyfel, er i Dewi Eurig Davies, Llywydd y Clwb yn 1939 ddweud fel hyn:

"Yn y gorffennol, talodd y Clwb ormod o sylw i'r Saesneg....... Haws dweud na gwneud, ond yn y dyfodol bydd rhaid talu mwy o sylw i'r Gymraeg. Cenedl o Gymry ydym, y

mae ein Ysgol Sir mewn tref hollol Gymreig."

Ysgrifennodd Margaret Eluned Roberts (Davies gynt) ataf yn yr iaith orau fel hyn:

"Pan oeddwn yn y dosbarthiadau iau (dros hanner canrif yn ôl) 'roeddwn yn llawn eiddigedd o weld y disgyblion hŷn yn cael aros ar ol i fynychu'r Clwb. Yna, wedi cyrraedd y pedwaredd dosbarth, 'roedd yr awr fawr wedi cyrraedd i ni gael ymuno â'r cwmni dethol.

'Roedd y noson yn cael ei rhannu'n ddwy ran, a chystal i mi gyfaddef fan hyn mai ychydig o gof sydd gennyf o'r rhannau cyntaf. Bu rhaid dod o hyd i ôl rifynnau o'r Ddolen, ac o'u darllen a gweld fod rhai o fawrion y genedl, megis Dewi Eurig, wedi bod yn llywyddion, gwelais y fath arlwy oedd yn cael ei gynnig i ni yn y Clwb. 'Roedd yna gyfle i ddisgyblion ddarllen papurau ar destunau arbennig, cymryd rhan mewn dadl gyhoeddus, eisteddiad o'r cwrt bach, Eisteddfod ffug, Etholiad ffug, gornestau gwybodaeth gyffredinol a hyd yn oed gornestau sillafu. Trueni mawr na fuasai gornestau sillafu'n cael eu cynnal y dyddiau hyn! Diddorol oedd gweld rhai o destunau'r trafodaethau a'r papurau a ddarllenwyd. 'Roedd un wedi'i baratoi ar "Y newid oedd wedi cymryd lle yn Aberarth"! 'Roedd yn amlwg hefyd fod y staff mor barod i roi eu gwasanaeth drwy roi darlithiau, rhoi hanes eu gwyliau, ac yn y blaen.

Coron y nos oedd yr ail hanner, sef y dawnsio a'r gêmau a'r brenin oedd Mr W. J. Jones o barchus goffadwriaeth. 'Roedd e'n bresennol bob amser ,ac ef oedd yn trefnu'r gemau ac yng ngofal y radiogram. 'Roeddem ni'r merched wedi meistrioli'r gelfyddyd o ddawnsio yn eithaf da - diolch i rai fel Margaret Lloyd (Makin nawr) a ganodd y piano am oriau rhwng gwersi ac amser cinio. 'Rwy'n siwr i Margaret chwarae "You are my Honey Honeysuckle" gannoedd o weithiau. Felly 'roedd gennych ferched yn hyddysg yn y foxtrot, y quickstep a'r waltz yn ceisio rhannu'r gelfyddyd honno gyda'r bechgyn, a rheiny ddim yn frwd iawn, a dweud y lleia.

Ar ddiwedd y noson, 'roedd y ffaith ein bod yn cael mynd gartref ar fws hwyrach nag arfer yn bwysig. Ar ddiwedd tymor y Nadolig, 'roeddem yn cael parti. I ni'r plant ar ddiwedd y tridegau a dechrau'r pedwardegau 'roedd hynny'n ddigwyddiad amheuthun.

'Rwy'n siŵr na ddywedais air yn gyhoeddus tra'n mynychu'r Clwb - 'roeddwn llawer yn rhy swil. 'Does ond gobeithio fod rhywfaint o'r profiadau gawsom yn y Clwb wedi dylanwadu arnaf. Erbyn hyn 'rwyf wedi dweud ambell i air yn gyhoeddus a datgan barn yn ystod treiglad y blynyddoedd."

John Raymond Jenkins describes the Club as:

"the highlight of school life. It is only in looking back that we realise the influence that any organisation has upon us. In those days, there were no local clubs in our communities at which one had the opportunity of expressing individual gifts. In the Club, there were opportunities to stand before an audience and do one's stunt. There

were Mock Trials in which certain pupils with a bent for advocacy would come up with the most ingenious "twists" to the Law. Then the charades at which elaborate scenes were enacted to illustrate the syllables of a word we wished to convey. I have a snapshot of myself dressed up as the Bishop for the Coronation of Elizabeth I, complete with cape and mitre, and the school window pole as the crozier. A foreshadowing of future achievements? Alas no. A vastly therapeutic exercise was the opportunity to vent the foibles and eccentricities of certain members of staff by impersonating them before an audience, and, indeed, before the particular members of staff themselves. This was done without malice or a desire to cause embarrassment and it says a great deal for the teachers concerned that they accepted it all in good fun. Having been a teacher myself since, I doubt if I would have been as magnanimous.

The kingpin of the Club, of course, was Mr W. J. Jones, that dear dignified chemistry teacher, that pacific disciplinarian and friend who had no need to assert his authority - his bearing and magnanimity ensured that we never crossed the boundaries of decency and propriety in Club activities. He was the epitome of the gentleman teacher. How well he was suited to his role as leader of the Club. The balance of liberty and control was perfectly poised, and, because of this, our enjoyment of the Club was complete.

Every Christmas we held the Club Christmas Party at which members of staff and their partners joined in the games and dances. What a thrill to us maturing boys to be held closely in a Tango or Veleta by a female member of staff on whom we had maintained a "crush" for several terms.

These were the joys of growing up in wartime. We were a privileged lot - privileged in being at Aberaeron County School - a school of modest size where we were all known by name and personality to a dedicated staff of teachers who had our individual well-bring at heart. That is what Education is all about."

Another Club enthusiast E. Aneurin Jones writes:

"Those of us of a certain age will remember an advertisement that insisted that "Friday Night is Amami Night", but for scores of past pupils of A.C.S., Friday night was, and is engraved on our minds as Club Night. It was a night that in those uncertain war-time days, lasted the whole week. It was arranged, anticipated, enjoyed and long savoured in retrospect. Club was a cocoon of fun and freedom in a very frightening world.

No doubt, the first half of the evening could be referred to as the soul of Club, but its heart lay in the dancing and games of the second half. Chairs would be stacked neatly and W. J. appeared as if by some sixth sense. The turn-table would move and the old 78s gave forth with - what else but the Paul Jones? Concentric circles - girls on the inside - moved around until the music stopped. The person opposite was your partner for the next few minutes. So the evening sped on - San Francisco, The Old Bull and Bush, The Polka, St. Bernard's Waltz, The Military Two-Step all wave their magic as the girls floated and the boys lumbered around the Old Hall. The boys usually sat on the high, wide window-sills, eyed the objectives, leaped down, and self-consciously walked across the Hall to seek the pleasure of a dance. The request was always polite, and acceptance gracious. Today's brashness would not have been acceptable.

To us, the Club was wonderful, wholesome and fulfilling. It helped us with the social graces, gave true pleasure and fostered friendships that have lasted fifty years and more. It engendered a healthy and natural respect between the sexes. Sex equality existed, and discrimination was unheard of. I do hope "The Club" continues to wield its magic. In my time it was an integral part of the essential A.C.S.".

Glynne Jones, who was a pupil when the school celebrated its half-century, writes today:

"Television was still unknown to us at school in Aberaeron in 1946. For our entertainment, we relied on film shows, dances and concerts at the local village halls, and in Aberaeron itself, the billiard hall was a powerful magnet.

At Aberaeron School, however, Friday evenings during the Autumn and Spring terms were eagerly awaited by the senior pupils. The School Club was in session.

Debates, mock elections, whist drives, talks by visiting speakers, form variety shows were numbered among the items presented for our entertainment during the first session on a Friday evening. The second half followed a regular pattern - draughts, chess, card games and, of course, dance music from our extensive collection of records. None of your reggae, rock, heavy metal, etc. ..... this was the real stuff - the waltz, the quickstep and the foxtrot - demanding balance, rhythm, timing and an ability to use the limited space available in the Old Hall. The gauche and the ungainly amongst us soon learned the basics!

The Club was unique in that it was run by us - the pupils. Its merits transcended mere entertainment. We had to draw up a programme for the two terms, post notices, keep minutes and accept responsibilities. Not only did the Club encourage the extrovert and the gregarious but it also opened the door for the bashful and the retiring. It was a valuable part of our school career, social, creative and an undoubted preparation for later life! The staff - W. A. Jones and T. H. Fox, who took it in turn to keep a benevolent eye on our Club evenings, gave us the opportunity to enjoy and to learn."

Henry W. Jones reminds us that:

"The early fifties saw the Club move to the new Hall. I think all who attended during those years would remember it with affection as an enjoyable extension to school Fridays - "a good thing", to use the erudition of the time. Varied activities like debates, talks, mock elections offered opportunities which many of us, alas were too dim, shy or plain lazy to grasp. But all eagerly looked forward to the dancing of the second half ...... Melys yw'r atgofion."

Christine Harries (Hides), a past President of the Club refers to the 1960s as:

"A time of change. My memories of the School Club were that it was a time of very great change. The 1960s, as everyone who is a little bit either side of fifty years old will know, was the "best" time to be a teenager. Club had just purchased a record player instead of a gramophone we had used for many years, and that would only play 78s. I was given the responsibility of going to buy the Top 20 on 45s. Two records I particularly remember are Chubby Checker's "Let's twist again" which was the new dance craze at that time, and the last record played at the end of each meeting was by Connie Francis and that was "Carolina Moon". "

Gareth Davies, Club President 1964/65 writes:

"Memories of School Club are still vivid in my mind. Friday evenings were undoubtedly the social highlight of the week when each of us would try and out-twist the other, or rock 'n roll to Elvis Presley. The dedicated weekly savings in order to present the Club with the latest smash-hit single, and the pride of hearing one's own name read out on its first playing.

Club offered much more than just dancing the evening away, but this was probably not apparent at the time. For those brave enough to volunteer, there would be the opportunity to sit on the panel of "Juke Box Jury" or "What's my Line?". More daunting would be the participation in lively debates. These events, for many of us, would have been our first introduction to public speaking, and helped to develop confidence and self-esteem. I can clearly remember delivering the President's Report on Speech Day in 1965 - I am convinced I still have the bruises as a result of my knees knocking violently together!

Aberaeron School Club was not just an institution, it was also an introduction to life ahead and a vital ingredient to the learning process."

Richard Hughes, on the other hand, remembers:

"Teachers dancing and a missing albatross. When asked to look back, across fifteen years, to my School Club days, these are the first two things that spring to mind.

The teachers were those responsible for our behaviour at the School Club discos, making sure that raging teenage hormones did not get out of control in the darkest recesses of the main Hall. Of course I realise now that they were charitable citizens giving up their spare time to enable a bunch of sixteen to eighteen-year-olds to enjoy themselves on a Friday evening. It's just that at that time some of them liked to appear in touch with the younger generation by jigging along to the music. This activity held the same sort of fascination to me then as I now get by watching the dancing on re-runs of 1970s editions of "Top of the Pops".

The "missing albatross" came from a Monty Python sketch in the year above mine -

Form VI Entertains. This was (maybe it still is?) an annual School Club tradition whereby the first year Sixth put on a show for the other members. Theirs was a well-rehearsed, polished affair, which was, in fairness, very funny.

The following year, I somehow became responsible for organising our effort. Despite great plans, all of which were much funnier in conception than in actuality, the show rapidly degenerated into a complete shambles, with key personnel going missing (à la Stephen Fry?), and certain members of the cast making rude gestures at the audience as the only way to get a laugh. All things considered however, I wonder if it was more in spirit with the tradition of the event than the professional affair which had preceded it."

I was pleased to receive confirmation from last year's Presidents - Miriam Owen and Tom Cotterill - of Club's continuing attraction despite changing circumstances and interests. I was happy to note their expressed wish that "every encouragement will be given to pupils to support the School Club for future years."

To bring the records right up to date, the present officials for the current session of School Club are:-

Presidents: Sian Griffiths and Dafydd Bevan.

Secretary: Karl Jenkins.

Treasurer: Helen Phillips.

Dafydd Bevan has written an impressive summary of his views on Club:

"This year's activities will start on October 10th with a Quiz which has already generated a high level of interest. We hope, this year, to keep that interest alive with a wide range of activities. Suggestions so far have been - a Hallowe'en Party, a Christmas shopping trip to Cardiff and a trip to see a West End show. There are also plans for activities which will not cost much money, the most obvious being the highlight of the School Club year - the traditional Christmas dance or "prom".

Most meetings will be on Tuesday nights but exceptions will have to be made for special activities. This year, being the centenary year of the School, we feel it is even more important to make this a good year for the School Club and keep up its long tradition."

Whatever the personal reflections and the ups and downs, the Club was an imaginative venture, designed to broaden the outlook by introducing young people in an informal manner to social, leisure and cultural exposures that were bound to influence their development. The School was fortunate to have those in charge who recognised these intrinsic values, and were prepared to secure such opportunities for the pupils in their charge. "Education" it has been said, "is the impact of one person upon another". That interaction was a crucial element of the School Club.

I am delighted to pay my personal tribute to all those who underpinned its activities, particularly as one remembers that this is the Seventy-fifth Anniversary of the Club's History.

Y DRYW

Cyril Jones

(*"Rather a timid pupil"*...Adroddiad ysgol 1960)

Maths o'dd y lesyn ac ma'n fyw fel ddo'
i'r dryw o'dd yn osgoi'i lyged e,-
a'i ŵn fel bran yn hedfan mewn i'w go'
o'r coridore hir tu fa's i rwm 2A.
"What is squared...squared?' yn eco yn 'i ben...
Ba-baglu balanso'r ateb ar raff iaith fain...
"Do you stammer boy...boy?' a'r eco nawr yn sen
am nad o'dd ystyr i *stammer* na siâp i'w sain.
Y crwt o'r nyth gaeedig, o bentre'r
wal lawn englynion...storiaes am fabi mewn hesg...
bron llanw'i drowsus yn sŵn crawc cwestiyne,
bron marw ise hwpo'i ben i'r ddesg.
Nawr, ma'r pin yn crafu i'w phren graffiti'i awen, druan,
a chwmpawd iaith a'i gylch e bron yn gyfan.
(1995)

❖

YR YSGOL A'R TRADDODIAD AMAETHYDDOL

Hywel Thomas (Llanarth) 1939 - 1943

In the Jubilee and War Memorial Number of "The Link" for the year 1946 it is recorded that the school acquired its garden in 1935. The late Mr. John Evans B.Sc., was appointed the school's first Agriculture Master a few years previously. The Chairman of the Governors from 1928 -1929 was the late Alderman John Jones, Penwern, Cilcennin. He was a most progressive farmer and a man of natural ability. It was mainly through his instigation that Agricultural Science became one of the subjects that was taught at the School. Under the guidance of Mr. John Evans, the school's model garden began to be developed.

Dyma ychydig o hanes yr ardd a'r berllan a gafwyd mewn llythyr oddiwrth Mr. Evan L. Williams B.Sc., Drenewydd, Powys (Llanarth gynt), Trefnydd Amaethyddol i Gyngor Sir Maldwyn am flynyddoedd lawer:

> *"Braidd yn niwlog bellach yw'r cof am y darn tir o dan yr ysgol a ddaeth i fod tua 1935, ac a fu yn 'nucleus' i'r fferm a ddaeth i fodolaeth yn ddiweddarach. Yr oedd y tir o dan borfa pan y'i prynwyd ond cafodd ei aredig a'i hau â cheirch y gwanwyn cyntaf. Yn anffodus, cafwyd cnwd rhonc ac aeth y cwbl yn fflat. Y flwyddyn ganlynol plannwyd coed afalau a ffrwythau eraill ar y rhan nesaf i'r "path" ac yn y gweddill "root crops", hynny yw, "mangolds a swedes". Gan fod cymaint o bryfetach yn y pridd, y broblem y flwyddyn honno oedd fod llawer o'r planhigion egwan yn cael eu tynnu o'r gwraidd gan frain a "jackdaws". Ar ôl y "root crop", aeth y darn yna o dan borfa a meillion - 'roedd "plots" o wahanol gymysgedd o borfa a meillion, rhesi o wahanol fathau a rhywogaethau ("species and strains") o borfa a clofer.*
>
> *Mr. John Evans (Carbon) oedd yn gyfrifol am y fenter yma, a'r unig berson arall a welais yn ymwneud â'r tir fel arbenigwr oedd Mr. Gwilym Jones, "Horticultural Instructor" y Sir, pan roddodd arddangosiad ar docio coed afalau i ni'r plant. Ymddiheuraf am nad oes rhagor o wybodaeth gen i, ond hoffwn ddweud fod Mr. John Evans, yn fy marn i, yn un o'r athrawon gorau yn yr Ysgol ac yr oedd ganddo wir ddiddordeb mewn Amaethyddiaeth."*

In his account of the School garden, Mr. Evan Williams referred to the fact that the children were present in the orchard when Mr. Gwilym Jones (who was the son of Alderman John Jones and Mrs. Jones of Penwern) was pruning the apple trees. The boys sometimes had to dig the garden and one of the pupils wrote a poem relating his experience and stand-point:-

Yr ysgol a'r ardd / The school and garden

The School Garden

All in a row, a sturdy band
We're Adam's sons in mud;
With spade and hoe we till the land
And curse the sprouting spud.
A pair of watchful eyes are thcy
That see no time is lost;
The tools are polished by the clay -
And all at our cost.
When Summer Days the garden tread,
With music in the air,
For "others" are the carrots red -
And "we" are left to swear.

Wyn Davies (Aberaeron) 1938.

In "The Link" for the year 1951, this is what appeared on the front page under Editorial:

> *"The Link comes out in an auspicious year: the year of the completion of our new buildings; the year in which we became fully "bilateral" (in the horrible modern jargon); the year in which we suddenly found ourselves a large school with a staff of 28 and more than 550 pupils; the year in which the curriculum was greatly widened to include such hitherto impossible subjects as shorthand, typing and metalwork; the year in which we first had a full-time music teacher; the year in which prefects first wore tassels on their caps! Truly, we can say with Virgil; "Magnus ab integro saeclorum nascitur ordo." But some may think it doubtful whether we can as truthfully add: "Iam nova progenies caelo demittitur alto." Let us hope that THE LINK is worthy of the occasion. If it is not, it is not for the want of trying."*

Fel y gŵyr yr rhan fwyaf ohonom, mab fferm yn ardal Ysbyty Ystwyth oedd Mr. J. T. Owen M.A., Prifathro yr ysgol yr adeg yma. Yr oedd Mr. Owen yn wladwr o'r iawn ryw, a sylweddolodd ar unwaith fod rhaid cael fferm i'r ysgol, er mwyn cynnal diddordeb bechgyn nad oeddent o dueddiadau academaidd. Daeth y cyfle yn nechrau'r pumdegau ac yr oedd Mr. John Evans B.Sc., yr Athro Amaethyddiaeth yn cydweld yn hollol. Gan fod y tir o gylch ac uwchlaw yr adeiladau newydd yn sych a llethrog, cadw defaid oedd yr ateb. Cafodd y Prifathro ei ddwyn i fyny yn sŵn brefiadau defaid a chyfarth cŵn, ac nid oedd corlannu, trochi a chneifio yn ddieithr iddo o gwbl. Penderfynwyd mai defaid oedd yr anifeiliaid i droedio'r tir yng ngolwg Bae Ceredigion. Bu adroddiad yn y Western Mail dyddiedig Rhagfyr 21ain 1952 a hefyd "Y Ddolen" yr un flwyddyn yn sôn am yr arloesi:

Western Mail 1952

"Mary had a little lamb - and as we all know, it followed her to school one day although it was strictly against the rule. In the light of modern educational developments, however, one can't help feeling that Mary lived before her time.

If she went to Aberayron (Cardiganshire) Secondary School today, for example, she would probably find her lamb quite welcome for keeping sheep has become part of the school course in agriculture science.

Three months ago, Mr. J. T. Owen (headmaster), got the county education committee to give a loan of £100 to enable the school to buy twenty store lambs. These were put out to graze on crops grown by the agricultural science pupils and after two months they were ready for the market. So well had they thrived, that the school - or rather the education committee - made a profit on them of 25s each. Another batch of twenty has been bought and these also look like bringing in a handsome profit.

"More important than the profit, however, is the practical instruction they provide for the agricultural science pupils. Under the tuition of the agricultural science master, the pupils prepare the ground and grow the crops for the sheep as well as the school canteen. They learn to recognise various diseases and pests and how to treat them. When the local vet was called in to inject the sheep against certain diseases, he gave the pupils a lecture on the subject.

"The experiment has been a most interesting one, and, at times, entertaining, especially when the boys were taught how to weigh the sheep," commentated Mr. Owen. "Some of the boys, in their eagerness to bring a lamb each to the scales, would try to get one by the tail or by means of a rugby tackle!"

Keeping sheep is only one aspect of the school's fascinating course in agricultural science. The main feature is crop production. In the one acre orchard, there are various kinds of fruit trees which are used to demonstrate the principles of manuring, grafting and spraying. Then there are the plots for demonstrating the Norfolk four course rotation system; the plots classifying the commonest botanical families, as well as another set of plots for the different species of grasses. Sometimes crops are grown which are new to the district, for example, lucerne and fodder beet.

An interesting experiment has also been carried out by Dr. Rice Williams, a Ministry of Agriculture soil chemist, on the manurial treatment of potatoes. Local farmers were invited to return to school temporarily for this demonstration.

Like most secondary schools, Aberayron has its workshop. In this case, the work done is designed to give the boys the knowledge and skill to tackle any of the small engineering jobs that are likely to be found on a modern mechanised farm. They are taught welding and brazing, drilling and soldering, etc. and how to repair the various kinds of farm machinery. The mysteries of the combustion engine and diesel engine are explained to them, and they are shown how to handle a tractor and other farm implements.

The girls have their own workshops. In addition to the usual domestic science subjects, they are given a course in crafts which covers embroidery, weaving, leatherwork, fabric printing and basketry. So successful has the course been that many girls have bought their own looms and tools after leaving school.

The reasons for providing this type of education for a proportion of pupils were explained by Mr. Owen. "The majority of our pupils are children born and bred on the land and their main ambition, especially the boys, is to return to live in rural surroundings when they leave school," he said. "This tendency may be due to several factors:

1. *many come from progressive agricultural areas;*

2. *there is in many of the surrounding villages a strong, healthy, communal life;*

3. *conditions today in the agricultural industry are such as to attract good quality pupils to the land including some whose academic achievements at school would warrant a successful career at a University.*

"This is as it should be. If we continue to export our best intellect to the black-coated professions then the cultural, social and even the agricultural life of the countryside is doomed. For this reason, I am convinced that it is our duty at school to foster in the abler pupils a regard for country life."

After saying that the agricultural industry today has been completely revolutionised and had become a very prosperous industry, Mr. Owen continued:

"This industry, which no country in future can afford to neglect, calls for a far more mechanically minded generation of land workers than ever before and I maintain that the foundation of this adaptability must be laid in the secondary schools. Naturally, all our pupils take certain subjects to satisfy their needs as members of the community."

"After these "core" subjects, come the optional subjects and agricultural science is one of them. It is taken by over fifty per cent of our pupils up to the General Certificate of Education standard. Among these pupils are some from urban areas whose knowledge of farming is negligible when they start the course."

The "Link" 1952

"Tua diwedd tymor yr haf, rhoed gwahoddiad i amaethwyr Cylch Aberaeron i ymweld â'r ysgol fel y caffent gyfle i sylwi ar y gwaith a wnaed gyda pharatoi plant i fyw bywyd a dilyn gorchwylion gwlad. Aed ar draws ac ar hyd y plotiau arbrawf, yr ardd gyda'i hamryw arbrofion ar datw, a'r berllan, lle caed anerchiad ar goed ffrwythau gan Mr. Gwilym Jones. Yna treuliwyd cryn amser yn y Siopau gwaith coed a metel, a chafwyd cyfle i weld plant yr ochr Fodern yn trin yr offer, ac yn troi allan lawer teclyn defnyddiol i fferm a bwthyn. Bu'r gwragedd hwythau yn yr ystafelloedd coginio, arlunio a chrefft. A ninnau'n byw yn sŵn dadleu pwyllgor a chynhadledd ar ddysgu Amaethyddiaeth fel gwyddor mewn ysgol am addysg dechnegol, yr oedd yn dda cael y cyfle hwn i geisio darbwyllo'r gwahoddedigion mai tan gronglwyd yr Ysgolion Sir y dylid cychwyn ar waith fel hyn. Ar derfyn y prynhawn caed cwpaned o de a'r athrawesau'n gweini. Hyderwn y gellir trefnu ymweliadau tebyg eto."

Wedi cael y fath lwyddiant wrth besgi'r ŵyn stôr teimlodd Mr. Owen a Mr. Evans mai'r cam nesaf oedd sefydlu diadell i fagu ŵyn. Mr. John Jones (Aberarth yn awr) a oedd yn ffermio Bryngwyn, uwchlaw yr ysgol, yn y blynyddoedd pell yn ôl bellach, ac ato ef y trowyd am gyfarwyddyd ynglyn â pha frid o ddefaid i'w cadw. Yr oedd y ddolen gyswllt rhwng y Bryn a'r Ysgol wedi dod i fod mor gynnar â dechrau y tridegau, canys dŵr a darddai yn ffynnon ar y fferm gnydiog yma a arweiniwyd trwy bibellau i ddiwallu holl anghenion yr Ysgol. Yr oedd Mr. John Jones y Bryn yn ŵr ifanc yr adeg yma ond yn brofiadol dros ben ym mhob agwedd o ffermio. Yn ôl Mr. Jones, tueddai Mr. J. T. Owen at gael diadell o ddefaid Cymreig pennau gwynion tra yr oedd Mr. John Evans yn ffafrio y ddafad benddu a oedd yn fwy o faint ac yn epilio yn fwy niferus. O dan arweiniad profiadol ffermwr y Bryn bu cyfaddawd a phrynwyd nifer o'r ddau frid.

Bu rhaid gosod terfynau addas er atal y defaid rhag crwydro a rhannau'r fferm yn gaeau hwylus yn ogystal. Pan oedd anhawster adeg geni'r wyn, John Jones a fyddai'n dod i'r adwy, ond yn ddiau yr oedd y plant a'r ddau Bennaeth yn dysgu yn gyflym o dan gyfarwyddyd y ffermwr deheuig. Yn y blynyddoedd yma, trochid y defaid mewn man pwrpasol yn y Bryn ac yno yr oedd y cneifio hefyd. Nid yn unig yr oedd cadw defaid yn dod ag elw i'r fenter, trwy werthu yr ŵyn a'r gwlân, ond yn ogystal, creai flas ar ddod i'r ysgol i blant y wlad, a maes o law daethant yn ffermwyr penigamp, yn yr ardaloedd amgylchynol. Yr oedd angen aredig darnau o'r fferm er cael dau laswelltyn i dyfu lle bu ond un gynt. I ymgymryd â'r gwaith o drin y tir prynwyd tractor Ferguson llwyd yn weddol rad, a'r peiriannau hefyd. Y gŵr a oedd yn gyrru'r tractor oedd y diweddar bellach, Mr. David Thomas Jones, Goitre, tyddyn bychan gerllaw. Yr oedd yn beiriannydd wrth reddf a'r wybodaeth drylwyr a oedd yn eiddo iddo, wedi'i loffa o feysydd ymhel â'r grefft dros nifer fawr o flynyddoedd. Clywais yr hanes yma gan Mr. John Jones, Aberarth, yn Nhachwedd 1995:

"Yn gynnar yn y dauddegau yr oedd y diweddar Mr. a Mrs. Ben Davies, Cefn Wig,

Aberarth, wedi prynu "Oil Engine" newydd sbon. Er ei bod yn gwneud y gwaith arferol ar y fferm sef malu a phwlpo a chaffo, yr oedd rhywbeth heb fod yn berffaith yn ei sŵn. Daeth Mr. D. T. Jones, y Goitre, heibio rhyw brynhawn a chyda'i glust wedi ei deneuo fel cerddor, i nodau peiriant, gofynnodd i Mr. Ben Davies a gawsai ei ganiatad i'w 'thynnu i lawr'. Bodlonodd y perchennog canys gwyddai fod y mecanic hunan-ddysgedig yn ŵr difeth. Wedi cyrraedd perfedd y peiriant canfuwyd fod un darn bach heb ei gysylltu yn berffaith. Gwnaeth Mr. Jones y cysylltiad priodol ac yna ail osodwyd y peiriant nerthol. Ni fu yr un trafferth ar ôl hynny a rhoddodd flynyddoedd lawer o wasanaeth gwerthfawr i'w pherchnogion."

Nid yw yn syndod o gwbl mai ef a ddaeth yn ŵr i drin y tir a gyrru y "Fergi Fach". Adeiladwyd sied gweddol rad fel cartref i'r tractor nepell o ffordd Gerallt. Yn ôl a glywais gan Mr. Gareth Owen, yr oedd ei dad Mr. J. T. Owen yn dychwelyd i'r ysgol un hanner dydd pan welodd Mr. D. T. Jones yn y sied a'r tractor wedi ei ddatgymalu a darnau ohoni ar y llawr, a'r mecanic â'i ddwylo a'i ddillad yn olew a "grease" i gyd. Yn ôl y mab, gwylltiodd y Prifathro a daeth geiriau nad ydynt mewn geiriadur dros ei wefusau, gan y credai fod ei beiriant annwyl wedi ei ddifetha. "Peidiwch â becso dim, Mr. Owen bach," meddai D. T. mor hunanfeddiannol ag y gall meidrol fod, "erbyn nos yfory, fe fydd hon yn gweithio yn well nag y gweloch chi hi erioed." "Gewn ni weld," meddai'r Prifathro â thôn o amheuaeth yn ei lais. Yr oedd gan Mr. Jones ddigon o hyder yn ei allu mecanyddol a bu'r hyn a ddywedodd yn hollol gywir. Rhoddodd y Ferguson flynyddoedd lawer o wasanaeth difeth wedi'r 'driniaeth' o dan law y "dewin" hwn.

O dan ei gyfarwyddyd sicr ef, dysgodd degau o blant o anian fecanyddol, lawer am y tractor a'r peiriannau a oedd ar fferm yr Ysgol. Yn ddios, y mae llawer ohonynt yn cofio gydag anwyldeb am yr amser a dreuliasant yng nghwmni Mr. John Evans a Mr. D. T. Jones yn plannu tato a cheisio 'cau y rhychiau' a'r scyfflo a'r howio cyn dod i dymor y tyfiant. Bu ambell gnwd tato yn drymach na'i gilydd ond yr oedd rhyw hwyl anghymarol wrth eu crynhoi. Yr oedd "rhin rhyw awch fel hen flys, yn llosgi rhwd a llesgedd oriau gwaith oddiar eu gwedd" Gan fod y bechgyn yn gryf ac ifanc a'r cyhyrau yn hyblyg, yr oedd y "sgrwb" wedi darfod erbyn trannoeth. Tyfwyd swêds yn ogystal ac fe'i defnyddiwyd i fwydo'r defaid yn hirlwm gaeaf. Nid oes dim yn well i lanhau y tir yn barod i'w ailhadu na'r llysiau gwyrdd yma, ac nid oes eisiau llawer o wrtaith arnynt.

Nid oedd yr un Ysgol Gyfun arall yn Sir Aberteifi â fferm yn eiddo iddi, ac ymfalchïai y Prifathro am hyn. Yr oedd peth o bridd tir y Dderw (lle ganwyd ef) ar ei esgidiau o hyd a medrodd, drwy y fferm, gyplysu dau fyd, yr academaidd a "chrefft gyntaf dynol-ryw".

Rhywbeth yn debyg a fu'r ffermio o flwyddyn i flwyddyn, ambell haf yn gynhesach na'i gilydd a'r cnydau yn fwy toreithiog wedi i'r glaw ddod yn ei bryd. Ffermwyr yr ardal o gylch Aberaeron a fyddai'n cneifio, a chywain y gwair, yn rhydd yn y blynyddoedd cynnar ac mewn byrnau yn ddiweddarach. Bu Mr. Morlais Davies, Mwdwl, a'i ddau fab Byron a Ceredig yn cneifio am flynyddoedd, a'r plant wrth eu bodd yn dal y defaid a rhoi'r gwlân yn becynnau twt. Bu Mr. George Lloyd, Pengarreg, a'i fab, Hugh, yn byrnio y gwair droeon. Wrth aredig y darnau braidd yn serth a'r graig yn agos, nid oedd y gwaith wrth fodd Mr. John Evans a bu "Rotovator" yn gwneud ei ran i baratoi gwell gwely i'r hadau porfa.

Soniodd un cyn-ddisgybl wrthyf ei fod ef ac un neu ddau arall o'i ffrindiau wedi cael cynnig i lywio y peiriant yma ar fan anodd. Pan welodd un o'r athrawon eraill hwy, gorchmynodd iddynt adael y gwaith. Bu'n eu dwrdio yn gas ac achwynodd wrth y Prifathro. Gan gymaint oedd diddordeb Mr. J. T. Owen yn yr agwedd yma o addysg bechgyn y wlad, dywedodd wrth yr achwynwr am anghofio am hyn gan ddweud "diolchwch na chafodd neb anaf." Ni roddai'r un dim fwy o fwynhad i Mr. Owen na gweld yr ŵyn bach yn prancio yn afieithus ar y caeau.

Wedi i Mr. David Thomas Jones ymddeol, apwyntiwyd y diweddar Mr. Artie Jones, Cefntyncoed a Glanyrafon, i gymeryd ei le a bu wrthi am flynyddoedd lawer hyd i afiechyd blin ei orfodi i rhoddi heibio'r gwaith. Y mae gan rhai cannoedd o blant atgofion hyfryd am y gŵr ffraeth a rhadlon hwn. Clywais am lawer o'r cyn ddisgyblion yn sôn amdanynt yn mynd yn eu tro i Farchnad Ystrad â llwyth o ŵyn yng nghefn y "Fan". Fel y dengys y lluniau, rhoddai'r bechgyn gymorth i ddal yr ŵyn i'w pwyso ac yr oedd Mr. J. T. Owen a Mr. John Evans gyda hwy ar yr achlysur yna. Dywedoodd un bachgen arall wrthyf fod y cnwd tato un flwyddyn yn eithriadol o doreithiog a bod un taten anferth a honno ar ffurf pêl rygbi. Ni fwytawyd hon, yn hytrach, fe'i harddangoswyd am wythnosau lawer, a chred y tynnwyd ei llun yn ogystal. Cafodd to ar ôl to o blant hwyl arbennig wrth gydweithio gyda Mr. Artie Jones, Mr. E. L. Davies, Mr. Tom Davies, Mr. D. Tudor Lewis ac ar ôl ymadawiad Artie, Mr. Jenkin Lewis.

Clywais y stori yma gan un bachgen arall. Un dechrau gaeaf, gofynnodd Mr. John Evans i'r bechgyn ar ddydd Gwener a ddeuent dydd Llun â'r sweden fwyaf a oedd ganddynt ar eu ffermydd. Hwyrach fod y cnwd yma yn cael ei dyfu ar ei fferm ef ond gwyddai i sicrwydd nad oeddent gymaint o faint â'r rhai a oedd ar fferm yr Ysgol. Felly mor llechwraidd â phosibl, aeth ef a'i ffrind pennaf, i chwilota ymysg y rhesi graenus, a thynasant un fawr a'i chuddio mewn twll dirgel yn y clawdd ac yr oeddent yn siŵr y byddent yn agos i'r brig. Bore Llun a ddaeth, a'r ddau yn cerdded yn dalog a hyderus at y guddfan. Er mawr siom iddynt yr oedd cwningod wedi dechrau gosod eu dannedd yn y sweden a'i anharddu. Nid oedd ganddynt felly yr un gobaith i gael y clod. Dyna un stori o blith cannoedd y gŵyr y cyn-ddisgyblion amdanynt.

Diau fod hedyn diddordeb mewn ffermio wedi ei osod yng nghalonnau y bechgyn cyn iddynt gyrraedd Ysgol Gyfun Aberaeron, ond o dan arweiniad goleuedig a thadol Mr. John Evans ynghyd â chefnogaeth lwyr Mr. J. T. Owen, daeth degau lawer ohonynt yn ffermwyr amlycaf ein Sir. Pwy all fesur yn iawn ddylanwad gweledigaeth lachar y ddau berson yma bron hanner canrif yn ôl bellach? Ymddeolodd Mr. J. T. Owen yn 1965 wedi gwasanaethu yr Ysgol am ddeugain a dwy o flynyddoedd, eu hanner union fel Athro a'r ail hanner fel Prifathro. Flwyddyn yn ddiweddarach daeth cwys Mr. John Evans yntau i'r pentalar a dyma'r adroddiad yn y "Ddolen" am yr achlysur:

Resignation - Mr. John Evans, B.Sc.

"The familiar figure of one member of staff, Mr. John Evans, will no longer be with us after the end of the Summer Term. He is retiring to a well-earned rest after giving thirty-three years' devoted service to the school as Head of the Science Department.

A native of the Swansea Valley, Mr. Evans graduated in 1923 at the University College of Wales, Aberystwyth with Honours in Botany. He embarked on his teaching career as Science Master at the former Central School, Lampeter, before being appointed to the post of Botany Master at Aberaeron in 1933.

Facilities for Science Teaching in those days were very limited compared with those of today. There was only one laboratory available - a Chemistry Laboratory.

The development of Agricultural Science together with its practical application with which Mr. Evans' name will always be inseparably linked at this school, was not to become a reality until an acre of land, the plot situated below the Gymnasium, was purchased for the school shortly before the War, thereby providing Mr. Evans with a badly needed outdoor "laboratory".

During the War, Mr. Evans' services were claimed by the Ministry of Agriculture when he left his teaching post for a temporary period to become Assistant Land Commissioner for Breconshire and Glamorganshire.

It was really after the War with the provision of the new Wing that Agricultural Science came into its own at the school. Backed by the foresight and enthusiasm of the Headmaster, Mr. J. T. Owen, Mr. Evans has seen the material facilities of his department grow so that at the present time the one acre of land available before the War has increased to approximately twenty acres. A flock of thirty-five ewes now grazes the hilly pastures and a new Agricultural and General Science Laboratory has been added to the Biology, Chemistry and Physics Wing.

Always kind in manner, sympathetic with his pupils and showing a rare understanding of their needs, he takes with him into his retirement the esteem and friendship of his colleagues and the affection and gratitude of both present and past generations of children."

Apwyntiwyd Mr. E. D. Williams B.Sc. fel Athro Gwyddoniaeth Amaethyddol i barhau'r hyn a gychwynwyd tua phymtheg mlynedd ynghynt. Yr oedd y fferm y pryd hyn yng ngofal Mr. Artie Jones a'i gydweithiwr Mr. E. L. Davies. Cynyddwyd nifer y ddiadell nes fod yna dros hanner cant o ddefaid erbyn dechrau 1968. Daeth mwy o gyffuriau i atal clefydau, a hyfforddai Mr. Williams y bechgyn a'r merched yn ogystal, sut i frechu'r defaid ac ar ba adeg i wneud hynny. Y mae un o'r bechgyn a oedd yn yr ysgol yn ystod tymor Mr. Williams sef Mr. Ian Evans o Dalgarreg, yn sôn am y blynyddoedd hynny. Bellach y mae Mr. Evans a'i briod, Mrs. Gwendoline Evans a'u dau blentyn yn byw yn Tirgwyn, Llwyndafydd. Dyma ei adroddiad:

Fferm yr Ysgol

1967 - 1971

"Pan oeddwn yn yr ail flwyddyn yn yr ysgol byddwn yn cael gwersi "General Science" gyda Mr. David Williams, a dyna lle byddem wrth ein bodd yn cael mynd allan i bwyso ŵyn er mwyn cofnodi'r "live weight gain" a injecto a doso'r defaid a'r ŵyn. Roedd yr ysgol yn codi tatw hefyd at ddefnydd y gegin. Erbyn cyrraedd y drydedd a'r bedwaredd flwyddyn, byddwn yn helpu mwy ar Artie ac Ifan a oedd yn gofalu am y fferm a thorri'r borfa a gofalu am y ddaear o amgylch yr ysgol. Os na fyddai'r gwersi eraill wrth ein dant, byddai modd colli ambell un er mwyn rhoi help llaw! Roedd 'na berllan 'fale yn yr ysgol hefyd, a rhaid oedd helpu i dynnu'r 'fale yn yr Hydref. Ond yr adeg mwyaf prysur oedd yr haf - adeg y cneifio a'r cynhaeaf gwair. Os yw'r cof yn iawn, George Pencarreg byddai'n cneifio ac yn cynhaeafu'r gwair a phlant yr ysgol yn helpu i ddal y defaid, pacio'r gwlân a chario'r bêls gwair. Os oedd rhaid mynd i gwato rhag rhywun neu rywbeth, wel y "Boiler Room" amdani, achos dyna lle 'roedd Artie ac Ifan yn mynd i gael eu tocyn hanner dydd!"

In the Western Mail for March 12th 1968 there appeared the following account:

Where Pupils have good wool mark.

"Boys and girls at a West Wales secondary school are getting first-hand training in animal husbandry - for the school has its own flock of sheep which has now grown to more than 50. Wool from the animals is used by the handicrafts class at Aberaeron Secondary School, Cardiganshire, to make materials for a variety of garments. The sheep are kept on the 20 acres of mainly hill land which the school has as part of its grounds. Ten acres of the land has been bought from a local farmer with money from the sale of lambs.

The school's groundsman, Mr. Arthur Jones, who looks after the sheep, told me that the flock, which includes several pedigree Clun Forest sheep had been started about 16 years ago. The flock of a dozen sheep and one ram the school bought has grown steadily over the years although most of the lambs are sold every year at local marts.

The agricultural science master, Mr. E. D. Williams told me, "The school has a lot of land and the best use we can make of it is to keep sheep. We also have an orchard and garden where we grow fruit and vegetables which are used in the school canteen."

Mr. Williams said that the flock of sheep was now providing an important part of the children's education, particularly as the school was in the heart of a rural area.

"We have to teach a very high standard of farming as we get a fair amount of criticism from farmers' sons and daughters. They compare our methods with those used at their own homes."

Mr. Williams said that the school had its own agricultural science laboratory and when they left school, the children who took agriculture had an excellent, first-hand knowledge of farming.

Money from the sale of the wool and lambs was used to buy food and agricultural machinery. Some of the wool, however, is bought by the school's handicrafts class, sorted, spun, dyed and woven on looms to make material for garments. It is also used at the school for knitting. The handicrafts mistress, Mrs. Nancy Evans, said that the girls found it particularly interesting to use school wool in their lessons."

Tua diwedd y saithdegau, cafodd Mr. Dai Lloyd, un o athrawon yr ysgol, y syniad y byddai'n werth amrywio ychydig ynglyn â'r fferm. Diau y sylweddolodd Mr. Lloyd nad oedd pob bachgen â diddordeb mewn defaid, trin tir a'r cnydau arferol. Yr oedd darn o'r berllan, a'r coed yn hen a diffrwyth, a phenderfynodd Mr. Lloyd, gyda chaniatad y Prifathro, Mr. D. J. Thomas, i'w gau yn ddiogel a chadw dofednod yno. Bu'n fenter arloesol a llwyddiannus a gwnaed elw ariannol hefyd. Pwy a wâd na heuwyd diddordeb mewn nifer o'r disgyblion, a dygodd hwnnw ffrwyth ar ei ganfed, maes o law. Dyma atgofion un o'r rhai y bu Mr. Lloyd yn eu hyfforddi, sef Mr. David J. Richards (Llanarth gynt) yn awr o Aberystwyth:

"I have fond memories of my time spent as treasurer of the school poultry farm. I learnt new skills and gained an insight into the farming industry both on a practical and financial level (albeit on a small scale).

On the practical side, we started with a disused orchard and through our efforts and hard work converted it into a small poultry farm. This involved repairing and erecting fencing and building pens for the chickens, ducks and geese and generally preparing the land in readiness for them. We had great fun digging out an area to be used as a duck pond by getting more than a little wet and muddy in the process!

Our next task was to go to an auction in Hereford to buy the poultry. The enthusiasm of our teacher, Mr. Dai Lloyd, ensured that our day was interesting, educational and a lot of fun!

We were then responsible for the birds and it was our duty to make sure they were well looked after until the time came for those which had been fattened up for Christmas to be killed and dressed. Because I had to feed the poultry, I missed assembly and I did not regret that at all!

On the financial side, when I was told I had to meet the bank manager to discuss opening a business account, an image sprang to mind of a fearsome, two-horned figure looming menacingly behind a desk. This was due to the comments I'd overheard as a child about the "Dreaded Bank Manager". What a relief it was to be greeted by a friendly-faced man who invited us into his office with a smile - phew!

I found I enjoyed learning about running a business - such as how to make a profit, taking into account hidden costs, and how to market and present a product to the customers.

To sum up, I can honestly say that the memories have stayed with me over the years and they inspired me to become my own boss, which I now am, as a business partner running a Butchery. But more than that, I was lucky to have been part of a great team of schoolfriends, mucking in together, which, along with the encouragement of the teachers - Mr. Lloyd, Mrs. Daniel, Mr. ap Dewi and the Headmaster, Mr. Thomas, made it a rewarding and worthwhile experience."

Y mae cannoedd o gyn-ddisgyblion yr ysgol yn sôn gydag anwyldeb a diolchgarwch, am y profiadau a gawsant ynglyn â'r fferm. Onid yw dynoliaeth yn eu dyled i'r arloeswyr ym mhob cylch o fywyd? Rhaid cydnabod hefyd, fod y weledigaeth lachar sydd bron yn hanner cant oed bellach, yn cael y sylw a'r gofal gan y rhai a ddaeth ar ôl Mr. J. T. Owen a Mr. John Evans. Y mae ymroddiad y gwŷr yma yn deilwng o glod a chydnabyddiaeth ac fe'i cant yn yr adroddiad canlynol gan Mr. Graham Hope, Dirprwy Brifathro, sy'n glo i bennod unigryw yn hanes Ysgol Gyfun Aberaeron.

"Over the last twenty years many changes have taken place in the field of education. The influence of T.V.E.I. courses and the introduction of the National Curriculum has changed the nature of the school curriculum. Likewise rapid changes in the agricultural industry have also taken place. Consequently, the way in which the school farm has been run has changed enormously."

Several members of staff have been involved in the running of the farm since the 1970s - Mr. Myrddin Evans, Mr. Meurig James and, more recently, Mr. Meirion Jones. All three staff have made a significant contribution to ensuring that the farm is still an integral part of the school.

Pupils still follow a Certificate of Education course in Agriculture and enjoy the experiences the school farm offers under the watchful eye of Mr. Meirion Jones. The purchase of a four-wheeled drive motorbike and trailer ensures that there are always sufficient volunteers to feed the sheep in the winter months! The flock now numbers ninety-four, ninety ewes and four rams; lambing occurs in mid-March in order to produce fat lambs for the autumn markets. Future pupils will have to rise to the challenge of producing quality sheep for a very discerning market. A new shed has recently been built on the school site and this will provide a much needed shelter for the coming lambing season.

Whilst the farm continues to provide a sound and valid educational experience for interested pupils, changes in school funding procedures have made it imperative for it also to be profitable. Animal husbandry has also changed dramatically, and Health and Safety regulations have become more stringent. Consequently, new and interesting challenges will be presented to the pupils of the 21st Century. Who knows, future developments could involve ostriches or emus, but only if the fences are reinforced!

Whatever happens, we must ensure that the foundations so carefully laid down many years ago are further developed. We must continue to promote the school farm as an exciting and unique educational experience for those pupils who wish to learn about countryside management and proceed to rural employment."

Carwn ddiolch yn ddiffuant i bawb a'm cynorthwyodd i gael yr hanes yma i olau dydd a rhwng cloriau Llyfr y Canmlwyddiant.

Were it not for the information I was given by so many people, my task would never have been completed.

❖

The poultry farm

CANT HEB FOD ALLAN - A HUNDRED NOT OUT

D. Geraint Davies

Dros y can mlynedd, mae nifer o agweddau wedi cyfrannu'n helaeth at lwyddiant Ysgol Gyfun Aberaeron. Fel yr ymfalchïwn yn nhraddodiad academaidd yr ysgol llawenhawn yng ngorchestion y meysydd chwarae. Yn araf bach yr heuwyd yr had ar ddiwedd y ganrif ddiwethaf, ond mae'r cynhaeaf dros y blynyddoed wedi bod yn ffrwythlon ac yn bell gyrhaeddol. Profwyd nifer o lwyddiannau lleol yn ystod y dyddiau cynnar, ond ers hynny mae nifer o athletwyr yr ysgol wedi amlygu eu hunain ar lwyfannau cenedlaethol a rhyngwladol. Mae'r bennod hon er teyrnged iddynt. Gobeithio hefyd y bydd yn ysbrydoliaeth i'w cyffelyb yn y dyfodol.

YR HANNER CYNTAF 1896 - 1945

Mae traddodiad yr ysgol ar y meysydd chwarae yn ymestyn yn ôl i'r dyddiau cynnar, a hyd yn oed yn 1897, cytunodd y Prifathro a'r Rheolwyr i dalu £2.2.0 *"for the use of a plot of ground for croquet for the girls."* Yn fuan cyflwynwyd hoci a phêl-droed, ac yn 1902 cyfeiriwyd at *"the progress made in athletics by the impetus given to football by Mr. Scott and the establishment by him of a hockey club which was now being well handled by Mr. D. Williams B.A."*

Bu rhaid aros tan 1904 cyn i'r athrawes gyntaf gymryd at awenau y tîm hoci merched gyda Miss Bennison *"undertaking to supervise and play with the girls while practising at hockey."* Hi hefyd, oedd yn gyfrifol ddwy flynedd yn ddiweddarach am archebu dwsin o ffyn hoci *"at a cost not exceeding 30/-."* Ar yr un adeg, profwyd haelioni'r Rheolwyr ymhellach, pan ganiatawyd gwariant o £2.2.0 i'r tim pêl-droed a £2.10.0 i'r tîm hoci.

Erbyn 1907, roedd dylanwad rhai o'r cyn-ddisgyblion ar y meysydd chwarae eisioes yn ymestyn tu hwnt i Geredigion :-

> *"In the Athletic world the Old Pupils are found to be doing fairly well. Miss E. V. Beckett, Mr Milton Davies and Mr Garfield Davies assist the Cardiff University firsts in Hockey and Association Football respectively. Mr T. Harold Evans is also doing very well at Aberystwyth at hockey. Mr D. W. Lloyd who did good service for his University, is a valuable asset to the Kilkenny Town and County Association football teams. Mr D. Thomas Jones has turned his affections from the East Cardiff Hockey Club to the Whitchurch club and is doing well for the latte.r.*

Yn ail rhifyn "The Link" yn 1908, ychydig o sylw a roddwyd i chwaraeon a bodlonwyd gyda rhestri'r swyddogion yn unig:-

"Turning to the question of officials, we find that the Girls' Hockey team is captained by Sally Owen, with Nesta Howell as vice-captain. Miss Owen B.A has been appointed secretary, and Olwen Davies, treasurer. Of the Boys' Association Football team, Ireneaus Jones has been elected captain, Scott Jones vice captain, Michael Davies as treasurer and Morgan D. Morgan and David Rees Davies as secretaries."

Eisioes fodd bynnag, chwaraewyd yn erbyn ysgolion eraill. Gan gofio cyflwr y ffyrdd a'r ffaith na ddaeth y rheilffordd i'r dref tan 1911, roedd hyn yn dipyn o gamp.

"The School Hockey and Football teams were carried in the brakes of Mr O. J. Jones and it was an education to sit behind the wonderful horses of "Owen the Van" and admire his control of the ribbons.

Our first winter trips in 1908, were to Llandysul a journey of four hours each way, the return journey in each case being made in the pouring rain - in an open brake.

These and subsequent trips were made enjoyable because the bulk of the boys were members of the School Male Voice Choir, trained by Mr E. O . James B.A. It was a case of singing the whole way home, many of the boys being first class soloists."

Roedd y cyfleusterau newid ac ymolchi llawn mor gyntefig â'r teithio:-

"Washing after games in those early days was primitive. If lucky, the boys would obtain pans of warm water from the kitchen, and taking these to the corridors would create an awful mess endeavouring to remove the grime of the playing fields."

Yn ystod tymor 1908-09, chwaraeodd y tîm hoci chwech gêm gan ennill dwy, colli dwy gyda'r ddwy arall yn gyfartal. Y canlyniadau oedd:

"Home Matches	*Away Matches*
Aberayron 1 Tregaron 0	*Aberystwyth 1 Aberayron 0*
Aberayron 2 Llandysul 1	*Llandysul 2 Aberayron 1*
Aberayron 2 Aberystwyth 2	*Tregaron 1 Aberayron 1 "*

O safbwynt nifer y gemau, braidd yn siomedig y bu'r tymor canlynol:-

"The girls have only played one match this season. They journeyed up to Tregaron with the amiable intention of giving the County School a thorough good drubbing. But as Bobbie Burns said, "The best laid scheme o' mice and men, gang aft agley." They were defeated but not disgraced by three - two. Next term, they mean to pay old scores back."

Y tîm a deithiodd i Dregaron oedd:-

"Mary Anna Jones, Nesta Howell, Grace Jones, Jane Davies, Lillian Howell, Nora James, Olwen Davies, Menevia Davies, Kathleen Jones, Olive Evans, and Lizzie Jones".

Cyffelyb bu hanes y tîm pêl-droed yn ystod yr un tymor. O dan gapteniaeth Penrhiw Evans:-

"the boys have played two matches this season. Although possessing a smart, vigorous team, ill-luck has dogged their footsteps so far. At Tregaron, they were defeated by two goals to one, and to their great surprise, Aberystwyth followed this up by defeating them on their home ground by five goals to one. But murmurs of revenge and growls of rage are heard on the football field, and these bode ill to the opposing teams for next term."

Gwireddwyd yr addewid, ac yn ystod y tymor canlynol daeth cyfle i dalu'r pwyth yn ôl :

"<u>Aberystwyth v Aberayron October 15th</u>

The boys opened the season well by defeating Aberystwyth 4-1. The scorers were Penrhiw Evans 2, Ernest Davies 2.

<u>Aberayron v Tregaron November 5th</u>

As was natural, this game was looked forward to with keenness. The opening stages proved even and interesting but gradually the Aeronites improved and won a hard game by 5-3. Scorers - Penrhiw Evans 3, Arnold Lewis, Ernest Davies."

Parhawyd yn ddi guro yn y ddwy gêm arall a chwaraewyd:-

"<u>Aberayron v New Quay October 19th</u>

In this match the visitors were completely outclassed, sufficent proof of this is, that a half back and a full back scored. The result was 7-2 in favour of the homesters. Scorers - Penrhiw Evans 3, Arnold Lewis, Aeron Jones, Peredur Jones, J.G Williams.

<u>Aberayron v Ystrad Meurig November 12th</u>

This was the first meeting of teams representing these schools. The result was a win for the homesters by 3-1."

Seren y tîm yn ddi-os oedd Penrhiw Evans. Bu'n gapten am ddau dymor gan goroni pob dim yn 1911, pan sgoriodd tair ar ddeg o goliau mewn dwy gêm; wyth wrth i'r tîm guro tîm tref Cei Newydd 10-0, a phump yn y fuddugoliaeth o 5-2 dros Dregaron.

❖

Bu 1913 yn garreg filltir yn hanes chwaraeon yn yr ysgol :-

"Lawn tennis has at last made its appearance at the school. The fixtures of the game having been obtained at the end of last year, through the energies of Mr W. J. Jones

and Dr. Davies to whom we tender our sincere thanks.

Early in the present year vague and mysterious shadows were seen in the misty twilight within the precincts of the school grounds. On closer inspection, these proved to be the "general factorum" and his business-like helpers, the budding professionals, who were doing their utmost in endeavouring to make their one and only lawn assume a playable condition. These worthy efforts met with their just reward and we were able to start tennis at the earliest possible date with the kind permission of Jupiter Pluvius.

The game was indulged in with the greatest zest by the girls of all the Forms, and play continued on every suitable occasion throughout the summer term and summer holidays, the weather proving most favourable.

On many Saturdays the pleasure of the game was greatly enhanced from a social point of view by the introduction of "al fresco" afternoon teas. These were a source of great pleasure to all concerned and were thoroughly enjoyed."

Am y tymor cyntaf merched yn unig oedd â'r hawl i chwarae tenis, ond yn 1914 :-

"Tennis at school this year was made more interesting because of the permission given to the boys to join in. Our membership therefore swelled enormously, and we had nearly 50 pupils making the most frantic efforts to lessen the bumps on our one and only tennis pitch."

Gyda'r aelodaeth newydd bu'n bosibl i drefnu'r twrnament llawn cyntaf:-

"In spite of rainy days, the tournament lasting over three weeks and running into 1161 games was carried to a successful end on June 20th when the finals of five events were played."

Final Results :-

Girls Singles: Edna Philips Jones beat Milwen Jones

Boys Singles: Morgan Davies beat Maldwyn Evans

Girls Doubles: Cybell Owen and Lizzie Jones beat Gwyneth Jones and Eluned Owen

Boys Doubles: Morgan Davies and Joseph Lewis beat Maldwyn Evans and Willie Jones

Mixed Doubles: Eluned Owen and David Lewis Jones beat Edna Philips Jones and David Higgon Jones

Umpire: Mr. W. J. Jones B.Sc".

Tenis i bob pwrpas oedd gêm y dref yr adeg yma. Chwaraewyd yn y 'Sports Club' wrth ymyl yr afon gyda'r clwb yn trefnu gemau cyson yn erbyn trefi cyfagos megis

Aberystwyth, Tregaron a Llambed. Felly, bu merched yr ysgol yn ddewr iawn i benderfynu *"after much consultation to send a challenge to the Town Tennis Club."*

> *"The fatal day dawned and it must be admitted that the girls had a severe shock when they saw the cream of the town players all "togged" ready for the fray...........at the sight of the splendid tea laid out for their benefit, their spirits rose again to their highest extent, and they prepared themselves confidently ....but they had a great shock when they found that their skill was not so great after all when pitted against the town professionals..................... we regret to say that the only fact worth mentioning is due to the powers of Bessie Davies and Eluned Owen, who actually beat a strong pair of town players in the last set of all................they maintain however that they would have done better on their own courts."*

❖

Dechreuwyd ar gyfnod newydd o gystadlu gyda sefydlu tri thŷ'r ysgol yn 1919. Enwyd y tai er anrhydedd i dri Cadeirydd cyntaf Bwrdd Rheoli'r Ysgol sef Major Price-Lewes D.L, Y.H, Tyglyn Aeron (1894-1911), Dr John Davies, Tanyfron (1911-1915) ar Henadur J. M. Howell Y.H, Portland House (1915-1927).

Ar y cae pêl-droed y gwelwyd y cystadlu cyntaf yn 1919 gyda Thanyfron yn cipio'r bencampwriaeth. Blwyddyn yn ddiweddarach, dechreuwyd y gystadleuaeth hoci gyda Thanyfron eto yn fuddugol, a'r bencampwriaeth tenis a rannwyd rhwng Portland a Thyglyn. Bu'r 1920au yn sicr yn oes aur i dîm tenis Portland gan iddynt ennill neu rannu'r bencampwriaeth wyth mlynedd yn olynnol. Cymerwyd cam pellach gyda chynnal mabolgampau cynta'r ysgol yn 1926.

Yn fuan iawn, fe ddaeth y mabolgampau yn ddigwyddiad pwysig yng nghalendr yr ysgol gyda nifer o "sêr" yn amlygu eu hunain. Yn 1932, Glanmor Evans *"was the hero of the day. Without doubt, his fine running and jumping were largely instrumental in giving Tanyfron the victory. Evans was an easy Victor Ludorum and was awarded the Senior Boys' Medal."* Parhaodd ei orchestion i'r flwyddyn ganlynol:-

> *"Tanyfron were again successful in winning the Cwmere Sports Cup in 1933 with a total of 137 points, Tyglyn running second with 104 and Portland third with 95. As in 1932, Glanmor Evans (Ta) again distinguished himself, winning the Senior Boys' 220 yards, Long Jump, 100 yards and gaining second place in the Hurdle and Obstacle Races. Allen Jones also helped his house to victory by winning the Senior Boys' 440 yards and the Mile. Tanyfron won the Relay race, but Tyglyn retaliated with a gallant victory in the Tug-of-War, a victory which gained them 10 points.*

Outstanding Tyglyn personalities were Tom G. Jones, Jack Lewis who won the Junior Boys High Jump and Lorna Lloyd, prominent in Junior Girls' events. Portland, although third were in no way disgraced, Megan Jones winning no fewer than four events (Senior Girls) for this house."

	1919	1920	1921	1922	1923	1924	1925	1926
Football	Tanyfron	Tyglyn	Portland	Tanyfron	Tyglyn	Portland	Portland	Port/Tyg
Hockey		Tanyfron	Tanyfron	Tyglyn	Tyglyn	Tyglyn	Portland	Port/Tan
Tennis		Port/Tyg	Portland	Portland	Port/Tyg	Portland	Portland	Portland
Sports								Tyglyn

❖

Ar ddechrau'r 1930au roedd pêl-droed yn dal yn boblogaidd:-

"During 1931-32, the school football team had a very good season. Twelve matches were played of which six were won, five lost and one drawn. For the first time in the history of the school, the Theological College were beaten at home and away. Other good performances were the victories over Tregaron County School and St John's College, Ystrad Meurig at Aberayron. The victories were largely due to the able captaincy of Gwilym Morgan."

"There was keen rivalry in those days," meddai, *"House matches provided great rivalry with the whole school allowed down to the Square Field to support. There was no P. E. teacher at the time with the academic masters taking it in turns to referee matches. On such a wet Wednesday afternoon, it was a common sight to see the masters in the centre of the field clad in wellingtons, raincoat, trilby hat and an umberella refereeing."*

Mae hefyd yn cofio am gêm o rygbi ar Gae Sgwâr ar ddechrau'r 1930au *"with the goal posts adjusted."*

"The match was arranged by Mr Fox, a rugby enthusiast from South Wales who had just joined the staff. He and I played together in the centre in the game against New Quay."

❖

Roedd Mr. T. H. Fox yr athro Lladin a Mr. W. E. Jones, athro Saesneg yn gricedwyr da ac o ganlyniad i'w hymdrechion:-

"The cricket season 1934 was memorable in that the game was made part of the school curriculum on the Boys' side. Interest in previous seasons had been more or less spasmodic, but last season the playing of matches increased enthusiasm. Aberayron Town, Tregaron County School, New Quay and Llanarth were met and interesting games resulted. It was not surprising that this revival of interest should coincide with the visit of Mr Woodfull and the Australian Test Team to this country - there was a marked interest in the B.B.C. Test broadcasts which were received on our new school Radio set.

Perhaps the most interesting match was that against Tregaron County School. School batted first and opened nervously, being finally dismissed for the small total of 22. Tregaron however, could only reply with 30. The school recovered confidence by the second innings and going in again knocked up 61 wickets for 5 wickets declared. This left Tregaron 54 to make for victory, but they could not stand up to the fast bowling of Allen Jones and Glanmor Evans and were dismissed for 22. Aberayron thus winning by 30 runs."

	1931	1932	1933	1934	1935
Football	Tanyfron	Tanyfron	All square	Tan/Tyg	Tyglyn
Hockey	Portland	Portland	Tan/Port	Tanyfron	Portland
Tennis	Tyglyn	Tyglyn	Tyglyn	Tyglyn	Tyglyn
Sports		Tanyfron	Tanyfron	Tyglyn	Tyglyn

Parhaodd dylanwad Mr Fox ar y gêm i mewn i gyfnod yr Ail Ryfel Byd:-

"That we played at all was due to our Latin Master, Mr. Fox." meddai Aneurin Hopkins, un o chwaraewyr brwd y cyfnod. *"He umpired all our games, school and house matches, he organised the erection of "The Net" in a corner of the field, and supervised the cutting of the wicket and outfield. His enthusiasm was backed by the Headmaster's encouragement.*

We were able to play matches against Tregaron, Ardwyn, Llandysul and the evacuated National School at New Quay. Ardwyn's ground was excellent, it was a real pleasure to play there. Tregaron's wicket was also excellent but Llandysul's was dangerous. Not only was it bumpy and bare, it had a scattering of stone and shale to add to its perilous nature."

Gan gofio pwysigrwydd y gemau tai yr adeg honno, nid syndod mai gêm fwyaf cofiadwy Aneurin Hopkins yw un rhwng Tyglyn a Thanyfron yn 1943:-

"Mr. Howell Evans decided to dismiss the school after dinner and all the pupils were exhorted to attend. Mr. Fox was the umpire. Tyglyn won the toss and Douglas Lewis

and I opened the batting. After hitting and thrashing for an hour or so, Ivor Jenkins the scorer, shouted from the pavilion verandah that I had made a century.

Stuart Griffiths bowled the next ball, a long hop which I top-edged and skied. Stuart caught it. Ivor then shouted as I walked back to the pavilion that on a recount I had made only 98. Ivor eventually qualified as an accountant."

Yn ddigon naturiol, fe gafodd y rhyfel dipyn o effaith ar fywyd yr ysgol, ond ar ddiwedd yr "hanner cyntaf" roedd chwaraeon yn dal i ffynnu. Yn ystod tymor 1944-45:-

"This year's football team may justly regard itself as being one of the best the school has had for the past twenty years. We began the season in rather low spirits since our former captain, M. Price was callled to the ranks of the Bevin Boys. His successor, H. Rees, fully merited his appointment, if we judge from subsequent play...............our crowning achievement came in the defeat of Ardwyn on their home ground. A.C.S. teams had failed to accomplish this for the last 25 years. After an exciting game, in which we led throughout, the match ended 6-4 in our favour."

Ni chafodd y tîm criced gystal lwc:-

"Much to the disgust of the probable members of last year's XI no inter-school matches were held during the season. We had looked forward to yet another successful season but our hopes were dashed mainly because of war-time travelling conditions."

Un gêm yn unig a chwaraeodd y têm tenis:-

"This was against Rosemead on Wednesday May 24th. The first string - Gwenllian Parry and Rhiannon Davies - played Rosemead's first string, and after a very exciting game, which lasted for nearly two hours, Aberayron won ....The second string of Valerie Jones and Sheila Rees lost ....the strings were then reversed. Both first strings won and thus the final result was a draw."

Tymor siomedig a gafodd y tîm hoci. Dim ond un gêm a enillwyd allan o bump, gan ysbrydoli Glenys Ball i gyfansoddi'r gerdd ganlynol:-

HIT, HIT, HIT.

Hit, hit, hit,
At that small white ball, O girl!
And I would that your stick could master
The sticks that around you swirl.
O well for their goal-keeper`s task
As she shouts to encourage her side!
O well for the team that has scored,
As they run to their places with pride.
And our enemy's ball goes on
To its haven beyond the post:
But O for a hit from that awkward stick,
That but of one goal we might boast!
Hit, hit, hit!
At the edge of the goal, o team!
But the tender grace of the match you have lost,
Alas, you will never redeem!

Daeth diwedd, felly, ar hanner cyntaf cyffrous. Gwawriodd cyfnod newydd wedi'r rhyfel. Megis dechrau fodd bynnag oedd y stori gan i'r cyffro barhau i mewn i'r ail hanner.

Tyglyn 1919

Tanyfron 1919

Portland 1919

Seymour Rees,   Naid Uchel

Hoci / Hockey 1919-20

Pêl-droed / Soccer
1919-20

Hoci / Hockey 1920-21

Pêl-droed / Soccer 1920-21

Tîm Hoci hŷn / Senior Hockey team
1925

Pêl-droed / Soccer
1926

Rygbi a Pêl-droed / Rugby and Soccer
1958

Gymnastics, 1950s

Hoci Hŷn / Senior Hockey
1959-60

Rygbi Hŷn / Senior Rugby
1961-62

Hoci Hŷn / Senior Hockey, 1961-62
Jennifer Jones, Mary Lewis, Llinos Davies, Ann Rees, Mrs. Valmai Jones, Teresa Hughes -Jones, Joyce Edwards, Barbara Davies,
Eirlys Davies, Enfys Morgan, Mari Williams (Capt.), Eleanor Jones, Beryl Jones, Deanne Swetman.

Tîm Iau / Juniors
1963-64

Rygbi Hŷn / Senior Rugby
1965-66

Hoci Hŷn / Senior Hockey
1966-67

Pêl-rhwyd / Netball
c. 1971

Hoci / Hockey
c. 1971

Rygbi / Rugby 1971-72

Mr D. Lloyd, Alun Rees, William Thomas, John Severs, Richard Phillips, Clive Parker, Brian Evans -Jones, Roger Jones, Dilwyn Patterson, Mr G.G. Davies.

Huw Griffiths, David Rees, Jeffrey Hubbard, Adrian Evans, Graham Hope, John Jenkins, Malcolm Rees, Peter Merritt Clive Thomas, Wyn Evans, Edmund Matthews.

YR AIL HANNER / THE SECOND HALF

Wrth i fflam erchyll yr Ail Ryfel Byd ddiffodd o'r diwedd yn 1945, cynheuwyd gobaith yr oes newydd. Gyda'r gobaith, daeth cyfle o fewn yr ystafell ddosbarth ac ar y meysydd chwarae. Bu'r campau yn foddion i anghofio am y gorffennol, ac yn Ysgol Aberaeron aethpwyd ati i gryfhau y sylfaen gystadleuol gadarn a oedd eisioes wedi ei gosod.

Wedi hir ddisgwyl, agorwyd y gampfa newydd. Yna yn 1948, roedd yr ysgol yn dathlu llwyddiant Gordon Griffiths, y cyntaf o ddisgyblion yr ysgol i'w ddewis i chwarae dros ei wlad:-

> *"I was chosen to represent Wales against Ireland at Belfast. I spent many hours speculating as to what kind of place Ireland would be and what kind of reception we should be met with. Eventually the day of departure arrived, and after meeting the rest of the tean at Liverpool we embarked on the "Ulster Monarch" en route for the Emerald Isle.*
>
> *On the Saturday morning prior to the match, the team was given a tactical talk by the trainer. In the afternoon, the event for which we had come over was played at Cliftonville Park where we won by four goals to nil. After the game, we were entertained to dinner by the Irish F.A and at ten o'clock set sail for home."*

Yn dilyn y gêm yma, chwaraeodd Gordon Griffiths yn erbyn Lloegr yn High Wycombe ar Chwefror 28ain 1948, gyda Chymru yn colli 4-3, ac hefyd mewn gêm gyfartal, 3-3, yn erbyn yr Alban ym Mangor ar Ebrill 3ydd. Bu hefyd yn ffodus i chwarae dros Gymru mewn twrnament ieuenctid yn Llundain yn erbyn Lloegr, yr Eidal, Gwlad Belg, yr Iseldiroedd, Awstria a Gweriniaeth Iwerddon.

❖

Daeth trobwynt pwysig yn hanes chwaraeon yn yr ysgol ar ddiwedd 1947, pan gyflwynwyd rygbi gan Mr Gwynfil Rees:-

> *"Fy ngwaith cyntaf yn yr ysgol oedd bod yn gyfrifol am yr holl wersi ymarfer corff i'r bechgyn, addysg grefyddol i'r ysgol i lefel "O", a hefyd Cymraeg i lefel "O". Ond yn arbennig iawn, fe ofynnwyd i mi ddydd yr apwyntiad, a fuaswn yn addo cychwyn rygbi yn yr ysgol. Addewais yn frwdfrydig iawn, heb feddwl am foment am yr holl broblemau. Wedi arfer dysgu bechgyn Dyffryn Aman a Dyffryn Gwendraeth, a'r fraint o gael Carwyn James yn gapten fy nhîm olaf yn ysgol y Gwendraeth - bechgyn â rygbi yn eu gwaed - ni sylweddolais y gwaith anodd o ddysgu bechgyn pêl-droed sut i chwarae â'r bêl hirgron."*

Erbyn diwedd y tymor hanesyddol hwnnw roedd y tîm yn "barod" am y gêm gyntaf:-

> *"After only two trials, a match was arranged against Holyrood School at Llanilar. The team was finally chosen and the sixth of December saw a very happy crowd of players and supporters board a "private" Crosville bus bound for Abermad. When we arrived we were given a warm reception.*
>
> *As we trotted out on to a muddy ground, we wondered what was in store for us. We kicked off and we have to admit that our opponents were on top during the opening stages. Following a fine three-quarter movement, the Holyrood captain burst through for an unconverted try. It was not long before we were in further trouble when the same "menace" raced over our line for a second try. The kick being from a difficult angle, the try was unconverted. Then an amusing incident was witnessed, when one of our forwards dashed over the line, raced behind the posts, but alas, in his excitement, he did not place the ball. Encouraged by this fortune, the homesters increased their lead by a try between the posts. Their captain made no mistake with the kick and we were eleven points down.*
>
> *Now we started a comeback which illustrates the never-say-die attitude of A.C.S. Five minutes before the interval, Evans opened our account after a spectacular dash. The try remained unconverted. After receiving a "pep talk" by Mr Rees during the interval, we came out for the second half in a determined spirit, and to the surprise of the home supporters we penned our opponents in their "25". The home line had a charmed life for the next quarter of an hour. Our supremacy was rewarded when Roy once more proved too slippery a handful for the home side. He went over between the posts and I managed to convert it from an easy position. As time went on the game faded away and with only two minutes remaining, Brennig and Terry made a brilliant opening and the latter gave me a peach of a pass and I crossed the line in the corner. The try was not converted due to a slight misunderstanding.*
>
> *The draw was a fair result and a true reflection of the play. Terry Evans, Brennig Williams, Roy Evans and John Bowen were prominent members of our side.*
>
> *Then came what we probably remember best. The delicacies which were set before us would not have disgraced Princess Elizabeth's Wedding Feast. After tea, we were escorted to our bus by our rivals and their Headmaster. After three cheers and a friendly goodbye, we returned singing the melodious strains of "Sosban Fach."*

Dechreuad digon boddhaol felly i'r fenter, ond o fewn y flwyddyn daeth cymorth ychwanegol i'r adwy :-

> *"Cafodd Mr. Bill Lewis ei apwyntio i'r Staff, a chefais fraich ac ysgwydd gref i'm cynorthwyo gyda rygbi a mabolgampau. Cawsom lawer o hwyl, ein dau, wrth y gwaith, a hoffwn feddwl i ni lwyddo i osod sylfaen gadarn i dimau da y dyfodol."*

Yn ystod tymor 1948-49 y cyflwynwyd y gêm i'r ysgol hon, a chwaraewyd pedair gêm o dan gapteniaeth Rhys Harries, Terry Evans yr is-gapten a Billy Jones yn ysgrifennydd:-

> *"Four fixtures were arranged, our first being at home against Ardwyn, a team noted for its prowess in Rugby. A large crowd had gathered to witness this match, and they were rewarded with a fine, open game. Throughout the first half we battled gamely, but could not match the speed and skill of the Ardwyn backs, and our line was crossed three times. We fared better in the second half, however, and the Ardwyn line had several narrow escapes, but in spite of this, our opponents added a goal and a penalty to their score. Finally we lost by 17 points to nil.*
>
> *Cardigan were our next visitors and they too scored 17 points without reply. In the return game with Ardwyn we again failed to score, being defeated by 19 points to nil.*
>
> *Undaunted by these defeats, we visited our old rivals, Tregaron, in jubilant spirits. For this match, Tregaron school had been given a half-holiday, so their team was not lacking in vocal support.*
>
> *Tregaron, assisted by a strong following wind, kicked off, and in fifteen minutes they crossed our line. A.C.S. were soon on the offensive and from a line-out near the Tregaron line, D.B. Evans dived over to score our first try. We assumed the lead when Ifor Herbert touched down for an unconverted try near the corner flag. Tregaron rallied, and scored a converted try. Being now behind, the A.C.S. team gave of their best, and Terry Evans gathering a loose ball, crossed for an unconverted try. We finally ran out winners by 9 points to 8 to register the first rugby victory in the history of A.C.S."*

❖

Cafodd Mr Gwynfil Rees ddylanwad hefyd ar fabolgampau'r ysgol. Yn 1948:-

> *"The Clerk of the Course, Mr I. G. Rees introduced this year some new events for the Boys. These were throwing the Javelin and Discus and putting the Shot. In the last event, the Seniors used a heavier shot than the other boys but they could not throw it as far as the Juniors threw their shot ....No competitor was allowed to try more than three events and instead of champions being chosen on the total number of points gained, medals were given for certain track events. Those who won medals were Jean Davies for the 100 yards Junior Girls; Gwenda Evans for the 220 yards Senior Girls; Billy Messer for the 600 yards walk for Junior Boys; Rhys Harries for the 880 yards Middle Boys and Gwyn Thomas who won the Mile for Senior Boys."*

Yn yr un flwyddyn, penderfynwyd cystadlu am y tro cyntaf erioed fel ysgol ym Mabolgampau Sir Gaerfyrddin:-

"On the morning of June 8th 1948, a twenty-eight seater bus carried a team of Aberaeron County School boys for the first time to a County Athletic Championship Meeting at Carmarthen. Our athletes were, to say the least slightly apprehensive and the ony calm person in the bus was Mr. Gwynfil Rees, with whom the idea had originated. Entering the field did little to dispel our qualms. A list of nineteen schools appeared on the programme. Their competitors seemed to be perfectly self-confident and we began to doubt the wisdom of our coming.

The first few races seemed to bear out the truth of our thoughts. Disappointment followed disappointment .... the heat however, of the Middle School 440 yards was greeted with newly aroused optimism and indeed, Rhys Harries ran an excellent race to finish first. In the final, he figured prominently, coming home second.

Failure in the Junior Long Jump did little to damp our enthusiasm, for the next item, the Junior Walk, was won by Billy Messer. Kenneth Jenkins was next on the list, and he, running very well, won his heat in the 110 yards hurdles. Later, with our excitement at its highest pitch, he won the finals of the same race.

The atmosphere in the homeward bound bus was very different from that prevailing on the way down. The successful competitors were haloed in pride while the unsuccessful entrants were not inconsolable. For had they not played their part in maintaining the name of their School in yet another new venture?"

Parhau a wnaeth y datblygiadau newydd ym myd mabolgampau. Yn 1950:-

"The first annual meeting of the Cardiganshire S.S.A.A was held at Cardigan. As a new venture, it met with great success and was very well attended. The A.C.S. was particularly successful in obtaining eleven "firsts". Graham Thomas made a personal success of the meeting by winning the Senior High Jump, Long Jump and the Hop, Step and Jump. Aberayron brought back the "Brynawelon" Senior Trophy largely on account of his achievements."

Blwyddyn yn ddiweddarach yn 1951:-

"A novelty in West Wales Athletics was introduced this year when a three-county athletics championship was held at Carmarthen. The competing counties were Cardiganshire, Carmarthenshire and Pembrokeshire. In the Mile Walk, Billy Messer gained first place and in the Junior 660 yards Walk, Alwyn Evans was a very good second. Other A.C.S. competitors present were James Burns, John Davies, Uriel Evans and Caerwyn Watts."

Yna yn 1952 cymerwyd cam mawr arall:-

"For the first time, girls' events were included in the County Sports. These events included sprints and jumps for all three age groups : Junior, Middle and Seniors. It was unfortunate that such field events as the shot, javelin and discuss were not included, but

we are promised that the pleasure of seeing young maidens tottering under the weight of the shot, and coiling themselves into grotesque postures in an endeavour to throw the discus will be ours next year. With due fairness, however, to the fair sex, we must congratulate the girls of this school who won outright the Junior, Middle and Senior awards in this year's meeting - a really splendid achievement."

❖

"School Athletic Records 1948-58

Boys Senior

100 yds- John Davies (P) (1954) - 10.5 sec.

200 yds - John Davies (P) (1954) - 24.4 sec.

440 yds - John Davies (P) (1953) - 57 sec.

880 yds- Jimmy Burns (P) (1951) - 2min. 19.2 sec.

1 mile - Gwyn Daniel (P) (1955) - 4min. 55.4 sec.

1 mile walk- W.G Messer (Ta) (1951) - 7min. 57sec.

110 yds. Hurdles - John Davies (P) (1952) - 15.2 sec.

High Jump - G. Thomas (Ta) (1948)

Emyr Jones (Ty) (1956) - 5ft 1in.

Long Jump - John Poole (Ta) (1951) - 18ft 9in.

Hop, Step, Jump - Derek Jones (Ta) (1956) - 36ft 5in.

Pole Vault- Terry Evans (P) (1951)

John Poole (Ta) (1951) - 8ft 9in.

Javelin - John Rees (Ta) (1957) - 126ft 7in.

Discus - H.W Jones (Ta) (1951) - 98ft.

Weight - Walter Jones Ta) (1958) - 37ft 4in.

Boys Middle

100 yds - Rhys Harries (P) (1948)

Emyr Jones (Ty) (1954) - 11sec.

Caerwyn Watts (Ty) (1954)

220 yds - William Morris (Ta) (1957) - 24.8sec.

440 yds - William Morris (Ta) (1957) - 57.2sec.

880 yds - Boyd Williams (P) (1957) - 2min 16sec.

3/4 mile walk - J. Jones (P) (1954) - 5min. 38.3sec.

110yds Hurdles - Gwyn Daniel (P) (1952) - 15.5sec.

High Jump - Tom Jones (P) (1957) - 5ft 1in.

Long Jump - David Jones (Ty) (1957) - 17ft 3in.

Hop, Step, Jump - David Jones (Ty) - (1956) -3 6ft7in.

Pole Vault - Tom Jones (P) (1957) - 8ft 10in.

Javelin - B. Hubbard (P) (1948) - 110ft

Discuss - Ronnie Evans (Ty) (1956) - 104ft 7in.

Weight - John Price (P) (1949) - 41ft 11in.

Girls Senior

100 yds - Jean Davies (P) (1949) - 12.2sec.

220 yds - Doris Davies (Ta) (1952) - 30.5sec.

Hurdles - B. Edwards (Ty) (1952) - 18.1sec.

High Jump - Janine Evans (Ta) (1957) - 4ft 6in.

Long Jump - Delphine Lintern (P) (1957) - 14ft 10in.

Hop, step, Jump - Glenys Daniel (P) (1955) - 32ft 2in.

Discus - Doris Davies (Ta) (1953) - 71ft 8in.

Weight - Margaret Williams (Ta) (1956) - 24ft 4in.

Javelin - Delphine Lintern (P) (1957) - 68ft 8in.

Girls Middle

100 yds - Carol Evans (Ty) (1957) - 12.3sec.

220 yds - Doris Davies (Ta) (1952)

Glenys Daniel (P) (1953) - 30.8sec.

Hurdles - Margaret Lewis (P) (1953) - 15sec.

High Jump - Glenys Daniel (P) (1953) - 4ft 3in.

Eluned Daniel (P) (1957)

Long Jump - Carol Evans (P) (1958) - 31ft 9in.

Hop, step, Jump - Glenys Daniel (P) (1953) - 31ft 9in.

Javelin - Rosa Wyatt (Ta) (1954) - 47ft 7in.

Discus - Margaret Williams (Ta) (1955) - 64ft 7in.

Ar y cyfan, bu'r pumdegau yn dipyn o "oes aur" yn hanes mabolgampau'r ysgol. Yn 1953, cynhaliwyd Pencampwriaeth Ysgolion Cymru yn Aberystwyth, *"with the school having no less than a dozen athletes wearing the royal blue vest. Aberayron pupils successful in gaining places were Derek Jones, 2nd Junior High Jump; John Davies, 3rd 880 yards Senior."*

Teithiodd saith i Gwmbrân y flwyddyn ganlynol, tra ym Mae Colwyn yn 1955 daeth Ronnie Evans yn drydydd yn y ddisgen iau. Yna yn Aberystwyth ym Mehefin 1956, *"no fewer than six new county records were set up by pupils of Aberaeron County School. In winning the Junior Girls' Cup, the Junior Boys' Cup and the Middle Boys' Cup our boys won 12 first places and 18 second and the girls won 3 first and 3 second."*

❖

Datblygiad arall ar ddechrau'r pumdegau oedd cyflwyno pêl-rwyd fel ail gem y gaeaf i'r merched:-

> *"For the first time, netball was recognised as one of the school games. It was not surprising that we gained only one victory in our opening matches against Lampeter, Dinas and the Convent."*

Yn ystod y tymor canlynol gwelwyd "*a considerable improvement in the team's play. Many matches had been arranged but only six were played:*

Aberaeron 9 Convent 6

Aberaeron 9 Cardigan 20

Aberaeron 16 Dinas 0

Aberaeron 5 Ardwyn 11

Aberaeron 17 Dinas 0

Aberaeron 0 Ardwyn 20"

❖

Dechreuodd y pumdegau yn y modd gorau posibl i'r tîm pêl-droed:-

> *"The School XI once again enjoyed a particularly successful season winning all games played. It is well to mention here that the triumphs of the team were due in no small*

measure to the football strategy of Mr. Alcwyn Evans and Mr. Jack Rees who converted a moderately good side into a forceful combination."

O dan gapteniaeth John Price, y canlyniadau gorau oedd curo Llanbed 9-0, Tregaron 10-3 a Llandysul 10-3 gyda John Davies yn sgorio 17 gôl yn ystod y tymor.

Yna yn dilyn tymor cyffredin iawn -*"the apathy into which the School XI descended this season is something which has puzzled many of our soccer critics"* - daeth tro ar fyd unwaith eto. Yn ystod 1952-53 gyda Henry Jones yn gapten *"the team had a very successful season - played 6, won 4, drawn 2. Furthermore, two of the School XI deserve mention. They are Marsden Hubbard and John Davies. Marsden having gone through a series of trials was selected to represent Wales against Scotland in a Youth International. John represented the Welsh Air Training Corps on three occasions."*

Erbyn canol y pumdegau tymor yn unig a neilltuwyd i bêl-droed. Droeon amharwyd ar nifer y gemau a drefnwyd gan dywydd garw ac er i'r ysgol gynhyrchu nifer o chwaraewyr disglair, teimlai llawer bod y bêl hirgron bellach yn dechrau ennill goruchafiaeth. Dechreuodd tymor 1957-58 yn y modd gwaethaf posibl i'r tîm :-

"The season began on a very dismal note, for we lost the opening game with our old rivals Tregaron 5-0 away. In this game, the Soccer Code played at Aberayron sunk to its lowest ebb for many years."

❖

Ym myd rygbi yn ystod tymor 1952-53:-

"It is worthy of note that in the match between Cardiganshire Schools and Pembrokeshire Schools four members of the Aberayron team were selected for Cardiganshire. They were: Terry Evans, John Davies, Gwyn Griffiths and John Watson. Of these, Terry and Gwyn were also selected to play for the combined Cardiganshire-Pembrokeshire XV against Carmarthenshire. In the same season a new enterprise was the formation of a Junior School XV."

Yn ystod 1953-54, ni chollwyd yr un gêm, ond yn anffodus ni chafwyd yr un lwc yn ystod y ddau dymor canlynol:-

"Several of the matches were lost through unfourtunate lapses and often we were robbed of victory by bad luck, such as an awkward bounce which gave our opponents the chances they wanted. Our loss against Cardigan at home will always be remembered as the victory of which we were robbed because our School rugby posts at one end have a noticeable inclination from the vertical."

Dychwelodd y dyddiau da gyda'r capten Elgan Davies yn amlwg wedi ei blesio gan berfformiadau tymor 1956-57:-

"A notable feature of our team this year has been the joy and abandon with which it has played its rugby. The team was more balanced than in recent years and consequently more combined teamwork was produced and better rugby played. This is borne by the fact that we provided five players for the County team against Pembrokeshire in Geraint Evans, Ronnie Evans, Tudor Griffiths, John Rees and myself."

Yn ystod y tymor canlynol, ymunodd Tom Jones, William Morris ac Ian Thomas a Geraint Evans a Ronnie Evans yn y tîm, tra ar ddiwedd y ddegawd yn 1959 cafodd capten y tîm Hywel Davies a Hywel Williams gyfle i chwarae yn nhreialon tîm ysgolion Cymru:

"Undoubtedly Hywel is the best centre in Cardiganshire at the moment. A fine attacking player and a strong tackler with excellent handling. Captained Cardiganshire against Pembrokeshire."

❖

Drwy gyfnod y pumdegau cystadlwyd yn gyson ar y cae hoci ac ar y cwrt pêl-rwyd. Ar y cyfan, profwyd tipyn o lwyddiant er i un sylwebydd gynnig yn 1957 *"our record for this season would be best sent to the Chemistry Lab, and under the guidance of Mr Thomas, it should be ceremoniously blown up to be forgotten for ever."*

Un enghraifft dda o'r llwyddiant oedd 1954-55, tymor gorau'r cyfnod i'r tîm hoci:-

	1952	1953	1954	1955	1956
Hockey	Tanyfron	Portland	Portland	Portland	Portland
Netball		Tanyfron	Portland	Portland	Portland
Tennis	Tyglyn	Tyglyn	Tyglyn	Tanyfron	Tanyfron
Football	Allsquare	Portland	Tyglyn	Tanyfron	Tanyfron
Cricket					Tany/Tyg
Rugby	Portland	Portland	Portland	Tyg/Port	Portland
Sports	Portland	Portland	Portland	Portland	Portland

"Despite the loss of some of its star players the hockey team had a very sucessful season. Much of the credit must go to our new games mistress, Miss Owen, who gave us every encouragement and help. Out of the nine matches played, six were won, two drawn and only one lost."

❖

Gwawriodd y chwedegau yn llawn gobaith a brwdfrydedd. Gyda phawb yn barod i arbrofi ac i fentro, daeth nifer o gyfleoedd newydd i ran disgyblion y cyfnod:-

"One of the most popular of the recent innovations into school life is the "Gym Club". Strangely enough, no one can remember exactly when it was started, apparently it grew into its present form sometime in 1958. We meet in the gymnasium every Wednesday during the dinner hour. For the three quarters of an hour that we are together, everyone is busy trying to improve his technique under the watchful and critical eye of Mr. Pascoe."

Clwb i'r bechgyn yn unig oedd hwn fel y Clwb Pêl fasged a sefydlwyd yn 1961:-

"This game has recently become increasingly popular and many viewers have seen the giants of the Harlem Globetrotters demonstrating their supreme skill on television. Whilst we do not claim that we will ever rival the Globetrotters in either speed or skill we can surely match them in enthusiasm.

As the boys are improving every day it would be a good thing to have an inter-school competition in basketball. We have actually played Cardigan who came to play cricket but it being a wet day, we went into the gymnasium and both the Juniors and Seniors and Senior Girls (tennis team members) played. Our school team won every group easily, showing once again our prowess in yet another sport."

❖

Ar ddechrau'r chwedegau daeth y gêm saith bob ochr yn boblogaidd ym myd rygbi ac yn yr ail gystadleuaeth flynyddol a chwaraewyd yn Llanbed yn 1960 enillwyd yr adran iau gan dîm yr ysgol :-

"The Junior VII was most successful running out eventual winners. Their progress was: Round I defeated Llandysul 8-0, Semi Final defeated a scratch VII 25-0, Final defeated Cardigan 11-0.

Junior VII team : Anthony Swetman, Wyn Davies, Haydn Davies, John Williams (captain), Eric Jarman, Roger Davies, David Hough, Nicholas Williams.

Law yn law â'r fuddugoliaeth yma:-

"For the first time the inter-house rugby competition was held in the form of a seven-a-side tournament in three sections - Senior, Junior and Lower Junior. Two points were awarded for a win and one for a draw. After an interesting, vigorous and keen afternoon's play, the final house placings were : Tyglyn 7pts, Tanyfron 6pts, Portland 5pts. Tyglyn, therefore were Rugby Champions of 1960."

Coronodd John Williams ei gyfnod fel capten y tîm iau:-

"The captain of the Junior XV, John Williams, was selected to play for the Probables in the Welsh Schools Under 15 Final Trial - the furthest any Cardiganshire schoolboy has gone to date."

Bu'n gyfnod o arloesi hefyd i'r merched:-

"For the first time in 1963 the school took part in a County Netball Tournament - four secondary schools competing. The Senior team lost two events, mainly owing to weak finishing. The Juniors, however, did very well, but they too were defeated by 7-2 in the final against Ardwyn."

Cafodd y tîm iau dipyn o lwyddiant yn ystod tymor 1964-65:-

"After being entered for the Urdd Junior Netball cup they worked hard and enthusiastically to reach the semi finals against Llandaff Secondary School. In the quarter finals, they won 16-11 against Gwendraeth Secondary School, the Carmarthenshire under 15 Netball Shield winners."

Bu'r tymhorau ynghanol y chwechdegau yn ddigon llwyddiannus i'r timau hoci. Yn

	1957	1958	1959	1960	1961	1962	1963	1964	1965	1966
Sports	Port	Port	Port	Tyg	Tan	Tan	Tan	Tan	Tan	Tan/Port
Rugby	Tan	Port		Tyg	Tan	Tan	Tan	Tan	Tan	Tan
Cricket	Tyg		Tyg	Port	Tan	Port	Port	Tan	Ta/Po/Ty	Tan
Hockey	Ta/Po/Ty	Tyg/Tan	Tyg	Tyg	Tyg	Tyg	Tan	Port	Port	Port
Netball	Port	Tan/Po	Tyg	Tyg			Tan	Tyg	Tan	Tyg
Tennis	Tyg	Tan	Port	Port	Tyg/Tan	Po/Tyg	Port	Tyg	Tyg	Tyg

1963-64:-

"As a result of the County Tournament five of our girls - Eirlys Williams, Teresa Jones, Krystina Michalska, Ann Rees and Annwyl Owen - were chosen to play in the final selection match. From this match Annwyl and Teresa were chosen to play for Cards. XI."

Yna yn ystod tymor 1965-66:-

"The Hockey XI can certainly claim to have enjoyed one of its most successful seasons remaining undefeated in all its school matches. In the Easter Hockey Tournament at Aberystwyth when the team was engaged against Senior sides it reached the final of the Tournament when it was defeated 3-0 by the Leominster XI, a team consisting of several Senior Herefordshire County players. Carol Davies, a member of the team, was honoured by being invited to play for the South Wales Girls Hockey XI, this being the second occasion only on which a Cardiganshire pupil has been selected."

❖

❖

Daeth un o lwyddiannau mwyaf y 1960au ar y cae rygbi yn ystod tymor 1964-65:-

> *"It is with great pride that the School heard of the selection of Nicholas Williams as a member of the Welsh Secondary Schools Rugby XV. Although only sixteen years of age Nicholas made a most favourable impression on the selectors in all the trials, and in the international with France at Dujon he gave an outstanding performance, scoring two of the three tries."*

Profwyd llwyddiant cenedlaethol hefyd ym myd athletau:-

> *"In the 1967 National Sports held in Carmarthen, Keith Jones won the Junior Pole Vault thus becoming the first Aberaeron pupil to gain first place in an event at the championships."*

Blwyddyn yn ddiweddarach yng Nghwmbrân enillwyd y Ddisgen Hŷn gan Colin Evans.

❖

Yn ystod y cyfnod yma, ni chyfyngwyd y disgyblion i'r campau traddodiadol yn unig:-

> *"Sailing is a rapidly growing sport and this was certainly borne out by the response from pupils to the formation of a school Sailing Club. Membership (2s 6d) is restricted to the upper school and every member must be able to swim.*
>
> *The local Yacht club boats were placed at the disposal of members. The highlight of the year was the one-day sailing instruction given by the Central Council of Physical Recreation. This proved to be of great benefit to all the members."*

Erbyn dechrau'r 1970au roedd yr awydd i deithio tu hwnt i Geredigion wedi cydio yn y timau rygbi ac aethpwyd ar daith hanesyddol a bythgofiadwy i Baris:-

> *"During the five day stay in the French capital the Senior and Junior XV teams played two matches against Lycée Chaptal and Lycée I. B. Say. On the Tuesday the teams travelled to the outskirts of Paris to play Lycée Chaptal whose pitches were situated in the shadow of Stades Colombes. The games proved to be hard and exciting and resulted in the two teams winning their respective matches.*
>
> *The Thursday proved to be another sweltering hot day and the temperature was in the nineties when the teams played Lycée I. B. Say. Straight from the kick off it was apparent that they were up against much tougher opposition than any they had experienced on the trip. Both the Juniors and Seniors played hard and never relented. However, playing against boys who were older and stronger, they were finally defeated."*

Amlygodd nifer o fechgyn yr ysgol eu hunain ar y cae rygbi yn ystod y saithdegau. Daeth nifer ohonynt yn agos iawn i ennill eu capiau. Un o'r cyntaf yn nhymor 1970-71 oedd Alun Rees:-

> *"He has been prominent in this sport since he came to school and it was inevitable that his prowess would attract attention outside the sphere of this school. This happened to the extent that he reached the final trial for the Welsh Schoolboys XV. This is an excellent achievement in itself as those who are aware of the keen competition that exists in Wales to get into the national team, understand only too well".*

Daeth ei haeddiant yn ystod tymor 1973-74:-

"Honours of the season went to Alun Rees who played in a representative match for West Wales against Australia at Stradey Park. The whole team were delighted with his selection and he had an outstanding game against the tourists."

Yn ystod tymor 1975-76 roedd Nigel Davies yn curo ar yr un drws rhyngwladol :-

"Nigel was invited to join the Welsh Secondary Schools Senior Squad in November and eventually played in the Final Trial. As a member of the squad he was presented with a W.S.S.R.U. official track suit along with an official sweater bearing the Welsh feathers but unfortunately, once again no cap came his way."

Yn yr un tymor:-

"Meirion Jenkins and Tim Lewis had a long and arduous trail to the Final Trial of the Junior (under 15) section by covering the length and breadth of South and West Wales. Both had a sound trial but alas, once again, a cap eluded both these outstanding Juniors."

Yn ystod tymor 1977-78, tro Ian Rees oedd hi i fynd am y cap :-

"Congratulations to Ian Rees, the second player within the last few years to be selected for the Welsh National Squad, but once again, no cap came our way. Ian did have the consolation, however, of playing in the Probables side in the Final Trial and being awarded an official tracksuit and tie."

Bu gêm olaf tymor 1973-74 yn dipyn o achlysur mewn mwy nag un ystyr:-

"Our last match of the season was against a Canadian touring side, the Victoria High School from Vancouver Island. After a disappointing first period, Aberaeron turned on the brand of rugby in the second half that provided good entertainment for the big crowd and finally ran out comfortable winners at 26-13.

The occasion warranted the official opening of the new pavilion on the rugby field. Past and present pupils alike will always remember the old tin shed and its primitive facilities and the trek back up to school after Saturday morning matches. Our modern spacious pavilion surpasses all the changing facilities that we visit in the whole of Dyfed."

Roedd adeiladu yn amlwg yn y gwaed yr adeg yma oherwydd dyma gyfnod cynllunio'r pwll nofio:-

"After a Public Meeting called by Councillor T. G. G. Herbert, Aberaeron it became clear that there was a very strong desire to provide the Aberaeron and district children the facility to become competent swimmers and thereby increase the safety of swimming in the sea. At the meeting Councillor Herbert was elected Chairman, Mr G. Bruce, Vice Chairman, Mr D. J. Thomas, Secretary and Mr Bebb Jones, Treasurer.

As well as the Managment Committee, there are three sub-committees, Financial and General Purposes: Chairman - Mr Haydn Rees, Secretary - Mr D. J. Thomas; Technical : Chairman - Councillor J. O. Williams, Secretary - Mr Iorwerth Evans;

Fund Raising : Chairman - Mr Hefin Davies, Secretary - Mr Dan Evans."

I goroni holl fwrlwm y flwyddyn daeth llwyddiant cenedlaethol i'r ysgol ar y cwrt tenis:-

"The standard of tennis in school is extremely high as can be seen from the results and also from the fact that we produced the Welsh champion in the Nestle's schols Tournament namely Anne Rees. Anne went on to play against the winners of Scotland, Ireland and England at Queen's Club London where she was beaten by the eventual champion."

Heb os, uchelgais fwyaf unrhyw ddisgybl fyddai i gynrychioli ei wlad. Dyna hefyd yr uchelgais a ddatgelodd Mr. Bill Lewis i ddarllenwyr cylchgrawn yr ysgol yn 1978:-

"Chwarae fel maswr i Gymru gyda Mr. Gwynfil Rees a Mr. Alan Pascoe yn y canol, Arwyn Lewis "scrum half", Iori Evans ac Alun Davies ar yr esgyll dri-chwarter, Griff Davies yn fachwr, Jack Rees a John Roberts "props", Dai Thomas a John Jones yn ail reng, Dai Lloyd a Dan Evans yn "flankers", Tudor Jones rhif wyth a Myrddin Evans yn gefnwr. Rheolwr y tîm Alcwyn Evans a Ron Mathews yn hyfforddwr."

Fel yn y gorffennol, daeth cryn lwyddiant i athletwyr yr ysgol yn ystod y saithdegau. Ym Mhencampwriaeh Cymru yng Nghaerdydd yn 1972, daeth Ian Lewis yn ail yn y ras dros y clwydi i fechgyn iau. Tair blynedd yn ddiweddarach enillwyd yr un ras gan Tim Lewis ac aeth ymlaen i:-

"He was first in the Welsh Games Youth section at Cwmbrân, he represented Wales at the games in Yeovil and was also selected for Wales (under 20) versus Combined forces."

Nid dyma ddiwedd ar ei orchestion oherwydd yn 1978, daeth yn Bencampwr Cymru unwaith eto yn y ras 110m dros y clwydi. Yn yr un cyfnod, daeth Ian Rees hefyd yn bencampwr Cymru yn y ddisgen hŷn.

Megis dechrau fodd bynnag oedd y llwyddiant, oherwydd flwyddyn yn ddiweddarach :-

"Mair Evans, Angela Parry, Glynis Jones, Helen Riddell and Alan Jones went through to

the National Sports in Cwmbrân, where Mair came first in both the 100m and the 200m, Angela first in the 3,000m, Glynis third in the 100m and Helen third in the javelin. Mair and Glynis both formed part of winning relay teams and Alan Jones ran in a relay team that came second."

Yn ystod tymor 1978-79, yn dilyn bwlch o dros bymtheg mlynedd, ail-ymddangosodd pêl-droed fel un o gemau'r ysgol:-

> *"The senior side had entered the Ivor Tuck competition and were drawn against Brecon High School in the first round. Against a school where soccer is part of the curriculum we won 3-1 before going on to beat Llandrindod Wells heavily in the next round. In the semi finals we were drawn against Newtown, and in atrocious conditions the team put up a good performance before losing by four goals to one."*

❖

Mae pymtheng mlynedd olaf yr "ail hanner" wedi bod yn benllanw i orchestion disgyblion yr ysgol ar y meysydd chwarae gyda nifer helaeth yn ymddangos ar lwyfannau rhyngwladol. Y cyntaf ohonynt oedd Alan Austin Jones a enillodd gap i dîm rygbi Ysgolion Cymru ar ddiwedd tymor 1980-81. *"Jones the Sprint is Welsh Hero"* oedd pennawd y "Western Mail" yn dilyn buddugoliaeth Cymru o 30-6 dros Dde'r Alban ar y Maes Cenedlaethol, gydag Alan yn croesi am *"the try of the game."*

> *"Jones was given the ball just outside his own 25 yard line by centre Simon Hill and in true sprinter's fashion he put his head down and aimed for the try line. It seemed as if the retreating Scottish cover would intercept the winger but he maintained his pace to outstrip the defence and round off a tremendous piece of individual play with a touchdown near the posts."*

Yn ystod yr un tymor, chwaraeodd Philip Gatehouse, Anthony Lewis a Huw Jones i dîm rygbi Ceredigion yn erbyn Gogledd Cymru. Aeth Anthony ymlaen i chwarae dros Geredigion / Gogledd Cymru yn erbyn Sir Benfro, tra enillwyd Pencampwriaeth saith bob ochr iau y sir gan dîm yr ysgol. Enillodd y tîm hŷn Bencampwriaeth hoci Ceredigion ac yna dod yn ail ym Mhencampwriaeth Dyfed. Yn dilyn hyn, dewiswyd Elizabeth James, Rhian Evans a Sharon Thomas i dîm hoci'r sir.

Tymor y tîm pêl-droed hŷn oedd 1981-82 yn enwedig yng Nghwpan Ivor Tuck, sef cystadleuaeth i ysgolion uwchradd Cymru:-

> *"Our first round opponents were Newtown at home and we turned in a magnificent performance to register a 4-1 win. Llandrindod conceded to us the second round tie and then it was on to Llanidloes. On a cold January afternoon we started badly but came*

back strongly to win 4-1. With this win we had reached the Mid Wales final of the competition and our opponents were Welshpool at home. Although we dominated the game and scored an early goal luck deserted us and they scraped a last minute equaliser to force a replay. In the replay, Welshpool took the lead before we equalised in the second half. The hunt was now on for the winning goal, again we had our chances but in the very last minute with extra time looming, a defensive lapse gave Welshpool the winning goal."

Yn wobr gysur, llwyddodd y tîm i ennill Pencampwriaeth Ceredigion drwy guro Llandysul 6-1 yn y rownd derfynol.

Ym myd hoci, enillwyd Pencampwriaeth Ceredigion gan y tîm hŷn am y drydedd flwyddyn yn olynol. Dewisiwyd Sharon Lloyd, Glynis Jones, Diane Jones a Carys Evans i dîm y sir, tra yr aeth Sharon a Glynis ymlaen i chwarae dros Orllewin Cymru.

Llwyddiant hefyd, i'r tîm pêl-rwyd gyda Carys Evans, Eilyr Jones a Louise Evans yn cael eu dewis i dim Ceredigion.

Ar ddechrau tymor 1982-83, dewisiwyd Glynis Jones, Sharon Lloyd, Carys Evans, Ruth Herbert, Hilary Owen, Caroline Davies a Sandra Jones i dîm hoci Ceredigion.

Dewisiwyd Glynis a Sharon i dîm Gorllewin Cymru tra ar ddiwedd y tymor, enillodd Glynis ei lle yng ngarfan dan 21 Cymru i fynd i Jamaica. Yn dilyn hyn, aeth ymlaen i chwarae i'r tîm ym Mhencampwriaeth Prydain yn yr Alban. Enillwyd Pencampwriaeth Pêl-rwyd y sir a dewiswyd Nicola Stevens, Glynis Jones, Emma Bryn-Jones, Sharon Lloyd a Helen Wright i chwarae dros Geredigion. Aeth Sharon ymlaen i chwarae dros Ddyfed tra ar ddiwedd y tymor, daeth yn Bencampwraig Cenedlaethol Chwaraeon yr Urdd. Enillodd Sandra Jones Bencampwriaeth Badminton Ceredigion o dan 16.

Yn ddi os, tymor Sharon Lloyd oedd tymor 1983-84. Yn dilyn llu o lwyddiannau eraill:-

"Her ultimate ambition was deservedly realised when she achieved a Welsh "cap" in her favourite sport of hockey. She was selected to represent Wales at schoolgirl level and compete in the Home Countries international at Keele and later at an international tournament in Berlin."

Ar ddechrau'r tymor enillodd Sandra Jones Bencampwriaeth Tenis Dyfed o dan 16 gyda Richard Jones yn ennill y gystadleuaeth i fechgyn o dan 18. Enillwyd Tarian Ceredigion gan y tîm Pêl-rwyd iau a dewisiwyd Sandra Jones ac Adrienne Causer i dîm dan 16 Dyfed. Enillodd Roger Rees Bencampwriaeth Coits Cymru, dewisiwyd Michael Evans a Steven Robinson i dîm rygbi Ceredigion, tra y cipiodd Mathew Jenkins y cyntaf yn yr adran bechgyn hŷn yn rasus trawsgwlad Ceredigion.

Y nesaf i amlygu ei hun ar y cae rygbi rhyngwladol oedd Michael Evans a ddewisiwyd i Ysgolion Cymru yn ystod tymor 1984-85 :-

"It is a long hard road to gain the ultimate honour. No trial was easy. Here was an unknown player, the other two full backs - one had been in the squad the previous season, the other had gained under 15 and under 16 caps - were well known to the

selectors.

Michael fortunately improved with every game to stand head and shoulders above the opposition. His displays were such that there could never have been any doubt as to who was the first choice full back. He played against New Zealand, Scotland, France, Ireland, England and toured Zimbabwe in the summer of 1995."

Daeth rhagor o lwyddiant i ran Sandra Jones ym myd tenis:-

"In both Llanelli and Swansea tournaments she wins the under 16 title and is runner-up in the under 18 doubles. She reaches the quarter finals of the under 16 singles in the Junior Welsh tournament at Cardiff as well as the semi final stage of the under 18 doubles. After such a fine season she is selected for the under 18 South Wales Junior County team."

Enillwyd Pencampwriaeth tenis dan 12 Ceredigion gan Barry Morris, a dewisiwyd Louise Bradshaw fel aelod o garfan hoci Dyfed. Daeth llwyddiant hefyd, i dîm criced y staff. O dan gapteniaeth Mr Meurig James, enillwyd y gynghrair leol drwy guro Llanon yn y gêm olaf.

Yn ystod tymor 1985-86, chwaraeodd Gareth Harries i dim pêl-droed Ysgolion Dyfed, tra enillodd Dean Simmons dwy fedal aur a thair arian wrth gynrychioli tîm saethu Dyfed. Llwyddiant hefyd ym myd athletau gyda Nia Cross yn dod yn drydydd ar y waywffon ym Mhencampwriaeth Cymru.

Profodd 1986-87 yn dipyn o dymor i'r tîm hoci hŷn:-

"It was arguably the most successful season ever for the Senior XI. The winning of the Ceredigion Championships in September was a prelude to a series of fine victories which culminated in the team's appearance in the final of the all Wales Championships at Colwyn Bay in April 1987.

Representing Dyfed after victories against Llanelli, Carmarthen and Pembroke, the team fought their way into the final after victories over Mid Glam, Gwent and Clwyd, and Gwynedd in the semi final. Against Clwyd in the final, the school failed to capitalise on their superior play and went down to a solitary late goal in extra time."

Dewisiwyd pump o'r tîm sef Lisa Cross, Sandra Jones, Meinir Evans, Mererid Richards a Catrin Woods i chwarae dros Ddyfed. Ym myd trawsgwlad, daeth Mari Jones yn chweched ym mhencampwriaethau Cymru yn y Drenewydd cyn cael ei dewis i gynrychioli Cymru yng Ngogledd Iwerddon. Cafodd lwyddiant hefyd ym mhencampwriaethau athletau Cymru yng Nghwmbrân. Daeth yn ail yn yr 800m a'r 75m dros y clwydi tra yn yr un bencampwriaeth enillodd Lisa Cross y 400m, merched hŷn. Ym myd rygbi dewisiwyd Richard Evans i garfan Cymru o dan 15.

Mewn cymhariaeth, bu tymor 1987-88 yn gymharol dawel. Chwaraeodd Eifion Roberts, Arwyn Davies, Iwan Thomas, Huw Evans, David Floyd a'r ddau Richard Evans i dîm rygi hŷn y sir ac enillwyd y gystadleuaeth saith bob ochr gan y tîm iau. Enillwyd twrnament hoci Ceredigion unwaith yn rhagor tra y chwaraeodd Mererid Richards mewn gêm brawf i'r tîm cenedlaethol.

Yna yn y tymor canlynol, daeth llwyddiant ysgubol gyda phedwar disgybl yn cynrychioli eu gwlad. Mari Prys Jones yn mynd o nerth i nerth ar y trac ac ar y cwrs trawsgwlad tra yn yr un gamp Darren Lewis yn dilyn ei wythfed safle ym Mencampwriaethau Cymru yn dod yn unfed ar hugain ym Mhencampwriaeth Prydain. Capiau hefyd i Catrin Woods a chwaraeodd i dîm hoci dan 19 Cymru mewn twrnament yn erbyn Gwlad Belg, yr Iseldiroedd, yr Almaen, yr Alban a Lloegr, ac i Alan Morgan a chwaraeodd i dîm pêl-droed dan 15 Ysgolion Cymru yn erbyn yr Alban yn Galashields.

Ar ddiwedd y ddegawd, yn ystod tymor 1989-90, parhau a wnaeth y llwyddiannau. Ym myd trawsgwlad daeth Andrés Jones yn Bencampwr Siroedd Cymru o dan 13, a dewisiwyd Angharad Howells i'r tîm iau Cenedlaethol. Hefyd, cynrychiolodd Angharad ysgolion Cymru yn y 1500m, merched iau; rhedodd Daisy Maund y 3000m, merched canol; dewisiwyd Emma Thomas i redeg y 100m ar 200m yn y Gemau Celtaidd, tra y rhedodd Mari Prys Jones y 300m dros y clwydi i'r tîm iau cenedlaethol yn ogystal â'r 400m dros y clwydi iîr tîm llawn.

Ymlaen felly i'r nawdegau, a mwy fyth o ddisgyblion yn camu ymlaen i redeg dros eu gwlad. Yn ogystal â'r "hen" wynebau, Felipe Jones, Alan Jones, Angharad Morgan, Yvonne Evans a Kay Vobe yn gwisgo'r "vest" goch. Yna, i goroni pob dim, yn Ebrill 1993 derbyniodd Alan Jones a Angharad Howells anrhydedd bellach wrth iddynt gael eu dewis fel capteniaid timau'r bechgyn a'r merched trawsgwlad Cymru.

Rhaid cofio hefyd am lwyddiannau eraill y blynyddoedd diwethaf. Daeth Menna Williams a Kelly Lee yn Bencampwyr Karate Myfyrwyr Prydain; enillodd Brett Stones, Rupert Wood, Gethin Boyle a Richard Zlotnicki Bencampwriaeth sgïo Ysgolion Dyfed; ym myd criced, teithiodd Geraint Lewis gyda thîm Dyfed i Zimbabwe; amlygodd Chris Kay ei hun yn y pwll nofio, tra i'r tim rygbi, un o'r uchafbwyntiau oedd y daith fawr i Canada yn Hydref 1993.

Wrth baratoi i ostwng y llenni ar ganrif o gystadlu, mae un enw o bosibl o'r cannoedd yn sefyll allan. Rhaid cydnabod llwyddiant Andrés Jones ym myd trawsgwlad. Bu 1995 yn hynod llwyddiannus iddo. Ym mis Ionawr, cynrychiolodd Prydain Fawr allan ym Mhortiwgal, yr athletwr cyntaf o Geredigion i wneud hynny. Mae hefyd wedi rhedeg mewn amryw rasus rhyngwladol yn y wlad yma ac ar y cyfandir. Llongyfarchiadau iddo, ac i bawb arall sydd wedi cadw'r fflam gystadleuol ynghyn dros y can mlynedd ddiwethaf. Gobeithiwn am gystal llwyddiant wrth gamu ymlaen i ganrif ac i fileniwm newydd.

Rygbi / Rugby
1973-74

Rygbi / Rugby
1981-82

D. J. Thomas, O.B.E., B.Sc.
Prifathro, 1973-1993

RECOLLECTIONS & REFLECTIONS

D.J. Thomas O.B.E., B.Sc. - Headmaster 1973 - 1993.

During my period as a student, I used to travel home to Carmarthenshire for the occasional weekend, and the only way to return to Aberystwyth on a Sunday was on a Western Welsh bus, which stopped in Aberaeron. In Aberaeron, one had to wait two hours for the Crosville connection to Aberystwyth. Try to visualise Aberaeron, nearly fifty years ago, without a single shop or cafe open, on a wet and windy Sunday afternoon with not even an adequate shelter from the elements. It was not an experience that would help create a very favourable impression of Aberaeron and I swore then that I would never set foot in such a miserable and unfortunate place! A few years later I was eagerly submitting my application for the post of Chemistry teacher at the school and, fortunately for me, I was appointed - the beginning of thirty eight years of service in the school and the county, eighteen years as a teacher of science and twenty years as Headmaster. Nearly all my professional life has been connected with the school - a period of great joy and personal pleasure as well as hard work.

I recall very little about my appointment except that Alderman E. Glyn Davies, Aberarth was Clerk to the Governors and he was the one who ushered me into the council chamber at the Town Hall for my interview. I was told afterwards that one of the Governors, who by then was old and doddery, had my name written on a piece of paper in his waistcoat pocket - a reminder of how he was to vote when the time came! Such was the effectiveness of the "no canvassing" rule in those days! Six appointments were to be made to the staff on that day in May 1955, and there were at least twenty candidates sitting uncomfortably in a downstairs room waiting to know their fate. I was one of the lucky six and Mr. J. T. Owen's words on my appointment still remain with me - "You have been appointed to a good school with high standards. We will always expect you to maintain those standards."

Wise leadership

I was privileged to serve under both Mr. J. T. Owen (ten years) and Mr. Griff Davies (eight years). It was a privilege I valued tremendously - there was no better way to learn my craft as a teacher and headmaster. I valued their friendship, their wisdom, their professional guidance and most of all their sincerity. They were both driven by the conviction that Aberaeron was the best school in the county and they were determined to maintain the high standards so characteristic of the school. I shall always be grateful to them for providing me with opportunities to develop and progress and to undertake responsibilities which eventually led to my appointment as headteacher in 1973. I was as aware then, as I was throughout my period in office, that I had to work very hard to emulate my predecessors and to achieve and maintain their standards of performance.

Mr J. T. Owen O.B.E., M.A. succeeded Mr Howell T. Evans as headmaster in 1944 assisted by a staff of fourteen. Mr Owen's period of office was one of great change brought about by the Butler Act of 1944. There were substantial building extensions (the New Block) opened in 1950. This was necessary to accommodate all the pupils in the area who were of secondary school age. The establishment of a bilateral school was a period of tremendous change which required breadth of vision and a very positive sense of direction, at the same time, retaining the values and particularly the scholarship of the past. Such natural leadership was ably provided by Mr. J. T. Owen. In addition, he was a renowned scholar and was highly respected within his native county. Mr. Owen retired in 1965 after a period of 42 years at the school as teacher and headmaster - an illustrious career dedicated to the school.

Mr. Griff Davies was appointed to replace him after years in educational administration as Further Education Officer and Deputy Director of Education for Cardiganshire. Mr. Davies brought his own substantial administrative and personal skills to the school; consolidating the values and ethos of the school and successfully leading it through a further period of change. There were major developments during this period related to the Raising of the School Leaving Age (ROSLA). These included the provision of a new Technical block and a much needed new canteen as well as a planned movement towards the comprehensive principle. Mr. Davies' inside knowledge of how local government operated proved invaluable to the school during intensive periods of negotiations. This period of progress and innovation under wise and intelligent leadership was brought to a premature end by Mr Davies' retirement due to ill-health in 1973.

Childhood & Youth

As I recall the days of my youth and schooling in rural Carmarthenshire, I see much which is familiar to me in the situation in Cardiganshire, particularly half a century ago. I was the son of a farmer who was lucky enough to win a scholarship to Whitland Grammar School - an achievement for someone from a non-academic background, who was destined to pursue the family's farming tradition. Secondary education was a compulsory interlude - faced with many problems and difficulties particularly financial ones. One had to stay in lodgings for a whole week in Whitland, all of six miles away! All pupils had to be indoors by 6.30 p.m. in the winter and 7.00 p.m. in the summer. This was also the situation in Aberaeron at that time, and one heard many tales of Mr. J. T. Owen walking around Aberaeron and New Quay, causing confusion amongst the pupils who were breaking the rules.

During this period at school, (1940-1947), I was left with a recollection of a much restricted curriculum compared with today, often taught with inadequate facilities, inadequate accommodation and a particular pressure on space. Nevertheless, this was a happy period of new experiences, of inspired teaching and the opening up of a new world. Such was the impact of the school on me, that I made a decision early on that I would continue with my education and abandon farming as a career. This was not an easy decision to make in those days, when farming was a way of life and sons were expected to inherit the family farm with all its responsibilities. These were also the problems of sons and daughters of farmers in the outlying districts of Aberaeron - resulting in a high proportion of them leaving school early at fourteen years of age and not completing their examination course. The most immediate task was that they should earn a living and help to relieve the poverty which was rampant in those days.

All young men in those immediate post-war days had to complete their National Service at eighteen years of age unless they were exempted. Farming was an accepted exemption, but I chose to go to the Army - The South Wales Borderers - for two years and to serve most of my time in Cyprus guarding the Illegal Jewish Immigrants, who were then on their way back to set up the new Israeli nation. On my "demob", I was more than a little lost with no career advice and guidance, and eventually applied for, and was accepted at, Aberystwyth to study Agriculture. My period there was enjoyable but not to be remembered for any outstanding academic successes! On the miraculously successful completion of the course, I was appointed as a Science teacher at Brynhyfryd School, Ruthin. Two years later, I was fortunate to come to Aberaeron and to spend the rest of my professional life there.

Aberaeron - Post War

Aberaeron school in the immediate post-war days was rich in talent, both in pupils and staff. The achievements, both curricular and extra-curricular were substantial. At that period there were about 350 pupils, morning assembly was held in the old hall (Library) and the school was approached by a narrow path from South Road. It was during this period 1947/48 that Mr. Gwynfil Rees and Mr. Bill Lewis introduced rugby to the school - a move that was to have a substantial effect on local leisure activities. It started as one term of soccer and one term of rugby, until eventually all the Cardiganshire schools changed to rugby. During the summer months, both cricket and tennis flourished until the County Athletics Association was formed, leading to the eventual demise of cricket as the concentration during the brief summer term shifted to the selection of the county athletics' team. Nearly thirty years later, both soccer and cricket were to return to the school curriculum, as well as the development of a proud athletics record.

During this post-war period, Mr. J. T. Owen was supported by a very able staff who had recent grammar school experience. Though some had served the school since pre-war days, others were appointed in the late 1940s having served in the Forces throughout the war. They did not all relish the forthcoming changes to bilateral education and some found it difficult to abandon their grammar school techniques and teach to a broader and wider audience, a high proportion of whom were not going to achieve "O" levels or their equivalent. Their wealth of experience however, and their flexibility, plus the influence of new young staff provided for the transition to bilateral education. Apart from those already mentioned, other long serving members of staff included Mr. W. A. Jones, Senior Master, (later Dr. W. A. Jones), Miss Elaine Lewis, Senior Mistress, Miss Maria Evans, Mr. John Evans, Mr. Jack Rees, Mrs. Olive Rees, Mr. Morgan Price, Mr. T. H. Fox, Mr. Alcwyn Evans, Mr. Ron Matthews, Mrs. Gwyneth Matthews, Miss Mair Meganwy Jones, Mrs. Nancy Evans, Mr. Tudor Jones, Miss Rhiannon Davies, Mr. Alun Davies, Mrs. Ann James, Mr. Merfyn Griffiths, Mr. Sidney Evans and Mr. D. Hughes Jones.

Bilateral Education

The old "County Intermediate School" became a bilateral school in 1948. Mr. J. T. Owen said at the time - "We stand at the threshold of an era of revolutionary changes, and great challenges will be presented in designing curricula appropriate to the pupils' needs. We will have to provide a menu far more appetising and nourishing than anything yet provided in our secondary schools, if we want to make all our 11+ pupils feel it is better to be in school than at work." The problem identified by Mr. J. T. Owen was one of major proportion - to convince those who would normally have left at fourteen years of age that there was a purpose and essential reward in their compulsory extended studies. By careful planning and a substantial degree of flexibility, a great deal was achieved in spite of the immediate difficulties of accommodation. Pupils were taught in various venues in the town including the old National School (now the Masonic Lodge) until the "new building" with its new hall, staff rooms and laboratories was completed and opened in December 1951 by Dr. T. H. Parry Williams, the eminent Welsh scholar and poet. This was the beginning of a new and fruitful period in the life of the school; a period of innovation and consolidation.

Agricultural Education

One of the unique features of the curriculum offered at Aberaeron was the central role of agricultural education as a medium of scientific enlightenment and also as an attempt to develop and enrich the skills which came so naturally to the sons and daughters of farmers. In the early 1930s, the opinion of the headmaster and Governors in relation to the role of agriculture was so positive that they appointed Mr. John Evans as a teacher of agriculture. This appointment was seen as one of great importance and the Chairman of the Governors referred to it in his Prize Day address as "a move which would do much to raise the standard of agriculture in the county and one that would impress upon pupils the dignity of work on the land."

These were high ideals, and to a large measure they were achieved mainly because of Mr. John Evans' patience, enthusiasm and active encouragement for so many pupils as groups and individuals. The school had slowly acquired land and eventually the school garden and the school farm became important units and vehicles of learning. The school farm was for many years unique in the county and in Wales, proving to be a valuable medium for scientific education for the sons and daughters of farmers and farm workers who were destined to return to their farms to enrich the rural life of Wales economically and socially.

In recent years, the demands of the curriculum have changed substantially making it difficult to retain this aspect of education. Hopefully as the curriculum continues to change, the farm will be returned to its full value as an educational tool. In the meantime, the school still uses the land and it is vitally important that it should retain it at all costs - particularly as further devolution takes place - it will them become a very valuable asset.

The first eighteen years

Those eighteen years as a member of the staff were happy and productive ones, working in a smallish school of barely 600 pupils with a dedicated staff sharing the joys of some remarkable achievements. I soon realised it was a "good school" and that I had a part to play in maintaining standards and traditions. Miss Elaine Lewis who was, by then, one of the characters on the staff often used to say - "I could write a book.... about the early years." I also feel that I could probably do the same. There would be so much to say, so much to record of those days of change and progress, successes and failures but most of all the development of happy relationships and the sense of belonging to "a family".

They were pleasurable, hard-working years and without doubt my mentors in the science department were Mr. John Evans and Miss Maria Evans. In those days I had a strong, healthy voice and it was claimed that on a fine summer's day when all the windows were open that my chemistry lessons interrupted the more cultured activities which took place in the middle block! The pattern of separate staff rooms continued for many years, but in those days all the men squeezed into a small room which is now the Bursar's office. Every break-time, there were fifteen to twenty bodies strewn over chairs and window-sills, totally engulfed in cigarette smoke. Those were the days when it was the "in thing" to smoke and nobody had heard of "passive" smoking. There we set the world to rights listening to the wisdom of Gwynfil Rees, Bill Lewis and Jack Rees and the barbed witticism of John Roberts. Often the calls of the "bell" were not heeded and J. T. Owen would open the door, look around, not needing to say anything - a tactic I was often to employ later.

Social aspects

During those early years on the staff, there was a vital social aspect as well as a professional one. Most teachers lived in Aberaeron and met regularly outside school. Many of us played golf, cricket, tennis or bowls, participating in local events and generally supporting the local community. This to some degree was expected of you and many of us served on the local council and numerous other organisations. I can recall an enraged councillor saying publicly that the "town was run by the school".

Inter-school staff activities were the norm, particularly staff cricket matches which were played regularly in the late 50s and 60s. Ceredigion schools staff teams played on a weekly basis and the competition was intense but friendly. Cricket was the only game I played reasonably well - particularly as a bowler, using my height to propel the ball at reasonable speed. It is but a few years ago that I was approached in Aberaeron town by an ex-student colleague whom I had not seen for forty years. He hesitantly approached me, asking nervously if I was "Dai Fast Bowler" - a boost for the ego as one approaches retirement!

An incident in a staff cricket match in Llandysul which remains clearly in the memory is of the late Mr. Tudor Jones, fielding close to the bat, being hit by a fast moving ball which struck a box of matches in his pocket. These burst into flame as well as his trousers, causing him much consternation and pain but not generating as much sympathy from his colleagues as he had hoped.

These inter-school occasions certainly helped to develop good working relationships amongst the staff. Today such a relaxed approach is not possible - staff could not find the time to play cricket and the competitive academic atmosphere which dominates would make one regard a colleague from another school as a professional opponent to be treated with suspicion.

Extra-curricular activities

I enjoyed participating in school events and was for years involved with stage lighting in a very amateurish way. Because one taught science, it was assumed that one had knowledge of electricity and therefore an enthusiastic inclination towards stage lighting. Nothing could be further from the truth in my case but, nevertheless I, along with many others, spent many hours annually, climbing ladders, moving lights, shifting dimmers, generally living precariously both in electrical and physical terms. The pleasure of watching hundreds of pupils express themselves so confidently on the stage with such skill and obvious enjoyment was ample reward.

In 1960, I took my first school group abroad, the first of about ten subsequent enjoyable experiences which I was able to share with other staff and my own family. Apart from my army experience, I had not been abroad myself; this was a new venture full of pitfalls as I was soon to discover. That first trip was to Venice and Rome by train and involved a party of seventy-two - much too large a group, with no Italian speaking staff and only one pupil with an Italian background.

As ever it was difficult to strike the right balance between authority and freedom. After all this was a holiday paid for by the pupils. On the other hand, in the interests of safety and the well-being of the majority, there had to be positive guidelines and observation of some basic rules. Venice was a comfortable experience - no roads to cross, only canals to fall into! Rome was a different matter - attempting to cross any street on your own was a nightmare - taking seventy people across was an onerous responsibility, faced with the volatile driving of exuberant Italians. Such exuberances were also evident in the way they pursued our girls.

The wonders of these two cities made it all worthwhile; the pupils came away suitably motivated, horizons broadened and imaginations stirred. That first trip was a painful lesson for me; many others followed and they were all enjoyable mainly because the pupils responded and always behaved themselves, and on many occasions were congratulated on their high standard of behaviour. Taking trips abroad is a high-risk occupation with heavy responsibilities. Aberaeron has by now developed a tradition for foreign trips, all well controlled and supervised, by dedicated and responsible staff.

The school has had a long-standing and highly successful exchange with St. Anne's School in Brest, Brittany. It has now been operating for well over twenty years since it was established by Mr. Alan Pascoe and Marie Louise Moal - our then Breton Assistante. Not only have generations of pupils benefited from the relationship, but very close friendships have developed between the staff of the two schools. I was privileged on many occasions to enjoy the generous hospitality provided by Marie Louise, Jeannine, Danièle, their families and many others, and also to entertain them in Aberaeron. Strong bonds have developed, based on mutual respect and the sharing of our Celtic heritage.

Promotion

My sudden elevation from the ranks to the Headship certainly produced challenges and many problems. I was inexperienced to say the least, and this soon became obvious during the first term - but one learnt quickly; there is nothing like the school of experience. I was very privileged to have received the unanimous support of the Governors on my appointment and this continued during those early days. In particular, Cllr. J. O. Williams O.B.E. New Quay was a very staunch ally and supporter. I will always be grateful to him for his outstanding commitment to the school and the community.

Staff reaction, as far as I could gauge was mainly favourable, with some exceptions who shall remain nameless! Pupils, I felt, were supportive as I was known to them. Roger, my only son, had just completed his sixth form course and started his medical studies as I took over. This made it easier for me from some points of view and probably much easier for him - but of course, I was no longer receiving any pupil feed-back.

I can still recall that first staff meeting and that first assembly at the beginning of the new term. To stand on the school stage at any time was awe-inspiring and until the end of my professional career I was never totally at ease knowing that one small incident could so easily destroy the reverence and controlled responses one was trying to achieve.

As far as I was concerned, school assemblies were Christian assemblies, with a Christian message in whatever diluted form, to be conveyed to the pupils. For the majority of pupils, this was their only contact with the Gospel and this was reflected in their near-total failure to sing the most familiar of hymns. It was an opportunity to raise awareness of the Christian faith and to provide the occasional moral message.

I would add that generally, schools are fairly moral places - much more so than the world outside. They try to operate according to a moral code and certainly in Aberaeron we considered it part of our ethos and responsibility to help pupils to distinguish between right and wrong. As teachers, we have always appreciated the importance of standing up for certain beliefs and values - often a difficult and unpopular task in this day and age.

Assemblies were also vital in order to maintain the identity of the school as an organisation and to instill a sense of belonging. They were occasionally a place for admonishment, but more importantly an opportunity to collectively recognise the achievements of all the pupils both in and out of the school; not only those who excelled academically, but all achievements at all levels. We all need such basic support in order to spur us on to further achievements - we all benefit from a recognition of success and particularly from sharing that success with others.

That first term was a testing time. I had to prove to myself and to others that I was capable of doing the job and eventually to add my own distinctive flavour to it. There were very many errors of judgement, many uncertainties in those early days, but we all survived and eventually, I learnt to enjoy the responsibility and hopefully to exercise authority wisely and well - but others will judge that.

Comprehensive Schooling

The change from Intermediate (Grammar) school to Bilateral happened at a precise date. The change from Bilateral to Comprehensive is not to be as clearly defined and catalogued. What one can say is that it happened in the late 1970s as the result of a series of events including the abolition of the 11+. However, it also involved reorganisation within the school in order to provide a common curriculum at least in the early years of secondary schooling. It also meant the introduction of new examinations with clear and well defined pathways and targets for each pupil. The essence of bilateral education in its simplest terms was that all pupils would be provided with secondary education but not necessarily following the same curriculum. A move towards comprehensivisation was a move towards an opportunity for all pupils to share the same basic experiences up to school leaving age. This involved streaming, setting and occasionally mixed ability classes and a variety of other strategies in order to enable each child to work towards a realistic goal.

I was, and still am, committed to the comprehensive ideal particularly in a rural community, where all pupils go to the same school and have the same high standard of opportunity provided for them. By today, comprehensive schools have become the subject of so much adverse political comment. The emphasis is on the manipulation of exam results and league tables, without reference to the origin of the pupils and the selectivity of the school. The truth is that the achievements of the rural Welsh schools particularly in Cardiganshire are extraordinarily high in providing not only academic distinction, often higher than that of many selective schools, but also providing a high quality of education for all their pupils. I am proud that I have been part of the achievements of Aberaeron school with outstanding examination results over the years and providing care and consideration for all its pupils. Our stated aim over the years has been to provide "equality of value" to each pupil's education. This has often meant redirection of scarce resources to support non-academic pupils - an expensive but very necessary feature of any caring school.

Schools generally, and comprehensive schools particularly, are blamed for all the ills of society - they have become political footballs unfairly maligned by politicians and newspapers. It is claimed that schools no longer teach traditional values hence the drug culture and the increase in the crime rate etc. The truth is that the problems of schools are the problems of society which cannot be cured during a seven-hour school day. In any school, it is vital to create a community not based on fear but on respect. The concept of the authoritarian teacher or headmaster feared by all is outmoded and outdated. It is true that one set out to create this impression at times, as such a display of authority was often necessary, but the real basis of any success we all achieved at Aberaeron has been a development of a mutual respect and understanding between the pupil and teacher. Long term relationships can only be maintained if there is this respect and a sense of fair play. We were fortunate in Aberaeron to have a caring staff who were expert in their academic and their pastoral activities and who were always seeking to improve the child's experience in and out of the classroom. I was privileged to work with an excellent responsive staff whose standards were always high.

Teaching methods

As a school, we did not escape the changes in teaching methods during the sixties, with the advent of "child-centered" education. If it achieved nothing else, it certainly put extra pressures on teachers who were now required to change their roles within the classroom. The concept of the teacher being in charge of his class with children sitting in neat rows of desks was out of favour. We were now into a routine based on the child's natural inclination to discover for himself with the teacher becoming a facilitator. This pattern resulted in much more movement and noise and apparent indiscipline. Not only did this produce great changes within the classroom but it substantially increased the load on individual teachers who were now involved in extensive preparations to meet the needs of individual pupils.

Many teachers rejected these methods, refusing to abandon their traditional and very successful methods, but also benefiting considerably from some of the excellent literature and techniques developed in the new schemes. The theories of the sixties are now being abandoned and a much more disciplined and authoritarian approach is returning to the classroom to meet the demands of the National Curriculum. In Aberaeron in the main we were always very traditional, and generally not given to excesses - but much of value has been gained over the years from the new methods. It is a simple fact of life that good teachers will inspire their pupils whatever methods they use.

The hidden curriculum

It was always, with rare exceptions, a privilege and a pleasure to gain a positive response from the majority of the pupils. I have long since discovered that children need what we all need from time to time - support, encouragement, help to overcome failure and recognition of achievement at whatever level. Children respond to punishment, provided it is fair and there is forgiveness and a sympathetic ear. My real basic pleasure in my role as teacher and headteacher was working daily with pupils helping to resolve their problems. That is an aspect of the work that I still miss. So much is to be gained by the child from the school's "hidden curriculum" - things that were not written into policies or job descriptions, but which developed naturally in a healthy and successful environment. I refer to attitudes, relationships, care and concern and active encouragement. One of the major factors relating to the past successes of Aberaeron School is that the staff had high expectations of their pupils. The pupils responded to such expectations, achieving academic success and inheriting worthwhile social values. It can all be summarised in the one phrase "knowing your pupils" - as important for the headmaster as it was for any member of staff. In oversimplified terms teaching is about "relationships" and "compromise". Relationships in this context means the ability to communicate, to care, to understand and therefore to relate. Nothing in a school situation was black and white and the ability to compromise was a vital factor if one was to succeed as a teacher. To compromise does not mean to concede but to show a spark of humanity and goodwill which avoids the humiliation of individuals already under stress.

Parental expectations

Another factor relating to the success of pupils in this locality is parental expectation and involvement. Education has always been highly valued in the poorer and deprived rural areas of Cardiganshire mainly as a channel, an avenue for success and an escape from the community. The same pattern still prevails but to a lesser degree and the loss of our most able children continues to be a worrying factor. However this is partly counteracted by the influx of people who are able to commute to their work, often bringing new life to small villages and occasionally problems too!

In my first twenty years in the profession, meeting a parent was a rare event - it indicated that a very serious issue was to be discussed. Little information was conveyed to parents about their children's progress and it was always assumed that the school knew best. The last twenty years has seen the development of a welcome partnership between parents and schools with regular discussions and transfer of information. Schools have become increasingly accountable for their actions, policies and procedures and parents in the main are well informed and very cooperative. Unfortunately it is often difficult to get parents of problem pupils to come to the school, indicating that the real problem is not school based but home based.

Generally I have enjoyed meeting most parents, but not all! Those parents of Welsh stock who were born and bred in this community often still find it difficult to bring themselves to visit the school let alone to interview the headmaster. There is a natural inbuilt deference to the patterns of the past when the schoolmaster's word was taken as law and not to be questioned. Such a deference is nearly always accompanied by a gratitude to the school for their efforts. A small minority of newcomers to the community were not as reticent or shy, being well practised in making unrealistic demands on the school - often to conceal and overcome their own deficiencies. In such cases the school had certain duties and responsibilities and had to take great care that pupils already rejected at home were not again rejected by the school. Physical threats which required police assistance have occurred in the headteacher's room at Aberaeron on more than one occasion. They were fortunately few and far between and the vast majority of parental interviews were constructive, helpful and friendly.

Growth of the school and in-migration

One feature of the recent period has been the growth of the school from around 650 pupils in 1973 to over 900 pupils in 1993. There were two main reasons why this occurred. One was the increase in popularity of the school, as reflected in its examination successes, so that many pupils from outside the catchment area chose to come to Aberaeron. This in itself was a pleasing recognition of the standards achieved by the staff and the school and to some degree, this was self-perpetuating as generally very able pupils chose to come to the school, thereby further enhancing the quality of the examination results.

Another factor of course, was the in-migration which took place in the late seventies and through the eighties, often bringing as many as fifty to eighty new pupils to the school during the course of the year. This influx lasted for a period of about 10 years gradually reducing by the late eighties but not stopping altogether by any means. The effect on our school community was substantial but the effect on primary schools in the locality was often overwhelming. This influx, although welcome in many respects, brought a wide variety of pupils of varying backgrounds and levels of ability; the majority blissfully unaware of the complexities of settling down in a cultural background which was so different even to the point of having its own language!

The majority of pupils were successfully integrated into a caring school community particularly in the cases where the pupils were able and committed to succeed and with a stable home background. Others found the change difficult leading to frustrations on the part of pupils and parents often resulting in antisocial behaviour in and out of school. One has to say that some of the pupils were ill-served by their parents' decision to transfer active and able-bodied youngsters from the heart of Birmingham, Wolverhampton and London to the loneliness of a neglected farm cottage miles away from the nearest neighbour and civilisation. Add to that the confusion of a new language and culture, often combined with a disintegrating family unit and it was clear that the experiment in their case was doomed to failure.

Every effort was made to accommodate the newcomers and immerse them in our way of life - at least we were able to distribute them to different forms allowing them to become absorbed in our school community rather than dominate it as occasionally happened in small primary schools. The reasons for the change of environment and the move to rural Wales were often flimsy, but one can understand the need and the urgency to get away from deteriorating urban situations in order to give the children a new opportunity. I know that in most cases we were able to provide that opportunity and that there are many grateful parents and pupils still in the community who will confirm this.

School buildings

Another obvious consequence of the increased numbers was the pressure on space. Apart from the erection of the new Technical Block as the result of ROSLA (Raising of the School Leaving Age) in the late 1960s and the new canteen opening in 1973, no other permanent new buildings have been provided since the 1950 extension. We were now in Dyfed and all their building projects were concentrated on the old Carmarthenshire area where so many schools needed upgrading. All we could manage to obtain to meet our expanding and urgent needs were additional mobile classrooms, so that currently the school looks like a shanty town with 20 or so of these mobile units. Additionally the old "School Canteen" which was condemned by the then Director of Education of Dyfed, Mr. John Phillips, in 1973 was eventually converted into three classrooms and a very useful Community Hall. All these rooms are still in daily use well over 20 years later, as also is the gymnasium, built for a school population of 200 - 300 over 50 years ago.

The promise has been made for major building investment in 1996. This is long overdue but of course Dyfed will have ceased to exist and one wonders whether Ceredigion will be able to honour the pledge and provide the capital investment necessary and also to combine this with a major leisure development so essential for the young and old in this central area of Ceredigion.

When the New Block was built in 1950, the architectural fad was for flat roofs. This barrack-like structure with its unattractive flat roofs has caused great annual expense in order to repair the leaks. The Old Building (1898) still retains its character with the original bell still in the copper dome, and even after being exposed to the open elements for over a hundred years, is still far more weatherproof than anything else on the school campus.

T.V.E.I.

As a school, we were privileged to be selected in the middle eighties as a T.V.E.I. school (Technical and Vocational Educational Initiative). This involved being part of a pilot scheme in the county, encouraging the use of the new technology and involving enterprise activities, as well as developing new bilingual curricula in technological subjects. This development was not totally popular with some of the more traditionally minded staff, but it did provide more investment in computers, building modifications and increased staffing and technological support. We were well placed at the end of the five year period to meet the rapid changes that were to follow. Many of these changes have been essential but the time has long since been reached when schools need a period of stability for consolidation. There are many aspects of the recent numerous education acts which are to be welcomed, including the National Curriculum and the regular testing on a national scale. Teachers and pupils, however, have become overwhelmed with the sheer mass of paperwork, the rapidity and frequency of changes often resulting in burn out of staff and early retirement. The most valuable aspect of education in establishments like Aberaeron is the stability of the teachers and their much valued experience. So much of this is being lost to the detriment of the pupils.

Managerial role

Over the years, the headmaster's role has changed beyond recognition. During my first five years, little changed in my role - I performed it in much the same way as Mr. J. T. Owen and Mr. G. G. Davies did before me. The last ten to fifteen years has been a period of constant change and adaptation starting with T.V.E.I. and subsequent curricular changes leading to the National Curriculum. The managing role of a headmaster was slowly increasing but the amount of financial management was still small because the major resources were still held at County Council level. Major decisions were also still being taken at Pibwrlwyd, and the Governors dealt with minor matters of no great significance.

Gareth Owen yn cyflwyno llun o aelodau hen deulu Tyglyn i'r ysgol ar achlysur ei ddarlith "My Reverend Cousin" Tachwedd 1980

D. J. Thomas, Jack Rees, Gareth Owen a Fran Owen

Enillwyr cystadleuaeth "Sain"

However, the power was slowly being transferred to schools and the concept of a headteacher as a manager was being developed, leading eventually to Local Management of Schools. In order to achieve this, I was regularly away from school attending meetings and courses being trained for my new role. This concept of management was extended to the rest of the school with three Deputy Heads, Heads of School, Heads of Year and Heads of Department. The concept of line management was introduced, totally undermining the teacher who simply wanted to teach his subject.

One consequence of all this was over the years, teachers also were called upon to attend courses on a frequent and regular basis often to the detriment of their subject teaching. All this was a matter of concern to the staff and to myself, and I was amazed how few complaints were received from parents over the years because of the absence of subject teachers. Presumably pupils did not talk about it at home but welcomed the respite provided by yet another supply teacher!

It is inevitable that a large complex organisation like Aberaeron School must have some sort of management structure but there are inherent dangers of which I was well aware. One obvious one was that the school would become bureaucratised with too much emphasis on having everything on paper, forgetting the personal relationships at pupil and staff level which are so essential for success. While it was convenient for me at times to have responsibilities shared for some failure on the part of "Management", it was also very necessary to avoid any gulf developing between management and staff and also to avoid the development of little "empires" at various levels - all of which could impede the efficient running of a school. I prided myself on having my door open at all times to staff and pupils who had problems to share. Such close contact was vital and it was often necessary to short-circuit the management system and simply to listen and share people's problems.

Schools these days at least appear to be democratic with staff meetings, committees, school councils, parent meetings etc. Certainly no person, not even the headteacher, can work in isolation; current accountability demands consideration of other viewpoints and a very positive response from the management of the school. This is good up to a point and I welcomed it, but it did create a false impression and expectancy that all demands will be met, when many of them were unrealistic and impracticable.

Local management of schools

One of the major changes that has befallen schools not welcomed by all headteachers was L.M.S. (Local Management of Schools) referred to earlier. I welcomed it, as it gave more (if not total) control to schools and less to the L.E.A., in the way that the money allocated to schools should be spent. This happened as a result of a new Education Act in 1989. Up to that point we handled about £40,000 only of our income mainly for purchase of materials and equipment. Everything else including teachers' salaries and maintenance of buildings was handled by the L.E.A. In 1990, we were allowed to control a budget of about £1.75 million - a frightening responsibility. New computer equipment was provided, a Bursar was appointed and headteachers and certain senior members of staff received effective training. What it did was to enable us to control our own destiny and to decide for example how many teachers we wished to employ and what repairs we wanted undertaken during the course of that year. The system has now progressed to an even higher degree of involvement with about 90% being devolved to school. It has proved to be a particularly effective innovation with control at local level with a corresponding reduction in County Hall staff. It also has many threatening aspects, as the income is dependent on annual pupil numbers, creating unacceptable fluctuations of income. All staff have become more cost conscious and much more accountable to departmental heads. We have all learned to budget for the coming year and to live within that budget.

Staff and staff appointments

Staff appointments have always been the responsibility of the Governors. I would dare to suggest that they enjoyed this - it was a duty undertaken with relish and sincerity, always, or nearly always listening to the advice of the headmaster. Occasionally, in the earlier years particularly, local pressures would result in the name of a dubious candidate emerging in the discussions but, I can say with some pride, that they always responded to professional advice and gentle persuasion! If the appointments weren't always a success it was probably more due to the quality of the advice given than to any failure on the part of the Governors. In the early days, the candidates came to the County Hall and later, to the school for an interview, with no contact with staff or the headteacher beforehand. Usually, of course, not only had their references been taken up but the telephone grapevine had been active - so that the candidate was not a totally unknown quantity. In recent years, we provided a complex framework of interviews, taking up the whole day, with visits to the departments and interviews by the heads of department and deputy heads. Such a process was revealing for both sides, occasionally resulting in the candidate leaving before the main interview! This more professional approach should, in theory, provide an improved quality of staff. I am not in fact sure that it made much difference and that in the final analysis the natural instincts of the Governors were as good a mechanism for choice as all the complex structures created by the school.

Some schools and other institutions have already moved beyond this into the world of psychological and psychometric testing, but perhaps a more sensible development is that the candidate should be asked to take an actual lesson under observation. The real truth that I discovered early in my career was that interviews and the other methods used in appointments were at the best only very rough guides - so much eventually depended on the quality of the individual, their staying powers in the classroom and their ability to establish sound, healthy relationships with pupils and colleagues. The unsung heroes of the teaching profession are those who can consistently, week in week out, year in year out, stand in front of a class and deliver a well prepared lesson with the same enthusiasm daily. Fortunately, Aberaeron has a very high proportion of teachers of such quality - teachers who consider their classroom performance to be of paramount importance. These dedicated people are the backbone of a successful school; the silent majority often do not emerge in the race for promotion. They are the solid contributors who win the respect of their pupils. Whatever the method of appointment used in a school, it is true that you have to live with people before you know the outcome of your choice. I certainly made mistakes when offering professional advice to my colleagues on the Governors. I had to live with some of them for a long time! I would add that they were a small minority and most have moved on to higher things - often promotion is the quickest path out of the classroom!

Aberaeron has been well blessed with quality staff over the years and the current situation is no exception. Not only are they able and knowledgable in their subject but they are caring and concerned about each child as an individual. As indicated, the pressure in teaching these days is immense, resulting in a new and increasingly familiar phenomenon of early retirement. Teaching was always a career for life - women retired at sixty and men at sixty-five. The original schemes for early retirement introduced about ten years ago were designed to provide attractive packages for staff who were to be made redundant due to falling school roles. By now, it is seen as a route of early escape from an over pressurised situation at classroom level. As a consequence, Aberaeron along with most schools in Wales, has lost many fine teachers in their early and mid fifties; people who were very competent and experienced and were at the peak of their professional life with at least ten more years service to offer to the community and the school. Their departure has depleted the school of top quality staff, who felt they were no longer able to maintain their standards within their classrooms because of the extra pressures of administrative work, the multiplicity of external examinations and a variety of other factors which have nothing to do with classroom teaching. The current government has responded to the problems of inner city schools by imposing unnecessary structures on all schools thereby making quality education more difficult to achieve in areas like Aberaeron where high standards were always the norm.

The language issue

The Governors have, in latter years, been much concerned with the language issue and the bilingualism of the school. This was probably one of the most difficult and sensitive issues that I had to deal with and it was emotive in the extreme. The headteacher was nearly always in a no-win situation. For the Welsh speakers and some learners who were aware of the decay of the language, drastic and rapid steps had to be taken on a wholesale basis to preserve the language. At the least this involved making Welsh the first language of the school and providing opportunities for more subjects to be studied through the medium of

Welsh. At the opposite end, there were those who resisted any change and who insisted that it introduced elements of racism, as Welsh was a dying language, and that English was the universal language. The majority of parents were not over enthusiastic about either point of view but expected the school to provide an opportunity in both languages but retaining an element of choice in all subjects. Often it was difficult to convince Welsh speaking parents that their children should follow a particular subject through the medium of Welsh.

Add to that the fact that all these parental views were reflected in the views of the staff and occasionally in those of the pupils and one can see that it was potentially a seething cauldron of discontent that could erupt and become a political and media issue - something dreaded by all headteachers. The pressures were enormous, aggravated by the complexities produced by the large number of people who had moved into the catchment area. At times, one felt that one could no longer continue to walk the political tightrope and, at the same time, produce an effective and a practical answer. The language issue was not an obvious and open one amongst the pupils although occasionally, quarrels of a personal nature were translated into linguistic ones. In the early days of my headship, the proportion of Welsh to English speakers stood at about 50/50, but by the late eighties this had changed to about 65/35 in favour of English speakers. It was clear that the Welsh language was being pushed into a secondary situation in its own heartland. It was vital that action should be taken to halt the decline and to re-establish the Welsh language as the prime language of the school, even if it was no longer the language of the hearth or the community.

These vexed questions were addressed regularly at staff and governors meetings and we took some positive steps in the mid-eighties to develop a coherent language policy. This involved:-

a) making Welsh the first language of communication within a bilingual situation in the school.

b) making an increasing number of subjects available for study through the medium of Welsh.

c) ensuring that it was reflected in our staffing policy and that all members of staff appointed were Welsh speakers.

All this was not achieved overnight and not without some pain and many mistakes. As far as communication at school, year and form level was concerned all announcements were made in Welsh followed by English. Many claimed that it should be in Welsh only and while this argument had validity, one also had to ensure that the important things were understood by all the pupils. One could not afford to create second class citizens who were not allowed to participate fully in school life because they did not understand what was going on. Apart from the fact that it could have unfortunate practical consequences it would have also created much opposition and this was to be avoided at all costs. If the plan was to succeed, the school en-mass had to be supportive. It was particularly difficult trying to appear to be moderate and reasonable about the issue, yet, at the same time, carry through a positive policy with some determination.

The provision of Welsh medium choices in several subjects to G.C.S.E. level was in many ways a substantial curricular headache resulting in staff changes and a reduced choice in the English language. The county allowed one extra member of staff to meet the difficult and virtually insoluble problems. Add to this the fact that so often there was a low uptake in the Welsh medium subjects initially, leading to a substantial imbalance of numbers, often as low as single figures in Welsh and the upper thirties in English. Slowly, with gentle encouragement and persuasion, these problems were overcome but not without much distress. I felt strongly that no child should be disadvantaged because of the language factor, a principle which is not always easy to reconcile with a language policy.

Gradually, a working policy was evolved which was eventually adopted by Dyfed as a pattern for its Naturally Bilingual Schools (as opposed to Welsh Medium Schools). Briefly, pupils were split into three groups with the Welsh speakers taking 60% of their subjects at G.C.S.E. level through the medium of Welsh; good learners 40% and learners 20%. The policy has been modified over the years but it is pleasing to note its general acceptance, now much strengthened by the Dyfed categorisation policy in primary schools. When I left in 1993, although over 60% of our pupils were learners, at least half of them were very good learners having been through the primary school system in a Category A school. All our official catchment area schools except one were, in those days, Category A, providing mainly Welsh medium education at primary school level. The secondary school situation is a natural progression from this situation.

A vision for the future

Apart from ensuring a good basic education for all, the language issue is, without doubt, the single most vital issue which affects the school. I know that the pattern has been set, the policies written and rewritten and the school still has the vision and the will, and most of all, the dedicated staff to ensure that the school becomes more than the mirror image of society. It needs to provide the leadership and the platform for the restoration of true bilingualism in the community. In the first edition of the "Link" in 1907, a report is given of the Presidential address of the debating society, given by a much respected member of staff, Mr. E. O. James. It is reported that Mr. James spoke inspiredly on the topic of "The Vitality of the Welsh Language". The article went on to say "when listening to Mr. James we felt proud of the fact that we were Welshmen and, as long as the Welsh language is taught by gentlemen who are as enthusiastic in their work and as patriotic as he is, we further add that it will be practically an impossibility for the Welsh tongue to die out." Who would have foreseen the events that were to follow in the next ninety years with the language on the verge of decay before it was to experience a revival in urban and rural areas? It is no longer a field for "gentlemen" to operate in but it needs the same patriotism and enthusiasm that Mr. E. O. James possessed. The school requires wise and inspired leadership and a vision about the role and survival of the language in Cardiganshire. In retrospect, I would not claim that we took appropriate action to alleviate the problem but we did take some steps to try to remedy the situation. A great deal still remains to be done and nothing will be achieved without the commitment and dedication which already exists on the staff and Governors and among the majority of parents. If the Welsh language dies in the heartland of Ceredigion, then it is unlikely to survive at all. Aberaeron School has a vital role to play in ensuring that survival.

Primary Schools

Reference has been made to the Primary Schools language categorisation. There were in excess of twenty schools in the catchment area and I had a very happy relationship will all of them. In a large number of cases, the headteachers were old pupils of the school but, that apart, I was always conscious of their loyalty and support. Gone are the days when new pupils came to the "Big School" without any form of induction and introduction. The transfer itself is now a cottage industry with visits by secondary school staff to the primary schools and visits by pupils and parents to the secondary school. This type of contact is certainly good for the new pupils, easing the pain and anxiety of the transfer considerably. Apart from that, all secondary schools are in open competition with one another and the schools close to the boundary of the catchment area often receive more frequent visits!

Ancillary Staff

A school cannot operate without the support of non-teaching staff who play a key role in the organisation. In the early days there was a caretaker, farm-worker / gardener, the canteen staff, cleaners and of course the school office staff. They were all dedicated people who loved their work and totally identified themselves with the school. They were typified by Mrs. Nell Davies, who was the school secretary for thirty-seven years, giving outstanding service to three headmasters. Her knowledge of the pupils, their background and family was encyclopaedic, eliminating the need for reference to complex records. I had the privilege of working with her for many years and enjoying the full benefit of her vast store of knowledge. The school office staff by now includes a bursar, whose role is to manage the school budget, a particularly difficult task in these days of cuts and deficits.

Until recently, the canteen and cleaning staff were directly employed by the school, but now, as with everything else, they have been privatised. This change hasn't always resulted in increased efficiency even though there has been a visible increase in the number of officials! Over the years, most employees had a long and much valued association with the school, resulting in a personal commitment and pride in the job, each person accepting full responsibility for the standard of their contribution. The old canteen, although housed in totally inadequate wartime prefabricated buildings, always provided quality food much enjoyed by staff and pupils. In this respect, nothing has changed and the food in the "new" canteen has maintained that same superb quality, much to my personal satisfaction and pleasure!

As the school expanded into the high-tech. age, help was essential in the laboratories, computer rooms, technology workshops and resource centres. Photocopying, hardly known fifteen years ago, has now become an essential school activity. Well qualified technicians were appointed and their contribution has been of the highest order, not only supporting teaching staff but also taking an active interest in the welfare of the students and participating fully in the life of the school.

Disadvantaged and disabled pupils have in recent years been encouraged to integrate into a normal school situation and Aberaeron was in the forefront, providing staffing and building changes, particularly ensuring access for wheel chairs into nearly all the classrooms. The school was recognised as the natural centre for all Ceredigion pupils and the success of the scheme was, to a large degree, dependent on the outstanding service of the care-assistants, who have teaching as well as caring responsibilities. The Special Education Department has thrived because they have provided stability and encouragement for numerous individuals who were dependent on their perseverance and reassurance. I particularly enjoyed my association with the Special Education Department and benefited considerably from sharing experiences with pupils and staff. There was so much sensitivity, so much humour, such effort and a tremendous sense of achievement.

Community Activities

The Swimming Pool was not, of course, part of the school as it was run by its own management committee with wide representation from within the school's catchment area. I was privileged to be its first secretary, a post I held for over twenty years until my retirement. The campaign for the establishment of the pool was initiated by County Councillor T. G. G. Herbert in the winter of 1971/72, with the pool completed by Penguin Pools in 1976. The school of course used the pool, exclusively between 9.00 a.m. and 4.00 p.m. during term time, and as such I had a dual role and involvement. It has proved to be a tremendous amenity for the locality, hopefully soon to be complemented by a leisure-centre on the school campus. I enjoyed my association with the pool and particularly with its staff who were always efficient and totally supportive.

The community aspects of my work were much enhanced by our Evening Class activities. In terms of a part-time centre, we were acknowledged to be the most active in Dyfed, with often over thirty classes being held weekly during the winter months. Over the years there has always been much interest in the area in the additional educational and recreational activities provided by the Evening Institute. Our centres extended throughout the school catchment area, using village schools and village halls, with the majority of classes being held in the secondary school. In recent years, with the loss of financial support from the county, there has been some reduction in activity. This is a cause for some concern as I feel strongly that such opportunities should continue to be provided in the often deprived rural communities subject to isolation and poverty.

School Governors

The plethora of education acts in the late eighties and early nineties resulted in a new governing body with representatives of parents being elected to office for the first time. The teaching staff also have their representatives and also for the first time, the headteacher actually becomes a governor of his own school. The Local Education Authority representatives remain, and others have been elected by the governors, from the community. The net result is a governing body whose numbers were increased from twelve to sixteen with people of substance with the interest of the school at heart. Because of the complexities of the school structure and the substantial changes that have taken place in recent years all governors were required to undertake training in order to develop expertise in financial and curricular matters. Suddenly they were making decisions about the allocation of a budget of nearly £2 million that had been devolved to the school. In order to do this they had to understand the problems of staffing, curriculum development, provision for the National Curriculum and the bilingual aspects, among a myriad of smaller issues. Perhaps, more importantly, they needed to understand the knock-on effect in a school situation where changes produce a chain reaction and where decisions taken were long term ones which could not be readily changed or abandoned for several years.

The training provided for the new governors was very professional and it must be stated that they responded very professionally so that Aberaeron now has an excellent team of governors, well versed in the complexities of modern management and whose advice I welcomed and respected. By now they are experts in their particular fields, serving on various sub-committees including Finance, Curriculum and Staffing, and Buildings. This pattern has certainly increased accountability with parents and teachers having a direct input into the running of the school. Some schools have even experimented with having pupils on the governing bodies but I don't anticipate such moves in Aberaeron in the immediate future.

My abiding recollections of the governors meetings will be that in the main, though not always, they were happy occasions with a great deal of good humour and professional discussion. There were often situations when there were frank exchanges of opinions and in latter years the governors were very well informed and the level of discussion was high. Usually decisions were arrived at by consensus, underlining the spirit of goodwill and the sense of ownership of the school which is a feature of the new governing body. I enjoyed the governors' meetings and I shall always be grateful to so many individuals who, over the years, showed a great deal of support and loyalty towards the school and myself.

Pastoral problems

An increase in school population and the in-migration certainly contributed to the nature and the frequency of the pastoral problems faced in the school. As society disintegrates and the traditional home patterns are cast aside, there is a residue of child suffering which is heart-rending and distressing. In the early years, marriage break-ups were a rarity and there was a stable, caring family relationship. As previously indicated, in recent years many of those who came in to the community did so in order to create a new life for themselves and their new family unit. Many fortunately succeeded, but far too many failed, leaving scarred children, some of whom were not to recover in time for them to benefit from their education. All schools, including Aberaeron, had to create a complex pastoral system, with Heads of Year and Heads of School and Form Teachers, who had been trained in their pastoral role. It was no longer enough to mark the register and have a quiet chat at the end of a lesson. Usually one had to liaise with Social Services, often denying access or contact to one or other of the parents, as well as discussing a variety of issues with the Police. Fortunately, one is referring to a minority of pupils with problems, but a large enough minority to take up an inordinate amount of staff time. A school can only reflect the society in which it exists, and however formidable our problems, they were small compared with the urban areas and inner cities. I am often angered by the demands made upon schools by politicians with the expectation that they correct all the ills of society, measuring the success of schools with no reference to their socio-economic background and the problems that they inherit.

School events

I have already referred to my enthusiasm as a teacher at the school to all forms of activities outside the classroom. As Headmaster, I was in a very privileged position to encourage such activities, vital for the balanced development of the child. So many opportunities were created outside the classroom by enthusiastic teachers who were prepared to devote their own time, skill and enthusiasm to the formation of many clubs and societies, the school magazine, school productions, school trips and games. The activities of the School Club or Institute are being fully chronicled in a separate article, but one can refer with equal enthusiasm to the Urdd, the Science Club (which I formed with Mr. Dan Evans over thirty years ago), Drama Groups, Chess Club, Ski Club and various subject groups. Additionally, there are enthusiastic sports groups meeting regularly on evenings and weekends. As indicated, various exchange groups have operated over the years and two or three holiday groups visit the continent annually. Such devotion on the part of the Aberaeron School staff is not the norm elsewhere and the efforts of the teachers on behalf of their pupils should be recorded and appreciated.

The school performances, averaging two a year, have become a feature of school life often involving a hundred or more pupils, produced and directed most professionally at all times. The Eisteddfod has a special place in the history of the school - the first Eisteddfod was held in 1908 on the same inter-house basis and it has survived until now - this in itself is a miracle. Past generations of pupils and parents and even grandparents still maintain their allegiance to Portland, Tanyfron or Tyglyn and when supporting their children in the Eisteddfod will insist on sitting with their House, thirty or forty years later. The Eisteddfod is unique in that it is an all day affair often not finishing until 10.00 p.m. Parents and the public are always invited to the afternoon and evening sessions and they respond with enthusiasm to the extraordinary talent that is on display. Over the years, the programme has been modified to meet the needs of the "Pop" generation and also the newcomers in our community. Still, however it retains its special flavour, characterised by House cries, teddy bears in green, blue and purple and yellow and the incessant chanting of the Houses. The school Eisteddfod and the public performances generally were occasions I enjoyed tremendously, and also occasions when I was proud to be associated with Aberaeron School.

There were, of course other occasions when the public was involved like the "Alderman E. Glyn Davies Memorial Lecture" established by Mr. G. G. Davies, my predecessor as a tribute to the past leader of Cardiganshire County Council. We were privileged to have several fine addresses over the years of high quality, in many cases, the lecturers being old pupils of the school. Other events which stand out include the excellent sponsored walks in which the whole school participated, raising as much as £12,000 in one day - a tremendous response from parents and pupils.

"The Link" is unique in many aspects if only that it continues to be published annually with a few exceptions since its origin in 1907. A Past and Present Pupils Association was started in 1904, and a magazine committee established in 1906, in order to "further and strengthen the feeling of good fellowship and friendship between past and present pupils". Mr. Gwyn Jones, the first headmaster, wrote in the first edition - "the magazine will serve as a record of all the varied interests and activities of the school and as an expression of its many aspects. It will act as a link putting old pupils in touch with the present life of the school."

To a large degree, it has achieved this end and, remarkably, continues to do so. It has faithfully recorded school activities, it has noted achievements of groups and individuals and it has recognised success at all levels. During its grammar school days, the magazine reflected the best that was produced in the school and carried winning entries of the school Eisteddfod and other external competitions. Gradually the old pupils' link has lessened so that, by now, it is a very effective and expanded school magazine reflecting the nature of a comprehensive school community with a broad range of content. It involves about two hundred pupils annually in its management and its contributions. It is a substantial magazine and, more importantly, it is still here when most other school magazines have disappeared. Its survival and expansion is due in no small measure to staff involvement and dedication - so many have been involved. I am grateful to them for their leadership, particularly Miss Sue Roberts in recent years.

Officials and Inspectors

I was appointed to my post as Head of Aberaeron about six months before Cardiganshire was merged with the other two counties to form Dyfed. I had a brief period of service under Dr. Henry Jones, the Director of Education for Cardiganshire, then Mr. John Phillips, Ceredigion's Deputy who became Dyfed's Director of Education. More recently Mr. John Ellis has been in control in Dyfed and I have always valued the happy relationship which existed and the full support received at all times. The Area Education Officers during this period were Mr. Alwyn Jones, Mr. Dave Williams and currently Mr. Roger Williams who will be Cardiganshire's new and first Director of Education. All have been supportive, providing encouragement and sound professional advice. Mr. Dave Williams of course had a particular interest in Aberaeron as he was an old pupil of the school. I enjoyed working with the county officials and always valued their expertise and professional guidance.

Individual inspectors often visited the school on an irregular basis. I personally recall being visited by an inspector when I was in my first year of teaching in Brynhyfryd School, Ruthin, in November 1953. After that, nobody actually visited my class during the whole of my twenty years as a classroom teacher. My next most memorable experience was the full inspection we had at Aberaeron in 1977, with nearly twenty inspectors spending a week at the school collecting information, making observations and comments. The experience was a very demanding and a stressful one for all the staff, as well as myself, but the results were very pleasing and encouraging, giving the school a justifiable boost and commendation. In spite of the upheaval and the confusion and the stress caused by such inspections, I do feel that there is much to be said for the new system, where schools are inspected at least every five years, with Aberaeron by now nearing the top of the list. I'm sure that the quality of education still offered at the school will produce yet another glowing report.

Community involvement

One cannot be involved in a leadership capacity in a large school without being part of the community and being involved in the community that the school serves. I was for years prior to my appointment as headmaster, a Youth Club leader at Aberaeron and New Quay and that was as good a place as any to learn one's craft and to understand youth culture and peer pressure. As a school, we were actively involved in fund raising for the swimming pool, an amenity which has served the school well for twenty years. Aberaeron is a community school with its Evening Institute and Community Hall, and a meeting place for many groups and societies. Recent developments in the school library to create a resource centre for the community confirm and expand the community interests.

Thoughts of retirement

I greatly enjoyed my role as Headmaster at Aberaeron, but of course, there were low periods when one felt deflated and defeated. Such a difficult period was that of the extended teachers' strike in the 1980s when one had to cross swords with respected colleagues at the same time agreeing with their aims and ambitions and sharing their concerns about the effect of their actions on the pupils. At least I was not at the helm during the teachers' strike of 1926 which went on for months and involved staff at Aberaeron and several other Cardiganshire schools - that was Mr Howell T. Evans' problem. It is also recorded in the annals of the school that the pupils went on strike in the later 1920s in a protest about a decision made by the headmaster. They apparently sat in the Square Field for an hour until they were persuaded to return to school. It is not only the youth of today who rebel!

I left with many regrets about things not achieved and, certainly, I consider that my inability to get a major investment in new buildings to replace the mobile classrooms and the ancient gym was a cause of regret. However, promises have now been made. I sincerely hope that they will be acknowledged and kept by Cardiganshire after local government reorganisation.

Towards the end one still had a vision, but was often lacking in energy. When I could not face the unexpected and the practical, like the water leaks and the fireworks or the distressed child and the awkward parent and perhaps most of all, the disgruntled member of staff, then it became obvious that it was time to go. My year out of school in 1991-92 as Appraisal Director for Dyfed confirmed that the problems one had to face in the outside world were less immediate and not as pressing as school ones. In the main, one could always phone or write tomorrow but school was not like that - today's problems had to be solved today. This inertia was an adequate sign that it was time to go. Anyway, forty years was enough in any profession, and thirty eight of those in Aberaeron, indicated that it was time for a change for both myself and the school. I was very fortunate during my period at Aberaeron not only to have an excellent staff at the school but also excellent Deputy Heads who shared the responsibilities. When it got to the point that they knew more about what was happening in the school than I did, then it was time to consider retirement.

Teaching may not be the most lucrative of careers, but it certainly gives one the greatest job satisfaction. It is also, by now, probably one of the most stressful occupations but it still is a particular pleasure to share in the successes of so many people, at any level not only at Oxbridge level, and to acknowledge these successes. Basically you need to love children in order to enjoy your job as a teacher. I was privileged to be in that position.

I survived because my wife shared my love for the school and encouraged me to devote myself totally to the school and spend every night and most weekends at my desk. A sympathetic ear, the occasional word of support and advice and the sharing of confidences provided the necessary reassurance and stimulus. Without such support, you cannot undertake the onerous duties involved, and I am very grateful to her for that support during the whole of my forty years in the profession.

The appointment of Miss Marina James is a pioneering one, being the only secondary school Headmistress ever appointed not only in Cardiganshire, but in the whole of Dyfed. I knew her as a pupil and later as a valued colleague and an outstandingly effective Deputy Headmistress. She will be an inspired leader, sensitive to the needs of this unique rural community and supported by a solid core of outstandingly able and caring staff.

It was a privilege to serve the school community and to be completely identified with it. Aberaeron School's standard of care and performance will survive any rigorous inspection procedure and emerge with distinction and march forward with confidence to the next century.

❖

Geraint Roberts, Cadeirydd y Llywodraethwyr yn cyflwyno anrheg i D. J. Thomas ar achlysur ei ymddeoliad. Haf 1993.

Staff yr Ysgol / School staff
1993

Alan Jones
Tîm Rygbi Ysgolion Cymru

Michael Evans
Tîm Rygbi Ysgolion Cymru

Glynis Jones
Tîm Hoci Ysgolion Cymru

Sharon Lloyd
Tîm Hoci Ysgolion Cymru

PRIFEIRDD YSGOL ABERAERON

Hywel Teifi Edwards

Rwy'n cofio i fi weld seremoni Cadeirio'r Bardd am y tro cyntaf erioed rywbryd cyn diwedd yr Ail Ryfed Byd yn Neuadd Goffa, Aberaeron adeg Eisteddfod yr Ysgol, a neb llai na'r cyn-ddisgybl, W. Beynon Davies, a oedd yn athro yn Ysgol Ramadeg Ardwyn ar y pryd yn beirniadu - athro y cefais achos droeon ymhen blynyddoedd i edmygu ei ddysg, yn ogystal â'r fraint o elwa arni pan ddôi gyda'r 'saint' i Gregynog ym mis Awst i fwynhau 'Wythnos Gymraeg' Adran Efrydiau Allanol, Prifysgol Cymru, Aberystwyth. Y prynhawn pellennig hwnnw yn y Neuadd Goffa, fe fyddwn i'n barod i gredu mai ef oedd traddodiad barddol y Cymry - pe gwyddwn bryd hynny fod y fath beth yn bod! Argraffwyd ar fy meddwl gan ei osgo a'i draethu fod cadeirio bardd yn fusnes o bwys. Ac mi roedd, wrth gwrs, ac y mae o hyd yn y Gymru hon, diolch byth.

Fe ofalodd athrawon yr hen ysgol yn ystod fy nghyfnod i ynddi (1946-1953) - Miss Gwyneth Parry (Mrs. Matthews yn ddiweddarach), Miss Mair Meganwy Jones, Mrs. Nansi Jones, Mr. Gwynfil Rees, Mr. Tudor Jones ac wrth gwrs, y prifathro ei hun, Mr. J. T. Owen - fod seremoni'r cadeirio 'yn bwrw ei swynion ar bob rhyw synnwyr' yn ddi-ffael bob blwyddyn. Ymdawelai llwythau Tyglyn, Tanyfron a Portland fel petai Arthur Frenin ei hun ar y llwyfan, ac ymdrechai'r barbariaid dua'u lliw ymddwyn fel petai ganddynt ddiddordeb ysol mewn beirdd a barddoniaeth. Teyrnasai 'hedd yr eisteddfod' dros bob man - nes codi o'r bardd buddugol i'w gyfarch gan sgrechfeydd gorfoleddus ei lwyth a rhegfeydd -nid anhyglyw - y darostyngedig rai. Yn fy achos i - 'blydi Portland!' neu 'blydi Tanyfron!' fyddai tan gabl.

Rwy'n cofio mai prifardd yr ysgol pan ymunais â hi oedd Ifan Dalis Dafis a gafodd ei gadeirio am y trydydd tro o'r bron yn 1947. Aeth yn ei flaen i ennill dosbarth cyntaf yn y Gymraeg yn Aberystwyth a threulio cyfnod hir yn ddarlithydd yng Ngholeg y Drindod, Caerfyrddin. Hen Gardi o Gymro braf - ond ei fod yn un o bethau Portland! Ta waeth, daeth merch i wared Tyglyn o wae wedi diflaniad Ifan Dalis - daeth Ceril Jones i hawlio'r gadair am bedair blynedd o'r bron rhwng 1949-52 a'n llanw ni'r Tyglyniaid glas ag ymffrost Thatcheraidd gwbwl annioddefol. A phan aeth hithau ymlaen i Aberystwyth, wele lanc gwyrdd o lwyth Tanyfron, **o'r diwedd**, yn codi'n ei lle - sef Gerallt Wyn Davies. Gallaf ei weld y foment hon yn ymlwybro tua'i gadair ar y llwyfan fel petai'n gas ganddo fod y fath beth ag awen yn bod. Enbyd o beth yw gwyleidd-dra beirdd!

Gwaetha'r modd, doeddwn i ddim yn fardd, yn ifanc nac yn hen, hyd y gwn i, ac yn hynny o beth, fel y prawf rhifynnau'r *Link*, roeddwn yn dilyn yn ôl traed yr 'Abereirth' a'm blaenorodd. Rhyddiaith oedd dewis cyfrwng y ddau ddisglair o fferm Caebislan, sef Jac L. a Joan Williams, yn ogystal ag Aneurin Jones, Glynne Jones a Bertha Lewis. Rwy'n cofio i fi yn 1953 ennill y wobr am ysgrif ar 'My Favourite Hobby' yn sôn am ddirgel ryfeddod maglu pysgod yn afon Arth - ac mae i'w gweld yn y *Link* dan enw Henry Wilcox Jones sy'n profi ei fod yn fwy o botsier na fi! Yr un flwyddyn, fe enillais y wobr am stori fer iasoer ac mae honno, hefyd, yn yr un rhifyn o'r *Link* dan y teitl 'Y Clochdy' - ac yn fy enw i. Wele gyfiawnder! Ond dim cadair - dim cymaint â stôl drithroed. Eto i gyd, yn Aberaeron yr agorwyd fy llygaid i weld cyfoeth ein traddodiad barddol ac yno y teimlais gyntaf ias y Gymraeg yn fy ngwaed.

Yn fy mlwyddyn gyntaf yn y chweched dosbarth, 1950-1, yr oeddwn i gael gwersi Cymraeg gan y prifathro, Mr. J. T. Owen, ond yr oedd mwy a mwy o'i amser yn cael ei lyncu gan waith bugeilio gweithwyr Gee, Walker and Slater a oedd wrthi'n codi'r estyniad i'r hen ysgol. Ni ddangosodd yr un Pharaoh fwy o ddiddordeb yn ei byramidiau nag a ddangosodd 'J. T.' yn yr estyniad i'w ysgol, ac fe fu'n rhaid i fi dalu pris ei ddiddordeb.

Un o'r llyfrau gosod oedd *Blodeugerdd o'r Ddeunawfed Ganrif.* Dôi i ddrws yr ystafell ddosbarth a dweud - "Chewch chi ddim gwers heddi. Trowch at 'Gywydd y Farn Fawr' a dadansoddwch y gynghanedd ymhob un llinell." Sôn am 'To Hell and Back'! Ac felly ymlaen drwy bob un o gywyddau Goronwy Owen a gweddill cynnwys y *Flodeugerdd* nes llanw cyfrol solet â llinellau dadansoddedig. Mae hi gen i hyd heddi. Druan ohonof! Rwyf wedi bod yn 'anghytbwys ddisgynedig' fyth ers hynny, yn gallu nabod cynghanedd fel shot ond heb lunio cymaint â chwpled cywydd yn fy oes. Ychydig a feddyliodd Gee, Walker and Slater eu bod, wrth ehangu hen ysgol, fwy na thebyg yn claddu darpar brifardd hefyd!

Pan drosglwyddodd Mr. Owen ei ofal amdanaf i Mrs. Matthews a Miss Mair Meganwy Jones, fe gafodd y *Flodeugerdd* lonydd a rhois innau'r gorau i gyfrif pennau 'mysedd yn fy nghwsg. Cefais fy nwyn at *Ysgubau'r Awen* Gwenallt a'm perswadio i ddarllen cerddi ac ysgrifau T. H. Parry-Williams er mwyn gwella fy Nghymraeg. 'Wele gwawriodd dydd i'w gofio. . .' yn fy mywyd. Cefais fy meddiannu gan y ddau ac y maent yn dal i fyw ynof o hyd. Y mae darganfod gogoniant iaith yn un o ddarganfyddiadau mwyaf ysblennydd bywyd ac fe ddigwyddodd i fi yn fy hen ysgol wrth ddarllen cerddi dau fardd eneiniedig.

Pan agorwyd yr adeilad newydd yn swyddogol ar 20 Rhagfyr 1951, y siaradwr gwadd oedd neb llai na T. H. Parry-Williams. Dyna'r tro cyntaf i fi ei weld a'i glywed ac rwy'n cofio o hyd wefr ei Gymraeg wrth ymateb i gyflwyniad ei hen ddisgybl, ein prifathro ni, Mr. J. T. Owen, na pharablodd yr un Cardi erioed ragorach iaith na'i iaith ef. Awr riniol i fi oedd honno ar bnawn Iau, 20 Rhagfyr 1951; awr sylweddoli yr hoffwn geisio siarad fy iaith rhywbeth yn debyg i'r ddau Wydion ar y llwyfan.

Y mae gwerth parhaol pob iaith fel cyfrwng patrymu a throsglwyddo'r profiad dynol yn dibynnu ar ddawn trin geiriau awduron ac ar allu ac awydd darllenwyr i ymateb mor llawn â phosibl i'w llên. Mewn cyfnod pan mae gwir berygl i'n dibyniaeth ddyddiol ar y cyfryngau cyfathrebu ein tlodi'n ieithyddol - waeth pa iaith a siaradwn - y mae o'r pwys mwyaf fod ein hysgolion a'n colegau yn cynhyrchu darpar awduron a darllenwyr sy'n parchu iaith fel cynsail pob diwylliant. Yn nheyrnas gwarineb, nid ar 'sound bites' y bydd byw dyn ac y mae angen gallu dweud mwy na 'grêt' ac 'O.K.' i ddiogelu gwerth diwylliant. Heb iaith, heb eiriau, heb flas at eiriau, salw fydd bywyd pob cymdeithas.

Dyna pam y dylem ni, sy'n ddisgyblion a chyn-ddisgyblion o'r ysgol hon, ymfalchïo yn ei phrifeirdd a'u gwerthfawrogi yn y ffordd orau trwy eu darllen - yn sicr - a'u hefelychu, hefyd, os tybiwn fod gennym awen. Yn sgil buddugoliaethau cenedlaethol diweddar Idris Reynolds a Cyril Jones, fe drefnwyd noson o ddathlu yn Neuadd yr Ysgol a roes bleser i bawb a ddaeth ynghyd. Yr oedd gan yr hen ysgol bob hawl i ddathlu ac at hynny onid yw'r Cymry dros y canrifoedd wedi gwneud yn fawr o'u beirdd yn gyhoeddus. Digon gwir. Y deyrnged fwyaf i fardd, fodd bynnag, fel i bob awdur arall, yw darllen ei waith a sôn amdano ac amdani. Chwedl John Milton: 'Fit audience let me have though few.'

Byddai'n dda gen i feddwl fod disgyblion Ysgol Aberaeron - hen ac ifanc - yn gwybod am gampau ein prifeirdd. A gaf i eu nodi'n fras heb geisio'u gwerthfawrogi mewn ysgrif fer fel hon. Fe fyddai'n dda gen i petai cystadleuaeth arbennig yn Eisteddfod yr Ysgol bob blwyddyn yn rhoi cyfle i werthfawrogi rhyw agwedd ar eu gwaith gan y byddai hynny'n sicrhau y byddai iddynt ddarllenwyr ifanc, cyson yn Aberaeron. Y mae digon eisoes wedi'i gynhyrchu i gynnal cystadleuaeth o'r fath am hir amser fel y prawf yr amlinelliad hwn o'u cyflawniadau.

J. M. Edwards (1903-78). Enillodd Goron yr Eisteddfod Genedlaethol deirgwaith: 'Y Pentref' (1937 Machynlleth); 'Yr Aradr' (1941 Hen Golwyn); 'Peiriannau' (1944 Llandybïe). Cyhoeddodd naw cyfrol o farddoniaeth a chyhoeddwyd *Y Casgliad Cyflawn* yn 1980. Y mae 'Peiriannau' heb os yn bryddest arwyddocaol ac y mae'n sicr fod J. M. Edwards ymhlith beirdd gorau'r ganrif hon.

L. Haydn Lewis (1904-85) Enillodd Goron yr Eisteddfod Genedlaethol ddwywaith: 'Ffoadur' (1961 Dyffryn Maelor) a 'Meini' (1968 Y Barri a'r Fro). Cyhoeddodd bedair cyfrol o gerddi gan gynnwys *Cerddi Argyfwng* (1966) - cyfrol ei frwydr yn erbyn torcalon yn dilyn marwolaeth drasig ei ferch, Carol, un o'm cydfyfyrwyr yn Adran y Gymraeg yn Aberystwyth. Diolch fod barddoniaeth wrth fynegi ing yn gallu gorseddu harddwch bywyd a diolch am ddewrder beirdd.

Geraint Bowen (1915-). Enillodd Gadair yr Eisteddfod Genedlaethol yn Aberpennar, 1946, pan ddyfarnwyd ei 'Awdl Foliant i'r Amaethwr' nid yn unig yn orau ond yn un o awdlau gorau'r Gymraeg. Y mae *Cerddi* (1984) yn cynnwys cynnyrch y cynganeddwr grymus hwn dros nifer o flynyddoedd ac y mae'r ffaith iddo olygu'r *Faner* rhwng 1977-78 a llanw swydd yr Archdderwydd rhwng 1979-81 yn hawlio iddo le arbennig ymhlith prifeirdd Ysgol Aberaeron.

Donald Evans (1940-). Yn holl hanes yr Eisteddfod Genedlaethol, nid oes ond tri phrifardd dwbwl-ddwbwl, sef T. H. Parry-Williams, Alan Llwyd a Donald Evans. Yn 1977, cipiodd y Gadair a'r Goron yn Wrecsam am awdl 'Llygredd', a phryddest, 'Hil', ac yn 1980 ailadroddodd y gamp yn Nyffryn Lliw am awdl 'Y Ffwrnais' a dilyniant o gerddi, 'Lleisiau'. Ac erbyn hyn, y mae wedi cyhoeddi naw cyfrol o gerddi sy'n tystio i'w awen ddiflino a'i afael sicr ar y mesurau caeth a rhydd. I Donald y mae barddoni yn gyfystyr â byw.

Idris Reynolds (1943-). Enillodd Gadair yr Eisteddfod Genedlaethol ddwywaith: 'Y Daith' (1989 Dyffryn Conwy) ac 'A Fo Ben . . .' (1992 Aberystwyth). Y mae wedi cyhoeddi un gyfrol hyfryd o ganu cynganeddol (gan mwyaf) eisoes, sef *Ar Lan y Môr . . .* (1994) ac yn ddiau fe ddaw eraill i'w dilyn o law bardd sy'n etifedd teilwng o'r traddodiad barddol yng ngodre Ceredigion.

Cyril Jones (1947-) Enillodd Goron yr Eisteddfod Genedlaethol yn Aberystwyth, 1992 am ddilyniant o gerddi ar y testun 'Cyfannu' a gallwn edrych ymlaen at gyhoeddi ei gyfrol gyntaf o farddoniaeth cyn bo hir gan ei bod hi'n amlwg nad awen ar gyfer cystadlu'n unig yw ei awen yntau chwaith.

Roeddwn wedi bwriadu cynnwys cerdd gan bob un ohonynt i gloi'r ysgrif hon gan mai'r deyrnged orau y gallwn ei thalu iddynt fyddai rhannu fy mhleser yn eu canu ag eraill. Ond nid raid imi wneud gan fod y pedwar sydd eto'n fyw wedi'u comisiynu i farddoni ar gyfer y gyfrol ddathlu, sydd hefyd yn cynnwys bobo gerdd gan J. M. Edwards a Haydn Lewis. Boed i'w darllen godi awydd i ddarllen mwy o'u gwaith, heb sôn am godi awydd yn rhai o ddisgyblion Ysgol Aberaeron i'w hefelychu.

Bodlonaf ar ddweud cymaint â hyn amdanynt. Y mae'r chwech yn feirdd sy'n mynegi'r profiad dynol a'u cyfrifoldeb i'r byd sydd ohoni trwy ymlynu wrth ddiwylliant eu hiaith a'u cymdeithas arbennig hwy. Wyneb yn wyneb â her bywyd, nid mater o 'ganu a gadael iddo' yw barddoni iddynt ac nid trwy wneud sioe o gatholigrwydd awenyddol yr ânt ati i ddangos eu bod yn ddinasyddion byd. Ar sail eu gofal am y byd sydd wrth eu traed y gwelant eu rhan fel beirdd yn y frwydr fyd-eang barhaus dros warineb.

A da hynny. Yn nhermau iaith, gwe o fydoedd yw'r byd yr ydym yn byw ynddo ac y mae i dranc unrhyw un o'r bydoedd hyn oblygiadau dynol cyffredinol. Yn iaith diwylliant, dylai pob dyn fod yn geidwad ei frawd a'i chwaer, ac yr oedd Cyril Jones wedi hen ddysgu'r wers honno cyn iddo gwrdd â'i gyd-deithiwr ifanc yn Kenya. Haeddai fwy na choron petai ond am hynny.

Y mae cymdeithas sy'n ddibris o'i phriod iaith yn ddibris o'i phrofiad ei hunan ac o'r gwerthoedd sydd wedi cyfeirio'i bywyd dros gwrs hanes. Dyna pam fod ennill brwydr y Gymraeg yn fater hollbwysig i bawb sy'n poeni am gyflwr gwarineb y gwledydd ar drothwy'r unfed ganrif ar hugain. Nid brwydr blwyfol mohoni, ac fe wêl y ganrif nesaf ei hymladd ledled daear wrth i'r anniwylliant Eingl-Americanaidd fygwth tagu mwy a mwy o ieithoedd brodorol.

Fe adawodd y Celtiaid lawer trysor i dystio i gyfoeth y diwylliant a fu gynt yn ogoniant y gwareiddiad Ewropeaidd. O'r trysorau hynny, y pennaf yw'r Gymraeg a'r traddodiad llenyddol sydd wedi gosod cymaint bri ar farddoniaeth. Yn y farddoniaeth honno y mae clywed calon cenedl yn curo a gweld ei dychymyg ar waith. Diolch i feirdd Cymru, gallwn heddiw ymborthi ar brofiadau'r canrifoedd wrth wynebu gobaith a phryder y milrif ac fe allwn ni, wrth ddathlu canmlwyddiant ein hen ysgol, ymfalchïo am iddi adael ei stamp ar chwech o brifeirdd a gyfrannodd, ac sy'n para i gyfrannu, at stoc y profiadau hynny. Gwnawn yn fawr ohonynt. Darllenwn eu cerddi a'u noddi â'n gwerthfawrogiad. Y maent yn prydyddu parhad y Cymry ar lan y môr:

Ym maeau yr hil bydd ymwroli
Tra mab i'w annog, tra Mabinogi,
A'r môr yn dweud y stori - ar y traeth
Tra tant o hiraeth, tra ton yn torri.

❖

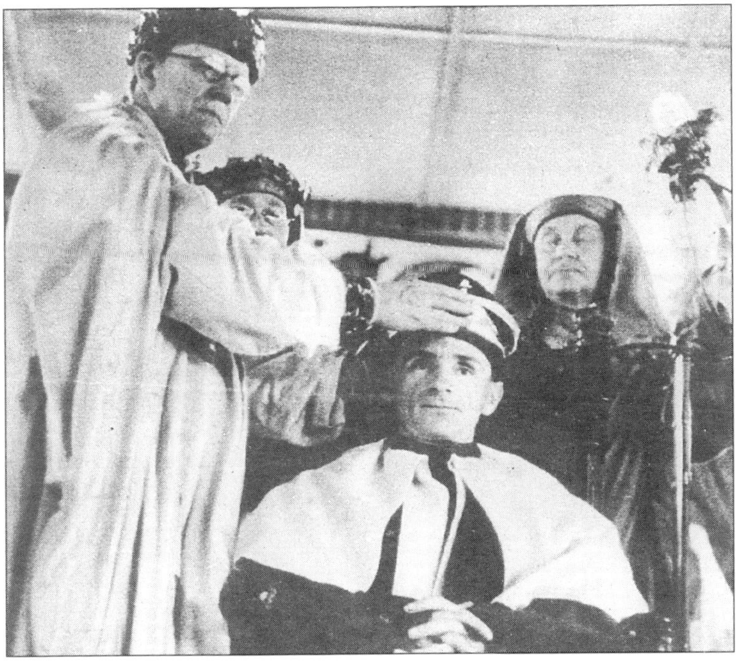

J. M. Edwards

L. Haydn Lewis

Geraint Bowen

Donald Evans

Idris Reynolds

Cyril Jones

EDRYCH YN ÔL / LOOKING BACK

Aberaeron County School 1958 - 65

Margaret Bevan (nee Parry)

When I walk up the school hill towards Aberaeron Comprehensive School these days to a parents' evening or a school production, I still feel a sense of excitement, even nervousness, at returning to my old school. I look over my shoulder hurriedly in case Mr. W. A. Jones is wheeling his bike along silently behind me, about to order me back to the bottom of the lane again because I've forgotten to wear my school beret. I peep through the window of the basement classroom where Mr. Sidney Evans kept an avuncular eye over Form 1A in 1958. I glance through the window of the men's staff room (now the Conference Room), half expecting to see Mr. Gwynfil Rees or Mr. Tudor Jones engaging Mr. Jack Rees and Mr. Bill Lewis in animated conversation, or Mr. John Roberts, behind them, chuckling at the success of his latest practical joke. Then, as I return to reality, a curious feeling of resentment at all that is different takes over. Where have the cloakrooms in the Old Building gone? Why banish the Maths Department to a miserable Portakabin? What right have the staff to invade Miss Elaine Lewis' Cookery Room? I am even irritated by the potted plants that surround the schools entrance and the pictures which adorn the corridors of the Old Building. Thirty years on, with Marina James, Wynne Harries, John Evans and Richard Griffiths sitting where J. T., Twm Chem, Mathews Maths and Dan Phys once sat watching them and me, how could this be my school?

When, as a small child, I was taken for a walk to see the big children's school, I vividly remember being told by a well-meaning adult that, if I did well at the primary school, I would go on to the old building, but, if I did not, I would go to the new building (which even then had workmen busily repairing its roof). It was therefore with some dismay that on my first day I found myself herded along with another hundred new pupils into the large hall in the new building. There we remained - the girls dressed in box-pleat gymslips seated along one wall, the boys in grey, short trousers and knee-length socks, along the other - for three long days, until we sat a thinly disguised 11+ to separate the sheep from the goats. True, we all went to the same school but those who were assigned to forms A and B passed, and went to the grammar forms where they were taught by subject specialists, given use of the best classrooms and text books, and entered for external examinations; forms C and D made up the moderns who took second place. In 1958, Aberaeron School was a bilateral school; comprehensive education was still some years away. But bilateralism itself was an enormous leap forward from traditional grammar and secondary modern education. Those pupils who were too traumatised by their first weeks experience to do themselves justice had several opportunities to prove that they had been misjudged, and it would be possible to list among my own contemporaries a senior scientist, a doctor and several teachers who would have had no chance of success under the selection processes that existed elsewhere at that time.

Indeed, in many ways, Aberaeron School catered admirably for the needs of its pupils. To me and to others in the academic forms, the school farm may have meant no more than the stench of rotting cabbages or the sight of an occasional heifer greeting us through the Cookery Room window, but for many, Artie, the school groundsman, and his tractor were the means not only of retaining enthusiasm among those whose interest would long have waned elsewhere but also of securing a committed band of agricultural workers for local farms. The Woodwork and Metalwork rooms too produced some highly skilled craftsmen, who, had their schooling been delayed until the nineties, might have experienced the joys of redesigning theatres or bridges in D. T. lessons but without learning the skills to plane a piece of wood. There have been other curriculum changes since 1965. To pupils nurtured on the National Curriculum, it will seem strange that we could escape Chemistry by opting for Art, or Maths by taking Music or Domestic Science (for girls, of course) or Woodwork (for boys only). The bizarre choice between Latin and French has long been removed and the demise of Latin is something which only Mr. Bill Lewis and Mr. Meurig Evans live to regret. Welsh-medium education was in its infancy and, although some pupils studied History and R. I. (not yet R. E.) through Welsh in the first two years, the majority of us only met Welsh within the curriculum in Welsh classes, where we were divided, like choosing steak in a restaurant, into those who took easy, medium or hard .

Welsh-medium education may not have been a feature of the school in the late fifties or the early sixties, but the ethos was certainly predominantly Welsh. As someone whose first language was English, I was very aware that most pupils spoke Welsh to each other and to the staff. Most pupils were the children of ex-pupils, their family connections and history known down to the smallest detail to all the staff. Newcomers from other parts of Wales were rare and those from England were a novelty. Nevertheless, English was the formal language of communication in the school, whether for announcements by the Head in assembly (which all pupils attended every morning) or over the Tannoy, which invaded every classroom even more during Mr J. T. Owen's day than it did in his successors (though the present staff may find this difficult to believe). School productions, however, alternated, as they do now, between English and Welsh; *She Stoops to Conquer* with Timothy Thomas and *Pelenni Pitar* with Alan Evans - Mr. Tudor Jones being the unifying factor, since he starred in them all.

There was more to the ethos of Aberaeron School in the sixties than simply Welshness. There was a sense of loyalty and affection which bound the staff and pupils alike. The atmosphere of the school Eisteddfod typified this by arousing in all an unparalleled enthusiasm and sense of involvement by pupils and staff. The staff indeed gave the school its unique character. It would be possible to list the names of teachers whose inspiring lessons will always remain in my mind; it would be possible to name staff who encouraged and helped me and others throughout our school years. It would be possible ... but it would be invidious to mention names. I am not looking back through rose-tinted spectacles when

I say that all the staff were wholly committed to the welfare and progress of every pupil in their charge.

It is perhaps because of the sense of security and happiness which the school fostered that the most abiding memories are the plethora of small but precious images, insignificant to any who did not share the experiences. I wonder whether Mr. David Thomas, then Chemistry teacher, remembers the circus of performing fleas with which he entertained us to capture our interest at the beginning of a lesson? Does Miss Maria Evans, our awe-inspiring form teacher for four long years, remember the occasion when she was struck speechless for a week after we presented her with a lamp as a Christmas present in the fifth year? Does Mr. Alcwyn Evans realize that we always knew how he cheated in Tanyfron's favour whenever the golliwogs were raised in the eisteddfod to indicate the respective positions of the three houses? Are Mr. and Mrs. Pascoe aware of the romantic interest which the first years of their marriage excited in the entire female population of the school? Does anyone else still remember Mr. Ron Mathews' cynical comments or ponder the implications of his cryptic remarks? How many other ex-pupils recall Mr. Gwynfil Rees holding the whole school spellbound with his inimitable stories between items on eisteddfod day? Do others remember with affection Mr. J. T. Owen sweeping at speed through the corridors, his gown flowing grandly behind him, turning suddenly to congratulate a pupil on some achievement or stopping to tell another how he taught her father before her?

Yes, Aberaeron School in the sixties was a very special place. Can I really be blamed for resenting all changes, even if they do represent progress?

❖

Fy atgofion personol fel disgybl yn Ysgol Sir Aberaeron

Elenid Non Hughes (Jones)

Mae'n anodd credu rhywsut bod 35 o flynyddoedd wedi mynd heibio ers i mi gychwyn yn ddisgybl 11 oed yn yr ysgol uwchradd yn Aberaeron. Ysgol Sir Aberaeron - y Cownti Sgŵl - oedd hi bryd hynny wrth gwrs. Profiad eithaf anodd i mi oedd symud o ysgol fach yn y wlad i ysgol a ymddangosai yn anferth a dieithr yn fy marn i ar y pryd. Ond gydag amser ymgynefinais â'r lle a gwneud ffrindiau da, a braf yw gallu dweud fy mod yn parhau i gadw cysylltiad ag amryw ohonynt hyd y dydd heddiw er ein bod yn byw ymhell oddi wrth ein gilydd yn ddaearyddol.

Fel disgybl yn yr ysgol rhwng 1960 a 1967, roeddwn i yn ymwybodol trwy gydol yr amser fod yna dair carfan o blant yno, sef plant Cei, plant Aberaeron a phlant y wlad ac yn naturiol roeddwn i yn disgyn i gategori "plant y wlad", gan fy mod yn dod o Lwyncelyn, rhyw ddwy filltir i'r de o Aberaeron. Fel un o blant y wlad, cludwyd fi a'm chwiorydd a phlant y pentref i'r ysgol ar fws Crosville gwyrdd yn y blynyddoedd cynnar. Bws Synod Inn y galwem ni ef gan ei fod yn dod o'r cyfeiriad hwnnw, ac ar y bws hwn fel ar bob bws ysgol arall roedd yna nythaid o blant direidus, ond plant annwyl a naturiol iawn bob amser. Yr adeg honno, un o reolau euraidd yr ysgol oedd bod yn rhaid i bob plentyn wisgo cap ysgol wrth deithio ar fws ysgol; roedd hi'n gas gen i wisgo cap ysgol, a dweud y gwir roedd hi'n gas gen i wisgo unrhyw beth ar fy mhen o ran hynny. Yn y cyfnod cynnar hwnnw roeddwn i'n blentyn eithaf nerfus, ac fel newydd-ddyfodiad bach i'r ysgol roeddwn i'n awyddus iawn bob amser i gadw at bob rheol oedd yn bodoli ac felly, yn ôl y drefn, roeddwn yn gwisgo fy nghap newydd ar fws Crosville Synod Inn bob amser. Ond un bore, ac mae'r atgof yn fyw o hyd, cofiaf amdanaf yn eistedd yn fy sedd ar y bws ar y ffordd i'r ysgol a'r cap ar fy mhen yn barchus. Y funud nesaf cipiwyd ef yn ddiseremoni oddi ar fy mhen gan un o'r cryts drygionus a'i luchio allan drwy ffenestr y bws! Lloriwyd fi gan deimladau cymysg - roeddwn yn gallu gweld doniolwch y sefyllfa ond eto ar yr un pryd roeddwn yn teimlo'r chwithdod o golli darn hanfodol o'r wisg ysgol heb sôn am ddarn o fy hunan-barch! Bu'n rhaid i mi gael cap newydd arall wrth gwrs, a gallaf eich sicrhau na wisgais i fy nghap o gwbl ar fws Synod Inn fyth ar ôl hynny! Buan y dysgais bod rhai rheolau yr adeg honno megis heddiw wedi eu creu ar gyfer eu torri! Atgofion hapus sydd gennyf am deithio ar y bws hwnnw serch hynny gyda'i gymeriadau lliwgar, brith! Weithiau pan fyddai bws Synod Inn yn torri i lawr roeddem ni blant Llwyncelyn yn cael ein cludo i'r ysgol ar fws merched Cei, bws Western Welsh coch. Roedd merched Cei yn gwisgo eu capiau yn daclus a thrwsiadus ar eu pennau bob amser wrth deithio ar y bws. Rwy'n cofio i mi gael gorchymyn go chwyrn un tro gan un o'r "prefects" (uwch-swyddogion i blant heddiw) ar y bws hwn i wisgo fy nghap **ar unwaith**, ac yn fwndel o nerfusrwydd dyma fi'n ufuddhau fel ci bach. Ie, "Caps on, girls" oedd hi ar y bws hwnnw bob amser! Wrth edrych yn ôl, rwy'n gwenu wrth gofio am y pethau bychain hyn, pethau dibwys iawn i bobl eraill wrth gwrs ond pethau sydd wedi mynnu aros yn fy nghof i serch hynny.

Rhaid oedd i ni ddisgyblion ysgol yr adeg honno wisgo'r cap ysgol i fynd lawr dre bob amser cinio hefyd. Pe anwybyddem y rheol caem gosb haeddiannol gan un o'r uwch-swyddogion - yr "hundred lines" bondibethma rheiny sy'n dal yn fytholwyrdd ym mhob ysgol hyd heddiw, am wn i. Profiad braf oedd cael mynd lawr dre amser cinio, gwisgo cap neu beidio, a chael prynu gwerth chwe cheiniog (yr hen arian wrth gwrs), neu bedair ceiniog os oedd yr arian yn brin, o losin bron bob dydd a'u bwyta'n awchus wrth gerdded nôl i'r ysgol erbyn dau. Roedd y siop losin wrth y Cae Sgwar yn gwneud elw da ar ein corn ni blant yr adeg honno, yn enwedig ni blant yr ysgol Iau. Cefais gryn flas ar y "caramels", yr "aniseed balls", a'r "marshmallows" am flynyddoedd lawer. Rwyn cofio'n dda am berchennog y siop losin yn dweud wrthyf un tro pan ofynnais am chwarter (100g i blant heddiw) o farshmallows, a golwg ddifrifol ar ei wyneb, "Chi'n gwybod, rych chi'n cael bargen wrth brynu rhain, mae eisiau lot ohonyn nhw i wneud chwarter." Am funud pendronais dros yr hyn a ddywedodd, chwarter yw chwarter meddyliais wrthyf fy hunan, ond wedyn deallais beth oedd ganddo o dan sylw - roedd e yn llygad ei le wrth gwrs! - roedd "marshmallows" yn cael eu gwerthu yn rhydd yr adeg honno bob amser ac nid mewn pacedi parod fel y'u gwerthir nhw gan amlaf heddiw a chan eu bod mor ysgafn, fe gaech lawer iawn ohonynt am chwarter (100g). Fel Cardi o'r iawn ryw, prynais lawer o farshmallows ar ôl hynny a chael gwerth fy arian bob amser!

Symud ymlaen wedyn a chyrraedd yr ysgol ganol, a minnau tua phedair ar ddeg oed. Dyma'r adeg pan ddechreuais ddod yn ymwybodol o hinsawdd politicaidd y dydd yng Nghymru, deffroad yn nhwf cenedlaetholdeb a gweithgarwch Cymdeithas yr Iaith, er na chymerwn ran weithredol o gwbl yr adeg honno. Rwy'n cofio un tro am fy ffrind o berfeddion cefn gwlad a minnau yn eistedd ochr yn ochr a'n gilydd yn yr ystafell Hanes, a'r pwnc o dan sylw oedd Y Ddeddf Uno 1536. Roeddem ein dwy wedi anesmwytho cryn dipyn yn ein seddau wrth nodi'r ffeithiau a chanfod yr anghyfiawnderau dybryd a oedd ynghlwm wrth yr uniad rhwng Cymru a Lloegr. Dechreuasom ochneidio a sibrwd pethau eithaf anghynnes o dan ein gwynt, a'r diwedd fu i'r athro Hanes golli ei amynedd tuag atom gan weiddi'n chwyrn, **"Pope Jones, and Free Wales Army, keep your comments to yourself!"** Gair bach o eglurhad, neu ryw fath o eglurhad beth bynnag: roeddwn i yn ferch i weinidog, felly dyna egluro'r "Pope Jones", ac roedd fy ffrind yn genedlaetholwraig bybyr, y fwyaf un yn ein blwyddyn ni ac o bosib yn yr ysgol gyfan yr adeg honno, felly dyna egluro'r "Free Wales Army", boed hynny'n gam neu'n gymwys wrth gwrs! Prysuraf i ddweud fy mod yn hoff o fy athro Hanes, yn fwy felly nag o'r pwnc ei hun yn aml, a dyfalwch pa ddwy a ymunodd a'r dosbarth Hanes yn y chweched dosbarth? Ie, neb llai na "Pope Jones" a "Free Wales Army"!

Yn yr ystafell Hanes honno, a minnau yn fy mhedwaredd blwyddyn yn bedair ar ddeg oed, rwy'n cofio'n dda fel y bu i mi wylo'n dawel i mewn i fy hances boced trwy gydol y wers un bore gan ymdrechu i gymryd nodiadau synhwyrol ond heb fawr o lwyddiant, ac ar yr un pryd yn gobeithio'n daer nad oedd neb wedi sylwi ar fy nagrau. Bore dydd Llun llwydaidd oedd hi ym mis Tachwedd 1963 a minnau wedi fy ysgwyd gan lofruddiaeth John F. Kennedy yn Dallas, Texas ar y dydd Gwener blaenorol. Roedd hi'n niwlog a glawog y tu allan ar y bore dydd Llun hwnnw yn Aberaeron, fel pe bai natur gyfan yn cydymdeimlo â'r ddynoliaeth yn ei phrofedigaeth. Brawychwyd y byd i gyd a siglwyd finnau hefyd gan y digwyddiad erchyll.

Ystafell arall rwy'n ei chofio'n dda yw'r ystafell Goginio. Roedd hon fel pin mewn papur bob amser ac aroglau glan "Domestos" ynghyd ag aroglau coginio'n treiddio drwyddi. O bryd i'w gilydd, caem y cyfle i goginio rhywbeth ein hunain a dyna gyffrous oedd cael mynd â'n campweithiau adref i'w dangos a'u bwyta'n awchus ar diwedd y dydd. Un diwrnod, rwy'n cofio ffrind i mi o'r un pentref wedi gwneud pwdin reis yn y wers Goginio yn yr ysgol. Os meddyliwch chi am funud, peth anodd iawn yw cario pwdin reis mewn dysgl am ddwy filltir heb iddo droi a cholli ar hyd bob man, ac yn gall iawn roedd fy ffrind wedi rhagweld y broblem hon ac wedi dod a hen dun biscedi i ddal y ddysgl reis yn sownd yn ei lle. Ar diwedd y prynhawn, roeddem ein dwy wedi dod oddi ar y bws ac wedi cyrraedd gât ei thŷ hi pan ofynnais iddi'n frwd ac yn llawn chwilfrydedd am gael gweld ei phwdin reis cyn iddi fynd i'r tŷ. Cytunodd hithau'n llawen, ond yn anffodus wrth dynnu'r caead i ffwrdd llithrodd y tun a'i gynnwys o'i gafael a disgynnodd y cyfan - y tun, y ddysgl a'r reis - yn glewt ar y concrit caled wrth ein traed. Roedd y ddysgl reis yn yfflon rhacs a'r pwdin yn ymledu yn un soegen wleb ar y palmant o'n blaenau. Wel, sôn am chwerthin a wnaethom ein dwy wrth geisio codi'r darnau! Yna'n araf, gwawriodd realaeth y sefyllfa arnom a sobreiddiasom drwon wrth ddychmygu beth fyddai ymateb ei mam pan ddeuai adref o'r dre yn hwyrach y noson honno. Es adref gan bwffian chwerthin ond fedrwn i ddim llai na theimlo'n euog hefyd. Paham oedd rhaid i mi fod mor fusneslyd? Wedi'r cwbl, roeddwn wedi hen ymgyfarwyddo â gweld pwdin reis ers cyn cof, gan ein bod fel teulu yn ei gael yn rheolaidd bob dydd Sul i bwdin!

Ond pwdin na fu erioed ormod ohono i mi oedd Eisteddfod Gŵyl Ddewi Ysgol Aberaeron. Roedd hon yn eisteddfod arbennig iawn yn y cyfnod roeddwn i yn yr ysgol ac mae hi'n parhau felly hyd heddiw mae'n debyg. Cynhaliwyd y rhagbrofion yn y bore a chofiaf am feirniaid cenedlaethol o fri yn dod i roi eu gwasanaeth. Dechreuwyd ar y cystadlu cyffrous o'r llwyfan am 2 o'r gloch y prynhawn, saib wedyn tua 4 o'r gloch ac ail-gychwyn ar weithgareddau'r hwyr tua 5.30 o'r gloch ac ymlaen wedyn nes gorffen tua 10 o'r gloch y nos. Roedd y neuadd dan ei sang gan blant a rhieni cynhyrfus. Roeddwn i ar ben fy nigon ar y diwrnod hwn bob blwyddyn, ac yn cystadlu ymron ar bob cystadleuaeth llwyfan oedd ar gael. Byddwn yn canu unawdau a deuawdau, yn adrodd yn Gymraeg a Saesneg a chanu'r piano, a byddwn wrth fy modd yn cymryd rhan mewn partion canu, yn arbennig felly cerdd dant, ond rhaid i mi gyfaddef roedd cymryd rhan mewn parti cyd-adrodd yn dân ar fy nghroen a cheisiais fy ngorau glas - a llwyddo'n bur aml hefyd - i osgoi cymryd rhan yn y diflastod hwn, er mawr ddicter i ambell athro. Roedd tri thŷ yn cystadlu yn erbyn ei gilydd, sef Tanyfron, Tyglyn a Portland, a bob tro y byddai marciau'r tri thŷ yn cael eu harddangos ar y bwrdd du, fe fyddem oll yn ein tro yn cael caniatad i weiddi bonllefau'r tai. Wel, sôn am hwyl a sbri gogoneddus wrth lafarganu'r synau hyn! Aelod o dŷ Tanyfron oeddwn i, y tŷ gwyrdd, a cheisiaf yn awr am y tro cyntaf erioed yn fy mywyd ysgrifennu i lawr fonllefau'r tai. Erbyn heddiw, ar ôl pendronni uwch ben y bonllefau hyn, rwyf yn fwyfwy argyhoeddiedig yn fy meddwl fod ethos y jyngl yn perthyn yn gryf iddynt! Beth bynnag, dyma fel rwy'n eu cofio gan obeithio fy mod yn weddol agos at fy lle o ran cywirdeb:

Dyma fonllef Tanyfron:

Swm Swm Saca, Swm Swm Se,
Bwshaba, Bwshaba, Bwshaba Be,
Scabo, Scabo, I Ia Io,
TANYFRON.

A dyma fonllef Tyglyn:

Wi Wi Waca, Wi Wi Wa,
Waca Wi, Waca Wi, Waca Wi, Wa,
Gishi, Gishi, Gishi,
TYGLYN.

A dyma fonllef Portland:

Ti Lasha Basha, Ti Lasha Ba,
Gorabela, Gorabela,
Jing, Jing, Jingo,
PORTLAND.

Er holi amryw ynghylch tarddiad ac ystyr y bonllefau hyn, nid wyf eto wedi cael esboniad boddhaol. Ni wn i am un ysgol arall sy'n llafarganu y fath synau adeg eisteddfod. Fel ym mhob eisteddfod, y "côr mawr" oedd uchafbwynt y cystadlu, a chymaint yn dibynnu ar y gystadleuaeth olaf honno. Dyma gyfle i bob un disgybl ymddangos ar y llwyfan, y gwych, y canolig a'r gwael yn gymysg oll i gyd. Anghofiaf i fyth mo'r wefr o fynd adre ar y bws ysgol ar ddiwedd yr Eisteddfod a hithau wedi 10 o'r gloch y nos a phawb ohonom yn crochlefain ein bonllefau tai, y sŵn yn fyddarol a'n gyddfau yn gryg. Druan o'r gyrrwr bws - ni feddylion ni blant am un eiliad fer erioed am yr effaith a allasai'r gweiddi croch fod wedi ei gael ar glyw y sant amyneddgar hwnnw.

Bu gen i drwyn da a sensitif erioed, a chofiaf yn glir hyd heddiw am yr arogl unigryw hwnnw yn yr Hen Adeilad, yr "Old Block" fel y'i gelwid gennym ni blant. Roedd yno rhyw arogl fel arogl llwydni a llwch yr oesoedd yn gymysg. Serch hynny, roedd y rhan hon o'r ysgol yn llawn cymeriad. Roedd yno lyfrgell hardd, ystafell urddasol a chain, a ninnau ysywaeth, fodau meidrol y chweched dosbarth, yn ei chamddefnyddio o bryd i'w gilydd wrth anghofio mai lle i fyfyrio'n dawel y dylasai llyfrgell fod. Rwy'n cofio un tro ar diwedd tymor a'r arholiadau wedi gorffen i mi gael stŵr gan un athro am fod mor haerllug a dod â fy ngwau i'w wneud yno! Nid lle i wau a gwagsymera oedd llyfrgell i fod! Yr athro oedd yn iawn wrth gwrs.

Yn y bloc newydd dros y ffordd, roedd yr arogl yn wahanol eto, ond yr hyn sy'n aros yn fyw iawn yn fy nghof i yw arogl ffiaidd y sylffwr deuocsid yn codi o'r labordy Cemeg ac yn drewi'r bloc gwaelod yn gyfangwbl! Llawer gwaith y cerddais y coridor gwaelod hwnnw gan wasgu fy ffroenau at ei gilydd rhag cyfogi! Doedd wyau drwg ddim ynddi! Er gwaetha'r drewdod, roedd gennyf rhyw ostyngedig barch tuag at y rhai a ymddiddorai yn y Gwyddorau yn y chweched dosbarth ac roeddwn yn llawn edmygedd o'r rhai a astudiai Gemeg, a'r rheswm am hynny oedd am i mi fy hunan fod mor ddi-glem yn y pwnc o'r cychwyn cyntaf. Gwelaf y gwyddonwyr gwybodus yn glir o flaen fy llygaid yn awr, yn ddisgyblion ac yn athrawon, oll yn gytun yn eu cotiau gwynion, wrthi'n gydwybodol yn gwneud arbrofion, arbrofion a oedd tu hwnt i'm amgyffred a'm deall i gan eu bod yn fy nhyb i yn perthyn i arall-fyd.

Ond pawb at y peth y bo ynte, a chefais innau gryn fwynhad wrth astudio Cymraeg, Saesneg a Hanes i Lefel "A". Yn y chweched dosbarth, deuthum i werthfawrogi cyfeillgarwch cyfoedion, athrawon a phrifathro yn fwyfwy eto. Buan iawn y daeth yr amser i ymadael a'r ysgol a throi am y coleg ym mis Medi 1967. Teimladau cymysg oedd gennyf ar ddiwedd fy rhawd yn Ysgol Aberaeon. Yn naturiol, roeddwn yn hiraethu wrth ymadael â hafan ddiogel yr ysgol gymdogol hon, er i mi deimlo lawer tro ei bod hi braidd yn Seisnigaidd. Roeddwn hefyd yn gwerthfawogi ac yn diolch am yr addysg a dderbyniais a'r cyfle a gefais yno i berthyn, i ffurfio barn a dechrau tyfu ar daith bywyd.

Bron i 30 mlynedd yn ddiweddarach edrychaf yn ôl ar fy nghyfnod yn ysgol Aberaeron fel un hapus yn fy mywyd. Rwy'n dal i feddwl am "fy hen ysgol i" gyda rhyw gynhesrwydd yn fy nghalon. Buasai'n braf medru camu'n ôl o bryd i'w gilydd i gyfnod fy nyddiau ysgol yn Aberaeron i ail-fyw y profiadau gorau! Ond wrth gwrs, rhaid gochel rhag sentimentaleiddio oherwydd gwyddom i gyd, bob un ohonom:

"Ddoe i neb ni ddaw yn ôl."

❖

Aberaeron y saithdegau. Celfyddydd a datblygiad.

Y Parch. Meirion Morris B.D.

I fachgen oedd newydd gyrraedd ei arddegau, yn byw yn un o'r pentrefi tawel oedd yn bwydo'r ysgol yn Aberaeron, mi 'roedd fy ymweliad cyntaf â'r lle yn frawychus ac yn creu cryn bryder. Nid oedd sôn eto am yr ymweliadau hynny o flaen llaw, sydd i fod i'n gwneud yn gyfarwydd â'r lle cyn cyrraedd, ac yr oedd fy unig argraffiadau wedi'u meithrin wrth wrando ar fy chwiorydd hŷn yn adrodd hynt a helynt eu bywydau yno.

'Roedd yn yr ysgol yn Nhalgarreg oddeutu 48 o blant, pan y bu ymadael a dal y bws am y tro cyntaf i fynd ar daith awr foreol, i fyd newydd a phrofiadau newydd. Yno yn disgwyl amdanaf, 'roedd 650 o ddisgyblion, yn cyfarfod mewn gwasanaeth boreol, pawb mewn rhesi, fel milwyr yn disgwyl eu gorchymynion dyddiol. Yno hefyd eisteddai y staff, yn hanner cylch taclus ar y llwyfan, ac yn y canol mewn clogyn du, y Prifathro. Yng nghanol y geiriau o groeso, teimlais y cynnwrf yna yn fy stumog oedd yn esgor o sefyllfa o ofn a dychryn, wrth i dawelwch y gwasanaeth gael ei dorri gan floedd, wrth i fachgen ddod o dan lach am liw ei grys, a hynny ar ddiwrnod cyntaf y tymor!

> Cyrhaeddais yr ysgol ar ddechrau tymor D. J. Thomas fel Prifathro, oedd newydd ei apwyntio y flwyddyn flaenorol. Mi 'roedd yr ysgol wedi symud o fod yn "County", neu ysgol Sir, i fod yn ysgol Gyfun, ac mi 'roedd y bathodyn a wniodd mam ar fy siaced yn cyhoeddi hynny yn glir. O gyrraedd, mae'n amlwg o edrych yn ôl fod yr ysgol yn dechrau dod i delerau â hyn, yn addysgol ac yn gymdeithasol. Dyma'r cyfnod pan y gwelwyd y gwrthdaro rhwng y dulliau newydd o addysgu, a'r hen ddull, y rhai a welai'r ysgol fel lle i feithrin pobl ifanc, a'r rhai a'i gwelai fel lle i ddysgu, a hynny drwy orchymyn a ffeithiau, di-ymwâd. Dyma y cyfnod pan y deuai addysg drwy gyfrwng y Gymraeg i sylw y llywodraethwyr, a hynny ar yr union amser pan 'roedd yr ardaloedd o amgylch yn cael eu boddi fwy-fwy gan fewnlifiad o bobl oedd â'i gwreiddiau yn Stoke a Birmingham. Mi 'roedd y cyfnod yn un o newid nid yn unig i fachgen ifanc o'r wlad, ond i'r ysgol hefyd.

Wrth edrych yn ôl ar fy nghyfnod yno, mae'n anodd mesur maint y dylanwad a gafodd y sefydliad hwn ar fy mywyd. Mae'n anodd hefyd maintioli y newidiadau a gymerodd le o fewn i'r ysgol, a hynny am fod fy nghwybodaeth o'r hyn a fu a'r hyn a ddaeth wedi fy ymadawiad yn gyfyngedig. Priodol felly yw sôn am yr hyn yr wyf yn ei wybod orau amdano, sef y blynyddoedd hynny a brofais fel disgybl, gan adael y gweddill i hanes cyffredinol.

O ran y dull o addysgu, yr oedd yr ysgol yn y cyfnod hwn wedi mabwysiadau dull llai cwrs o ddosbarthu y disgyblion o fewn blwyddyn. Diflannodd 1a, 1b, 1c a 1d, ac yn ei lle daeth cyfnod 1N, 1S, 1E a 1W, y llythrennau yn cyfeirio at bwyntiau y cwmpawd, gan osgoi i raddau yr awgrym o symud i lawr o "A" i "D". Ond ar yr un pryd, mae'n ddiddorol wrth edrych yn ôl, i sylwi fod y llythrennau blaenorol yn dilyn wyddor Saesneg, ac ni chlywyd neb erioed yn cyfeirio at fy nosbarth i fel 1 Gogledd. Mi 'roedd dod i'r afael â dwy-ieithrwydd yn rhywbeth yr oedd yr ysgol eto i ddod i delerau ag ef. O'n cwmpas yr oedd y frwydr o blaid statws cyfartal i'r iaith yn dechrau amlygu ei hun, yn y frwydr dros arwyddion yn bennaf, ond ni chafodd hyn ei effaith yn yr ysgol, nes iddi nesau at yr 80au, pan y cyflwynwyd addysg ddwyieithog a bandiau oedd yn adlewyrchu gallu amrywiol o fewn cyd-destun iaith gyntaf y plant.

O eistedd yn y 'stafell ddosbarth, mi 'roedd yr addysg hefyd yn adlewyrchu y traddodiad hyn. Dysgwyd y pynciau inni yn Saesneg, ac yn yr iaith honno hefyd yr oedd pob cyfathrebu, os oedd yna drafodaeth neu gwestiwn yn esgor o'r wers. I fachgen oedd wedi derbyn ei addysg gynradd yn gyfangwbl yn y Gymraeg mewn awyrgylch gwbl Gymreig, mi 'roedd y sioc ddiwylliannol ieithyddol hon yn golygu fod angen amser i addasu ac arfer. Mae'n sicr fod profiad plant Cei Newydd ag Aberaeron o ganlyniad yn wahanol wrth iddynt setlo i mewn i fywyd yr ysgol yn gynt. Mae'n anodd credu erbyn hyn fod yna sefyllfa yn Aberaeron, a hynny ond ugain mlynedd yn ôl lle byddai'r Prifathro yn eich cyfarch yn y coridor yn Saesneg, ac yn siarad Cymraeg yn rhugl o'i weld yn y capel neu ar y stryd. Fel y medrwch grynhoi o'r sylwadau hyn, fe gafodd y sefyllfa hon gryn effaith arnaf, a da medru tystio i'r camau breision a gymerwyd yn ystod y 70au i newid yr awyrgylch.

O ran ei faes, gwyddonydd oedd y Prifathro newydd, ac i raddau, mi fyddai hyn i'w weld yn y modd trefnus a systematig yr oedd yn dymuno gweld bywyd yr ysgol yn cael ei gynnal. Mi 'roedd ymweliad â'i ystafell neu glywed ei lais ar y sustem sain yn creu ofn, ac mae'n ddiogel fod hyn wedi arwain at y mesur o ddisgybliaeth a welwyd yn bodoli o fewn bywyd y sefydliad. Meddai ar lais fel taran, oedd yn treiddio y coridorau, wrth i rhywun gael gwahoddiad i'w swyddfa, i gael sgwrs am hyd ei wallt, neu am eu dewis o fag i gario ei lyfrau. 'Roedd ganddo faich arbennig dros weld y plant yn gweithio er mwyn sicrhau llwyddiant mewn arholiadau, a fyddai yn ei dŷb yn diogelu gwaith a sicrwydd yn eu dyfodol. Yn yr un cyfnod, gwelwyd nifer y di-waith yn genedlaethol yn croesi un milliwn, ac ardaloedd gwledig yn dioddef yn arbennig yn sgîl hyn. Cofiaf yn dda yr anogaeth hyn yn cael ei ail-adrodd yn fynych yn ystod y gwasanaethau boreol, er mwyn ein hannog i weithgarwch, yn arbennig o gwmpas yr arholiadau.

Wrth ddweud hyn, nid dyma'r unig bethau y gwelwyd eu pwysleisio yn ystod y cyfnod. Mi 'roedd yn yr ysgol weithgareddau hefyd oedd yn ceisio ehangu gorwelion addysg, drwy feithrin yn y disgyblion allu i ragori mewn cyfeiriadau eraill, ochr yn ochr ag yn yr ystafell arholiad. Yn ystod y 70au, fe amlygwyd hyn orau yn y cyngherddau a'r sioeau yr oedd yr adran Ddrama a'r adran Gerdd yn eu cynnal o gwmpas adeg y Nadolig. Perfformiwyd operau cerddorol, megis Nia Ben Aur, Joseff, A Christmas Carol a Godspell, ynghyd â chyngerdd mwy tradoddiadol bob yn ail flwyddyn. Yn y perfformiadau hyn, gwelwyd gwedd mwy celfyddydol i'r ysgol, ynghyd â dangos hefyd allu a dawn y to newydd o athrawon a ddaeth i'r ysgol. Un o'r athrawon Drama cyntaf hynny oedd Cleif Harpwood, oedd ar y pryd yn parhau yn aelod o'r grwp enwog, Edward H. Dafis, un ar y pryd oedd yn byw ym mhentref enwog Derwen-Gam, ac a oedd yn ddiweddarach i fynd ymlaen i weithio i'r cyfryngau yn cynhyrchu rhaglenni. Un arall oedd Malcolm Williams, un oedd wedi ymddangos eisioes ar y teledu ym myd darlledu Cymraeg. Adleisiwyd yr agwedd meddwl newydd hyn yn yr adran Gerdd wrth i Gareth Hughes Jones gael ei apwyntio i ofal yr adran.

Mi 'roedd y bechgyn hyn yn ifanc, yn llawn brwdfrydedd a gallu creadigol, ac fe gefnogwyd eu gwaith a'i hymdrechion, wrth i'r cynyrchiadau blynyddol ennill mwy a mwy o fri, ac o dan Neville Evans, i rai o'r disgyblion ddechrau astudio Drama fel pwnc arholiad. Yn y cyfnod hwn hefyd, gwelwyd nifer o'r disgyblion yn ymddangos yng nghynyrchiadau cenedlaethol cwmni theatr yr Urdd, a chwmni theatr Ieuenctid Cymru a Phrydain. Ar yr ochr gerddorol, mi 'roedd yna eisioes nifer o ddisgyblion wedi ennill bri ag amlygrwydd o ganlyniad i'w gallu lleisiol, rhai sydd yn awr yn parhau yn enwog, ac ar yr un pryd, gwelwyd disgyblion yn cael lle yng Ngherddorfa'r Sir, a Cherddorfa Ieuenctid Cymru. Gwelwyd y doniau hyn yn cael eu amlygu o fewn yr ysgol yn yr eisteddfod flynyddol, a mawr oedd y paratoi a'r disgwyl am y diwrnod hwn. Ar ddechrau y cyfnod, 'roedd y neuadd yn llawn ar hyd y diwrnod, wrth i'r disgyblion gystadlu yn frwd, i ennill y darian i'w tŷ. Er hynny, wrth i'r blynyddoedd fynd heibio, ac wrth i'r ysgol newid o fod yn un naturiol Gymraeg, mi 'roedd y disgyblion oedd yn meddu brwdfrydedd yn prinhau, a mwy yn edrych ar y diwrnod fel gwyliau answyddogol. Er hynny, yma y gwelwyd meithrin doniau cyhoeddus, oedd i ddod â bri i nifer ar lwyfannau lleol a chenedlaethol.

Ochr yn ochr â hyn, gwelwyd y datblygiad a gyfeiriwyd ato yn null y dysgu, a cafwyd nifer o athrawon newydd i ateb y gofyn. Daeth addysg drwy gyfrwng y Gymraeg o fewn gafael y disgyblion hynny a fynnai hynny, gyda'r rhan fwyaf o'r pynciau ar gael yn awr, a hynny i fyny i safon arholiad allanol, yn y ddwy iaith. Cododd yr ymwybyddiaeth o Gymreictod yn yr un cyfnod a chlywyd iaith y coridor yn newid. Ymhlith yr athrawon newydd, gwelwyd pobl fel Geraint Davies, Meurig James, Non Mathias ac Emyr Llewelyn. Fe hyfforddwyd y rhain mewn sefydliadau oedd wedi mabwysiadu dulliau llawer iawn mwy rhyddfrydol o addysgu, ac fe gyflwynwyd grwpiau a trafodaethau fel rhan sylfaenol o fywyd y dosbarth. Ar yr un pryd, gwelwyd llacio rhywfaint ar reolau bychan mewn perthynas â disgybliaeth. Gwelwyd hefyd ddiddordeb newydd yn y gofal dros ddisgyblion unigol, wrth i gyfnod bugeiliol gael ei sefydlu ar yn ail fore, yn lle y gwasanaeth. Yn ystod y cyfnod hwn, rhoddwyd cyfle i'r disgyblion i drafod unrhyw broblem oedd yn codi o'u bywyd yn yr ysgol. I ba raddau y bu'r cyfnodau hyn o gymorth, mae'n anodd maintioli, ond mae'n amlwg fod yna le yn awr ar y cwricwlwm i anghenion personol ochr yn ochr ag anghenion cyfun. Fe welwyd y datblygiad hwn yn cyd-fynd gydag argyhoeddiad personnol y Pennaeth am werthoedd moesol Cristnogol, a mewn perthynas â hyn gwelwyd ymweliadau gan y Rheithor lleol. Bu i'r cyfan sefydlu patrwm o addysg safonol a gofal personol fel dwy ochr i'r un geiniog ym mywyd yr ysgol.

Wrth nodi'r newidiadau a ddigwyddodd mewn perthynas ag addysg, mae'n rhaid nodi fod yna nifer o bethau cyffrous arall wedi digwydd yn y cyfnod. Ynghyd â datblygiad pynciau newydd fel Drama, fe welwyd hefyd gyflwyno cyfrifiaduron i fywyd yr ysgol, yn ogystal â'u cyflwyno i rai o'r disgyblion. Yn y cyfnod cynnar hwn, gan y rhai oedd â diddordeb mewn gwyddoniaeth, gwelwyd yr awydd pennaf i feistrioli y cyfrwng newydd hwn, ond buan y bu i'r diddordeb ehangu. Mae'n deg wrth basio i nodi fod y diddordeb mewn gwyddoniaeth, a'r amlygrwydd a roddwyd i ddysgu y pynciau gwyddonol yn haeddu sylw mwy manwl nag y medraf ei roi yma. Gan mai yn y celfyddydau y bu imi ymddiddori yn bennaf, mae'n amlwg mae i'r cyfeiriad hwnnw y mae'r cyfraniad hwn yn mynd hefyd. Gwelwyd nifer o'r disgyblion yn llwyddo yn eithriadol yn y pynciau hyn, ac yn mynd ymlaen i yrfaoedd llwyddianus ym maes ymchwil gwyddonol ynghyd â swyddi o fewn meddygaeth a mil-feddygaeth ag ati. Wrth nodi hyn, mae'n debyg fod y ddealltwriaeth yn glir yn y cyfnod hwnnw, fod y plant galluog i gyd i fod i ymgymeryd â dewisiadau ym myd gwyddoniaeth, gan adael y celfyddydau i ddisgyblion â llai o allu. Clywais un o'r athrawon yn adran y celfyddydau yn adrodd unwaith am un o'i gyd-weithwyr yn sôn am y celfyddydau fel pynciau hamdden.

Wrth ystyried bywyd yr ysgol, a'r bywyd y tu allan i'r addysg ffurfiol, mae'n amlwg ddigon fod nifer o'r problemau cymdeithasol sydd bellach yn gymaint ran o fywyd yr ifanc, heb ddod i amlygrwydd yn ystod y cyfnod. Mae'n debyg mae bygylu oedd un o'r problemau mwyaf a welwyd ym mherthynas y plant â'i gilydd, er fod yna ymdrechion lu wedi'u gwneud i geisio ateb y broblem. Mi 'roedd yr awyrgylch o ddisgyblaeth a nodwyd eisioes a oedd yn bodoli tu fewn i'r ysgol yn golygu nad oedd y broblem yn cael tir da i dyfu. Yr unig sôn am gyffuriau yn y cyfnod hwnnw oedd y tuedd ymhlith rhai i ysmygu, heb fod yna fawr o gyfeirio at unryw gyffuriau eraill.

Gwelwyd yn ystod y cyfnod nifer o gymdeithasau yn ffynnu, megis yr Urdd, lle gwelwyd llwyddiant yn y cyfarfodydd wythnosol ac ar lwyfan mwy eang, gyda nifer o aelodau yr adran yn dod i amlygrwydd. Mi 'roedd yna hefyd gymdeithas Gristnogol, ac er nad oedd gennyf fawr o ddiddordeb ar y pryd mewn dim mwy na chrefydd arwynebol, mi 'roedd nifer o'r athrawon a'r disgyblion yn cwrdd yn wythnosol. Ymhlith y cymdeithasau eraill roedd y clwb gwyddbwyll, y clwb ffilmiau, y clwb gwyddoniaeth, y band chwyth, band pres a'r gerddorfa, ynghyd â phethau eraill oedd yn ceisio cyrraedd ehangder y diddordebau a feddai'r disgyblion. Gwelwyd yr un diddordebau hefyd ym maes chwaraeon, gyda rygbi yn flaenllaw ymhlith y bechgyn, ynghyd ag athletau a rhywfaint o chwaraeon ymylol, a pêl-rwyd a hoci yn dal eu tir yn niddordebau'r merched. Mae'n debyg mai'r un datblygiad a fu yn ystod y cyfnod oedd adeiladu y pwll nofio, a chofiaf yn dda y rhan fwyaf o'r disgyblion yn cynnal taith noddedig i godi arian tuag at y gwaith, ynghyd â nifer o weithgareddau amrywiol arall. Gwelwyd hefyd rywfaint o ddiddordeb newydd mewn pêl-droed, yn arbennig yn sgîl apwyntio Mr. Geraint Davies i'r adran Hanes, un oedd yn treulio ei amser sbâr fel canolwr neu refferi o Sadwrn i Sadwrn.

Yn dilyn y bywyd cymdeithasol hyn, mae'n deg nodi fod y disgyblion yn ôl yr arfer yn rhannu yn rhwydd o ystyried diddordebau gwahanol a chefndir diwylliannol a ieithyddol. Mae'n amheus i ba raddau y llwyddwyd i integreiddio y gwahanol ffrydiau o blant a ddeuai erbyn hyn i'r ysgol. Nid oedd hyn ond yn ymateb naturiol a disgwyliedig, ac yn wir yn amlygu y gwirionedd nad ydy disgyblion yn dysgu fawr iawn o sgiliau cymdeithasol mewn sefydliad o'r fath, gan fod y strwythur yn ffafrio dysgu plant i ddod ymlaen gyda plant o fewn eu grwpiau a'i hoedran eu hunain. Fe fu i hyn i arwain at rhai tensiynau fel y gellid ei ddisgwyl, ond erbyn diwedd y 70au, nid oedd y broblem wedi datblygu yn achos gofid.

Wrth geisio maentumio dylanwad y blynyddoedd hynny arnaf, mae'n amlwg ddigon fod yna nifer o bethau cyffrous wedi digwydd imi a'm tebyg oedd i fowldio i ryw raddau ein bywyd a'n barn, ac i adael argraffiadau oedd i barhau. Codwyd ein hymwybyddiaeth ynglyn â llawer o'r problemau sydd wedi dod i fwy o amlygrwydd ers y cyfnod, ond ar yr un pryd, cawsom hefyd feithrinfa oedd yn cyfrannu addysg sylfaenol drylwyr, ynghyd â chyfleoedd i ddatblygu diddordebau personnol. Mewn gwersi a gweithgareddau eraill, dysgwyd ni i feithrin barn oedd yn resymol a chyfrifol, a chyfrannwyd inni y gallu a'r hyder i dorri ein cwys yn y byd. Wedi gadael yr ysgol a symud i fyd addysg pellach ac yn ddiweddarach i fyd gwaith, 'roedd y feithrinfa hon i roi y gallu inni ddarganfod ein hunain, a'n lle fel dinasyddion. 'Roedd y balans a ganfuwyd rhwng addysg ffurfiol ac addysg alwedigaethol a dderbyniwyd yn dilyn patrwm gweddill y byd academaidd, ac yn adlewyrchu blaenoriaethau y Pennaeth a'r athrawon.

❖

"Twelfth Night"
1987

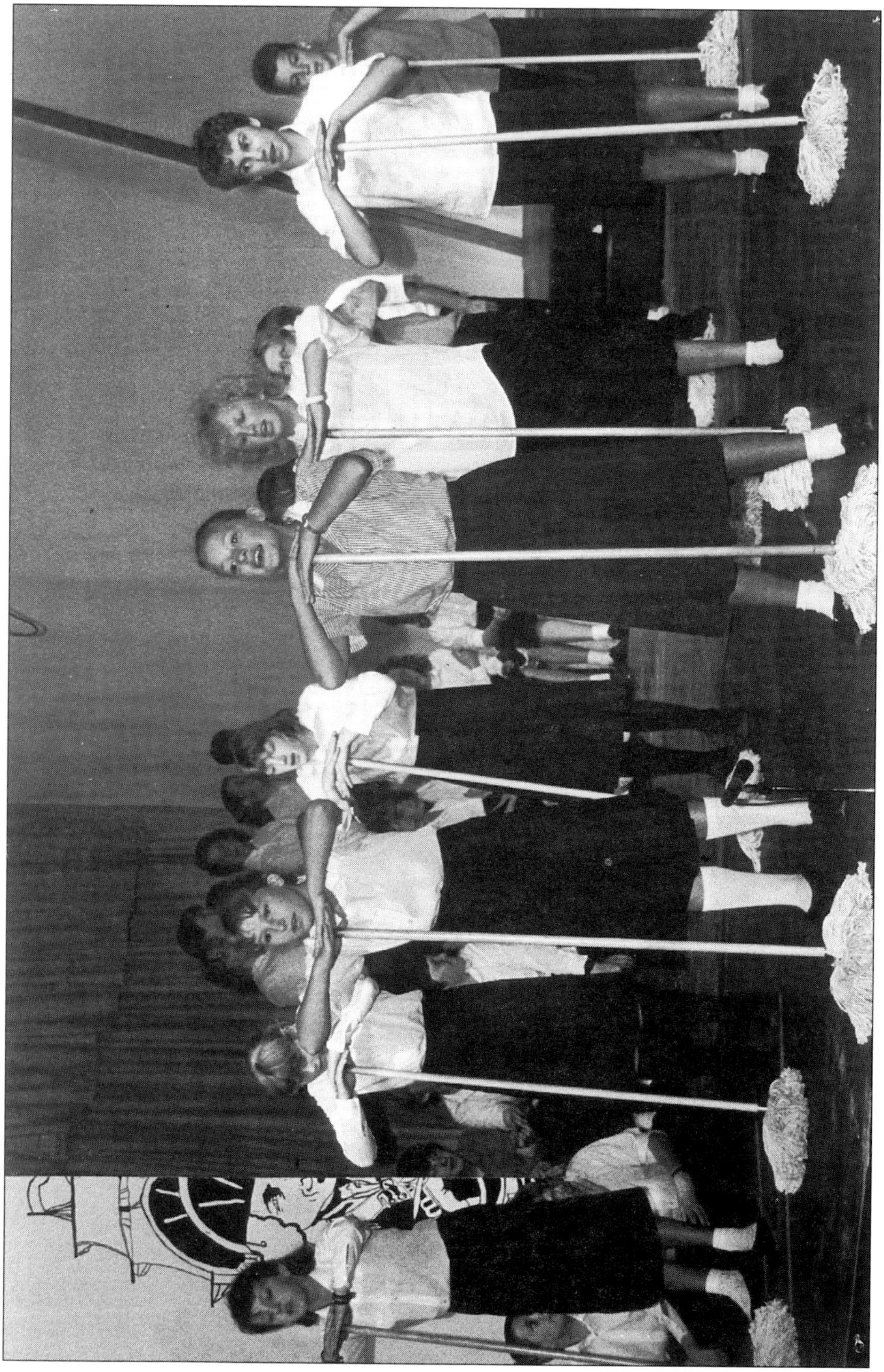

"Hip Hip Horatio"
1988

My years in Aberaeron Comprehensive School

Lisa Pascoe (1977 - 1984)

When I was asked to write about my memories of Aberaeron School, I was a little worried that, having left well over 10 years ago, I would encounter at least a little difficulty in recalling my school life.

It wasn't difficult at all. In fact , how can one forget anything about a period which plays such an important part in our most formative years? My most vivid recollection of those days was that the school, besides being a busy centre of the usual educative processes was also a hive of extra-curricular activity. I was very lucky to have been involved in the musical side of these activities; the concerts, the drama productions, the Eisteddfodau. In particular, I can recall that fateful concert when we battled through the 1812 Overture to the sound of taped cannons in the background under the staunch guidance of Mr. Gareth Hughes-Jones, the then Head of Music. How relieved he was when we all ended on the same note! The late Mrs. Gwyneth Matthews, then teaching Welsh, and a lady of sharp wit confided to my mother that she thought we had "met our Waterloo"! Various musicals were put on during my time at Aberaeron, but the one that I remember with the most fondness is "Godspell". There was a great sense of teamwork between staff and pupils - and the fun we had during rehearsals.....I wonder what "Jesus" (Morus Puw Morris) and "Judas" (Richard Jones) are doing now? How can I forget the excitement and thrill of the eisteddfodau which were, and still are, fiercely fought between Tyglyn, Tanyfron and Portland? Portland, my house, had been third for most of my years at school, despite the commitment of staff and pupils alike. How great it felt when we won the competition in my final year!

I have very clear memories too of teachers and lessons at Aberaeron. On the whole, I enjoyed my subjects and the relationships I built up with the staff. Being taught by both parents was an interesting experience, although it did mean that I could get away with very little! I enjoyed all my subjects but I must admit that my interest mostly lay with languages and literature. I still remember to this day many of the quotations I learnt from "Romeo and Juliet" and the poem "Sohrab and Rustum" and from the striking poetry we studied in our Welsh Literature lessons with Mrs. Ann James - such as these lines from "Wrth fy Nrws" by Nesta Wyn Jones:

"Hen wynt, beth yw'th stori heno,
A'th ffroen wrth dwll y clo?
Beth welaist ti wrth bererindota'n ddiamcan
Dros wead ein tipyn byd?"

French, however, was my favourite subject and I continued with this and Music at Exeter University, and I recognise the great debt I owe to the school for the groundwork it afforded in the basic principles of education and the work ethic that served me so well during my advanced studies.

I could go on; memories may fade but they never disappear and the more I think, the more they come flooding back. I am now a teacher of languages in Bristol and am very happy in my work. Despite the pressures of the current educational climate, it is good to note that relationships between pupils and staff remain strong. I remember my school days with fondness and often with a certain sadness that they will never return. I hope that the present pupils at Aberaeron and indeed my own pupils will enjoy their school years as much as I did, and that the school will continue to prosper and serve the needs of the young people in the area as successfully as it did for me and my generation. "Vive Aberaeron".

❖

Atgofion

Eleri Siôn (1982 - 1989)

Pe bai rhywun yn gofyn i mi am yr hyn a roddodd Ysgol Gyfun Aberaeron i mi, y ddau ansoddair sy'n saethu i'r meddwl yw "Cyfle" a "Sbort". "Cyfle" oherwydd y rhestr faith o gyfleoedd a gefais i, boed yn ymddangos ar y llwyfan fel cantores, adroddwraig, actores, cyflwynwraig; ymddangos ar y cae chwaraeon fel chwaraewraig hoci, pêl-rwyd, rhedeg, taflu'r jafelin a'r ddisgen; ymddangos mewn print ac yn ffodus, fe gefais i amser i ddilyn amryw o gyrsiau addysgiadol!! Yr ansoddair arall yw "Sbort", oherwydd y mwynhad a gefais i wrth gymryd rhan yn yr agweddau yma. Er hynny 'roedd yna straen weithiau i ddal popeth!

Os oedd yna dyndra ym mywyd ein llenorion mawr megis Saunders Lewis a T. H. Parry Williams, 'roedd yna dyndra yn ogystal yn fy mywyd i. Nid rhwng crefydd a seciwlariaeth, cariad ac Eros, ond rhwng canu ac adrodd ac ymddangosiadau cyhoeddus a chwaraeon. 'Roedd y naill beth mor bwysig â'i gilydd i mi, ond oedd fyw i mi fynd adre yn ddi-lais ar ôl chwarae gêm o hoci ar brynhawn dydd Gwener cyn cystadlu mewn Eisteddfod ar brynhawn Sadwrn!

Yn yr 1980au, 'roedd Ysgol Aberaeron yn beiriant creu chwaraewyr hoci a rygbi penigamp, ac yn 1989, yn fy mlwyddyn olaf i, fe gafodd tair ohonom drial i dîm hoci Cymru - Catrin Woods (a enillodd ei chap), Elin Lloyd a minnau. O'm rhan i, yr athrawes Anne Hubbard a chwaraewyr megis Glynis Jones a Sharon Lloyd a'm hysbrydolodd i, i frwydro ymlaen drwy dywydd oer y gaeaf. Buom yn bencampwyr Ceredigion am nifer o flynyddoedd ac yn 1987 fe gollon ni deitl "Pencampwriaeth Ysgolion Cymru" mewn amser ychwanegol - tipyn o gamp i ysgol wledig fel ni!

Byddai'n stori wahanol yn yr haf, gyda'r borfa newydd-dorri yn crasu yn yr haul lawr ar y cae athletau. Fy hoff gamp oedd taflu'r waywffon neu'r "jafelin". 'Roeddwn i'n ymwybodol iawn o 'nghoesau, felly fel rhan o'mgwisg athletau, 'roedd pâr o "deits" du. Pan welodd yr athrawon ymarfer corff, sef Chris Jones ac Alun Rees y coesau duon a'r jafelin yn dod tuag atynt, fe waeddon nhw: "Fatima Whitbread! Ble wyt ti'n mynd?" Pe bydden nhw <u>ond</u> yn gwybod y gwir, o dan y "teits" 'roeddwn i'n gwisgo corset i gadw'n stumog i fewn, ac o'n i ar fy ffordd nôl i'r ystafelloedd newid achos 'roedd "cramp" yn fy mola i!!

Fy mhrif atgofion o'm hamser i yn Ysgol Aberaeron oedd yr achlysuron cyhoeddus fel yr Eisteddfod, y Cyngherddau a'r Sioeau. Mi fyddai fy mrawd a minnau bob amser yn hwyr oherwydd 'roedd rhaid i'n rhieni orffen yr holl waith ar y fferm cyn ein hebrwng i Aberaeron. 'Roedd yna asbri a chyffro ar bob un achlysur gyda phawb yn uno â'i gilydd a gweithio fel tîm. Felly, beth bynnag oedd y digwyddiad, naill ai cystadlu mewn chwaraeon neu berfformio ar lwyfan, 'roedd y teimlad o fod yn rhan o un teulu mawr yn un cryf iawn.

Erbyn diwedd yr 1980au, 'roedd dylanwad yr iaith Saesneg yn ddylanwad amlwg ar fywyd yr ysgol. Yn fy marn i, er hynny, ni wnaeth hyn darfu gymaint â hynny ar ysbryd ac egni'r gymdeithas Gymraeg. Os rywbeth, fe gryfhaodd hyn y teimlad o genedlgarwch ac uwchraddoldeb y Genedl Gymraeg. Dyma lle daw'r gair "cyfle" i'r amlwg unwaith eto. Gan ein bod ni'n ddwyieithiog, byddai'r cyfleoedd yn dyblu, ac weithiau mi fyddem yn teimlo rhyw anniddigrwydd oddi wrth y disgyblion di-Gymraeg. Felly, mae yna agweddau positif iawn yn brigo o fynychu Ysgol Ddwyieithiog!!

Erbyn hyn, 'rwy'n gweithio yn y byd cyfryngol - rhywbeth 'roeddwn i wedi breuddwydio am wneud am flynyddoedd. Yn eironig iawn, mae'r tyndra rhwng y chwaraeon a'r ochr perfformio wedi diflannu ac 'rwy wedi gallu uno'r ddwy agwedd â'i gilydd drwy weithio ar raglenni chwaraeon o bob math boed ar y teledu neu ar y radio. 'Rwy'n sicr o un peth, ni fyddai hyn wedi digwydd ar wahân i'r cyfleoedd a gefais, a'r agwedd a ddatblygais tra mod i yn Ysgol Aberaeron. Un person a oedd yn flaenllaw yn fy arwain ar y llwybr yma oedd Mrs. Lona Brierley, Pennaeth yr Adran Gerddoriaeth, a hoffwn i ddiolch iddi hi am ei chymorth a'i chefnogaeth ar hyd yr adeg.

Ar y funud, 'rwy'n gweithio ar gyfres goginio o'r enw "Dudley" sy'n f'atgoffa i o'r wers goginio gyntaf a gefais erioed. Yn y wers, fe lwyddodd fy ffrind Tess a minnau ddistrywio pryd o fwyd mor sylfaenol â "toasted sandwich". Os ydych yn gyfarwydd â "flamed" neu "charcoal grilled burgers" fe wyddoch am be 'rwy'n sôn!

Felly, yr hyn a roddodd Ysgol Gyfun Aberaeron i mi oedd "cyfle" a "sbort"...o!...a chyn i mi anghofio, fe gefais i addysg weddol hefyd!!!

❖

Wi wa waca
Wi wa wa
Waca wi waca wi
Wa wa wa
TYGLYN yw y
gorau gorau gorau

Ti la sha ba
Ti la sha basha
Gorebela gorebela
Jing jinga jingo
PORTLAND yw y
gorau gorau gorau

Swm swm saca
Swm swm se
Bwsha ba bwsha ba
Bwsha ba bei
Sgarbo sgarbo i ai o
TANYFRON

ER COF AM HOWELL T. EVANS. M.A.

L. Haydn Lewis

Daethost yn nyddiau cyfyng yr ymryson fawr
A'r byd ym mlinder ynfyd y gyflafan hir,
Daethost heb utgorn rhwygol - fel y tyrr y wawr,
Er bod sibrydion lawer am dy oleuni clir.
Cofiwn dy ddyfod a'n chwilfrydedd taer ei ryw
Tithau'n hamddenol ond effro i gyd;
Bechan yr ysgol - pam y doist yn llyw
Iddi a'th yrfa eisioes oll mor glyd?
Buan y lluniaist iddi drefn a newydd radd,
Ninnau ni wyddem pa ryw ryfedd raid
Ynot a'n daliai i'n dinistrio a'u lladd -
Blant yr afonydd drefn a fu gynt o'u plaid!
Distaw dy gynnwrf a'th fwriadau lu
Eto terfysgwr oeddit fel y dydd a'r haul;
Tyner a thirion hefyd a difost dy wyneb cu,
Cyfaill a phennaeth dysg yn dy holl draul!
Dewn ein hanes cudd, a diwyd ffyddlon was
Lewych dy Gymru hen a'i helynt ffrom,
Saesneg oedd dull d'ymddiddan ond ni chollwyd blas
Angerdd dy galon gywir - ni chawsom siom!
Cofiwn hir ddyfal aberth un a garai'n bur
Lwyddiant dy lafur ym mhob rhan o'n bau;
Claer ei serchowgrwydd, a'i ffyddlondeb fel y dur
Erot, ac erom, oedd yn llwyr-barhau.
Distaw y bwriaist heibio bwys a hyd y gwaith,

Gorau Ymgais Gwybodaeth

Troist i fyfyrdod tawel dy gyfrinion mwyn;
Bychan ein meddwl pa mor fyr dy daith
Drannoeth y gado o'r athrofa fwyn!
Yma mor ddistaw heddiw dy ymadael di;
Nid wyt "bresennol" fel y mynnit gynt;
Mwyn athro tirion mor ddidwrf wyt ti
Heddiw'n ymddeol i'th dragywydd hynt!
Arall a ganodd am orweddfa'i dad a fu -
Hwnnw a fu yn fugail plant am lawer oes,
Minnau, pe meiddiwn, i'r athrofa gu
A'i phennaeth mwyn a ganwn yn un hiraeth croes!
Distaw yw sŵn dy ymdaith, ond atgofus yw
Dydd dy ymadael ymaith a'th lescau i'r bedd;
Dirion Benadur hawddgar nid yw'r rhin yn wyw
Yma'n dy ddarfod y mae'n llawn o'th wedd!

❖

I MR. J. T. OWEN, O.B.E., M.A.

(Wrth ymddeol o fod yn Brifathro Ysgol Uwchradd Aberaeron, 1965)

John Roderick Rees

Teilwng yw cyrraedd talar
O'i hir gwys ar erw a gâr;
Yn deg am ddwy a deugain
Y bu'n arddu, llyfnu'r llain.
Unlle nid oes heb fanllef
I'r sglein ar ei ysgol ef.
Ei fyd oedd eisteddfodau,
Ŵr â min ym myd dramau;
Rhin ydoedd i'w feirniadaeth,
Dug ei siŵr, garedig saeth.
Heb air llanw, hwb i'r llenor,
Lle doi'r ddawn y lledai'r ddôr.
Un a gâr faes agored,
Awr bêr ei fwynder a fed.
Rhostir braf, ceulan afon,
Yn ei si mae hyfryd sôn.
Hoen gŵydd a'r unigeddau
Y cwm am y byd yn cau.
Fab y Dderw*, erys derw da
Yn irdwf yn y gwrda,
Rhuddin hen werin waraidd,
Mor gryf ydyw mêr y gwraidd.
Ei gaer fu Aberaeron
Rhoes ei oes i warchod hon.

* Y Dderw, Ysbyty Ystwyth, lle magwyd J.T. Owen

D. J. THOMAS, O.B.E., B.Sc.

SONNET TO D.J. FROM THE STAFF

Kay Pascoe

How shall we miss thee? Let us count the ways.
We'll miss the booming bass on tannoy loud,
The stride on stage on full assembly days,
The dark brown mane, aquiline profile proud.
We'll miss the initiatives, the "forward plan",
The morning meeting's cheery "Bore Da",
The talks on litter, dress and earring ban,
All these will be remembered near and far.
The willingness to grant the hour free
For graduations, rugby trips, the rest,
Will with affection e'er recalled be,
And talked of warmly as the very best.
We'll miss you, and this sonnet kindly meant
Brings wishes for a long retirement.

❖

Andrés Jones
Tîm Rhyngwladol Prydain / Great Britain International
Portugal 1995

Gwisg ysgol / School uniform
1950s / Summer dress / Present day
Carys Jones, Menna Davies, Meryl Lloyd

John Eilir Lewis B. Sc.
Prifathro 1993 - 1995

JOHN EILIR LEWIS B.Sc.
PRIFATHRO 1993-1995

Yn dilyn ymddeoliad Mr. D. J. Thomas yn 1993, penodwyd Mr. John Eilir Lewis yn Brifathro. Symudodd i Aberaeron o Lanfair Caereinion, lle bu'n Brifathro yr Ysgol Uwchradd yno am naw mlynedd.

Magwyd Mr. Lewis yn Swyddfa'r Post, Ponthirwaun, ger Aberteifi a derbyniodd ei addysg yn Ysgol Gynradd Trewen, Ysgol Ramadeg Aberteifi a Choleg Prifysgol Cymru, Aberystwyth, lle graddiodd mewn Daeareg a Daearyddiaeth. Wedi cwblhau cwrs hyfforddi ol-raddedig aeth yn athro ysgol i Croydon. Bu hefyd yn athro yn Swydd Stafford, Hayes, Middlesex ac Uxbridge. Yn 1982, penodwyd ef yn Ddirprwy Brifathro yn Ysgol Uwchradd Y Drenewydd, ac o 1984 hyd 1993, bu'n Brifathro Ysgol Uwchradd Caereinion lle sefydlodd ffrwd Gymraeg llwyddiannus.

Dros y blynyddoedd, arweiniodd sawl taith addysgol i'r cyfandir gan gynnwys y Pyreneau, y Dolomitau a'r Alpau, Norwy a'r Arctig, y Sahara a Gwlad yr Iâ, ac yn 1992 bu'n gyfrifol am daith gyfnewid i Chile, yn Ne America. Yn 1980, gwnaed ef yn Gymrawd o Ymddiriedolaeth Goffa Winston Churchill am ei fentrau gyda phobl ieuanc.

Yn anffodus, byr bu cyfnod Mr. Lewis yn Aberaeron gan iddo gael ei daro gan salwch ar ôl 14 mis yn unig yn y swydd, a gyda thristwch y derbyniwyd ei ymddiswyddiad yng Ngorffennaf 1995. 'Roedd yn amlwg fod ganddo weledigaeth glir ar gyfer y dyfodol ac 'roedd yn anffodus na chafodd y cyfle i ddatblygu, gydai'i frwdfrydedd a'i egni arferol, y cynlluniau oedd ganddo ar gyfer yr ysgol a'r gymuned.

Mr. Lewis received his early education at Cardigan Grammar School and later graduated in Geology and Geography at University of Wales, Aberystwyth. He was appointed Headteacher of Ysgol Gyfun Aberaeron following a period of nine years as Headteacher at Caereinion High School, Powys. Prior to this, Mr. Lewis was Deputy Headteacher at Newtown High School and had previously taught in Croydon and Hillingdon.

Over the years, Mr. Lewis led many expeditions abroad including the Pyrenees, the Dolomites, the Alps, the Arctic, Norway, the Sahara and Iceland. In 1992, he took part in a Group Study Exchange visit to Chile, South America.

Unfortunately, Mr. Lewis was only at Aberaeron for a short period as he became ill after being in the post for only 14 months. It was with deep sadness that his resignation was received in July 1995. He had a clear vision for the school and the community and it is unfortunate that he was not able to implement his numerous plans.

YR YSGOL HEDDIW / THE SCHOOL TODAY

Y Prif Fachgen, Aled Jenkins a'r Brif Ferch, Caryl Lewis

Does dim byd yn edrych mor fawr â'r ysgol gyfun pan rydych chi newydd adael diogelwch yr ysgol gynradd yn unarddeg oed. Mae'r lle yn ymddangos fel cwch gwenyn a'r gweithwyr yn prysuro o amgylch ei goridorau di-ddiwedd. Ond ar ôl wythnos, mae'r arswyd yn cilio a'r adeiladau'n lleihau'n rhyfeddol. Ymhen ychydig wythnosau mae yna gylch o ffrindiau newydd i'ch diddori a dysgwch fod athrawon yn medru gwenu. Dyma'r broses sy'n rhaid i bawb ei hwynebu a'r broses sy'n agor drws addysg i tua cant pedwardeg o blant lleol yn Ysgol Gyfun Aberaeron bob blwyddyn.

Ar ddechrau'r flwyddyn gyntaf treuliom sawl noswaith yn clymu'r tei yn barod i'r diwrnod wedyn, ond yn wir, ymhen rhyw fis fe gollom flas ar y seremoni nosweithiol. Cyn hir, doedd dim amser, gan fod Ffrangeg i'w ddysgu a Gwyddoniaeth i'w ymchwilio. Yn yr ysgol, roedd ystafelloedd cyfrifiaduron i'w darganfod; C.D.T. i'w wneud a phrydau iachus i'r teulu i'w coginio yn yr Anecs. Roedd yma dîmau hoci a rygbi i'n denu, pwll nofio i'w defnyddio a chyrtiau tennis i chwarae arnynt. Pasiodd dosbarth un a dau yn un freuddwyd liwgar o chwaraeon, gwahanol wersi a ffrindiau newydd.

Yn y drydedd flwyddyn, fe ddechreuodd y gwaith fynd yn galetach. Canolbwyntiodd yr athrawon ar ein paratoi ar gyfer y cwrs T.G.A.U. Erbyn inni gyrraedd dosbarth pedwar nid dyna oedd ei enw mwyach. Fe newidiwyd ei enw i "Dosbarth 10" o dan y Cwricwlwm Cenedlaethol. Uchafbwynt y flwyddyn yma oedd wythnos o brofiad gwaith gydag unrhyw un a oedd yn ddigon caredig neu ddwl i'n cymryd! Bu'n rhaid trafod cryn dipyn ar ein gyrfa yr adeg hon.

Arholiadau allanol; ceisio am waith neu fynd ymlaen i addysg uwch. Dyma oedd rhai o broblemau'r bumed flwyddyn. Ar ôl yr arholiadau T.G.A.U., ac, yn waeth fyth, y canlyniadau, roedd rhaid dewis gadael neu aros a sefyll arholiadau lefel A neu gyrsiau fel G.N.V.Q., Sbaeneg neu Siapanëeg. Mae rhwng 160-170 o ddisgyblion yn y chweched dosbarth, ac roedd yn rhaid dewis pynciau addas.

Nid yn unig bywyd academaidd sy'n cael ei fwynhau yn Aberaeron. Mae yna lu o weithgareddau allgyrsiol i'w blasu. Y mae clybiau chwaraeon, sgio, rygbi, pêl-droed, pêl-fasged, hoci, pêl-rwyd, tenis, nofio a gwyddbwyll, heb sôn am y sioeau, yr Eisteddfod a'r mabolgampau blynyddol. Ceir hefyd Adran yr Urdd, Clwb yr Ysgol a'r Clwb Cristnogol. Trefnir teithiau i'r disgyblion, tripiau Saesneg i Stratford, teithiau i Lundain i'r dosbarthiadau Celf, tridiau yn Llangrannog i'r dysgwyr Cymraeg a phenwythnos yng Nglanllyn i'r dosbarthiadau Daearyddiaeth. Ceir hefyd ffilmiau Ffrangeg i'r dosbathiadau Ffrangeg a darlithoedd Gwyddoniaeth i'r gwyddonwyr. Yn allgyrsiol, ceir gwyliau blynyddol i Ffrainc a'r Eidal a gwyliau cyfnewid i'r plant sy'n dysgu Ffrangeg. Bu'r bechgyn hefyd yn chwarae rygbi yng Nghanada. Mae'r ysgol hefyd yn codi arian at nifer o wahanol elusennau ac yn annog y plant i gydweithio'n glos gyda'r gymuned trwy ddiddanu'r henoed ac yn y blaen.

Hyd yn oed yn ein hamser cymharol fyr yn yr ysgol, daeth nifer o newidiadau ar ein traws. Datblygodd yr adran gyfrifiaduron i feithrin ymwybyddiaeth o dechnoleg. Ychwanegwyd ystafell gyffredin i'r Chweched ac adnewyddwyd y Llyfrgell. Trowyd hi yn Ganolfan Wybodaeth gyfforddus gan galluogi pawb i ymestyn eu gwybodaeth drwy gyfrwng y meicrosglodyn! Caniatawyd i'r merched i wisgo trowsus gan siomi nifer o'r bechgyn a pheidiodd y "blaser" ysgol i fod yn hanfodol. Gwelsom apwyntiad y Brifathrawes gyntaf yn hanes yr ysgol, Miss Marina James. Daeth Siapanëeg a Sbaeneg i'r adran Ieithoedd Modern gan ehangu gwybodaeth yr ysgol o wledydd a diwylliannau eraill. Mae'n anodd meddwl nad yw'r plant lleiaf yn cofio'r dyn mawr yn y clogyn du a fu'n gymaint rhan o fywyd yr ysgol, Mr. D. J. Thomas. Clywn ei lais o hyd yng nghoridorau'r meddwl, "Braint nid hawl ydyw mynd i'r dref..."

A dyma ni yn ceisio cywasgu bywyd saith mlynedd i ychydig linellau. Mor hawdd ydyw rhoi darlun cyflym o'r ysgol ond nid yw'n gwneud cyfiawnder â'r profiad a gawsom yma. Rydyn ni'n dod i ddiwedd cylch yr ysgol. Yn awr, ni a'n ffrindiau sy'n helpu trefnu'r clybiau ac yn mynd â'r plant o'r ysgolion cynradd o amgylch yr ysgol i guro ar ddrws addysg. Yn y dyfodol agos, fe fyddwn ni'n agor drws addysg bellach a byd gwaith ac yn sicr, addysg Ysgol Gyfun Aberaeron fydd ein hallwedd.

❖

Although it is necessary to acknowledge that the transition from primary to secondary education is a considerable one, it is seldom as horrific as the lively mind of an eleven-year-old would like to imagine. Indeed, leaving the fold of primary school is the first liberating step to teen and subsequent adulthood. Aberaeron school receives an average influx of approximately one hundred and forty new pupils each year from primary schools in the vicinity. These pupils animate the old school by coursing around its corridors like fresh blood through its veins. They integrate quickly into the social framework of the school and become active participants in many activities. Preparing the school tie in nervous anticipation is a novelty that soon loses its gloss as life at school becomes a stable routine.

For us, the first and second years passed in a blaze of activity; making new friends and being introduced to new subjects such as French, Information Technology, C.D.T., Pottery and Science. There were various clubs and choirs to join and hockey or rugby to enjoy during lunchtimes. There was a swimming pool to investigate and healthy meals to cook in the Annexe. There were various outings, including one to a leisure park to broaden our circle of friends. The early years of secondary school were chiefly spent in adapting ourselves to our new environment and broadening our knowledge and horizons.

The third year brought with it more focused work, centering on preparation for the G.C.S.E. course we were to embark on the following year. Thanks to the National Curriculum, class names were changed in the fourth year and we became "Year 10". The excitement of the fourth year culminated in a week of work experience with a company or firm (preferrably one with a good insurance policy!) We were invited to give serious consideration to our careers at this stage.

The fifth year brought external exams. After the dreaded results, decisions had to be taken whether to stay on in school to study or to seek employment. Between 160 and 170 pupils return to prepare for A levels, G.N.V.Q., A.S. levels or to take Spanish or Japanese. The perk of being a sixth former soon followed with the much-coveted blue tie and a licence to sit during assembly!

To outline school life in purely academic fashion is to do it great injustice. There are a considerable number of extra-curricular activities to sample. There are various sports namely skiing, rugby, net-ball, basket-ball, hockey, football, tennis, swimming and chess, not to mention the annual shows, Eisteddfod and sports day. There are also clubs like the Urdd Movement, the School Club and the Christian Union.

Extra-curricular visits and outings are also arranged. English students enjoy trips to Stratford; Art students visit London galleries; Welsh learners enjoy a few days at Llangrannog; Geography students can study the beautiful landscape at Glanllyn; French students tackle French films in Theatre Mwldan and the Scientists frequent various lectures.

School-arranged holidays include annual trips to France and Italy and exchange visits for French and German students. The rugby boys have also played in Canada. In school there are always fund-raising activities and projects to promote school/community relations.

In our relatively short time at Aberaeron, many changes have occurred. The Information Technology department has expanded to meet the needs of the computer-literate children of today. A new Common Room was acquired to accommodate the increasing number of pupils who return to the sixth form. The library was given a make-over, transforming it into a high-tech. Information Centre. Girls were "liberated" and allowed to wear trousers. We also witnessed the appointment of the first Headmistress to the school, Miss Marina James. Japanese and Spanish crept into the Modern Language department, providing extensive information about different cultures. In our time, we also witnessed the retirement of a "larger than life" character in his long black gown, Mr. D. J. Thomas. His booming voice and purposeful stride will always be an integral part of our reminiscences of Aberaeron.

It only remains to relate the injustice we have done to the school by trying to sketch its virtues in words. Seven years of life packed into a few pages hardly begins to describe our time here. And so the circular motion of the school continues. Where we once trailed around the school in awe of its size, we now show the primary school children around. Our year helps to organise the clubs and events when once we were participants. The wheel has turned and we all now prepare to unlock the door of higher education or employment. Without doubt the education we have received at Aberaeron is our key.

❖

Tîm Gwyddbwyll / Chess Team
1995
Andrew Walden-Jones, Ceredig Jones, Mr. Rhys Roberts, Gwilym Jones, Toby Cotterill, Matthew Bowker, Lorraine Smithers, Barnaby Pole.

Joint Winner of the 1939-45 Reunion Group competition
Janine Hardy, 12A.

Joint Winner of the 1939-45 Reunion Group competition
Heather Green, 12B.

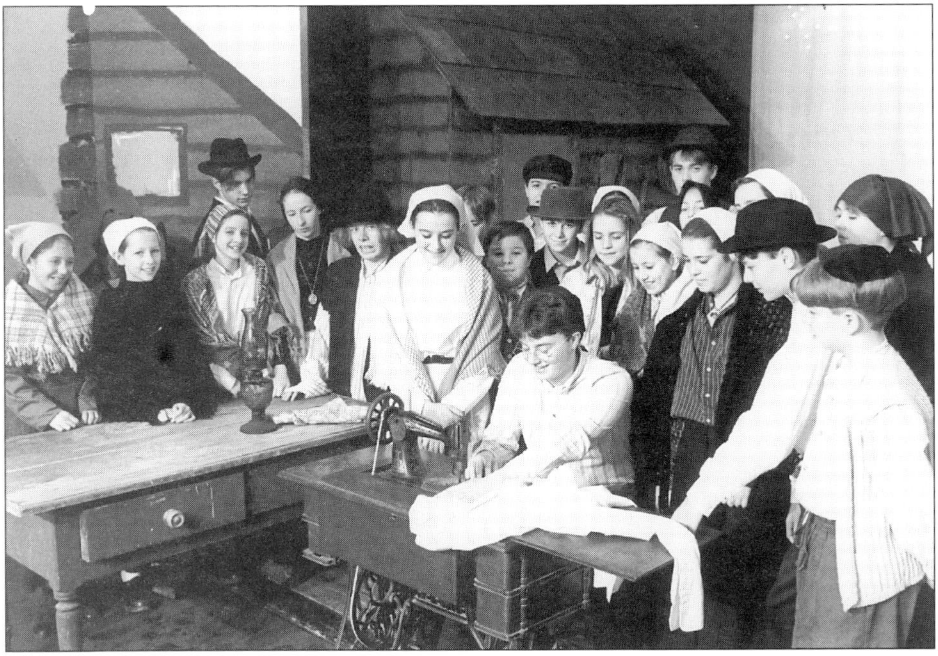

Crythor ar y To 1995

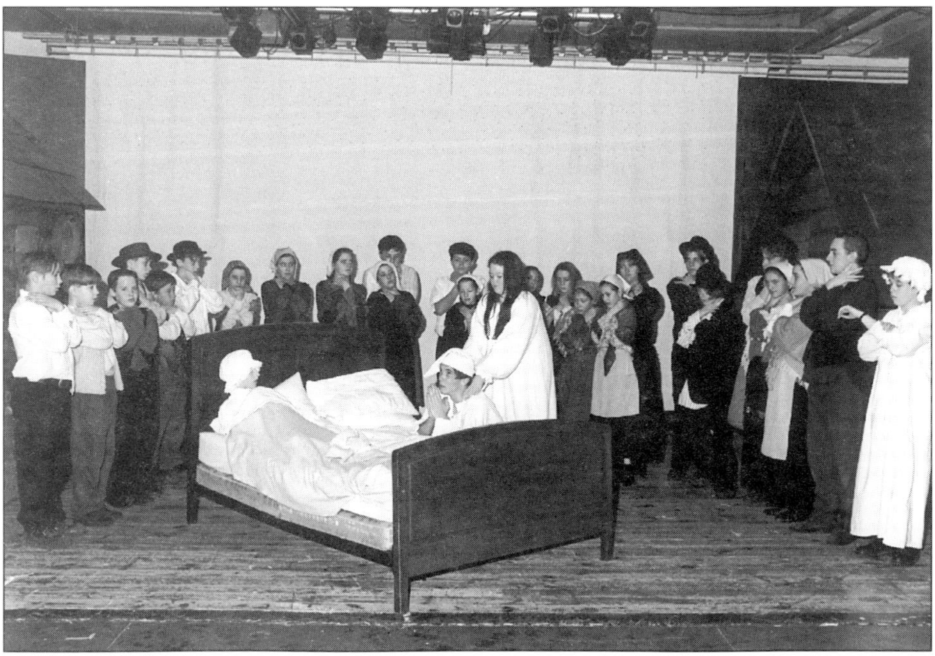

Crythor ar y To 1995

Gorau Ymgais Gwybodaeth

YSGOL ABERAERON

Idris Reynolds

Mae afon Aeron o hyd
Sy'n estyn o Lanrhystud
I odre bro Caerwedros
Hyd y wlad yn afon dlos;
O Lanon mae'i glannau hi
Yn ewynlliw hyd Wenlli.
Hyd wal y Cei deil y co'
Yn ei afiaith i lifo
Yn gytun â miwsig ton
Iwerydd Aberaeron;
Yn oriau'r trai eto'r un
Ydyw'r alaw'n Mydroilyn.
Ym Mhen Lôn mae hen, hen li,
Hen gerdd sy'n dal i gorddi
Drwy Drefilan a Llanarth
Hyd draethell bêr Aberarth,
A'r afon hon fwria hud
Ei hawen dros Ddihewyd.
Yn ei si mae'r ddau Gross Inn
Yn uno â Chilcennin;
Ar y ffin mae'r Felinfach
Yn oesol yn agosach,
A llafar yn Nhalgarreg
Ydyw tonc ei ffridiau teg.
Ym mhlwy Brynherbert mwyach

Ysgol Gyfun Aberaeron 1896 - 1996

Eto fyth mae'r geunant fach -
Un a red gan ddyfrhau
Hen barc helyg bro'r Ciliau,
A'r afon Aeron yw nant
Y mynydd heno 'Mhennant.
Tan fwa'r bont yn ferw byw
Hyder rhedegog ydyw;
Drwy gwm ei bwrlwm di-ball
Â'i fôr canrif arall,
A thrwy bob plwy boed cân plant
Ei hyfory'n llifeiriant.
(1995)

❖

Tîm Karate / Karate Team
gyda / with
Chris Jones (Head of P.E.), Marina James (Acting Headteacher), Roger Sayce (Coach), Anne Hubbard (P.E. Teacher)

Y Ganolfan Adnoddau newydd / The new Resource Centre 1996

J. Marina James
Pennaeth 1995-

HER Y DYFODOL

J. Marina James, Y Pennaeth.

Bu'r pymtheng mlynedd ddiwethaf yn gyfnod o newidiadau cyflym a radical mewn addysg yng Nghymru a gwelwyd ysgolion yn cyflawni llawer yn ystod y cyfnod hwn. Dechreuodd rhai o'r newidiadau hyn yn yr 80au cynnar gyda chynlluniau fel A.D.A.G. ond daeth y newidiadau mawr yn sgîl Deddf Diwygio Addysg 1988, Deddf Addysg (Ysgolion) 1992 a Deddf Addysg 1993. Gwelwyd newidiadau mawr i Gyrff Llywodraethol ysgolion, rheolaeth ariannol ar ysgolion, cyflwyno'r Cwricwlwm Cenedlaethol, system arolygu newydd, tablau perfformio, cofrestru agored a deddfwriaeth ynglŷn â disgyblion ag Anghenion Addysg Arbennig. Yn ogystal, cyflwynwyd yr opsiwn i gynnal ysgolion â grant. Rhoddodd y datblygiadau hyn lawer mwy o annibyniaeth i ysgolion gan greu hinsawdd hollol wahanol iddynt weithredu ynddi, a'u galluogi i lywio eu datblygiadau eu hunain gan bennu eu blaenoriaethau a dosrannu eu cyllid. Er hynny, bu'n rhaid addasu'n gyflym i'r holl newidiadau, gan roi sylw i agweddau newydd o reolaeth mewn ysgolion. Felly, yr her gyntaf i ysgolion yn ystod y blynyddoedd nesaf yw cwrdd â holl ofynion y deddfau hyn.

Mae'r byd 'rydym yn byw ynddo yn newid yn gyflym ac mae llawer o'r pethau sicr bellach wedi diflannu. Ni all unrhyw un heddiw ddisgwyl cael gwaith neu swydd am oes. Gwelwyd nifer o ddiwydiannau traddodiadol lleol yn cau dros y blynyddoedd, ac mae dod o hyd i waith addas yn mynd yn anos bob dydd, boed yng Ngheredigion, yng Nghymru neu dros Glawdd Offa. Rhaid i ysgolion y dyfodol felly, sicrhau bod disgyblion, wrth iddynt chwilio am waith, yn medru delio, hyd y mae modd, â'r prinder cyfleoedd fydd yn eu wynebu. Mae'n bosibl y bydd rhaid i bobl ifanc heddiw gael eu hyfforddi cymaint â phum gwaith yn ystod eu hoes. Hefyd mae'n debyg y bydd y newid a fu yn ddiweddar yn parhau gan efallai gynyddu yn gyflymach ac ymhellach.

Yng Nghymru, megis dechrau'n unig y mae posibiliadau'r technolegau newydd mewn sawl sector o'r economi, a gellir disgwyl newidiadau strwythurol pellach. Mantais dulliau cyfathrebu soffistigedig yw y byddant yn galluogi pobl i weithio lle bynnag maent yn dymuno, ymhell o ganolfannau diwydiannol os oes angen. Gall hyn fod yn fantais sylweddol i gefn gwlad Cymru gan y bydd yn galluogi nifer o fusnesau bychain i gael eu sefydlu ac a fydd yn rhoi hwb i economi'r ardaloedd gwledig gan ddarparu gwaith i'n pobl ifanc yn eu broydd genedigol.

Tasg addysgwyr sy'n gweithio gyda'r ifanc heddiw yw eu paratoi ar gyfer eu rôl fel dinasyddion ifanc, gweithwyr, dysgwyr drwy gydol eu hoes a rhieni, gan addysgu iddynt y gwerthoedd, gwybodaeth a'r sgiliau ar gyfer pob rôl. Dylai'r rhain wrth gwrs gysylltu â, ac adlewyrchu, gwir sefyllfa y cysylltiadau cymdeithasol ac economaidd lle maent yn byw. Rhoddir pwyslais gan y Llywodraeth presennol ar ddatblygu disgyblion fel unigolion crwn. Bydd angen i bob ysgol felly sicrhau cynnydd pob plentyn yn gymdeithasol yn ogystal ag yn academaidd. Er mwyn cynorthwyo disgyblion unigol i gyflawni eu potensial bydd yn angenrheidiol cael cwricwlwm a dulliau dysgu ac addysgu sy'n ddigon gwahaniaethol i gwrdd ag anghenion unigol.

'Rydym ar drothwy'r chwyldro mawr nesaf ym myd technoleg gwybodaeth - y traffyrdd gwybodaeth, a disgwylir i athrawon eu defnyddio i gefnogi'r amrywiaeth o ddulliau dysgu a ddefnyddir yn y dosbarth. O ganlyniad, gwelir athrawon fel rheolwyr y broses ddysgu yn hytrach na fel ffynhonnell gwybodaeth. Mae'n siŵr mai rhywbeth i'r gorffennol fydd gweld un athro yn unig yn rheoli dosbarth o ryw 25-30 o ddisgyblion gan geisio trafod lefelau cymhleth o wahaniaethu i sicrhau bod pawb yn elwa'n llawn o'r cyfleoedd dysgu. Bydd ehangu darpariaeth Technoleg Gwybodaeth, yn ogystal â chael cynorthwywyr i gydweithio gyda'r athro yn y dosbarth i gefnogi'r gwaith dysgu, yn galluogi disgyblion i ddilyn rhaglenni dysgu unigol, a thrwy hynny, eu galluogi i gyflawni llawer mwy. Gall Technoleg Gwybodaeth newid canolbwynt gwaith yr athro o fod yn un sy'n drosglwyddo gwybodaeth i ganfod anawsterau dysgu, cynllunio rhaglenni dysgu, asesu a chynorthwyo i ysgogi disgyblion. Mae'n bosib wrth gwrs y gall disgyblion ymestyn eu gwybodaeth trwy gael cyfleusterau Technoleg Gwybodaeth yn y cartref gyda'r ysgol fel llyfrgell a chanolfan wasanaeth gwybodaeth.

Mae'n siŵr y gwelir cysylltiadau rhyngwladol yn datblygu ymhellach trwy ymestyn y defnydd a wneir o loerennau i gysylltu ag ysgolion yn rhannau eraill y byd, o Japan i Unol Daleithiau America, gan ehangu addysg a phrofiad y myfyrwyr a'u paratoi i fod yn ddinasyddion rhyngwladol.

Yn sgîl dyfodiad yr Awdurdodau Unedig newydd, gwelir mwy o ymrwymiad i rannu holl adnoddau addysgol lleol, yn rhai dynol a materol, a bydd disgwyl i ysgolion y dyfodol gwrdd ag anghenion y gymuned leol, yn enwedig trwy weithio gyda'r darparwyr lleol. Gwelir felly addysg gymunedol yn cael ei ehangu ac ysgolion yn gweithio gyda'r gymuned er budd y gymuned. I wneud hyn, bydd angen cydweithrediad agos rhwng ystôd eang o gyrff a gwasanaethau lleol yn y sector stadudol a gwirfoddol. Derbynnir bellach nad yw addysg yn gorffen pan fydd myfyrwyr yn gadael ysgol yn 16 neu 18 oed, a rhoddir cryn bwyslais ar y cysyniad o addysgu pobl drwy gydol eu hoes, a hynny mewn amryw ffyrdd. Disgwylir i ysgolion ymateb i'r her yma, gan ehangu y gwasanaethau a gynigir ganddynt. Rhagwelir oedolion yn ymuno â chyrsiau Blynyddoedd 10 ac 11 (dosbarthiadau 4 a 5) a hefyd â chyrsiau'r Chweched dosbarth mewn pynciau megis Cymraeg, Saesneg, Mathemateg, Ieithoedd Modern a chyrsiau galwedigaethol fel Astudiaethau Busnes. Dymuniad rhai, mae'n siŵr, fydd ennill cymwysterau i'w paratoi i ddychwelyd i fyd gwaith tra bydd eraill eisiau astudio i helpu eu plant, neu am y boddhad o ehangu eu gwybodaeth. Gall disgyblion elwa o'r profiad hwn - byddant yn gweld oedolion yn gwerthfawrogi addysg ac wrth gwrs mae oedolion yn medru dod â phrofiadau go iawn i'r dosbarth.

Mae'n debygol hefyd y gwneir mwy o ddefnydd o adnoddau'r ysgol, yn arbennig technoleg cyfrifiadurol, ar gyfer gweithgareddau nos a darpariaeth hamdden ac addysgol dros y penwythnosau a gwyliau ysgol. Bydd angen cydweithio'n agosach gyda diwydiant yn arbennig ynglŷn â pharatoi disgyblion ar gyfer y byd gwaith. Awgryma'r Cydffederasiwn Diwydiannau Prydain (C.B.I.) y dylai'r sgiliau craidd canlynol gael eu cynnwys yng nghwricwlwm disgyblion 16-19 oed:

- cyfathrebu
- rhifedd
- technoleg gwybodaeth
- gwaith tîm
- datblygiad personol
- datrys problemau
- ieithoedd modern

Tra bod y Cydffederasiwn yn derbyn bod cymwysterau o hyd yn bwysig, mae'n pwysleisio bod hyblygrwydd yn allweddol ar gyfer y dyfodol, a bydd rhaid cael disgwyliadau uchel ymhlith athrawon, disgyblion a chyflogwyr, er bod hynny'n medru bod yn anodd mewn cyfnod o ddiweithdra uchel. Mae yna alw gan ddiwydiannwyr ac academyddion am gwricwlwm ehangach a mwy cytbwys i fyfyrwyr 16-18 oed yn hytrach na rhaglen gul o dri phwnc safon A, i alluogi ein disgyblion i gystadlu'n ffafriol â phobl ifanc mewn gwledydd eraill mwy llwyddiannus.

Mae'r Llywodraeth presennol yn credu bod addysg a chodi safonau addysgol yn flaenoriaeth allweddol i sicrhau llwyddiant economaidd, a thros y blynyddoedd nesaf bydd disgwyl i ysgolion anelu at y targedau a osodwyd ganddynt ar gyfer y flwyddyn 2000. Mae'r targedau yn cynnwys:

- bod hanner yr holl ddisgyblion 15 oed yn ennill Gradd A-C ym mhob un o'r pynciau Mathemateg, Gwyddoniaeth, Cymraeg (iaith gyntaf) neu Saesneg yn eu T.G.A.U.
- bod 85 y cant o bobl ifanc 19 oed yn ennill 5 T.G.A.U. gyda gradd C neu'n uwch, C.G.C.C. (G.N.V.Q.) canolradd neu C.G.C. (N.V.Q.) lefel 2.
- bod 60 y cant o bobl ifanc 21 oed yn cyrraedd 2 lefel A, T.A.G., C.G.C.C. (G.N.V.Q.) uwch neu C.G.C. (N.V.Q.) lefel 3.

Mae mwy a mwy o bobl yn galw am sefydlu Cyfundrefn Addysg Annibynnol i Gymru gan fod anghenion Cymru yn hollol wahanol i Loegr, a bod angen sicrhau bod Cwricwlwm ysgolion Cymru yn berthnasol i anghenion y disgyblion, ac yn eu paratoi ar gyfer eu cymunedau lleol. Fel ysgol draddodiadol ddwyieithog, mae'n bwysig ceisio sicrhau darpariaeth ddwyieithog ym mhob agwedd o fywyd ysgol er mwyn galluogi'r disgyblion i gymryd eu lle'n hapus mewn cymdeithas ddwyieithog. Bydd angen parhau i gadarnhau dwyieithrwydd y Cymry Cymraeg a dysgwyr da, i ddatblygu dwyieithrwydd y disgyblion â'r Gymraeg yn ail-iaith iddynt ac i feithrin dwyieithrwydd yr hwyr-ddyfodiaid. Mae'n bwysig hefyd datblygu ethos Gymraeg a Chymreig o fewn cyd-destun dwyieithog yr ysgol a sicrhau bod yr etifeddiaeth yn cael ei throsglwyddo i'r disgyblion ynghyd â'r ymwybyddiaeth o berthyn i wlad a diwylliant.

Er mai ychydig iawn o ddiddordeb a ddangoswyd yn Nyfed, ac yn wir, dros Gymru, mewn eithrio o ofal yr Awdurdod lleol, gallai'r pwnc llosg o ysgolion a gynhelir â grant godi ei ben eto, o ganlyniad i'r ad-drefnu ym mis Ebrill 1996, os nad yw'r gwasanaethau addysgol a ddarperir gan yr unedau unedig yn ateb gofynion yr ysgolion. Mae'n bosib y caiff ysgolion, er eu bod yn ymwybodol o'r angen am wasanaethau cynhaliaeth canolog i'w cynorthwyo i wynebu'r her, eu gorfodi i eithrio er mwyn gwarchod eu cyllid.

Mae'n debygol iawn y bydd llawer o newidiadau yn digwydd eto ym myd addysg a bydd y dyfodol yn Ysgol Gyfun Aberaeron, fel ysgolion eraill Cymru, yn gyfnod diddorol ac yn un fydd yn gryn her i bawb.

Tomorrow's School

We live in a rapidly changing world. Gone is the likelihood of a job or even a career for life. The potentials of new technology are in the early stages of recognition and the process of change is likely to accelerate faster and further.

The task of educators working with the young today is to prepare them for their role as young citizens, workers, life long learners and parents. It is the values, knowledge and skills for these roles that the young need to learn. A broad and balanced curriculum, with greater emphasis on vocational courses, needs to be offered to all pupils at all levels, including post-16. Qualifications remain important but flexibility will be the key to the future. The young of today face a world which is very different from that which faced their parents. Jobs, which will be of interest to some of them, have not yet been invented.

The School is rightly proud of the success it has enjoyed in all fields during the last one hundred years. The vision and leadership of the former headteachers has ensured that the School has always been held in high esteem and regarded as one of the best in the country. I have been very privileged to have worked in a team with two of those leaders and this gave me invaluable experience and insight into the role of a headteacher. Mr. D. J. Thomas was headteacher at the school for 20 years and I was fortunate to have been a member of the School Management Team for 9 years while he was headmaster. He proved to be a firm, strong, innovative and industrious leader who was totally committed to the life of the School. He was always proud of "his" school and ensured that all members of the School community played their part in the success of the School. He was aware that it was a privilege to be the Headteacher of Ysgol Gyfun Aberaeron and did his utmost to uphold the standards of this unique establishment. He was succeeded by Mr. John Lewis who unfortunately was only at Aberaeron for a short period as he had to retire because of ill-health. I admire Mr. John Lewis for the clear vision he had for the School and community and it is unfortunate that he was not able to implement his numerous plans. I look forward to furthering the School's high academic and cultural standards to enable pupils to fulfil themselves as rounded individuals. High priority will continue to be given to provide quality education.

The triangle of cooperation between the school, the parent and the pupil forms such an important part of a school's success that it must be at the core of the aims of the institution. Without the support of parents or the active cooperation of the home, success will be seriously limited. Prominent among the aims of the school is the provision of an environment in which the pupils are happy, feel valued as individuals and learn to cooperate with one another.

As part of its commitment to the local community, the School will continue to expand the services offered at the School and develop community education. The School's bilingual policy should continue to reflect the bilingual nature of the locality and provide for the varying linguistic attainments of pupils. The present and future generations need to understand that life-long education adds value, both to the quality of life of the individual and to the economic success of the country.

In order to deliver a high quality, relevant and cost-effective service, schools will need to keep abreast of changing technology and make widespread use of the Internet and other electronic information highways.

Another important priority for the School is to ensure that the much needed new block and leisure centre will be built at the School in the near future. Cyngor Sir Ceredigion has agreed that the £4 million development which will replace 22 mobile classrooms should get top priority in the council's education capital programme. Meanwhile, the introduction of the new Unitary Authorities in April 1996 will result in further changes.

Schools will need to meet the challenge of performance measurement, accountability, increasing legislation, international links and almost instant electronic communication. The role of the teacher will change significantly in the next few years away from being the provider of knowledge to being the facilitator of learning. However, preparing our young people for the ever-changing world of work, both today and tomorrow, should prove to be exciting and challenging for everyone.

❖

Staff yr Ysgol / School Staff
1996

Er Cof / In Memoriam

Margaret Ingrid Bowen, Cilborth, New Quay. Died August 20th 1980. In school 1968-1975.

Mum, Dad, Anne and Scott.

Joan (Evans) Burton, B.A., Ty Rhos, Ceinewydd. Cyn-ddisgybl ac Athrawes Saesneg yn yr ysgol hon.

Y teulu i gyd.

David Penri Davies, (1935-1990), 14 Brynymor, Aberaeron, (gynt o Felinfach). Yn yr ysgol 1947-1953.

Y teulu i gyd.

Glenys Mary Davies, (1924-1950), Albion House, Aberaeron. Cyn-ddisgybl yr ysgol hon.

Ei brawd a'i chwaer, Aylmer Davies a Joyce Jones.

Henadur Simon Davies, Greengrove, Felinfach. Llywodraethwr am lawer o flynyddoedd ac yn Gadeirydd y Llywodraethwyr ym 1949. Hefyd ei ferch Jane Davies, cyn ddisgybl a Llywodraethwraig yr ysgol.

Mrs. Mary Kathleen Davies.

Gwilym Evans Ellis, (1896-1961). Cyn Brifathro Ysgolion Cynradd Cilcennin ac Aberaeron.

Teulu Môr Ewyn, Aberaeron.

David Evans, Heulfor, Maenygroes. Cyn Brifathro Ysgol Gynradd Caerwedros. Yn yr ysgol 1938-1943. A'i fab, Christopher. Yn yr ysgol 1970-1977.

Aline, Alister & Vivian.

Er Cof / In Memoriam

Evan Owen Evans, (1897-1954), Arlwyn, Caerwedros. Morwr a chapten llong. Hefyd ei gefnder, John James Jones, M.A., (1892-1957), Aberystwyth a chynt o Gei Newydd. Bu'n Geidwad Cynorthwyol ac yn Geidwad yn Adran Llyfrau Printiedig, Llyfrgell Genedlaethol Cymru.

John Keith Evans.

Goronwy Evans, Gwynfryn, Llanrhystud. Yn yr ysgol 1977-1983.

Y teulu i gyd.

Howell T. Evans, M.A., Prifathro yr ysgol hon 1917-1944.

Ei feibion Lyn a Rhys Evans.

William Sydney Evans, M.Sc. Athro Ffiseg 1947-1959.

Mrs. M. Sydney Evans.

Rhian Heulyn (Roberts), gynt o Synod. Yn yr ysgol 1961-1968.

Y teulu i gyd.

Valmai Hubbard, Gorsaf Dawel, Aberaeron. Died 30th August 1974. Music Teacher.

All the family.

Mary (Evans) James, B.A. Cyn Brifathrawes Ysgol Llangoedmor ac Athrawes Ysgol Ferwig. Aelod o dîm Hoci'r ysgol yn 1917.

Teulu Pantrhew Fawr.

Benjamin George Jones, gynt o Banteryrod, Llwyncelyn. Cyn-ddisgybl 1926-1932.

Mrs. Menna Wynn Jones.

Gwilym Morgan Jones, Cilcennin ac Aberaeron. Cyn-ddisgybl yr ysgol hon.

David L. Jones.

Er Cof / In Memoriam

1022998 Flight Sgt. John Albert Jones, 51 Squadron R.A.F.V.R., Pontfaen, Ciliau Aeron. Buried in the British Military Cemetery, Venray, Holland, aged 23.

Teulu Pontfaen, Ciliau Aeron.

John Lloyd Jones, Penparcau, Llwyndafydd, (gynt o Pantlleine, Synod). Yn yr ysgol 1918-1922.

Mrs. Bessie Jones, Eilir a Brynmor.

Y Parchedig Edwin Pryce-Jones, M.A., Hafan, Llwyncelyn. Fu'n Gadeirydd y Llywodraethwyr yn yr ysgol hon 1964-65.

Megan, Mair, Elenid a Siân.

Owen Llewellyn Lewis, Westbourne, 29 Stanley Place, Cadoxton, Neath. In school 1936-1942.

Mrs. Thelma Lewis.

J.T. Owen, O.B.E., M.A., Afallon, Aberaeron. Athro (1923-1944) a Prifathro (1944-1965) yr ysgol hon.

Teulu Afallon.

Annie Margaretta (Roberts) Salmon, Nythfa, Cross Inn, Llandysul, (formerly Llwyncelyn), 1901-1980. In school 1912-1917.

All the family.

Joan (Griffiths) Thomas, Rhoslan, Llwyncelyn, 1921-1976. Yn yr ysgol 1933-1939.

Teulu Rhoslan.

Er Cof / In Memoriam

David Gwilym Williams, M.A., Ph.D., (1926-1987), Brynseilo, Nanternis ac ar ôl hynny, Eryri, Llanon. Ysgolfeistr a gweinyddwr. Penodwyd ef gan Gyngor Sir Aberteifi, ym 1966, yn Drefnydd Iaith y Sir a'i benodi gan Gyngor Sir Dyfed, ym 1979, yn Swyddog Addysg Rhanbarthol. -

Awen , Nest a Dilwyn.

TANYSGRIFWYR / PATRONS

John Ablitt, 3 Twthill Terrace, Caernarfon, Gwynedd.

Cynthia Adams, 10 Alban Square, Aberaeron.

Michael Brian Allanson, 220 Harrington Road, London.

Peter Emry Owen Andrew, Coedmôr, Synod.

Dr. Sandra (Jones) Barfield, (gynt Teglwyn, 28 North Road, Aberaeron), Cardiff.

Alastair & Alison Bell, Hafan Deg, Panteg Road, Aberaeron.

Ian & Erica (Bell) Bell, Hafan Deg, Panteg Road, Aberaeron.

Iola G. (Evans) Billings, 57 London Road, Coalville, Leicestershire.

Lenore (Evans) Bradshaw, Little Gables, Adlington Road, Wilmslow, Cheshire.

Robert, Lona & Gareth Brierley, Garthwen, 10 Penybryn, Ffosyffin.

Elinor Julian (Evans) Buse, 34 Heol Birchwood, Cyncoed, Caerdydd.

Margaret (Jones) Cockburn, Stanhope, Wellmeadow, Staunton, Nr. Coleford, Gloucestershire.

James & Alec Cowan, Blaencwmpridd, Synod Inn.

Cynog Dafis A.S., Crugyreryr Uchaf, Talgarreg.

Megan (Jones) David, Pontfaen, Ciliau Aeron.

A.E. Valmai Davies & S.E. Glesni (Davies) Evans, New Georgia, Llanarth.

Aled Rees Davies, Margaret Ann Davies, Berthlwyd, Llanarth.

Aneurin Rees Davies, Tynffynnon, Llanbedr Pont Steffan.

Anwen Grace (Evans) Davies, Hafod y Wig, Pencader.

Aylmer Davies, Sheil, Le Rond Collas, St. Martin, Jersey.

Barry & Mair (Evans) Davies, 51 Brookhouse Road, Walsall, West Midlands.

Byron S.C. Davies, Gwynfryn, Cilcennin.

Carolyn Davies, Brownhill, Synod Inn.

Carolyn Diane (Owen) Davies, Penygraig, Hermon, Cynnwyl Elfed, Carmarthen.

Mr. & Mrs. Dewi Davies, Andrew & Peter, Dolwerdd, Lower Regent Street, Aberaeron.

Edwin & Kay (Morgan) Davies, Ty Newydd, Brynog, Felinfach.

Eifion Davies, Blaenplwyf, Maesmynach, Llandudoch, Aberteifi.

Elgan Davies, Y Gwyndy, Ffordd Aberteifi, Castell Newydd Emlyn.

Eurof & Sarah Davies, Chestnuts, Heol Gwbert, Aberteifi.

G. Alun R. Davies, Maesydre, 11 Alban Square, Aberaeron.

G. Wyn Davies, 81 Petersfield Road, Hall Green, Birmingham.

Gareth & Terry (Bell) Davies, Bay End, 119 Sea Road, Westgate-on-Sea, Kent.

Gerallt & Gwenda Davies, Ceinfan, Heol Llyswen, Aberaeron.

Gwynfor Davies, (Caerwedros), Bourn Place, Nizels Lane, Hildenborough, Tonbridge, Kent.

Hannah Mary (Thomas) Davies & John Dylan Davies, Glynnant, Llanarth.

Hywel Davies, Cotness Cottage, Cotness Lane End, Laxton, Goole, N. Humberside.

Jackie Davies, Drefaes-Uchaf, Bethania, Llanon.

James, Kevin, David & Richard Davies, Plas Newydd, Llanarth.

Jennifer & Daniel Davies, 9 Cae Martha, Llanarth.

John & Nell Davies, Glangwenffrwd, Penuwch.

John Derick Davies, (gynt o Lanarth), Llysyfran, Penfro.

John Lloyd Davies, Sundial Cottage, 1 Eastback, Pembroke.

Keri Davies, Llysceri, Caerwedros.

Linda Davies, Tegfan, Aberaeron.

Lloyd & Beryl (Rees) Davies, Gwelfor, Synod Inn.

Mair (Jones) Davies, Min-y-Llan, Llanwenog.

Margaret Eleri Davies, Bryntirion, Ffordd Caerwedros, Llandysul.

Mary Kathleen (Davies) Davies, Cwmderwen, Narberth, Pembrokeshire.

Morfudd (Thomas) Davies, Llawr-y-Glyn, Godre Rhiwgoch, Aberaeron.

Dr. Neville Davies, Dremddu-Hall, Pont Creuddyn, Llanbedr Pont Steffan.

Nigel R. Davies, Wenallt, Belle Vue Terrace, Aberaeron.

Rhiannon Davies, Tremle, South Road, Aberaeron.

Richard Davies, Brynfa, Synod Inn.

Sandra, Jennifer & Nerys Davies, Brynonnen, Nanternis.

T.G. & H.E. Davies, 101 Denham Avenue, Llanelli.

Thomas Alan Davies, Gofynach Fach, Llanarth.

Wyn & Yvonne (Vaughan) Davies, Rhoshelyg, Lôn Penymorfa, Llangynnwr, Caerfyrddin.

Yolande (Jones) Davies, 78 Cardiff Road, Llandaf, Caerdydd.

Mary Eirian (Williams) Debbane, Ottawa, Canada.

Mary Eileen (Jones) Dobbin, 35 Cynan Close, Brynteg Parc, Beddau, Pontypridd, Mid Glamorgan.

Jenkin Gwyn Edwards, Nantcenin, Llanrhystud.

Wynford Edwards, Nantyneuadd, Cellan, Llanbedr Pont Steffan.

Betty Ellis, Môr Ewyn, Aberaeron.

Dewi Ellis, Nantgwynfynydd, Bethania, Llanon.

Alun Evans, Glennydd, Gorsgoch, Llanybydder.

Alun & Margaret (Roberts) Evans, Maes-yr-Einion, Synod Inn.

Sir Anthony Evans, Drokes, Bucklers Hard, Beaulieu, Hampshire.

Beryl (Evans) Evans, Cesena, 16 Market Street, Aberaeron.

Caradog Evans, Beechwood, Llanarth.

Clifford Evans, Angorfa, 7 Cambridge Close, Langland, Swansea.

David Roy Evans, Synod Uchaf, Synod Inn.

Davina Evans, Afallon, Caerwedros.

E.O. Evans, (gynt o Tremle, Derwen Gam), 6 Picton Crescent, Ceinewydd.

Eirlys Evans, Rhydfach, Llwyndafydd.

Elir Evans, Afallon, Caerwedros.

Eleanor (Savage) Evans, Maes Einon, Abermeurig, Lampeter.

Elizabeth (Thomas) Evans, Pannau, Llwyndafydd.

Elizabeth E. (Morgan) Evans, Lynn Evans, Pantrhew Fawr, Dihewyd.

Evan John Evans, Glanfa, Cilcennin.

Gareth & Eirwen (Davies) Evans, Hafod Iwan, Caerwedros.

Gwilym & Melita Evans, 18 The Rath, Milford Haven.

Gwilym Rhŷs Evans, 2 Camperdown Avenue, Chester le Street, County Durham.

Gwyneth Morfydd (Price) Evans, 19 Maes Aeron, Talsarn.

Jenkin Vernon Evans, Min-yr-Awel, 8 Poplar Road, New Barnfields, Newtown, Powys.

Joan (Williams) Evans, Troedybryn, Cei Bach, New Quay.

John Evans (Tubby), The Seahorse Inn, Uplands Square, New Quay.

John & Ithela (Davies) Evans, Neville Evans, Dolfor, Ffosyffin.

John Alan Evans, Murmur y Coed, Berllan Deg, Aberaeron.

John Cyril Evans, Redding, California, U.S.A.

John Keith Evans, Arlwyn, Caerwedros.

Judith & John Evans, Fernhill, Park Street, New Quay.

Dr. Keith Prosser Evans, Pantgwyn, 42 Glynderi, Carmarthen.

L.G. Evans (gynt o Tremle, Derwen Gam), 68 Gorsfach, Dafen, Llanelli.

Lloyd & Gwenda Evans, 37 Danycoed, Aberystwyth.

Mrs. M. Sydney Evans, Troed y Llan, Porthaethwy, Sir Fôn.

Mair Elizabeth (Richards) Evans, Margaret Delyth Evans, Brynwichell, Bethania, Llanon.

Maisie Evans, Brynmeillion, Llanon.

Maria Evans, Aldborough, 4 North Road, Aberaeron.

Maud (Jones) Evans, Blaenhafod, Ffostrasol.

Michael Stephen Evans, Murmur y Coed, Berllan Deg, Aberaeron.

Peter Rees Evans, 22 Pen-y-Fro, Pencoed, Bridgend, Morgannwg Ganol.

Sheila (Page) Evans, Bodawel, 2 Bennar Terrace, Church Street, Barmouth, Gwynedd.

Sian L. Evans, 86 Lillie Road, West Kensington, London.

Dr. Siôn Prosser Evans, 5 Clifton Terrace, Mumbles, Swansea.

Terris & Huw Rosser Evans, Anwen Rosser Williams, Ysgubor-Wyre, Llanrhystud.

Thomas Melfin Alfor Evans, Glyn-yr-Odyn, Aberaeron.

Tom & Margaret (Jones) Evans, Aeron View, Felinfach.

Trevor & Catherine (Roberts) Evans, Jayne Evans, Frondeg, Heol-y-Cwm, Francis Street, Ceinewydd.

Trevor Adrian Evans, Caerwen, 16 Brynderwen, Caerfyrddin.

William Evans, Rylwyn, Llanybydder (gynt Dihewid).

William & Myfanwy (Edwards) Evans, Gwynfryn, Llanrhystud.

Elizabeth (Evans) Evans-Moran, Elizabeth's Cafe Bar, 20 North Parade, Aberystwyth.

Keith Evenden, Trem y Gorwel, Synod Inn.

Rebecca (Cowan) Franklin, Blaencwmpridd, Synod Inn.

David Thomas Gatehouse, Marida, Lampeter Road, Aberaeron.

David Parry Griffith, P.O. Box 558, Hampton, New Brunswick, Canada.

Griffith Brian Griffiths, (gynt Plas, Llanarth), 31 Westwood Avenue, Ipswich, Suffolk.

Gwynne Griffiths, 54 Glan-y-Môr, Aberaeron.

Mary Rosina (Evans) Griffiths, Pentre, Padarn Crescent, Llanbadarn Fawr, Aberystwyth.

Merris & Glyn Griffiths, Plas Newydd, 19 Park Street, New Quay.

Richard & Ann (Lewis) Griffiths, Pantderi, Lampeter Road, Aberaeron.

Eifion & Ros Gruffudd, Steffan Gruffudd, Y Draingwynion, Llanddeiniol.

Professor Wynford L. Harries, 258 North Blake Road, Norfolk, Virginia 23505, U.S.A.

Deanne (Swetman) Hartwell-Jones, Royal Oak, 30 North Road, Aberaeron.

Eirlys Elenid (Humphries) Hatcher, The Laurels, Talygarn, Llantrisant, Morgannwg.

Dewi M. Henry, 2 Llanwern, Gilfachreda, New Quay.

Mair Heulyn (Roberts), Crudyrawel, Synod.

Meinir Heulyn (Roberts), Bronwydd, Heol Tŷ Fica, Pontypridd, Morgannwg Ganol.

Mrs M.D. (Evans) Hill (gynt o Tremle, Derwen Gam), Windrush, Penlan Road, Llandoch, Penarth.

Graham Hope, 5 Cwrt Deri, Cwmann, Lampeter.

Aneurin Hopkins, 381 Knightsfield, Welwyn Garden City, Hertfordshire.

Margaret Aline (Jones) Horton, Rhiwig, Cefn Wig, New Quay.

Dr. Anne E. (Jones) Howells, (gynt Teglwyn, 28 North Road, Aberaeron), Glyn Neath.

Glyn & Sheila (Lloyd-Davies) Howells, Sicar Uchaf, Brongest.

Vic Hubbard, Gorsaf Dawel, Aberaeron.

Geraint & Susan Hughes a'r teulu, 1 Cae Martha, Llanarth.

Gwyneth Jean (Evans) Hughes, White Haven, Court Road, Energlyn, Caerphilly.

H. Haf Hughes, Cwmere, Felinfach.

J. Denys Gwynne Hughes, Bronfa, South Road, Aberaeron.

Nellie K. (Williams) Humphries, Isfryn, Pentre'r Bryn.

A. Elin (Williams) Hurman, 5 Brongwyn Court, Penparc, Aberteifi.

Eleanor (Davies) Hutchins, Cysgod-y-Dail, Cross Inn, Llandysul.

Siân (Morris) Ioan, Croesheddig Newydd, Pentre'r Bryn.

Aled Rhys James (gynt Alban Stores), Brynhafod, Heol yr Odyn, Aberaeron.

Bert & Pat (Rees) James, 11 Dingat Close, Llandovery.

Eifion James, (gynt Alban Stores), Hampton Wick, Llundain.

Gareth James, (gynt Alban Stores), Tadley, Basingstoke.

Hywel James, (gynt Alban Stores), 88 Waterloo Road, Caerdydd.

Joyce (Evans) James, Brynog View, Felinfach.

Marina James, Ysgol Gyfun Aberaeron, Aberaeron.

S. Ann (Jones) James, Crug Awelon, Clogfryn, Aberaeron.

Nesta Jenkins, Alltwen, Cribyn.

Sal Jenkins, Brynowen, Llwyndafydd Road, Llandysul.

Thomas & Mair (Rees) Jenkins, Tegfryn, Dihewyd.

Meinir (Owen) Jerman, Chestnuts, Heol Gwbert, Aberteifi.

Phyllis Rees (Evans) John, 53 Caswell Drive, Caswell, Swansea.

Anne Jonathan, Fir Grove, 11 North Road, Aberaeron.

Aled Jones B.Sc., Afallon, Synod Inn.

Dr. Alwyn Jones M.B. B.Ch. B.Sc., Afallon, Synod Inn.

Anne (Evans) Jones, Afallon, Synod Inn.

Barbara Jones, Cefncarne, New Quay.

D. Cyril Jones, Cilcain, Tregynon, Y Drenewydd, Powys.

D.E. Alun & Erica (Davies) Jones, Min-y-Don, West End, Beaumaris, Anglesey.

D. John A. Jones HND, Bryntirion, Llanwnnen, Lampeter.

Dai & Delyth Jones, Post Office, Felinfach, Lampeter.

Dan & Miriam Jones, 7 Victoria Street, Aberaeron.

David Lewis Jones, 10 Heathfield Court, Heathfield Terrace, London.

David M. Jones, Nantypelle, New Quay.

David Michael Jones, Sundew, Slab Lane, West Wellow, Nr. Romsey.

E. Aneurin Jones, Meini Llwyd, Llanbedr Pont Steffan.

E. Eirona (James) Jones, Glanrhos, Synod Inn.

E. Linda Jones, Pantawel, Cribyn.

Dr. Gareth Jones, 9 Poolfield Drive, Solihull, West Midlands.

Glyn & Judith (Davies) Jones, Ger Wyre, Llangwyryfon, Aberystwyth.

Glynne Jones, 44 Park Hall Road, East Finchley, London.

Henry Wilcox & Ann (Richards) Jones, Glenview, Aberarth.

Heulyn Jones, 57 Spencer Road, Osterley, Isleworth, Middlesex.

Huw Aled Jones, Brynsaron, Saron, Caernarfon, Gwynedd.

Isabel Parry (Rees) Jones, Caeralaw, Llanarth.

Jane Dilys (Edwards) Jones, Mynydd Brith, Blaenpennal, Aberystwyth.

Jenkin Jones, Fronowen, Maestir Road, Llanbedr Pont Steffan.

John Brynmor Jones, 59 Parc y Coed, Creigiau, Caerdydd.

John Gareth Hedley Jones, 11 Wellington Gardens, Aberaeron.

Joyce (Davies) Jones, Riversdale, Lampeter Road, Aberaeron.

Kenneth Jones, Glascoed, Ciliau Aeron.

Lee Jones, Brynteg, Cribyn.

Lloyd Jones, Beryl Jones, Gethin Jones, Mynachlog Uchaf, Talgarreg.

M. Eluned (Rees) Jones, Hafan, Boncath.

Margaret Eirwen (Lewis) Jones, Glynhir, Brynhoffnant.

Margaret Heulwen (Morgan) Jones, Ty'r Esgob, Synod Inn.

Margaret Lloyd Jones, Kenton, Harrow, Middlesex.

Mary Anne Jones, Dwynant, Cribyn.

Menna Wynn-Jones, 1 Rosslyn House, 236 Kew Road, Kew Gardens, Surrey.

Meredydd Lewis Jones, 16 Elizabeth Close, Ivybridge, Devon.

Nancy (Evans) Jones, Sea Crest, Wellington Street, Aberaeron.

Nancy (Lloyd) Jones & Griffith Lloyd, Gynt o Glyn Derwen, Ciliau Aeron.

Nellie (Davies) Jones, Maesllan, Llanwnen, Llanbedr Pont Steffan.

Patricia A. Jones, Glanhathren, Cwmann, Llanbedr Pont Steffan.

Pennie Jones, 4 Chalybeate Gardens, Aberaeron.

Phyllis Anne (Harries) Jones, 8 Heol-y-Bont, Llanarth.

Ray (Evans) Jones, Hafod-yr-Ŵyn, Gors-goch, Llanybydder.

Rees-Tom Jones, 30-31 Rock Street, New Quay.

Rhodri D. Jones, 3 Wellington Street, Aberaeron.

Sarah M. (Davies) Jones, Brynhyfryd, Talgarreg.

T. James Jones & Catherine Eifiona (Jones) Carpenter, Glenora, North Road, Aberystwyth.

Professor Tecwyn Jones O.B.E., Perthygwenyn, New Quay.

Thomas Ernest Jones, Bryngwyn, Pentre'r Bryn.

Vernon Jones, Rhydfechan, Llanarth.

Noreen Kay, Chris & Niki Kay, Arnant, Cellan, Lampeter.

Thirza (Lewis) Lalloo, 33 Hobson Drive, Ilkeston, Derbyshire.

John & Maralyn (Davies) Lambert, Dyffryn Duar, Llanybydder.

Susan Lewes-Daley, Rosedene, Lampeter Road, Aberaeron.

Anne (Lewis) & Tudor Lewis, Gorslwyd, Cilcennin.

Ben Lewis, Awelon, 1 Greenland Terrace, Aberaeron.

Catherine Berys Lewis, Neuadd, Ffosyffin.

Dai & Mair (Herbert) Lewis, Ardwyn, 33 Sgwâr Alban, Aberaeron.

Mr. & Mrs. Daniel Lewis, Glasbant, Llwyncelyn, Aberaeron.

Delyth (Rees) Lewis, Nant yr Efail, Llangwyryfon, Aberystwyth.

Evelyn M. Lewis, 16 Alban Square, Aberaeron.

Francien Lewis, Gwelfryn, 10 Oxford Street, Aberaeron.

Handel Lewis, West Hill, Maenygroes, New Quay.

John & Doreen (Davies) Lewis, Gwyndaf & Caryl Lewis, Ffosdwn, Dihewyd.

Dr. John Antony Rees Lewis, Seaward, New Quay.

John Eilir Lewis, Hazeldene, Stryd y Fro, Aberaeron.

Margretta Geinor Lewis, Ddolwilym, Talgarreg.

Olwen (Jones) Lewis, Glyncoed, Llanbedr Pont Steffan.

Thelma (Davies) Lewis, Westbourne, 29 Stanley Place, Cadoxton, Neath.

W.J. Lewis, Pant-y-Berllan, North Road, Aberaeron.

Angharad Lloyd, Dolgwartheg, Heol Llyswen, Aberaeon.

Betsan, Buddug & Dafydd Lloyd, Adsolwen, Nebo, Llan-non.

Dafydd Gwilym Lloyd, Tegfan, Llanarth.

Evana (Evans) Lloyd, Dolgwartheg, Heol Llyswen, Aberaeron.

Hywel Lloyd, Dolgwartheg, Heol Llyswen, Aberaeron.

Janet (Davies) Lloyd, Tegfan, Llanarth.

Jennie (Davies) Lloyd, Llysowen, Lampeter Road, Aberaeron.

Lodwick & Delyth (Davies) Lloyd, Adsolwen, Nebo, Llan-non.

Roger & Mari (Jones) Lloyd, Tegfryn, Llanarth.

Thomas Jonathan Lloyd, Tegfan, Llanarth.

Llyfrgell Genedlaethol Cymru, Aberystwyth.

Nancy (Jones) Lovatt, Llanio, Heol y Gogledd, Aberystwyth.

Margaret (Lloyd) Makin, Minawel, 11 Market Street, Aberaeron.

Mary Dawn (Davies) Mayes, Claire Louise Mayes, Hedydd, Llanarth.

John Graham McLoughlin, 2 Bronllethi, Llanarth.

Margaret Lloyd (Davies) Medway, Delfan, Heol Brynglas, Llanbadarn, Aberystwyth.

Alun Morgan, Gynt o Panteg, Llanarth.

Angela Beaumont Morgan, Craig Ddu, Llannon.

D. Hywel Morgan, Swn-y-Nant, Maes-a-Môr, Cross Inn, Llandysul.

Dannie & June (Morgan) Morgan, Huw & Sian (Jenkins) Morgan, Michael & Eleri (Morgan) Robinson, Coedybryn, Synod Inn.

David & Dilwen (Jones) Morgan, Glas y Dorlan, Cross Inn, Llandysul.

Elen Ann & Llinos Morgan, Rhydeinon, Llanarth.

Ifor Morgan, Gynt o Panteg, Llanarth.

Nita Morgan, 13A Albert Street, Aberaeron.

Delyth Gwenllian Morgans, Blaenfallen, Talsarn.

Y Parch. Beti Elin Morris, Hafdir, LLanwnen Road, Lampeter.

Evan John Morris, Dafydd Griffith Morris, Drefach, Cross Inn, Llandysul.

Fred Moulton M.B.E. & Kay (Jones) Moulton, Aeron House, 15 Alban Square, Aberaeron.

Gwladys Eleri (Jones) Munien, Trevor & Nicholas Munien, 31 North Cottages, Napsbury, St. Albans, Hertfordshire.

Caroline (Evenden) O'Connell, 2 Fron Villa, Caerwedros.

David Arwyn Owen, Penygraig, Hermon, Cynwyl Elfed, Carmarthen.

Hermione Ware (Lloyd) Owen, Tyglyn, 115 Tyglas Road, Llanishen, Cardiff.

Owenna (Beynon) Owen, Murmur-y-Gân, Brynhoffnant.

Angela Page, Bodawel, 2 Bennar Terrace, Church Street, Barmouth, Gwynedd.

Mr. & Mrs. John Parkhurst, Esgaironnen Fach, Llanarth.

Margaret (Lloyd Evans) Parry, Redmires, Wrington Lane, Congresbury, Bristol.

Alan & Kay Pascoe, Aerondale, Lampeter Road, Aberaeron.

Glenys (Ball) Pashley, 11 The Gables, Oxshott, Surrey.

T.W. & Mair (Jones) Peasey, 18 Edward Fitzgerald Court, Woodbridge, Suffolk.

Eirlys (Rees) Peate, Bryn Heulog, Welsh St. Donats, Cowbridge, De Morgannwg.

Andrew & Nia (Davies) Phillips, Lunaria, Heol-y-Dŵr, Llanon.

Lilian (Evans) Phippen, Aberarth.

Marie (Perry) Pinwill, Bryn-y-Wawr, Synod Inn.

Roy & Myra (Williams) Pocock, Broneirian, Llanon.

Miranda & Barnaby Pole, Bath Villa, Cross Inn, Llanon.

Jean Pugh, Maldwyn Pugh and Islwyn Pugh, Aberaeron, Little Chalfont, Buckinghamshire and Hastings, Sussex.

Daniel, Mark & Lucinda Rees, Pantrhyn, Llawyndafydd.

David Wynn Rees, Pensarnau, Cross Inn, Llandysul.

Glyn, Hywel, Euryl & Meinir Rees, Castell-y-Geifr, Llanarth.

John Roderick Rees, Bear's Hill, Penuwch.

Jos Rees, Goitre, Llanarth.

Nansi (Jones) Rees, 1 St. Colms, Cromwell Road, North Berwick, East Lothian.

Idris Reynolds, Bryn Môr, Brynhoffnant.

Heather (Hopkins) Rice, Ceredigion, 143 Estcourt Road, Gloucester.

David & Beryl (Rowlands) Richards, 7 Goetre Fach Road, Killay, Swansea.

Irene (Evenden) Richards, Celyn-Aur, Marble Terrace, Llandysul.

Richard Glyn Richards, 20 Bryn yr Eglwys, Llanbedr Pont Steffan.

Beryl (Jones) Roach, 14 Brohenllys, Felinfach.

Eurwyn, Aled, Eifion & Lowri Roberts, Y Dorlan, Llanon.

Glyn Heulyn Roberts, Liscard, Rhes Rheidol, Aberystwyth.

Margaret E. (Davies) Roberts, Synod Parc, Synod.

Susan S. Roberts, Ysgol Gyfun Aberaeron, Aberaeron.

Alan & Alice (Edwards) Robinson, Awel-y-Don, Pentre Isaf, Llanrhystud.

Brian & Lynne (Jones) Robinson, Maengwyn, Rhiwgoch, Aberaeron.

Harold Robinson, 15 The Park, Christleton, Chester.

Wynne Rogers, Sian & Eleri Rogers, 4 Cross Inn Road, Caerwedros.

M.E. Idwen Rowlands, (Y Chwaer Gwenfryd, C.S.F.), St. Thomas' Lodge, 25 The Rath, Aberdaugleddau.

William Ll. Rowlands, Crud-yr-Awel, Maes-y-Trên, Felinfach.

E. Jean (Jones) & D. Roy Salmon, D. Robert, John H. & R. Heulyn Salmon, Broheli, Nanternis.

Sandra (Adams) Santos, 10 Alban Square, Aberaeron.

Christopher Sewell, 264 Staines Road, Twickenham, Middlesex.

Jane Lloyd (Jones) Shaw, Penlan Mabws, Llanrhystud.

Elizabeth Glenys (Davies) Sherwood, 23 Ashbourne Road, Ealing, London.

Cheryl Beaumont (Morgan) Stevens, Mark, Marisa & Morgan Stevens, Michelle (Stevens) Williams, Pen-y-Ffordd, Stryd Fawr, Llanon.

Teulu Cilgynlle Fawr, Ceinewydd.

Teulu Fronfedw, Ciliau Aeron.

Teulu Hafan, Llwyncelyn.

Alan Thomas, Llwynderw Fach, Llanarth.

Angharad & Teleri Thomas, Maesllan, Nanternis.

Ann Elizabeth (Griffith) Thomas, 14 Maes Gerddi, Porthmadog, Gwynedd.

Berwyn James Thomas, Felin-Huw, Cwmtydu, Llwyndafydd.

D.J. Thomas O.B.E. & Mrs. B. Thomas, 8 Dyfed House, Glenside Court, Tygwyn Road, Cyncoed, Caerdydd.

Parch. D. Nennog Thomas F.R.S.A., Brynlleine, Pentre'r Bryn.

David Hywel Thomas, Sassafras, Melbourne, Australia.

Delyth (Davies) Thomas, 43 Penbryn, Llanbedr Pont Steffan.

Gwyneth Parry Thomas, 2 Allen View, Cross Inn, Llandysul.

Gwynne Thomas, 7 Alltmawr Road, Cyncoed, Cardiff.

Helen, Mair & Owen Thomas, Rhoslan, Llwyncelyn.

Hywel Thomas, Delfan, Oxford Street, Aberaeron.

Linda & Anwen Thomas, Islwyn, Llanarth.

Mary Catherine Thomas, Tanyfron, Llanarth.

Nell Thomas & Hywel Thomas, Cnwc-yr-Ehedydd, Llanarth.

Pearl (Evans) Thomas, Hafod-y-Nant, Cylch-y-Llan, Cei Newydd.

Rhys & Eirlys (Jones) Thomas, Murmur-y-Môr, Gilfachrheda.

Tudor & Clare Thomas, Owen, Rhys & Catherine Thomas, Tŷ Rhos, Aberaeron.

Nigel & Christine (Phillips) Venville, Gorffwysfa, Llanarth.

Stuart & Edwin Venville, Gorffwysfa, Llanarth.

Beryl (Jones) Ward, Tretire Court, St. Owen's Cross, Hereford.

Alun & Myfanwy (Thomas) Williams, Islwyn, Llanarth.

Awen Ffrancon Williams, Corsham, Wiltshire.

Betty (Evans) Williams, 46, Erw Goch, Waunfawr, Aberystwyth.

Dai & Alwena Lloyd (Jones) Williams, Llawr y Glyn-Gwastod, Abermeurig.

David Lewis Williams, Arymor, Aberaeron.

Eleanor (Lewis) Williams, 33 Hobson Drive, Ilkeston, Derbyshire.

Evan Lewis Williams, Afallon, 7 Park Lane, Newtown, Powys.

Ffion & Ben Llwyd Williams, Llawr y Glyn-Gwastod, Abermeurig.

Griff & Shirley (Adams) Williams, 11 Glade Close, Coed Efa, Cwmbrân, Gwent.

Huw Gwynant & Dafydd Gwynant Williams, The Old Police House, Ceinewydd.

John H. Williams, 17 Heathwood Grove, Heath, Cardiff.

John & Wendy (Davies) Williams, The Old Police House, Ceinewydd.

M. Eileen (Evans) Williams, Bro Dirion, 10 Trefaenor, Comins-coch, Aberystwyth.

Margaret Williams, Pantcefn Fach, Llanarth.

Mari Ffion Williams, Nanteos, Synod.

Megan (Ellis) Williams, Derwen Gam, Ruthin, Clwyd,

Nan Rowena (Evans) Williams, Hafod-y-Gân, 24 Penlôn, Porthaethwy, Ynys Môn.

Richard Gwynant Williams, Llanrwst, Gwynedd.

Mr. & Mrs. Roger J. Williams, Maelgwyn, Rhydlewis.

P.R.G. Young, Penarddwylan, 4 Rhiwgoch, Aberaeron.

❖